About the Managing Editor

Nicolás Kanellos has been professor at the University of Houston since 1980. He is founding publisher of the noted Hispanic literary journal *The Americas Review* (formerly *Revista Chicano-Riqueña*) and the nation's oldest Hispanic publishing house, Arte Público Press.

Recognized for his scholarly achievements, Dr. Kanellos is the recipient of a 1990 American Book Award, a 1989 award from the Texas Association of Chicanos in Higher Education, the 1988 Hispanic Heritage Award for Literature presented by the White House, as well as various fellowships and other recognitions. His monograph, *A History of Hispanic Theater in the United States: Origins to 1940* (1990), received three book awards, including that of the Southwest Council on Latin American Studies.

Among his other books are the *Biographical Dictionary of Hispanic Literature of the United States* (1989) and *Mexican American Theater Legacy and Reality* (1987).

Dr. Kanellos is the director of a major national research program, Recovering the Hispanic Literary Heritage of the United States, whose objective is to identify, preserve, study, and make accessible tens of thousands of literary documents of those regions that have become the United States from the colonial period to 1960.

Reference Library of

HISPANIC AMERICA

Advisors

Dr. Edna Acosta-Belén, *Director, Center for Caribbean and Latin American Studies, University of Albany*

Dr. Rodolfo Cortina, *Director, Bibliographic Database, Recovering the U.S. Hispanic Literary Heritage Project, and Professor of Spanish, Florida International University*

Dr. Rodolfo de la Garza, *Professor of Political Science, The University of Texas at Austin*

Dr. Ricardo Fernández, *President, Lehman College, City University of New York*

Dr. Arturo Madrid, *Director, the Tomás Rivera Center, Claremont, California*

Dr. Michael Olivas, *Associate Dean of Law and Director of the Institute for Higher Education Law and Governance, University of Houston*

Contributors

Roberto Alvarez, *Department of Anthropology, Arizona State University*

Gilbert Paul Carrasco, *School of Law, Villanova University*

José Fernández, *Department of Foreign Languages, University of Central Florida*

María González, *English Department, University of Houston*

Gary Keller, *Bilingual Review Press, Arizona State University*

Thomas M. Leonard, *Department of History, Philosophy & Religious Studies, University of North Florida*

John Lipski, *Department of Modern Languages, University of Florida*

Tatcho Mindiola, *Mexican American Studies Program, University of Houston*

Silvia Novo Pena, *Department of English and Foreign Languages, Texas Southern University*

Manuel Peña, *Foreign Languages, California State University, Fresno*

Jacinto Quirarte, *College of Fine and Applied Arts, University of Texas, San Antonio*

Arturo Rosales, *Department of History, Arizona State University*

Guadalupe San Miguel, *History Department, University of Houston*

Federico Subervi, *Department of Radio-Television-Film, University of Texas, Austin*

Dennis Valdez, *Chicano Studies Program, University of Minnesota*

Jude Valdez, *College of Business, University of Texas, San Antonio*

Reference Library of

HISPANIC AMERICA

VOLUME

I

Nicolás Kanellos,
EDITOR

Distributed by Educational Guidance Service

Reference Library of Hispanic America is based upon *The Hispanic-American Almanac*, published by Gale Research Inc. It has been published in this 3-volume set to facilitate wider usage among students.

Nicolás Kanellos, *Editor*

Gale Research Inc. Staff:

Lawrence W. Baker,
Christine B. Hammes,
    Senior Developmental Editors
Rebecca Nelson, *Developmental Editor*
Peg Bessette, Kevin S. Hile,
Neil R. Schlager,
    Contributing Editors

Mary Beth Trimper, *Production Director*
Evi Seoud, *Assistant Production Manager*
Mary Kelley, *Production Assistant*

Cynthia Baldwin, *Art Director*
Barbara J. Yarrow,
    Graphic Services Supervisor
Mark C. Howell, *Cover Designer*
Arthur Chartow, *Page Designer*
Willie F. Mathis, *Camera Operator*
Nicholas Jakubiak, *Keyliner*

Benita L. Spight, *Data Entry Supervisor*
Gwendolyn S. Tucker,
    Data Entry Group Leader
Tara Y. McKissack, Nancy K. Sheridan,
    Data Entry Associates

 This book is printed on acid-free paper that meets the minimum requirements of American National Standard for Information Sciences Permanent Paper for Printed Library Materials. ANSI Z39.48-1984.

ISBN 0-8103-9621-1

Printed in 1994
Printed in the United States of America
for distribution by
Educational Guidance Service

Ofrezco esta labor a mi hijo adorado, Miguel José Pérez Kanellos, con la esperanza de que él, su generación y las que siguen puedan tener plena consciencia de su historia, sus artes, sus tradiciones y acceso a información básica acerca de su gente. Que el pueblo hispano y, particularmente los estudiantes, jamás vuelvan a carecer de básicos recursos informativos en sus bibliotecas y en sus escuelas. Que el pueblo americano en general tenga también acceso y plena conciencia de una parte importante—la contribución hispana—de la identidad nacional estadounidense y la abrace como suya.

I offer this labor of love to my adored son, Miguel José Pérez Kanellos, in hope that he, his generation, and those that follow will be able to possess a complete awareness of their history, arts and traditions and have access to basic information about their people. May Hispanic Americans of the United States, and especially Hispanic students, never again be impoverished of basic informational resources in their libraries and schools. May the American people in general have access to and a full awareness of an important part—the Hispanic contribution— of the national identity of the United States and embrace it as theirs.

N.K.

Contents

VOLUME I

VOLUME II

VOLUME III

Acknowledgments

My most sincere thanks to all the scholars who have contributed to this volume, for indulging me in my obsession and for producing such wonderfully researched and written chapters, despite the pressure I exerted on you for making deadlines and supplying illustrations and other materials. My thanks as well to my editors at Gale Research Inc., especially Christine Nasso, Christine Hammes, and Rebecca Nelson, whose guiding hand was always characterized by a gentle touch, whose advice was always offered with compassion and understanding. I feel very fortunate to have become part of the Gale family.

Thanks also to my scholarly advisors, especially Dr. Michael Olivas, who assisted me greatly in contacting contributors for this volume. My deepest appreciation and thanks to my assistant, Hilda Hinojosa, who helped organize, type, and maintain oral and written communications with the contributing scholars and with my editors. This, the largest project of my career as a scholar, was brought to press, with her able, efficient, and enthusiastic support.

And from my wife Cristelia Pérez and my son Miguel, I beg their forgiveness for the months that I spent communicating more with my computer screen than with them. Without Crissy's love, support, and understanding this project would never have gotten off the ground, much less seen the light of day. Thank you; I love you.

Nicolás Kanellos

Preface

Reference Library of Hispanic America is the research product of a national team of outstanding scholars who unanimously have invested their time, energy, and genius to create the first one-stop source for information about a broad range of important aspects of Hispanic life and culture in the United States. In their labors for *Reference Library of Hispanic America,* as well as in their day-to-day academic work, these scholars have actively engaged in the difficult task of working with original documentary sources, oral interviews, and field work to create a written record of Hispanic life where none existed before. These scholars are among the first in our country's academic history to research, analyze, and preserve much of the information offered here. The scholars, and this work, are dedicated to filling an informational void relating to the history and culture of Hispanics of the United States—a void that has existed for too long in libraries, classrooms, and homes.

Prior to this publication, the scant information that has been available has quite often resulted from prejudice, propaganda, and folklore (quite often created to support the political and economic exploitation of Hispanics) covering a people conquered through war or imported for their labor, but who were never fully incorporated into the national psyche, the national identity, or the national storehouse of educational, economic, and political opportunities.

The vast majority of Hispanics in the United States are working-class citizens. Even those Hispanics in the professional class often share working-class backgrounds. The majority of Hispanics in the United States are *mestizos*—the product of mixed races and cultures, for the American Indian and African heritages have blended in every aspect of everyday life to produce today's Hispanic peoples of the Americas. The Spanish language, which introduced and reinforced a common culture and religion for these peoples for centuries, serves as a unifying factor for Hispanics, regardless of whether or not the individual speaks Spanish in daily life. These central factors—social class, ethnicity, linguistic-cultural background—unify the people and the information presented in *Reference Library of Hispanic America,* while also respecting the tremendous diversity in racial, ethnic, geographic, and historical backgrounds that exists among Hispanics today.

The final result of this endeavor, we hope, is an easy-to-use compendium that presents an up-to-date overview of each subject, summarizing the known data and presenting new, original research. Moreover, *Reference Library of Hispanic America* has been written in a language and style that make it accessible to students and lay people. Illustrations—photographs, drawings, maps, and tables—bring the data to life. For further reading, subject-specific bibliographies (at the end of each chapter) as well as a general bibliography (on pages A-13 and A-14 of each volume) provide ready reference to other important sources. A complete index (on pages A-15 through A-40 of each volume) assists the reader in locating specific information. A glossary of Spanish terms (on pages A-9 through A-11 of each volume) has also been included to facilitate the reading of *Reference Library of Hispanic America*.

As this is the first edition of a very new type of resource, we are aware there may be some gaps in information, resulting from incomplete data or unavailable resources (be they documentary, informational, or human). However, great pains have been taken to ensure the accuracy of the data and the representativeness of the scholarly interpretation and opinion presented in each chapter. Research is ongoing and future editions of *Reference Library of Hispanic America* will update the present volume.

Nicolás Kanellos
University of Houston

Introduction

The Hispanic Population

With a Hispanic population of more than 22 million, the United States is among the largest Spanish-speaking countries in the world. According to the U.S. Census Bureau, the number of Hispanics in this country has grew by 53 percent from 1980 to 1990. It is projected that by the year 2000, there will be almost 33 million Hispanics living in the United States.

Reference Library of Hispanic America, based on *The Hispanic-American Almanac,* is a one-stop source for information on people of the United States whose ancestors—or they themselves—originated in Spain, the Spanish-speaking countries of South and Central America, Mexico, Puerto Rico, or Cuba.

While the Spanish language is a unifying factor among Hispanics, the diversity that exists within the Hispanic community continues to profoundly influence the collective American experience.

Scope and Contents

Reference Library of Hispanic America covers the range of Hispanic civilization and culture in the United States—providing a chronology and Historical Overview, presenting the facts and figures in such chapters as Law and Politics and Population Growth and Distribution, and discussing the arts, including Theater, Music, and Film.

Twenty-five subject chapters were written by scholars in the field of Hispanic studies. These experts have drawn upon the body of their works and new research to compile their chapters, ending each with a list of references that can be used for further research into any of the subjects covered in *Reference Library of Hispanic America.* A bibliography at the back of each volume of *Reference Library of Hispanic America* provides sources for general information on Hispanics.

Concise biographical profiles in many chapters highlight Hispanics who have excelled in their fields of endeavor.

A glossary of Spanish terms, found in each of the three volumes, facilitates the reading of the material.

The keyword index, also found in each volume, provides quick access to the contents of *Reference Library of Hispanic America.*

More than 400 illustrations—including photographs, drawings, tables, and figures—punctuate the discussion in each chapter.

Suggestions Are Welcome

The managing editor and publisher of *Reference Library of Hispanic America* will appreciate suggestions for additions or changes that will make future editions of this book as useful as possible. Please send comments to:

Reference Library of Hispanic America
Gale Research Inc.
835 Penobscot Bldg.
Detroit, MI 48226

Chronology

50,000-10,000 B.C. Asian peoples migrate to North and South America.

ca. 1000 B.C. Celts move into the Iberian Peninsula.

ca. 500 B.C. Carthagenians establish themselves on the south coast of Spain.

200 B.C. The Iberian Peninsula becomes part of the Roman Empire.

350-850 A.D. Teotihuacan civilization flourishes in the central plateau of Mexico.

500 A.D. Vandals and Goths invade and conquer the peoples of the Iberian Peninsula.

700-900 A.D. Nahua peoples gain ascendancy in Mexico's central plateau.

711 A.D. The Moors invade and conquer the Visigothic kingdoms of the Iberian peninsula.

718-1492. The Reconquest of the Iberian peninsula takes place. Queen Isabella and King Ferdinand unify Spain through their marriage in 1469, and culminate the Reconquest by defeating the last Moorish stronghold—Granada.

1000 Mayan civilization flourishes in the Yucatán peninsula and Guatemala.

1492. The native American population of the Western Hemisphere may have reached between thirty-five to forty-five million.

August 3, 1492. Christopher Columbus sails from the Spanish port of Palos de Moguer with three ships: the Pinta, the Niña, and the Santa María, his flagship.

October 12, 1492. The Spaniards land on an island called San Salvador—either present-day Watling Island or Samana Cay in the eastern Bahamas.

October 27, 1492. Columbus and his crews land on the northeastern shore of Cuba. Convinced that it is either Cipango or Cathay (in Asia), Columbus sends representatives to the Great Khan and his gold-domed cities, only to find impoverished Arawak living in *bohíos* (huts).

November 1493. On his second voyage Columbus discovers the Virgin Islands and Puerto Rico.

1494. After establishing Isabela on La Española (Hispaniola), the first permanent European settlement in the New World, Columbus sets sail and encounters Jamaica in the summer of 1494.

1508. Juan Ponce de León sails in a small caravel for Puerto Rico, where he establishes friendly relations with the native chieftain, Agueibana, who presents him with gold.

1509. Ponce de León is appointed governor of Puerto Rico.

1510. Diego Velázquez de Cuéllar departs with more than three hundred men to conquer Cuba, and lands at Puerto Escondido. He is successful in defeating Arawak chieftain Hatuey's guerrilla raids.

1511. Velázquez is commissioned governor of Cuba. That same year the Cuban Indians are subjected to the *encomienda*.

1512. The Jeronymite Fathers in La Española decide to save the decimated Arawak population by gathering them into missions. Soon, missions spread like wildfire throughout the Spanish Empire.

1512. The Laws of Burgos: Promulgated by the Crown, the regulations are in response to the extremely harsh treatment that desperate colonists in the Caribbean imposed on natives through the deplorable *encomienda* system.

1513. Juan Ponce de León lands on the shores of Florida, exploring most of the coastal regions and some of the interior. At the time, there were an estimated 100,000 native Americans living there.

September 27, 1514. Ponce de León is granted a patent, empowering him to colonize the island of Bimini and the "island" of Florida.

1515. Diego Velázquez becomes a virtual feudal lord of Cuba, and establishes what are to become Cuba's two largest cities, Santiago and Havana. He also directs the explorations of the Mexican Gulf Coast by Francisco Hernández de Córdoba and his nephew Juan de Grijalva. These expeditions betray the existence of civilizations in the interior of Mexico.

1518. Hernán Cortés sets out from Cuba to explore the mainland of Mexico in order to confirm reports of the existence of large, native civilizations in the interior.

1519. Alonso Alvarez de Pineda claims Texas for Spain.

1519. Hernán Cortés lands on the coast of Veracruz, Mexico.

1520. Explorer Alvarez de Pineda settles the question of Florida's geography: He proves it is not an island, but part of a vast continent.

1520s. Continuing their maritime adventures, the Spanish explorers cruise along the northern shore of the Gulf of Mexico, seeing Alabama, Mississippi, and Texas, and also sailing up the Atlantic coast to the Carolinas.

July 1, 1520. Under the leadership of Cuitlahuac, Moctezuma's brother, the Aztecs force the Spaniards out of Veracruz, just a year after the Spaniards had come into the city. The Spaniards called this *La noche triste* (The Sad Night). Moctezuma was stoned to death by his own people during this debacle.

1521. Cortés and his fellow Spaniards level the Aztec empire's city of Tenochtitlán, and begin building Mexico City on the same site.

1524. King Charles establishes the Council of the Indies, designed to oversee the administration of the colonies of the New World.

1536. Álvar Núñez Cabeza de Vaca returns to Mexico, indirectly involving Spain in exploring and colonizing what becomes the American Southwest: In Mexico City rumors were that Cabeza de Vaca and his companions had discovered cities laden with gold and silver, reviving the legend of the Seven Cities, which dated from the Moorish invasion of the Iberian Peninsula.

1537. Àlvar Núñez Cabeza de Vaca returns to Spain and spends some three years writing *La relación*, an account of his wanderings in the North American continent. Published in 1542, *La relación* is a document of inestimable value because of the many first descriptions about the flora, fauna, and inhabitants of what was to become part of the United States.

May 18, 1539. From Havana, Cuba, Hernando de Soto sets sail for Florida; he eventually reaches as far north as present-day Georgia and South Carolina. His expedition later crosses the Great Smoky Mountains into Tennessee. From the mountains, the expedition heads southwest through present-day Georgia and Alabama.

1540. There are an estimated sixty-six Pueblo villages in the area of New Mexico, growing such crops as corn, beans, squash, and cotton. On April 23, 1541, Coronado sets out to reach Quivira—thought to be the legendary Cities of Gold—near present-day Great Bend, Kansas.

1542. The New Laws are proclaimed. They are designed to end the feudal *encomienda*.

July 1542. Coronado returns to Mexico City with fewer than one hundred of the three hundred Spaniards that once formed part of his company.

September 28, 1542. Juan Rodríguez de Cabrillo, a Portuguese sailor commissioned by the viceroy to sail north of Mexico's west coast in search of treasures, enters what he describes as an excellent port—present-day San Diego, California.

1563. Saint Augustine, Florida, the earliest settlement in North America, is founded. It remains a possession of Spain until 1819.

1573. The Franciscan order arrives in Florida to establish missions, which a century later would extend along the east coast of North America, from Saint Augustine, Florida, to North Carolina. The Franciscans also establish a string of missions from Saint Augustine westward to present-day Tallahassee.

1580s. Diseases have all but wiped out the Indians of Puerto Rico. The flourishing of sugar production will now have to await the importation of large numbers of African slaves.

1598. Juan de Oñate begins the colonization of New Mexico.

1610. Santa Fe, New Mexico is founded.

1680. A Pueblo Indian named Popé leads a rebellion that forces the Spaniards and Christianized Indians out of northern New Mexico southward toward El Paso, Texas; they found Ysleta just north of El Paso.

1689. In part due to the need to provide foodstuffs and livestock to the rich mining regions in southern Mexico, the first royal *mercedes* (land grants) are granted to Spaniards in the fertile valleys of Monclova, in northern Mexico, just south of the present border.

May 1690. The first permanent Spanish settlement in Texas, San Francisco de los Tejas, near the Neches River, is established.

1691. Father Eusebio Kino, an untiring Jesuit missionary, makes the first inroads into Arizona. By 1700, Kino establishes a mission at San Xavier del Bac, near present-day Tucson; he later establishes other missions in Arizona: Nuestra Señora de los Dolores, Santa Gertrudis de Saric, San José de Imuris, Nuestra Señora de los Remedios, and San Cayetano de Tumacácori.

1693. Despite the fact that Texas is made a separate Spanish province with Don Domingo de Terán as its governor, the Spanish Crown orders its abandonment. Fear of Indian uprisings is the reason given by the Spanish authorities.

1716. Concerns about possible French encroachment prompt the Spaniards to reoccupy Texas in 1716 by establishing a series of missions, serving to both ward off the French and convert the natives to Catholicism. Of these missions, San Antonio, founded in 1718, is the most important and most prosperous.

1718. The San Antonio de Béjar and de Valero churches are built where the city of San Antonio is located today.

1760. After the Seven Years' War, which united France and Spain against Britain, France cedes claims to all lands west of the Mississippi in order not to give them to the victorious British. Overnight, New Spain's territory expands dramatically.

September 17, 1766. The presidio of San Francisco is founded, becoming Spain's northernmost frontier outpost.

1767. King Charles III expels the Jesuits from the Spanish Empire. This event opens the door for the Franciscan conquest of California. This conquest would never have been accomplished without Fray Junípero de Serra.

July 3, 1769. Fray Junípero de Serra establishes the first mission of Alta California in what would become San Diego. Serra eventually founds ten missions, travels more than ten thousand miles, and converts close to sixty-eight hundred natives.

1770-1790. At least 50,000 African slaves are brought to Cuba to work in sugar production.

1774. Pedro de Garcés, a Spanish Franciscan missionary, founds the first overland route to California.

1776. In the American Revolution, because of their alliance with France, the Spaniards are able to obtain lands all the way to Florida.

1776. Anglo-Americans declare their independence from England, and thirty-four years later Hispanics proclaim their independence from Spain. The thirteen former British colonies come to be known as the United States of America in 1781, and the newly independent people of New Spain name their nation the Republic of Mexico.

1783. Spain regains Florida. In July 1821, the sun finally sets on Spanish Florida when the peninsula is purchased by the United States for $5 million.

1790s-1820s. The Apache threat subsides because of successful military tactics and negotiations on the part of local Spanish leaders, and Hispanic settlements begin to thrive in Pimería Alta (California). At one point as many as one thousand Hispanics live in the Santa Cruz Valley.

1798. The Alien Act of 1798 grants the U.S. president the authority to expel any alien deemed dangerous. Opposed by President Thomas Jefferson, the Alien Act expires under its own terms in 1800.

1798. The Naturalization Act of 1798 raises the number of years—from 5 to 14—that an immigrant has to live in the United States before becoming eligible for citizenship.

1800. Large, sprawling haciendas with huge herds of cattle and sheep characterize the economy and society of northeast New Spain.

1803. A powerful France under Napoleon Bonaparte acquires the Louisiana Territory, from Spain which was ceded during the Seven Years' War in the previous century. Napoleon, vying for dominance in Europe and in need of quick revenue, sells the vast territory to the United States, thus expanding the borders of the infant nation to connect directly with New Spain.

1804. To the consternation of Spain, President Thomas Jefferson funds the historical expedition of Lewis and Clark. Spain is obviously worried that the exploration is a prelude to the settlement of the territory by Anglos.

1810. In Mexico, Father Miguel Hidalgo y Castilla leads the revolt against Spain.

September 16, 1810. With the insurrection of Father Miguel Hidalgo y Castilla, the Spaniards withdraw their troops from the frontier presidios.

1819. When Andrew Jackson leads a U.S. military force into Florida, capturing two Spanish forts, Spain sells Florida to the United States for $5 million under the Onís Treaty.

1820. Stephen Long leads a revolt, ostensibly as part of the Texas independence movement against the Spanish, but obviously he is acting as a filibusterer for his countrymen. Spain finally enters into delibera-

tions with Moses Austin, a Catholic from Missouri, to settle Anglo-Catholic families in Texas.

1821. Mexico acquires its independence from Spain. By this time permanent colonies exist in coastal California, southern Arizona, south Texas, and in most of New Mexico and southern Colorado. The imprint of evolving Mexican culture is stamped on today's Southwest. Soon after Mexico gains independence, Anglo-American settlers begin to move into the Mexican territories of the present-day U.S. Southwest, especially Texas.

1823. Erasmo Seguín, a delegate to the national congress from Texas, persuades a willing U.S. Congress to pass a colonization act designed to bring even more Anglo settlers to Texas. Between 1824 and 1830, thousands of Anglo families enter east Texas, acquiring hundreds of thousands of free acres and buying land much cheaper than they could have in the United States. By 1830, Texas has eighteen thousand Anglo inhabitants and their African slaves, who number more than two thousand.

1823. Fray Junípero de Serra's death does not stop missionary activity in California. His fellow Franciscans establish another twelve missions. The famous mission trail of California includes the missions San Diego de Alcalá (1769), San Carlos de Monterey (1770), San Antonio de Padua (1771), San Gabriel Arcángel (1771), San Luis Obispo de Tolosa (1772), San Francisco de Asís (1776), San Juan Capistrano (1776), Santa Clara de Asís (1777), San Buenaventura (1782), Santa Bárbara (1786), La Purísima Concepción (1787), Santa Cruz (1791), San José de Guadalupe (1797), San Juan Bautista (1797), San Miguel Arcángel (1797), San Fernando Rey (1797), San Luis Rey (1798), Santa Inés (1804), San Rafael Arcángel (1817), and San Francisco Solano (1823).

1829. Slavery in Mexico is abolished by the new republican government that emerges after independence.

1836. The Anglo settlers declare the Republic of Texas independent of Mexico.

1836. The Texas constitution stipulates that all residents living in Texas at the time of the rebellion will acquire all the rights of citizens of the new republic, but if they had been disloyal, these rights are forfeited. Numerically superior Anglos force Mexicans off their property, and many cross the border to Mexico.

1840. To meet the wage-labor demands, 125,000 Chinese are brought to Cuba between 1840 and 1870 to work as cane cutters, build railroads in rural areas, and serve as domestics in the cities. Also, the influx of European immigrants, primarily from Spain, increases during that period. Newly arrived Spaniards become concentrated in the retail trades and operate small general stores called *bodegas.*

1845. Texas is officially annexed to the United States.

1846. The United States invades Mexico under the banner of Manifest Destiny. The treaty of Guadalupe Hidalgo ends the Mexican War that same year. Under the treaty, half the land area of Mexico, including Texas, California, most of Arizona and New Mexico, and parts of Colorado, Utah, and Nevada, is ceded to the United States. The treaty gives Mexican nationals one year to choose U.S. or Mexican citizenship. Seventy-five thousand Hispanic people choose to remain in the United States and become citizens by conquest.

1848. The gold rush lures a flood of Anglo settlers to California, which becomes a state in 1850. Settlement in Arizona and New Mexico occurs at a slower pace, and they both become states in 1912.

1850. The Foreign Miners Tax, which levies a charge for anyone who is not a U.S. citizen, is enacted.

1851. Congress passes the California Land Act of 1851 to facilitate legalization of land belonging to Californios prior to the U.S. takeover.

1853. General Santa Anna returns to power as president of Mexico and, through the Gadsden Treaty, sells to the United States the region from Yuma (Arizona) along the Gila River to the Mesilla Valley (New Mexico).

1855. Vagrancy laws and so-called "greaser laws" prohibiting bear-baiting, bullfights, and cockfights are passed, clearly aimed at prohibiting the presence and customs of Californios.

1855. The Supreme Court rules that the Treaty of Guadalupe Hidalgo did not apply to Texas.

1857. Anglo businessmen attempt to run off Mexican teamsters in south Texas, violating the guarantees offered by the Treaty of Guadalupe Hidalgo.

1862. Homestead Act is passed in Congress, allowing squatters in the West to settle and claim vacant lands, often those owned by Mexicans.

April 27, 1867. Spanish troops stationed on Puerto Rico mutiny, and are executed by the colonial governor.

1868. Cubans leave for Europe and the United States in sizable numbers during Cuba's first major attempt at independence.

1868. Fourteenth Amendment to the U.S. Constitution is adopted, declaring all people of Hispanic origin born in the United States are U.S. citizens.

September 17, 1868. A decree in Puerto Rico frees all children born of slaves after this date. In 1870, all slaves who are state property are freed, as are various other classes of slaves.

September 23, 1868. El Grito de Lares, the shout for Puerto Rican independence, takes place, with its disorganized insurrectionists easily defeated by the Spanish.

October 1868. Cuban rebels led by Carlos Manuel de Céspedes declare independence at Yara, in the eastern portion of the island.

1872. Puerto Rican representatives in Spain win equal civil rights for the colony.

1873. Slavery is finally abolished in Puerto Rico.

1875. The U.S. Supreme Court in *Henderson v. Mayor of New York* rules that power to regulate immigration is held solely by the federal government.

1878. The Ten Years' War, in which Spanish attempts to evict rebels from the eastern half of Cuba were unsuccessful, comes to an end with the signing of the Pact of El Zajón. The document promises amnesty for the insurgents and home rule, and provides freedom for the slaves that fought on the side of the rebels.

1880s. In Cuba, slavery is abolished by Spain in a gradual program that takes eight years. The influx of new European immigrants has made Cuba more heterogeneous, leading to the social diversity that is still apparent today.

1880s. Mexican immigration to the United States is stimulated by the advent of the railroad.

1892. The Partido Revolucionario Cubano is created to organize the Cuban and Puerto Rican independence movement.

1894. The Alianza Hispano Americana is founded in Tucson, Arizona, and quickly spreads throughout the Southwest.

1895. José Martí and his Cuban Revolutionary Party (PRC) open the final battle for independence.

1896. A Revolutionary Junta is formed in New York to lead the Puerto Rican independence movement.

1897. Spain grants Cuba and Puerto Rico autonomy and home rule.

April 1898. The *USS Maine* mysteriously blows up in Havana Harbor. And on April 28, President William McKinley declares war against Spain.

May 1898. The U.S. military invades San Juan in pursuit of Spaniards, and is welcomed by the cheering crowds, longing for independence.

December 10, 1898. Spain signs the Treaty of Paris, transferring Cuba, Puerto Rico, and the Philippines to the United States.

1900s. Brutality against Mexican Americans in the Southwest territories is commonplace. Lynchings and murders of Mexican Americans become so common in California and Texas that, in 1912, the Mexican ambassador formally protests the mistreatment and cites several brutal incidents that had recently taken place.

1900. The Foraker Act establishes a civilian government in Puerto Rico under U.S. dominance. The law allows for islanders to elect their own House of Representatives, but does not allow Puerto Rico a vote in Washington.

1901. The Federación Libre de los Trabajadores (Workers Labor Federation) becomes affiliated with the American Federation of Labor, which breaks from its policy of excluding non-whites.

1902. The Reclamation Act is passed, dispossessing many Hispanic Americans of their land.

1902. Cuba declares its independence from the United States.

1910. The Mexican Revolution begins, with hundreds of thousands of people fleeing north from Mexico and settling in the Southwest.

1911. In Mexico, the long dictatorship of Porfirio Díaz comes to an end when he is forced to resign in a revolt led by Francisco Madero.

1913. Victoriano Huerta deposes Francisco Madero, becoming provisional president of Mexico.

1914. President Woodrow Wilson orders the invasion of Veracruz in an effort to depose Victoriano Huerta, who soon resigns.

1917. During World War I, "temporary" Mexican farm workers, railroad laborers, and miners are permitted to enter the United States to work.

1917. The Jones Act is passed, extending U.S. citizenship to all Puerto Ricans and creating two Puerto Rican houses of legislature whose representatives are elected by the people. English is decreed the official language of Puerto Rico.

February 1917. Congress passes the Immigration Act, imposing a literacy requirement on all immigrants, aimed at curbing the influx from southern and eastern Europe, but ultimately inhibiting immigration from Mexico.

May 1917. The Selective Service Act becomes law, obligating non-citizen Mexicans in the United States to register with their local draft boards, even though they are not eligible for the draft.

1921. Limits on the number of immigrants allowed to enter the United States during a single year are imposed for the first time in the country's history.

1921. As the first of two national origin quota acts designed to curtail immigration from eastern and southern Europe and Asia is passed, Mexico and Puerto Rico become major sources of workers.

1921. A depression in Mexico causes severe destitution among Mexicans who suddenly find themselves unemployed.

1925. The Border Patrol is created by Congress.

July 1926. Rioting Puerto Ricans in Harlem are attacked by non-Hispanics as the number of Puerto Ricans becomes larger in Manhattan neighborhoods (by 1930 they will reach fifty-three thousand).

1929. With the onset of the Great Depression, Mexican immigration to the United States virtually ceases and return migration increases sharply.

1929. The League of United Latin American Citizens is founded in Texas by frustrated Mexican Americans who find avenues for opportunity in the United States blocked.

1930s-1940s. With the onset of the Great Depression, many Mexican workers are displaced by the dominant southern whites and blacks of the migrant agricultural labor force.

1930. The United States controls 44 percent of the cultivated land in Puerto Rico; U.S. capitalists control 60 percent of the banks and public services, and all of the maritime lines.

1930. Within the next four years, approximately 20 percent of the Puerto Ricans living in the United States will return to the island.

1933. The Roosevelt Administration reverses the policy of English as the official language in Puerto Rico.

1933. Mexican farm workers strike the Central Valley, California, cotton industry, supported by several groups of independent Mexican union organizers and radicals.

1933. Cuban dictator Gerardo Machado is overthrown.

September 1933. Fulgencio Batista leads a barracks revolt to overthrow Cuban provisional President Carlos Manuel de Céspedes y Quesada, becoming the dictator of the Cuban provisional government.

1934. The Platt Amendment is annulled.

1938. Young Mexican and Mexican-American pecan shellers strike in San Antonio.

1940s-1950s. Unionization among Hispanic workers increases rapidly, as Hispanic workers and union sympathizers struggle for reform.

1940. The independent union Confederación de Trabajadores Generales is formed and soon replaces the FLT as the major labor organization in Puerto Rico.

1940. Batista is elected president of Cuba.

1941. The Fair Employment Practices Act is passed, eliminating discrimination in employment.

1941. With the U.S. declaration of war in 1941, Hispanics throughout the country enthusiastically respond to the war effort.

1943. Prompted by the labor shortage of World War II, the U.S. government makes an agreement with the Mexican government to supply temporary workers, known as "braceros," for American agricultural work.

1943. The so-called "Zoot Suit" riots take place in southern California.

1944. Batista retires as president of Cuba.

1944. Operation Bootstrap, a program initiated by the Puerto Rican government to meet U.S. labor demands of World War II and encourage industrialization on the island, stimulates a major wave of migration of workers to the United States.

1946. The first Puerto Rican governor, Jesús T. Piñero, is appointed by President Harry Truman.

1947. More than twenty airlines provide service between San Juan and Miami, and San Juan and New York.

1947. The American G.I. Forum is organized by Mexican-American veterans in response to a Three Rivers, Texas, funeral home's denial to bury a Mexican American killed in the Pacific during World War II.

1950s. Through the early 1960s, segregation is abolished in Texas, Arizona, and other regions, largely through the efforts of the League of United Latin American Citizens (LULAC) and the Alianza Hispano Americana.

1950s. Immigration from Mexico doubles from 5.9 percent to 11.9 percent, and in the 1960s rises to 13.3 percent of the total number of immigrants to the United States.

1950s-1960s. Black workers continue to be the most numerous migrants along the eastern seaboard states, while Mexican and Mexican-American workers soon dominate the migrant paths between Texas and the Great Lakes, the Rocky Mountain region, and the area from California to the Pacific Northwest.

1950s-1960s. As more and more Puerto Ricans commit to remaining on the U.S. mainland, they encounter a great deal of rejection, but at the same time demonstrate a growing concern for social and economic mobility. Their early employment pattern consists of menial jobs in the service sector and in light factory work—in essence low-paying jobs.

1950. In spite of the resurgence of Mexican immigration and the persistence of Mexican cultural modes, Mexican Americans cannot help but become Americanized in the milieu of the 1950s and 1960s, when more and more acquire educations in Anglo systems, live in integrated suburbs, and are subjected to Anglo-American mass media—especially television.

July 3, 1950. The U.S. Congress upgrades Puerto Rico's political status from protectorate to commonwealth.

1951. The Bracero Program is formalized as the Mexican Farm Labor Supply Program and the Mexican Labor Agreement, and will bring an annual average of 350,000 Mexican workers to the United States until its end in 1964.

1952. Congress passes the Immigration and Nationality Act of 1952, also known as the McCarran-Walter Act, reaffirming the basic features of the 1924 quota law by maintaining a restrictive limit on immigration from particular countries. Immigration from the Western Hemisphere remains exempt, except that applicants must clear a long list of barriers devised to exclude homosexuals, Communists, and others.

1952. Batista seizes power of Cuba again, this time as dictator, taking Cuba to new heights of repression and corruption.

1954. In the landmark case of *Hernández v. Texas* the nation's highest court acknowledges that Hispanic Americans are not being treated as "whites." The Supreme Court recognizes Hispanics as a separate class of people suffering profound discrimination, paving the way for Hispanic Americans to use legal means to attack all types of discrimination throughout the United States. It is also the first U.S. Supreme Court case to be argued and briefed by Mexican-American attorneys.

1954-1958. Operation Wetback deports 3.8 million persons of Mexican descent. Only a small fraction of that amount are allowed deportation hearings. Thousands more legitimate U.S. citizens of Mexican descent are also arrested and detained.

1959. The Cuban Revolution succeeds in overthrowing the repressive regime of Batista; Fidel Castro takes power. The vast majority of Cuban Americans immigrate to the United States after this date: between 1959 and 1962, 25,000 Cubans are "paroled" to the United States using a special immigration rule. Large-scale Cuban immigration to the United States occurs much more quickly than that from either Puerto Rico or Mexico, with more than one million Cubans entering the country since 1959.

1959. Most of the two million Puerto Ricans who have trekked to the U.S. mainland in this century are World War II or postwar-era entries. Unlike the immigrant experience of Mexicans, or Cubans before 1959, the vast majority of Puerto Ricans enter with little or no red tape.

1960s. A third phase of labor migration to the United States begins when the established patterns of movement from Mexico and Puerto Rico to the United States are modified, and migration from other countries increases. The Bracero Program ends in 1964, and, after a brief decline in immigration, workers from Mexico increasingly arrive to work under the auspices of the H-2 Program of the Immigration and Nationality Act of 1952, as well as for family unification purposes, or as undocumented workers.

1960s-1970s. The migrant agricultural work force is changing rapidly. With the rise of the black power and Chicano movements, the appearance of modest protective legislation, and the increasingly successful unionization efforts of farm workers, employers seek to recruit and hire foreign workers to replace the citizens.

1961. Aspira (Aspire) is founded to promote the education of Hispanic youth by raising public and private sector funds. Aspira acquires a national following, serving Puerto Ricans wherever they live in large numbers.

April 1961. Anti-Communist Cuban exiles who are trained and armed by the United States, attempt a foray into Cuba that is doomed from the beginning. The failure of the infamous Bay of Pigs invasion embitters thousands of exiled Cubans, while strengthening Castro's position at home. Many observers throughout the world criticize the Kennedy administration for the attempt to overthrow a legitimately based government.

1962. The United Farm Workers Organizing Committee in California, begun as an independent organization, is led by César Chávez. In 1965 it organizes its successful Delano grape strike and first national boycott. It becomes part of the AFL-CIO in 1966. Today the union is known as the United Farmworkers of America.

October 1962. Kennedy redeems himself from the Bay of Pigs disgrace by blocking a Soviet plan to establish missile bases in Cuba. Soviet Premier Khrushchev agrees to withdraw the missiles with the proviso that the United States declare publicly that it will not invade Cuba.

1964. Congress enacts the first comprehensive civil rights law since the Reconstruction period when it passes the Civil Rights Act of 1964. One result of the act is the establishment of affirmative action programs. Title VII of the Act prohibits discrimination on the basis of gender, creed, race, or ethnic background, "to achieve equality of employment opportunities and remove barriers that have operated in the past." Discrimination is prohibited in advertising, recruitment, hiring, job classification, promotion, discharge, wages and salaries, and other terms and conditions of employment. Title VII also establishes the Equal Employment Opportunity Commission (EEOC) as a monitoring device to prevent job discrimination.

1964. The Economic Opportunity Act (EOA) is the centerpiece of President Lyndon B. Johnson's War on Poverty. The EOA also creates the Office of Economic Opportunity (OEO) to administer a number of programs on behalf of the nation's poor. These include the Job Corps, the Community Action Program (CAP), and the Volunteers in Service to America (VISTA).

1965. The experienced *braceros* (manual laborers) inspire other Mexicans to immigrate to the United States. Many of these contract laborers work primarily in agricultural communities and in railroad camps until the program ends in 1965.

1965. A border industrialization program, the *maquiladora* (assembly plant), is initiated. Mexico hopes to raise the standard of living in its northern border region, while the United States hopes to avoid the possible negative political and economic consequences of leaving hundreds of thousands of Mexican workers stranded without employment as the Bracero Program is ended.

1965. Although the single aim of the Voting Rights Act of 1965 is African-American enfranchisement in the South, obstacles to registration and voting are faced by all minorities. The act's potential as a tool

for Hispanic Americans, however, is not fully realized for nearly a decade.

1965. For the first time, the United States enacts a law placing a cap on immigration from the Western Hemisphere, becoming effective in 1968.

1965. Fidel Castro announces that Cubans can leave the island nation if they have relatives in the United States. He stipulates, however, that Cubans already in Florida have to come and get their relatives. Nautical crafts of all types systematically leave Miami, returning laden with anxious Cubans eager to rejoin their families on the mainland.

1965. A major revision of immigration law results when Congress amends the Immigration and Nationality Act of 1952. The national origin quota system is abolished.

Late 1960s-early 1970s. Intellectual foment and rebellion reign in the United States. Caught up in the mood, young Mexican Americans throughout the country seek a new identity while struggling for the same civil rights objectives of previous generations. This struggle becomes known as the Chicano movement. The word "Chicano" is elevated from its pejorative usage in the 1920s when it denoted lower-class Mexican immigrants, and from its slang usage of the 1940s and 1950s, to substitute for "Mexicano."

1966. Hundreds of Chicago Puerto Rican youths go on a rampage, breaking windows and burning down many of the businesses in their neighborhoods. Ostensibly, the riots are in response to an incident of police brutality, but the underlying causes are broader, linked to the urban blight that characterizes their life in Chicago.

1966. A program is initiated to airlift Cubans to the United States. More than 250,000 Cubans are airlifted to the United States before the program is halted by Castro in 1973. About 10 percent of the island's population immigrates to the United States between 1966 and 1973.

1968. Chicano student organizations spring up throughout the nation, as do barrio groups such as the Brown Berets. Thousands of young Chicanos pledge their loyalty and time to such groups as the United Farmworkers Organizing Committee, which, under César Chávez, has been a great inspiration for Chicanos throughout the nation. An offshoot of both the farm worker and the student movements, is La Raza Unida party in Texas, an organization formed in

1968 to obtain control of community governments where Chicanos are the majority.

1969. After the establishment of the Central American Common Market in the 1960s led to economic growth and improved conditions in the region, the border war between Honduras and El Salvador leads to the collapse of the common market and the rapid decline of economic conditions in Central America.

1970s. Immigration and Naturalization Service (INS) Commissioner Leonard Chapman seeks to increase funding and expand the power of his organization, claiming that there are as many as 12 million undocumented workers in the country. Other observers most commonly place the number in the range of 3.5 million to 5 million people.

1970s-early 1980s. The rise in politically motivated violence in Central America spurs a massive increase in undocumented immigration to the United States.

1970. Eighty-two percent of the Hispanic population of the nation lives in nine states, with the proportion rising to 86 percent in 1990. The major recipients of Hispanic immigrants are California, Texas, and New York, and to a lesser degree Florida, Illinois, and New Jersey.

1970. A Chicano Moratorium to the Vietnam War is organized in Los Angeles. Journalist Rubén Salazar is accidentally killed by police.

1970. The struggle over affirmative action continues when opponents coin the term "reverse discrimination," suggesting that white males are victims of discrimination as a result of affirmative action on behalf of women, blacks, Hispanics, and other underrepresented groups.

1970. Brutality against Mexican Americans continues. In *López v. Harlow*, a case filed in an attempt to bring the violence under control, a police officer shoots and kills López, a Mexican American, allegedly in self-defense, because he thought López was about to throw a dish at him.

1970. The amendments constituting the landmark Voting Rights Act of 1970 add a provision that is designed to guard against inventive new barriers to political participation. It requires federal approval of all changes in voting procedures in certain jurisdictions, primarily southern states. This act prevents minority votes from being diluted in gerrymandered districts or through at-large elections.

1971. La Raza Unida Party wins the city elections in Crystal City, Texas.

1972. Ramona Acosta Bañuelos becomes the first Hispanic treasurer of the United States.

1973. The right of the Puerto Rican people to decide their own future as a nation is approved by the United Nations. In 1978, the United Nations recognizes Puerto Rico as a colony of the United States.

1973. An employment discrimination case, *Espinoza v. Farah Manufacturing Company*, argues discrimination toward an employee, Espinoza, on the basis of his citizenship status under the Civil Rights Act. However, the Supreme Court holds that there is nothing in Title VII, the equal employment opportunities provisions of the Civil Rights Act of 1964, that makes it illegal to discriminate on the basis of citizenship or alienage.

1973. The Labor Council of Latin American Advancement (LCLAA) forms to promote the interests of Hispanics within organized labor.

1974. Congress passes the Equal Educational Opportunity Act to create equality in public schools by making bilingual education available to Hispanic youth. According to the framers of the act, equal education means more than equal facilities and equal access to teachers. Students who have trouble with the English language must be given programs to help them learn English.

1975. The Voting Rights Act Amendments of 1975 extend the provisions of the original Voting Rights Act and makes permanent the national ban on literacy tests. Critical for Hispanic Americans, the amendments make bilingual ballots a requirement in certain areas.

1977. The INS apprehends more than one million undocumented workers each year.

1977. A group of young Cuban exiles called the Antonio Maceo Brigade travels to Cuba to participate in service work and to achieve a degree of rapprochement with the Cuban government.

1978. The median income of Hispanic families below the poverty level falls from $7,238 in 1978 to $6,557 in 1987, controlling for inflation.

1978-1988. Hispanic female participation in the work force more than doubles, from 1.7 million to 3.6 million. In 1988, 56.6 percent of Hispanic women are in the work force, compared with 66.2 percent of white women and 63.8 percent of blacks.

1978-1988. The proportion of Hispanic children living in poverty rises more than 45 percent, and by 1989, 38 percent of Hispanic children are living in poverty.

1979. Political upheaval and civil wars in Nicaragua, El Salvador, and Guatemala contribute to large migrations of refugees to the United States.

1980s. Japanese industrialists take advantage of the maquiladoras by sending greater amounts of raw materials to Mexico where they are finished and shipped duty-free to the United States.

1980s. The rates of immigration approach the levels of the early 1900s: legal immigration during the first decade of the century reached 8.8 million, while during the 1980s, 6.3 million immigrants are granted permanent residence. The immigrants are overwhelmingly young and in search of employment, and Hispanic immigrants continue to account for more than 40 percent of the total.

1980s. Programs to apprehend undocumented immigrants are implemented, and reports of violations of civil rights are reported.

1980. A flotilla converges at Cuba's Mariel Harbor to pick up refugees. By year end, more than 125,000 "Marielitos" migrate to the United States. Castro charges that the exiles he allowed to return on visits had contaminated Cubans with the glitter of consumerism.

1980. The Refugee Act of 1980 removes the ideological definition of refugee as one who flees from a Communist regime, thus allowing thousands to enter the United States as refugees.

April 1980. A bus carrying a load of discontented Cubans crashes through the gates of the Peruvian embassy in Havana and the passengers receive political asylum from Peru. Castro begins to revise his policy of gradually allowing Cubans to leave.

1980-1988. The Reagan administration maintains that affirmative action programs entail quotas, constituting a form of reverse discrimination.

1980-1988. The number of Hispanics in the work force increases by 48 percent, representing 20 percent of U.S. employment growth.

1986. After more than a decade of debate, Congress enacts The Immigration Reform and Control Act (IRCA), creating an alien legalization program: legal status is given to applicants who held illegal status in the United States from before January 1, 1982, until the time of application. The program brings legal status to a large number of undocumented Hispanics.

1987. 70.1 percent of Hispanic female-headed households with children are living in poverty.

1988. Ronald Reagan appoints the first Hispanic Secretary of Education: Dr. Lauro F. Cavazos.

1989. Median family income for white families is $35,210; for blacks, $20,210; and for Hispanics, $23,450. Per capita income is $14,060 for whites, $8,750 for blacks, and $8,390 for Hispanics.

1989. Immigration from the Americas rises from 44.3 percent in 1964 to 61.4 percent. Of the major countries, Mexico accounts for 37.1 percent of total documented immigration to the United States, the next highest number of immigrants being from El Salvador, 5.3 percent.

1990. George Bush appoints the first woman and first Hispanic surgeon general of the United States: Antonia C. Novello.

1990. The erosion of past civil rights legislation by the Supreme Court during the Reagan and Bush administrations results in efforts by representatives of civil rights, black, and Hispanic organizations to initiate a push for a new Civil Rights Act. A series of compromises produces a watered-down Civil Rights Act in 1991.

1991. The proposed North American Free Trade Agreement between Mexico, the United States, and Canada expands even further the *maquiladora* concept, offering potentially greater tax abatements for U.S. businesses.

March 1991. Unemployment among U.S. Hispanics reaches 10.3 percent, roughly double the rate for whites.

1

A Historical Overview

❋ Spanish Legacy ❋ The Indigenous Caribbean Populations
❋ The Indigenous Mexican Population ❋ The Spaniards in the Valley of Mexico
❋ Movement to the North ❋ Anglo Encroachment into the Mexican North
❋ Mexicans under U.S. Rule ❋ Africa and the Making of Society in Cuba and Puerto Rico
❋ Independence of Cuba and Puerto Rico ❋ Early Mexican Immigration to the United States
❋ The Mexican Revolution and Immigration to the United States
❋ The "Mexico Lindo" Generation ❋ Depression, Repatriation, and Acculturation
❋ World War II and the Mexican-American Generation ❋ From Chicanos to Hispanics
❋ Migration to the United States from Puerto Rico
❋ Early Settlement of Puerto Ricans in the United States ❋ The Great Migration
❋ The Revolution of Fidel Castro and Cuban Immigration ❋ Hispanic Identity in the United States

This chapter presents a history of the three major Hispanic groups that have made their home in the United States: Mexicans, Puerto Ricans, and Cubans. Their historical evolution has made each group unique unto itself, but several factors deeply rooted in the formation of their national and cultural identity bind them together. Foremost among these are their link to the mother country Spain and the geographical proximity the three nations share within the Caribbean and the Gulf of Mexico.

❋SPANISH LEGACY

The first task in understanding the Hispanic society in the United States is to view the long gestation period that went into the formation of each of the three main cultures: Mexican, Cuban, and Puerto Rican. All three share many things in common. The main language spoken by the groups is Spanish, most of the inhabitants are Roman Catholics, and much of the folklore is similar.

The Spanish spoken in the two Caribbean islands and in Mexico had its roots in Spain, because it is from there that the main thrust of colonization took place. The Castilian language spoken in Spain can be traced to a long evolution that began with the earliest

human inhabitants of the Iberian Peninsula over fifty thousand years ago.

The presence of Paleolithic man (game hunters and cave dwellers) is known because of archaeological evidence left by the culture, the most famous being cave drawings of the animals on which the dwellers depended for food. More advanced cultures are known as Iberian but not much is known about these early agricultural and village people except that they migrated to the peninsula from Africa several thousand years before the birth of Christ.

A few centuries later, about 1000 B.C., a wave of Celtic warriors, hunters, and part-time keepers of livestock converged on the peninsula from somewhere in present-day Hungary near the Danube River. They mixed with the Iberians and established a unique Iberian-Celtic culture. These Gaelic-speaking nomads eventually settled in almost every part of Europe. The strongest cultural vestiges with which most Americans are familiar are those of Scotland, Wales, and Ireland. In Spain and France, cultural manifestations from the Celtic period are also evident, although not as salient as in the British Isles. There is, for example, in northwest Spain a province known as Galicia, where Gaelic characteristics have lingered to the present time. There, such Gaelic modes as the bagpipe and the kilt are used in ceremonies.

Gaelic culture in the rest of Spain, however, was overwhelmed by a series of invasions and colonization efforts, which shortly before the birth of Christ greatly transformed the linguistic, racial, and economic systems of the peninsula. The first interlopers having significant influence in the evolution of the peninsula were the Greeks and the Phoenicians, who arrived about the same time as the Celts. Both groups went to Iberia to mine tin and establish a series of trading outposts. They were not prodigious colonizers, and Iberian-Celtic culture remained strong, although over time the more advanced cultural expression of the Greeks and Phoenicians became diffused among the earlier settlers. The Iberian-Celts developed sculpture and other artistic motifs that significantly took on the characteristics of Greek classical realism, and they borrowed technological innovations, such as transportation vehicles and mining techniques.

Later in the second century B.C. Carthage, a civilization greatly influenced by Greek achievements and centered along a large portion of the North African coast, challenged the expansion of the Roman Empire in Europe and Africa. The Carthaginians were not successful in the Iberian Peninsula, however. They were able to wrest away from the Greeks authority over the region, but in 133 B.C., the Romans defeated the Carthaginian army at Numantia. This was just one of the many Roman victories, that ensured the expansion of Rome into most of Europe, including the Iberian Peninsula.

The Roman colonization of Iberia was classic in every sense of the word. Unlike previous invaders, such as the Greeks, Phoenicians, and Carthaginians, they settled in, families and all, subordinated and enslaved the natives, and set up a plantation system based on slave labor. They remained in the peninsula until their empire began to crumble about A.D. 400. From the Latin-speaking Romans, Iberia acquired some of its most significant linguistic, cultural, political, and economic institutions, in turn giving Spain and Latin America many of their present-day characteristics.

For example, Portuguese and Spanish, which are spoken in Latin America, are only two of four main languages that evolved from the vulgarization of Latin in Iberia. Portuguese was taken to Brazil by the Portuguese, who were never completely under Spanish dominion. Castilian, the language we now call Spanish, became the dominant language everywhere in the Iberian Peninsula except Portugal. The kingdom of Castile managed to conquer and dominate every other region of Iberia except Portugal. It was

the Romans who distinguished between the western and eastern parts of the peninsula, giving the name "Hispania" to the east and "Lusitania" to the west. The word "Spain" came from "Hispania," and although Portugal did not retain "Lusitania" as a place-name, any term associated with that country or its language is still prefixed by "Luso-," just as "Hispanic" refers to Spain or its heritage.

The political system introduced by the Romans had a profound effect on the evolution of government structures at all levels in Spain, and by extension, in its colonies in Spanish America. Perhaps the most enduring feature of this legacy is the careful attention given to the formation of city political culture. The Romans called this process *civitas*. Anyone who travels in almost any town in Latin America can see a faithful replication of the town square, or *plaza*, with its main Catholic church engulfed in a carefully drawn complex of government buildings dominated by the municipal or state center. The Romans also thought that it was the responsibility of government to build a bathhouse, an amphitheater, and a coliseum near the town center, regardless of the size of the town. This tradition, of course, was followed in Latin America, where one can find similar institutions, even in small villages, if only in modest proportions. In the United States, such a civic impulse is certainly present, but not to the same degree as in Latin America. Many U.S. towns and cities took their shape in response to purely economic exigencies, and then some planning, or none at all, followed.

The legal and judicial system in Latin America is quite different from the common law tradition familiar to people living in England and its former colonies. The Latin American judicial system, drawn from the Napoleonic Code, does not have juries. Rather, judges make the final decisions on all cases brought before the courts. Apart from their language and governmental legacies, the Romans were influential in other areas as well. For example, the large farms and ranches found in Latin America, typical of the landholding system in Spain and Portugal, came from the Roman plantation system known as *latifundia*. Finally, Christianity especially its ensuing branch of Catholicism, was one of Rome's most enduring legacies. In Iberia, the religion became Rome's greatest cultural and historical hallmark, to be spread even further one thousand years later when Spain embarked on its own powerful empire.

Other ethnic groups followed the Romans into Spain, leaving a continuing heritage that also is part of the Hispanic tradition throughout Latin America and in the United States. The most aggressive of these were Germanic tribes that had been migrating from

Asia Minor, slowly penetrating every region where Rome held sway. Some Germanic tribes had been within the empire long enough to serve in Roman legions as mercenaries, and many others were romanized by them. When the Roman Empire fell, some of these Germanic tribes began to carve out their own fiefdoms along with other groups in the empire. But outside tribes, more barbaric and less inclined to Roman ways, poured into the former Roman realms, pillaging and carving out their own regional baronies. Vandals, Berbers, and Visigoths moved into the Iberian Peninsula but were eventually romanized. As Roman political influence declined, the Germanic barbarians, already having relinquished many aspects of their language, began to speak one of the variations of Latin evolving in the peninsula, and they embraced Christianity. The latter process was of such intensity that, as the Germanic tribes mixed with the inhabitants of Spain, who by then were an admixture of all the groups that had previously lived in Iberia, they all came to call themselves Christians as a means of identifying themselves ethnically.

Iberia was now lapsing into the Dark Ages, so called because the brilliance of Rome and all the achievements associated with the empire faded. This was the beginning of feudalism, an era in which hundreds of small baronies, carved out of the vastness of the Roman Empire, resorted to raiding each other for territorial aggrandizement. The economic system that had held the empire together evaporated, leaving in its place a factional economic and political system. Technologically, the Germanic tribes were backward, and they depended a great deal on raising livestock. From the empire of Rome they managed to salvage some rudimentary metallurgical and other techniques of production. Because a great part of their lives was spent raiding and pillaging, the tribes introduced to Iberia a warrior cult, which was perhaps the most important cultural ingredient of their society. Along with this came a rigid code of conduct that usually accompanied such societies. Adherence to Christianity, once they entered into former Roman realms, added a religious fervor to the military code. This impulse found its expression throughout Christian Europe in the Crusades against the Muslim infidels and in Iberia in a phenomenon known as the Reconquest.

Perhaps Iberia would have remained under the solid sway of feudalism, as did the rest of Europe, if it had not been for the invasion of Arabic-speaking Muslims from North Africa in the beginning of the eighth century. More commonly known as the Moors, these latest newcomers to the peninsula remained for eight hundred years and, next to the Romans, had the greatest influence on the culture of the Iberians. The invasion was spurred by the rise of an Islamic expansion impulse in North Africa that quickly engulfed the Persian Gulf all the way to India and north into southern Europe. This expansion was inspired by a religious fervor left after the birth of Mohammed, the founder of Islam, who was born in Mecca in the seventh century A.D.

The first Moors crossed the Strait of Gilbraltar in A.D. 713, and they brought to the peninsula such an advanced culture that its merits could not help but influence the moribund feudal structure left in the wake of Rome's decline. The Muslims left few stones unturned in their quest for technological and philosophical knowledge, borrowing and improving on much of what was known to the world at the time. From the Far East they acquired advanced metallurgical skills, including the making of steel, and medicinal knowledge. In the moribund civilizations of the West, Muslims stemmed the decline of Greek and Roman philosophical, agricultural, and architectural systems.

Years of survival in the desert engendered among the Arabs thorough knowledge of how to preserve and manage water resources. This ability, which they put to good use in much of the semiarid peninsula, was a useful inheritance for the Spaniards who settled in similar terrain in the Americas. The Moors pushed the Christians all the way to the northern reaches of Iberia, but many Christians remained behind Moorish lines, where they were tolerated and allowed to maintain and evolve their Christian and Castilian cultures. Along with the Moors came thousands of Jews, who were also tolerated in Islamic domains, and many of whom served as merchants, teachers, and medical practitioners in such great Muslim cities as Sevilla, Granada, and Cordoba.

The surge that pushed the Christians north lasted until the eleventh century, when the Moorish caliphate of Cordoba began to disintegrate into smaller, less-effective kingdoms. The Christian Castilians then embarked on a protracted effort to regain the lands they had lost to the Moors in the previous three hundred years. This Reconquest was attempted piecemeal fashion, since Castilians could not mount unified efforts, because both their economic and political systems were feudal.

The Reconquest lasted until 1492, when King Boabdil was ousted from Granada, the last Moorish stronghold, by the forces of the Castilian queen Isabella and her Aragonese husband, Ferdinand. The marriage of these two monarchs from neighboring Iberian kingdoms in 1469 unified the two largest kingdoms on the peninsula and eventually led to the entire unification of Spain. However, the whole peninsula was not to be consolidated in this fashion because the Portuguese, in the western portion of Iberia, managed by themselves to defeat and eject the Arab caliphs at the beginning of the fifteenth century, before Castile did.

Before the Catholic Kings, as Ferdinand and Isabella came to be known, could effectively accomplish this unity, however, the power of the feudal lords acquired by partition of former Moorish caliphates had to be curbed. Ferdinand and Isabella accomplished this by several means. First, they embarked on establishing political institutions that challenged the local rule of the nobility. Then, they linked the long struggle of the Reconquest to their own process of consolidation, thus appropriating the nascent nationalism evoked by that struggle to unify the disparate baronies of the peninsula.

In 1492, the Catholic Kings expelled the Moors and the Jews from Spain. In 1493, they acquired from Pope Alexander VI, who himself had been born in Spain, the papal patronage. This was a concession of major proportions, because it gave the Spanish monarchs complete dominion over the operations of the Catholic church in Spain. As one can imagine, this was a vehicle of great advantage for the consolidation efforts envisioned by the two monarchs.

The long initial struggle to fend off and finally push out the Moors engendered in the Germanic Castilians an even more resilient warrior culture that by 1492 was, no doubt, the most salient expression of their society. Values such as valor, honor, audacity, and tenacity were highly prized. But the Castilians inherited many other positive characteristics from the many groups that had invaded and inhabited Iberia. Little was lost from such exposure, so when Columbus sailed and encountered the New World in 1492, Spain was truly a compendium of its multiethnic past. This complexity of cultures became the Hispanic stamp imprinted on its colonies in the New World.

Columbus's fateful voyage certainly changed the course of history. It opened a vast new region for exploration and exploitation for the Europeans.

✳THE INDIGENOUS CARIBBEAN POPULATIONS

In Mexico, some twenty-five million Indians lived in the confines of what are now the central regions of the country. Their civilization was quite advanced, and in spite of major efforts by the Spaniards to eradicate indigenous culture, much has remained to this day. But in the Caribbean, the Indians were fewer, to begin with, and they were not as developed as those on the Mexican and South American mainland. Tragically, cultural and racial genocide took a greater toll in the Caribbean. The indigenous populations there were greatly reduced almost from the outset of the colonization process because of diseases, brought over by Spaniards, to which the Indians were not immune. Nonetheless, the inhabitants of Cuba and Puerto Rico have retained many vestiges of indigenous society. The largest non-Hispanic influence in the Caribbean came from Africa. Thousands of slaves were brought over first to work the mines, then to work the large sugar plantations that served the Spaniards as the mainstay of the island economies. Today the vestiges of this important heritage are seen in much of Caribbean culture and, of course, in the racial makeup of Caribbean peoples.

The indigenous groups in the Caribbean were composed mainly of Carib and Arawak, who lived in seminomadic villages throughout the Greater and Lesser Antilles which make up the bulk of the Caribbean islands, and as far south as the coasts of what are today Venezuela and the Guineas. The Carib were considered by the Spaniards to be fiercer than the Arawak, but both groups hunted, fished, and gathered wild plants, such as the manioc root, for food.

Their way of life had evolved very little in thousands of years. Since the traditional methods of obtaining food had always yielded results, few incentives existed for innovation. Their lives revolved around villages that they were prone to abandon when economic need dictated. Politically, they depended on a council of elders for guidance. Religious beliefs were linked to the hunting-gathering economy, and they relied primarily on shamans for observance of rituals. Village homes required very little to build. Those using palm leaves and wood ribbing were among the most sophisticated. Some lived in dugouts that were called *barbacoas*. When the Spaniards moved on to the Central American mainland, they remembered this word and applied it to the cooking of meat in pits, a common form of preparation in central Mexico. Hence, the word "barbecue" has stuck to this day.

Before the Spanish Conquest, the Taino Indians, an Arawakan group that dominated the islands of Cuba and Puerto Rico, had a highly developed social and political system. In the twelfth century, they had displaced, throughout the Antilles, the less developed Ciboney, who lived in cavelike dwellings and who foraged and fished to survive. Taino-Arawak settlement was based on fishing and extensive planting of corn, squash, and chile, the same foodstuffs cultivated on the Mexican mainland. Because of extensive dependence on fishing, the Taino had an extraordinary maritime ability and moved from island to island setting up villages whose populations numbered in the hundreds. But shortly before the Spanish occupation of the Greater Antilles, warlike Carib Indians swept into the Caribbean and drove many of the Arawak out and captured their women. As a result, to the Spaniards, Arawak became known as a language of females. Like the Arawak, the Carib were excellent sailors who crossed much of the Caribbean in huge canoes that were fitted with woven cloth sails and carried as many as fifty people.

The simple-life style of these island people was drastically altered after the arrival of Columbus and the Spaniards. The first island settled by the Europeans was Hispaniola, which is the present-day Dominican Republic. Columbus naively ordered his translator to enter into negotiations with the Great Mogul of India, insisting, as he did until his death in 1506, that he had found a direct route to India by sailing west from Spain. As quickly deduced by everyone, except Columbus it seems, what the great discoverer had encountered was a gigantic landmass that blocked direct passage to the real India; even so, the name "Indies" stuck. The name "America" was adopted in northern Europe because of the writings of Amerigo Vespucci, the Italian cartographer who explored the newly found lands. The Spaniards, however, always referred to the New World as Las Indias.

The fate of these "Indians," so called because of the colossal miscalculation made by Columbus, was tragic beyond almost any other experience of indigenous peoples in the Americas. From their rude conquest Columbus and his settlers envisioned rewards that the natives were ill prepared to deliver. Columbus, a Genoese from a seafaring merchant tradition, insisting that he was in Asia, expected to trade with the simple Carib and Arawak. The trouble was that the Caribbean natives had no surplus after they took care of their needs, and even if they had, their fare was of little use to Columbus in setting up trading posts.

Most of the Spanish settlers accompanying Columbus were steeped in the tradition of the Reconquest, and they counted on a subjugated population to do their bidding. They expected to establish feudal baronies. Columbus opposed such a tradition, but he capitulated nonetheless and gave his men *encomiendas*. Developed in feudal Spain, the encomienda was booty given to a Spanish conqueror of a Moorish caliphate. The award was usually the land that had belonged to the caliph, and according to Christian standards of the time, the prize was befitting a hero who had defeated the despised "infidels," as the

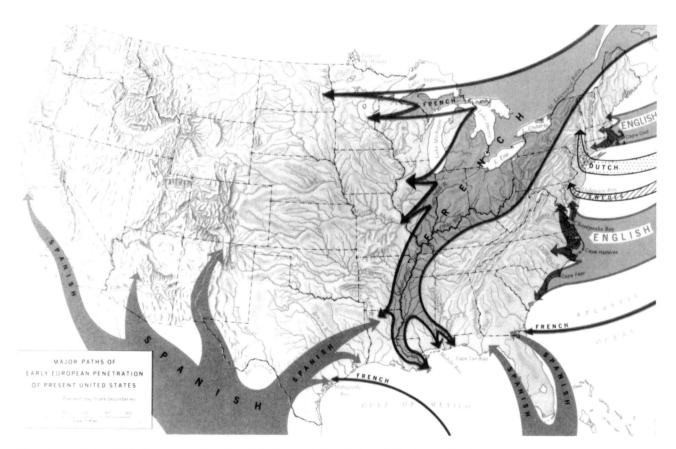

(Courtesy of the U.S. Department of the Interior and the National Park Service.)

Moorish Muslims were known. But just as the natives were unable to fit into Columbus's trade scheme, they were just as unsuited to provide labor or tribute, for that would have required them to have lived in a more sophisticated society.

The Spanish attempt to establish feudal baronies resulted in a debacle for all parties involved. But it was worse for the Indians, who were either worked to death in gold mines that yielded little gold or were forced to feed the demanding Spaniards. The result was mass starvation. The final blow in this endless chain of mistreatment was the introduction of European diseases, such as smallpox and measles, to which the natives were not immune. This inadvertent intrusion was the most tragic of the European offerings. Numbering over one million in the Caribbean islands before Columbus's voyage, the Indians were eventually decimated. Indian lineage however, was not extinguished altogether. There were numerous offspring of Spanish-Indian sexual liaisons, resulting in a small but formidable mestizo population, which continued the Indian genes in the islands.

The Conquest of Cuba

When Columbus and his Spanish sailors first arrived on the island that was named Cuba on October 27, 1492, they disregarded the Indian tribes that lived by subsistence agriculture and fishing. Columbus's attention was fixed on Hispaniola, where the first permanent Spanish colony had been established. It was not until 1508 that the island was systematically charted by Sebastián de Ocampo, who circumnavigated the island gathering information about the coastlines and harbors that would prove useful for the eventual occupation.

The first Spanish political system was not established in Cuba, however, until many years after Columbus's encounter with the natives of the Caribbean. Diego Velásquez de Cuéllar was commissioned governor of Cuba in 1511 after he had led an expedition that defeated the Arawak-Taino Indians. Velásquez, who first arrived in the New World at Hispaniola with Columbus's second voyage in 1493, was by then a veteran colonist with many years of experience in dealing with Caribbean natives. In the conquest, which was conducted in typical Spanish fashion, hundreds of men, women, and children were slaughtered. Many fled to the mountains or to other islands, such as Puerto Rico, only to be caught up with again in later expeditions.

Spared the encomienda for some nineteen years after the first arrival of Europeans in the Caribbean, Cuban Indians were finally subjected to the abhorrent institution after 1511. Columbus, who had expected trade, not feudal conquest, gave this prerogative

to his men in Hispaniola, setting the precedent for the next sixty years of Spanish conquest. Giving this grant was against Columbus's better judgment, but he found that he had no choice because it seemed like the only way to reward the Spaniards who demanded some kind of prize for their participation in the momentous expedition.

Velásquez had no such scruples, and the parceling out of human beings proceeded in hasty fashion. Velásquez himself became a virtual feudal lord of Cuba, and by 1515 he founded what became Cuba's two largest cities, Santiago and Havana. His power was such that he directed the explorations of the Mexican Gulf Coast by Francisco Hernández de Córdoba and his nephew Juan de Grijalva. These expeditions betrayed the existence of civilizations in the interior of Mexico, prodding Velásquez to put his brother-in-law, Hernán Cortés, in charge of the expedition that resulted in the conquest of Mexico. Velásquez remained governor of Cuba until the 1520s, and, like that of other Spanish conquerors, his rule left an indelible stamp on the formation of Cuban society.

The initial Cuban economy, based on raising livestock and placer mining of gold, was propped up with labor provided by the ubiquitous encomienda. Because of the demand for pork, cattle hides, and gold in the other Spanish colonies, especially after the conquest of Mexico, Cuba provided tremendous opportunity for the first settlers. Velásquez himself, who had gotten rich in Hispaniola by engaging in similar activity, repeated his endeavor in Cuba and prospered there as well.

Unfortunately, European disease and the forced labor in the mines took a grim toll and many Indians became ill and died, or were virtually worked to death. The amount of gold on the island was limited. Soon the supply was exhausted, frustrating the Spaniards to such a point that they made the Indians work harder so that decreasing sources could yield the same previous results. Indiscriminate livestock raising was also destructive to the Indian way of life. Huge, untended herds trampled the fragile crops, reducing the harvest on which the Indians depended as their main source of food. Ironically, the Spanish-based economy in Cuba declined very quickly because of competition from livestock raisers in Mexico and in other new colonies.

Then, when silver was discovered in the Zacatecas province of Mexico and Potosí in Peru, a rush to these areas depopulated Cuba when many fickle Spaniards left to find riches elsewhere. They clamored to leave for newly conquered Mexico and Peru, even though the Crown futilely imposed harsh sanctions to those that deserted their encomiendas. The near-abandonment of the initial economy was so disastrous for the Indians that it makes their unwilling sacrifice even more tragic. The surviving indigenous groups must have wished that more of the exploitative Spaniards had left and never returned. But the Cuban economy revived. Because of the ideal position of the island, it became an entrepôt for silver coming from New Spain (roughly the area of present-day Mexico) and Peru and for European goods destined for the rich colonial markets.

Havana's fine harbor allowed the city to achieve dominance by the mid-sixteenth century, even though it did not become the capital of Cuba until 1607. The British and French, anxious to capture the booty offered by incoming ships, subjected the city to numerous attacks. Fortifications made the city safer, and it soon became the most important naval and commercial center for the Spanish colonies in the Caribbean. Ships with gold and silver from Mexico and South America were formed into fleets at Havana in the 1550s so that the Spanish navy could protect them from pirates during the journey back to Spain. By the 18th century, Havana was the New World's greatest port.

The Conquest of Puerto Rico

Unlike Cuba, the island of Puerto Rico was not seen by Europeans until Columbus's second voyage to the New World in 1493. The Taino Indians living on the island called it Borinquen, but Columbus renamed it San Juan Bautista, even though he did not attempt to settle the island, concentrating instead on Hispaniola. As in Cuba, the Taino also received a few years of respite from the Spanish mistreatment. But sixteen years later, Ponce de León and a crew of fifty followers subdued the thirty thousand or so inhabitants of the island, and it was renamed Puerto Rico, or "rich port." The Spaniards overwhelmed the large population of Taino Indians by using terror tactics as they approached each village. Reducing the Indians' ability to resist Spanish incursions throughout the Caribbean was lack of cohesion and the poor communication among the scattered villages. If they had offered organized resistance, even in the face of superior weapons, horses, and other advantages held by the Spaniards, it would have been impossible for the Spaniards to succeed.

Following the pattern established in the Caribbean, in Puerto Rico the Spaniards immediately set out to raise livestock and other foodstuffs for the expanding colonial market. But sugarcane was also planted after the conquest, and the natives were pressed into the encomienda to tend to these crops. Harsh treatment and lack of experience with systematic labor rendered the Indians almost useless for work on sugar plantations, however. Besides, by the 1580s, diseases had all but wiped out the Indians of Puerto Rico. The flourishing of sugar production would have to await the coming of large numbers of African slaves.

✴THE INDIGENOUS MEXICAN POPULATION

In Mexico the greatest cultural influence, along with the Spanish language, was its momentous indigenous history. In 1518, Hernán Cortés set out from Cuba to explore the mainland of Mexico in order to confirm reports of the existence of large, native civilizations in the interior. He was originally commissioned by Diego Velásquez, the governor of Cuba, who had received reports of highly developed societies from previous explorers on reconnaissance trips along the Yucatecan and Mexican coasts.

As the Spaniards were to discover, the reports were indeed true beyond their wildest dreams. Civilization in southern Mexico, or Mesoamerica, as the area is known archaeologically, had its beginning in the vast migrations across the Bering Strait over fifty thousand years ago. The first humans to cross into the North American continent entered in waves before the strait was inundated by the melting polar caps in 10,000 B.C. Their livelihood depended on hunting the giant mastodons and other big game and gathering wild plants.

Social organization was limited, since they were mobile and traveled in small bands following the trail of animals. At best, they had a leader who ruled by consent of the other hunters and who had proved his worth in both hunting and defending his group from marauders. They lived in caves and rude shelters as they traversed the countryside in their pursuits. Their religious beliefs were simple. Like other Paleolithic big-game hunters from Europe, Africa, and Asia, they worshiped the very game on which they depended for food. Hence, drawings of mastodons and tapirs have been found on the bone artifacts they used as tools, leaving archaeologists to surmise that this was a form of worship.

Hunting and gathering, which provided a healthy, plentiful diet (Paleolithic man was bigger than present descendants), might have continued, but a significant climatic change about 7200 B.C. forever altered the course of human history in Mesoamerica. The area became more arid, creating the desert conditions we know today. The lush green land on which large animals depended for food disappeared. Humans had to turn to other sources of food and entered a stage designated the Archaic period. The former hunters became scroungers, depending on wild plants for their sustenance and to a lesser degree on smaller animals for protein. During this long period, which lasted until 2500 B.C., the gatherers became more and more adept at food acquisition and storage, but they also discovered that they could cultivate some of the plants for which they previously scrounged.

This discovery was the first major step toward civilization. Slowly, the inhabitants of Mesoamerica began to plant and irrigate the seeds of wild plants, such as maize, squash, beans, and amaranth. In the process, they also domesticated some of the wild animals they hunted. Unlike in the rest of the world, wild cattle and horses had not survived the decline of big game. Only the bison in the northern part of the continent lived on. Domestic animals included only turkeys and small dogs. Not surprisingly, the course of development for the Indians of the Americas did not include beasts of burden except for the Indians themselves.

Still, once domestication of both plants and animals pervaded Mesoamerica, in an era called the Formative period, 2500 B.C. to A.D. 250, material progress proceeded at an astonishing rate. First, villages appeared throughout the region as new techniques of cultivation resulted in flourishing plots of crops. Terracing, the plowing of platforms on hills, and *chinampas*, (man-made islands on bodies of water,) greatly increased the ability to produce. The resulting surpluses released many workers from agricultural work and made possible the emergence of specialists, such as potters, toolmakers, and even entertainers, such as musicians, acrobats and dancers.

In addition the simple metaphysical exigencies related to hunting and gathering gave way to a dramatic sophistication in religious practices, a process hastened by the ability to specialize. Farmers increasingly needed more precise prediction of the weather so that planting and harvesting could be planned accordingly. Shaman priests provided this valuable knowledge as they studied the heavens and acquired the astronomical skills necessary to forecast weather changes. Farmers looked to their religious leaders more and more for guidance, leading to a dependence that put the priests with their metaphysical teachings in leadership roles. Such control gave priests political power, which they exercised to their advantage. They demanded tribute and labor from the commoners and leaders alike, until the priesthood and the leadership converged into a theocracy.

At the end of the Formative period, religious leaders demanded the construction of huge temples and other religious institutions. It was at this point that religion started to assume such dominance that the Mesoamerican world revolved entirely around metaphysical arrangements. A pantheon of deities was inspired by the need to pay homage to the elements essential to agriculture. Thus, the most important gods were those that symbolized the sun, the mother earth, and, of course, water.

About A.D. 250, throughout the Americas pre-colombian civilization reached its apogee and human development entered into the era known as the Classical period. Large urban centers with specialized production techniques entered into trade arrangements with other cities. During the Formative period, between 1200 B.C. and 400 B.C., a high civilization (which in most of Mesoamerica did not appear until the Classical period) had emerged in selected regions of Mesoamerica. A society known today as the Olmec built large cities with ceremonial centers and advanced architecture, pottery, and art. But most important, the Olmec developed a knowledge of astronomy and math that allowed them to invent a calendar system almost as accurate as ours today. Such development was limited to La Venta and San Lorenzo on the Gulf of Mexico, while the rest of Mesoamerica continued in the village mode even after the decline of these great centers.

In the classical era, many communities, especially those of the Maya and Zapotec, whose centers were close to the old Olmec centers, probably were influenced by the older, declined civilization. The Zapotec, in fact, occupied Monte Albán, a city with marked Olmecan characteristics, while the Maya built centers like Chichén Itza in Yucatán and El Tajín in Vera Cruz. The Maya excelled in math and astronomy, a definite inheritance from the Olmec, and they produced the most delicate pieces of art in all the Americas.

The newer methods (terracing and chinampas) of cultivation were more beneficial to the societies of the hilly and lake-filled Valley of Mexico. There Teotihuacán, the most impressive center in the Classical period, was built twenty-five miles northeast of the what is now Mexico City. The city had over 200,000 inhabitants, huge pyramids, and a large market where the most advanced pottery and obsidian wares were traded.

Throughout Mesoamerica, thriving agricultural communities existed, dedicated to cultivating maize, the ears of which were about ten times larger than during its initial planting in the Archaic period. Maize was king, but an array of other crops were also important in the diet of Mesoamericans. Unfortunately, in the tenth century A.D., one by one the Classical centers in both the highlands and the tropical lowlands declined. Archaeological evidence points to several causes. In the Mayan lowlands, reliance on slash-and-burn agriculture probably led to the exhaustion of the soil. The method works as long as there is plentiful new land to be brought under cultivation. Also, another climate change (bringing even drier weather) prompted nomadic barbarians from the north, known as Chichimecas, to migrate to Mesoamerica looking for water. It is believed that these newcomers pillaged and sacked the cities of Mesoamerica one by one. The Classical period thus came to an end, and although the barbaric newcomers replaced and imitated the old civilizations, they never surpassed them in philosophical or technical achievement. Because of the warlike orientation of the new cities, the era has been called the Militaristic period. This was the state of society when the Spaniards arrived in the early fifteenth century.

The Toltec were the first of the former Chichimeca group of tribes to have approached the degree of development of their predecessors. Their most impressive city was Tula, about sixty miles northwest of the present-day Mexican capital. The center, known for its giant monoliths, which resemble sentries on guard, remained the most important city in the Valley of Mexico until it too fell to other marauding Chichimeca. The Toltec also occupied the city of Monte Albán, which had served the Zapotec before them. According to myth, it is to there that Quetzalcoatl, the god known as the plumed serpent, was banished and expected to return in the future. As with Tula, the Toltec also abandoned Monte Albán, probably for the same reasons.

One of the last Chichimeca tribes to enter the central valley was the Aztec, who just a few years prior had left their mythical homeland of Aztlán in search of a new home, as Huitzilopochtli, their god of the sun, had mandated. According to legend, they would know where to settle once they encountered an eagle devouring a serpent on top of *nopal* (prickly pear cactus) in the middle of a lake. They wandered south looking for the sign and finally saw it in the middle of Lake Texcoco, where they built Tenochtitlán.

This legend has a basis in truth. The Aztec arrived in the Valley of Mexico about the thirteenth century and were such a nuisance, since they continued the Chichimeca life-style of pillaging, that they were banished by Atzcapotzalco leaders to an island in the center of the lake, which they fortified and used as a base of operation. From there they imitated other city-states and built their own magnificent city, which surpassed all the others in size and beauty, while they defeated and dominated the other communities in the lake region. They went through several stages and emperors until the Spaniards conquered them in 1521.

The city was laid out in squares. Perfectly straight causeways allowed merchants to supply Tenochtitlán in the middle of the lake, while they took the city's products to the countryside and other communities. Bernal Díaz del Castillo, one of Cortés's soldiers, wrote his first impressions of the city some years later: "Gazing on such wonderful sights, we did not know what to say, or what appeared before us was real, for on one side were great cities, and the lake itself was crowded with canoes, and in the Causeway were many bridges at intervals, and in front of us stood the great City of Mexico."

The society, a theocracy, was made of distinct classes known as the *pilli* (aristocracy); the various knighthoods, such as the *jaguar*; the *pochteca* (merchants); and the *macehuales* (commoners). At the bottom were the *mayeques* (serfs), who tilled the land of the nobles, and the *tamines*, who were full-time bearers. When the Spaniards arrived, Moctezuma II was the most powerful and most famous of emperors. He was deified and given equal status with the Aztec sun-god, Huitzilopochtli. They were both demanding, but the sun-god was voracious in his appetite for human sacrifice. The bloody reputation that the Aztec acquired is due to the thirst of this deity.

The Conquest of Mexico

If there were any doubts among the Spaniards about the existence of an advanced civilization in the interior of Mexico, they were put to rest almost as soon as Cortés landed on the Gulf Coast at a bay he named Veracruz. The reports received from the natives first encountered on the Mexican mainland were too compelling for any misgivings. After scuttling some of his ships so that the four hundred Spaniards that accompanied him could not return, Cortés set out to find the source of this civilization. Cortés, an audacious conquistador from Estremaduera in southern Spain, had inherited that warrior mentality so deeply ingrained in that part of the Iberian Peninsula. In fact, the intrepid explorer was not interested in doing the bidding of his ostensible benefactor, a fact that Diego Velásquez had discovered too late. Cortés had left Cuba just before the governor gave orders to have him arrested. With the few hundred men he had recruited and organized into a conquest team, Cortés had sailed just in time. In the time-honored tradition of the Reconquest, Cortés wanted to subjugate the civilization of Mexico and establish himself as its feudal lord.

After declaring the landing site a town (Veracruz), the con quistadores set out for the city of Tenochtitlán, which was considered a populous center of great wealth and power. Along the way he and his men encountered resistance in Cholula, but through the intelligence and language-interpreting services offered him by an Indian maiden given to him by Indians in Tabasco, he was able to defeat the Cholulans and continue on to Tenochtitlán. On the way he picked up Indian allies from the city of Tlaxcala. This Indian group became a ready ally because the Aztec were their hated enemy. Various Aztec leaders had attempted to dominate them and force them to pay tribute, as they had done with other cities in the valley for years. But the Tlaxcalans resisted fiercely. Moctezuma, the Aztec emperor who ruled the great city of Tenochtitlán, had spies who had kept him informed of the progress of the approaching Spaniards ever since they had landed on the coast. But he did not know what to make of them. Paradoxically, he was at a loss as to how to deal with the intruders. The Aztec emperor actually thought that Cortés was the long-lost god Quetzalcoatl, and that the rest of the Spaniards were immortal. By the time the Europeans arrived at the city, Moctezuma was paralyzed with indecision and Cortés seized the opportunity to sequester the vacillating king in his palace. The Spaniards set up house inside the walls of the city, as did the thousands of Tlaxcalan allies. In the meantime, Diego Velásquez, chafing because Cortés undertook his venture without authorization, sent Pánfilo de Nárvaez to arrest him and bring him back to Cuba in irons. Cortés, through his own system of spies, learned of Narváez's arrival at Veracruz and left Tenochtitlán to deal with him. And in another incredible feat, Cortés persuaded the soldiers of his would-be captor to desert and join him.

Upon his return to Tenochtitlán, Cortés found the city in an uproar. In his absence, Pedro de Alvarado, the conquistador lieutenant, mistook an Aztec ritual for a planned uprising and gave orders to slaughter the Indians who were observing the ritual. This was the last straw for the countless Indians who could not understand why Moctezuma had been so passive. Under the leadership of Cuitlahuac, Moctezuma's brother, the Spaniards were forced out on July 1, 1520, just a year after the Spaniards had come into the city. The Spaniards called this *La noche triste* (The Sad Night). Moctezuma was stoned to death by his own people during this debacle.

Cortés was not a man to give up very easily and so he retreated to the town of Coyoacán, where he set up headquarters to plan the defeat of the city. He quickly built brigantines and armed them with cannons. With his own original soldiers, supplemented by the defectors from Narváez and the thousands of Tlaxcalans, Cortés laid siege to the city, not allowing supplies to go in. In time he attacked the starving Aztecs and the neighboring Tlatelolcans, who were also decimated by the European diseases to which the Mesoamer-icans were not immune. Cuitlahuac himself was a victim of the ravages.

Cuauhtemoc, from neighboring Tlatelolco, then took command. The siege finally forced a surrender, and Cuauhtemoc was captured with the defenders of the city and executed. He went on to become a hero in the eyes of Mexicans, while Cortés is vilified. Cortés had the city of Tenochtitlán razed, and the beginning of Spanish Mexico commenced with the building of a European city on top of the old Aztec capital. However, the old conqueror was eventually stripped of his power, banished back to Spain, and replaced by professional viceroys who ostensibly represented the needs of the Crown. The Spaniards then ruled Mexico until 1821, a full three hundred years after the conquest, indelibly stamping their Hispanic mark on Mexican society. Still, what is considered Indian remained in many ways.

✳THE SPANIARDS IN THE VALLEY OF MEXICO

After Cortés razed Tenochtitlán, he set out to build a Spanish city, ironically rescuing from the rubble the very same building materials used by the Aztec. His conquistadors then continued to explore and bring under Spanish rule other indigenous communities. Pedro de Alvarado ventured south to the Yucatán Peninsula and Guatemala, while Cortés's enemy and rival, Nuño de Guzmán, brutally subjugated the vast realm of the Tarascans to the west. Cortés dispensed encomiendas left and right as a way of rewarding his men, but he reserved for himself the largest encomienda of all, practically all of Oaxaca. In 1529, he was authorized to use the title El Marqués del Valle de Oaxaca.

In the initial years of the conquest, the encomienda remained, as in the Caribbean, the main prize sought by conquistadors. Many of the onerous aspects of the institution had been somewhat mitigated with the Laws of Burgos. Promulgated by the Crown in 1512, the regulations were in response to the extremely harsh treatment that desperate colonists in the Caribbean imposed on natives through the deplorable encomienda. Now Spaniards had to abide by regulations that forbade overworking the Indians and that required the *encomendero* (the recipient of an encomienda) to provide for the spiritual welfare of the Indians. This usually consisted of supporting a prelate and building a church within the jurisdiction of the encomienda grant. In New Spain, as the vast territory claimed by Spain on the North American continent came to be called, the encomienda became for the Indians an acculturation vehicle to Spanish ways.

The most important Spanish acquisition for the Indians, usually through the encomienda, was Catholicism. Spanish friars in the beginning of the colonization process exhibited a great amount of zeal, imbued as they were with an inordinate amount of idealism, which characterized the Catholic church during this period of internal reform. They traveled far and wide, proselytizing and winning over hundreds of thousands to the Christian faith. The converts were so numerous, however, that they could not really assimilate Catholicism completely and the tendency was to combine, syncretically, pre-Colombian beliefs with the new teachings.

Indians in the Valley of Mexico did make better adjustment to the encomienda than those in the Caribbean. Prior to the European conquest, Aztec and other dominant tribes had forced tribute from countless subordinated Indian groups, a process that anticipated the demands of the encomienda. Nonetheless, scant comfort can be taken in this, because it is only in relation to the extreme cruelty in the Caribbean that the measure is made. In reality, treatment of the natives by their new masters was as harsh, if not harsher, than under the Aztec. For one, the Spanish tribute demands differed drastically from what the natives were accustomed to providing. The Europeans had no use for the items considered to be the necessary tribute by the Aztec, such as feather cloaks, leopard skins, obsidian relics, earthen pottery, and foodstuffs, such as maize. They wanted pure gold to use as specie, wheat, European beasts of burden, and European domestic animals, such as sheep, cattle, and pigs. The natives were not really able to provide precious metals in any significant amounts, but the Indians had to alter their agricultural tradition in order to provide the food to which Spaniards were accustomed. In time the natives also began to consume new foodstuffs, and in the process modify their traditional food ways. For example, pork, beef, and mutton were combined with chile, maize, and other vegetables native to the Americas to form the basis for the Mexican food that we know today.

By 1540, another major phenomenon began to drastically change the social and racial character of central Mexico. The prodigious sexual appetite of the Spaniards led to numerous liaisons with the native women. From the moment they set foot on Mexican soil, the conquistadors violated the women of the conquered tribes and took them as concubines, with only a few marrying among the Indians. The consequence was a large progeny of children who were half Spaniard and half Indian. This new racial ensemble came to be known as mestizo, and after a few generations, the possible variations of mixture became so profuse that over one hundred categories existed by the end of colonial rule in 1821.

In 1504, Queen Isabella died, and twelve years later King Ferdinand succumbed as well. Succeeding them was their heir, Charles V, who was born to Juana la Loca, daughter of the Catholic Kings, and her Hapsburg husband Prince Phillip of Austria. Neither Isabella nor Ferdinand lived to see the conquest of the great Aztec Empire by conquistadors who were intent on making their prize a personal and feudal domain. It fell to the young king to wrest that realm away from Cortés and his encomenderos, a process begun almost as soon as the value of the conquest was realized. In 1524, Charles established the Council of the Indies, designed to oversee the administration of the colonies of the New World. An *audiencia*, a court of judges and administrators, was appointed in 1527 as a major step in asserting royal control. It was presided over by Nuño de Guzmán, who set out to destroy the power of Cortés, his old rival. But the rapacious Guzmán seemed to be a worse threat than the feudalistic Cortés, and the whole audiencia slate was replaced a year later by a president and judges more loyal to the Crown. To supervise and establish the Catholic faith, Juan de Zumárraga was named archbishop of New Spain in 1527.

The most ambitious move in the effort to consolidate royal power in New Spain was the appointment of Antonio de Mendoza, an extremely capable administrator who served the Crown well as viceroy for many years. In 1542, the New Laws were promulgated, a stroke designed to end the feudal encomienda, ensuring the predominance of Hapsburg control over the area. Mendoza found that he could not effectively implement the restrictive measures without provoking insurrection from the armed encomenderos, and so he opted for allowing the controversial institution to die out on its own. Encomiendas were only good as long as there were Indians to parcel out, but because of the horrible epidemics caused by European diseases, the indigenous population was decimated within a century.

In the meantime, the Spanish zeal for exploration and conquest led to incursions north of the Caribbean islands and Mexico into many regions of what is today the United States. Juan Ponce de León had sailed and landed on the shores of Florida in 1513, exploring most of the coastal regions and some of the interior. Continuing their maritime adventures, the Spanish explorers in the 1520s cruised along the northern shore of the Gulf of Mexico, seeing Alabama, Mississippi, and Texas and also sailing up the Atlantic coast to the Carolinas. Between 1539 and 1541, a large, well-equipped group of explorers led by Hernando de Soto journeyed into the interior of

North America looking for mineral wealth, through present-day Florida, Georgia, South Carolina, Alabama, Mississippi, Arkansas, Louisiana, and Texas.

At the same time that De Soto was in the midst of his exploration, Francisco Vásquez de Coronado prepared for a momentous trek that took him and another large group of Spaniards north to present-day Arizona, New Mexico, Texas, and Oklahoma. In 1541, he set out from Mexico City in search of the Seven Cities of Cíbola, a mythical region rumored to rival Tenochtitlán in wealth and splendor. To supply Coronado's party, Hernando de Alarcón sailed up the Gulf of California and took his three ships against the current of the Colorado River, reaching present-day Yuma, Arizona.

✳ MOVEMENT TO THE NORTH

In transcendental terms, Coronado's feat has great historical significance. But at the time, his explorations were considered a disappointment because of the failure to find the fabled cities of Cíbola and Quivera. Dispelling the myths of greater glory and riches in the far north dampened enthusiasm for any further forays so far from the viceroyalty of Mexico City. In addition, the discovery of silver in the immediate north, soon after Coronado returned empty-handed, ensured that the Spaniards would concentrate all their efforts closer to their home base, and the expansion and real settlement northward commenced in earnest. In 1546, Captain Juan de Tolosa, leading a small expedition of soldiers and missionaries into El Gran Chichimeca, as the wild region north of Querétaro was known, discovered a rich vein of silver in a mountain known as La Bufa. The strike was located in what is now the city of Zacatecas, some three hundred miles north of Mexico City. It was the first of a series of finds in a fanlike pattern spreading from Zacatecas into Guanajuato, Querétaro, and San Luis Potosí. The area is known as the Central Corridor because it is located on a plateau escarpment between two large mountain ranges, the Sierra Madre Occidental to the west and the Sierra Madre Oriental to the east. In the last half of the sixteenth century, Spanish officials in Madrid far from central Mexico, in Madrid, concentrated all their efforts on spurring mining activity both in New Spain and in Peru, where even greater silver deposits were uncovered.

But before the rich minerals could be adequately exploited, the Central Corridor had to be made safe from hostile Indian tribes. Although sparsely settled by the nomadic Chichimecas, the natives resisted the unwelcome intrusion of large numbers of Spaniards and mestizo workers, precipitating fifty years of Indian warfare. By the end of the sixteenth century, the nomads were brought under control through a combination of extensive military and religious proselytizing campaigns. As the mining regions were carved out from Chichimeca territory, thousands of mestizos, sedentary Indians from the former Aztec Empire, and Spaniards migrated to the *reales* (mining camps), settling permanently. The mining economy and the arid desert environment of El Gran Chichimeca engendered unique social conditions where a new Mexican ethnic identity was forged. Here the population was not as linked to either the large, sedentary Indian civilization and culture of the central highlands or the cities that were large centers of administration, commerce, and Spanish culture, such as Mexico City and Puebla.

While the inhabitants of the mining frontier drew on Spain and the more settled Indian areas for cultural continuity, the exigencies of the new environment generated an even more vibrant source of identity and culture. The process was carried north as the mining frontier moved in that direction in the seventeenth and eighteenth centuries. By 1800, the Spaniards had reaped $2.25 billion worth of silver from the vast array of rich mines. In the Spanish system, all wealth belonged to the Crown and the miner was granted a *real* (a royal concession giving him or her the right to exploit the mine). The Crown received one-fifth of all the take, or the royal fifth, however, these concessions would remain in the miner's family, ensuring a continuation of *patria potestad* (the original authorization) usually under a patriarch.

Life for miners was grim. The initial method used for mining was the rathole, in which a lode was followed by digging twisted narrow shafts with hand labor. Indian forced labor was first used through a system called *repartimiento*, but mining required staying power and skill, which Indian workers, forced to travel hundreds of miles on foot from their homes and sedentary life-styles in the highlands, would not muster. Within a few years the grantees of the reales turned to wage labor, and hundreds of thousands of mestizos, who were born in the decades immediately after the conquest in the highlands, poor whites, and acculturated Indians poured into the Central Corridor to work not only in mining but also on the haciendas, which specialized in raising livestock and agriculture for consumption in the reales. Thus, the hacienda became an indispensable corollary to mining, and within a few decades both of these activities determined the social arrangements of the region. The economy, based on wage labor, created a proletariat that was able to work in a more diverse opportunity structure than in the central highlands. For example, the *patio* amalgamation process, used to

free the silver from its ore base, was rather complicated. After the ore was excavated from the large
shafts, it was carefully sifted and gauged by women
and young boys, pulverized with huge ox-drawn mil-
lstones, and then spread out into pancakes called
tortas. It was here that the most important step took
place. The *azoguero* (mercury man) applied mercury
to the pile until the only portion of the torta that was
not mush was the pure silver. Each step required
thousands of workers, technicians, machines, and
beasts of burden and vast amounts of resources, such
as rope, leather, and iron.

This activity was carried farther north as smaller
mining operators followed the missionaries to the
frontier. In essence, a persistent pattern emerged in
which the missionaries tamed the Indians so that the
Hispanic miner could follow, once they were
"softened" to European ways. The missionaries provided the service unwittingly, but they served that
purpose nonetheless. Parral, at the northern end of
the corridor in Chihuahua, and Alamos, in Sonora,
were thus settled by Spanish-Mexicans. By the mid-
1600s, the mines had played out, so then miners in the
frontier were forced to settle down and turn to agri-

culture and the operation of smaller-scale mining
known as *gambusino*.

For today's Mexican Americans, the social and
cultural transformation of the Central Corridor is
particularly important, because the Hispanic culture
that emerged in northern New Spain (today's American Southwest) during the colonial period is an extension and reflection of the mining society in this
region. In addition, Mexican immigrants who in the
early twentieth century swelled existing Hispanic
communities throughout the United States came
from this region as well, reinforcing the unique Mexi-
canness that had already been established in the
Southwest.

The reasons for settling the extreme northern frontier of New Spain were not as related to mining as
they were in the case of the Central Corridor. Nonetheless, the process of colonization was a slow but
sustained extension of the northward movement that
started with the founding of the Zacatecas mines. By
the time Mexico acquired its independence from
Spain in 1821, permanent colonies existed in coastal
California, southern Arizona, south Texas, and in
most of New Mexico and southern Colorado. The

San José de Tumacacori Mission, Arizona. (Courtesy of the U.S. Department of the Interior and the National Park
Service.)

A *vaquero* in early California. (Courtesy of the Bancroft Library, University of California.)

imprint of evolving Mexican culture so evident in the Central Corridor was also stamped on today's Southwest. It contained a mestizo-*criollo* (pure-blooded Spanish descendant) racial mixture with a strong reliance on raising livestock, subsistence agriculture, and mining. Leaders of most colonizing expeditions were persons born in Spain, but the rank-and-file soldiers, artisans, and workers in general were of mixed blood (mestizos) or criollos born in New Spain.

The first foray out of the Central Corridor, after Coronado's unsuccessful trek, was in the 1590s into Pueblo Indian territory in northern New Mexico. Fifty years earlier, Coronado had written of these sedentary Indians who lived in large agricultural settlements containing multistory houses with well-ordered political and religious systems. His attempts to buffet them into encomiendas provoked fierce resistance, and as a result he and his party were forced to abandon New Mexico. This failure contributed to the overall disillusionment with exploration. Nonetheless, the possibility of exploiting the labor of the Pueblos and saving their souls, modest as this potential might have been, remained a lure after Coronado. The attraction glowed even more forty years later

when Antonio de Espejo reported in 1583 the possibility of silver deposits in New Mexico.

Spurred by Espejo's report, Juan de Oñate, the grandson of a Zacatecas mining pioneer from Spain, was granted a charter to explore into present-day New Mexico as early as 1595. In 1598 he and his group set out along the Central Corridor from the more civilized Zacatecas to the uncertainty of the north. Oñate's party, made up of Spaniards, criollos and mestizos, also contained Tlaxcalan Indians, who had remained loyal to the Spaniards, after helping Hernán Cortés defeat the Aztec in 1521. They served in menial positions as carriers, servants, and laborers. After reaching the Rio Grande, the explorers and missionaries then traveled along the river valley, established a minor post in present-day El Paso, and continued on up through upper Rio Grande valley into Pueblo Indian territory.

Oñate was ordered to return in 1608, but Franciscan missionaries and settlers remained attracted to the communities of sedentary Indians. Santa Fe was founded in 1610, followed by other settlements. The clerics wanted to convert the Indians, and the civilians hoped to put them into encomiendas and demand gold as tribute. The efforts to enslave the Indians backfired, however. In 1680, a Pueblo Indian named Popé led a rebellion that forced the Spaniards and Christianized Indians out of northern New Mexico southward toward El Paso, and they founded Ysleta just north of El Paso. The latter community is said to have housed the *genízaros* (acculturated Indians made up of Comanche captive-slaves), Christianized Pueblos, and the faithful Tlaxcalans. Sixteen years later, many of those settlers who had fled returned to northern New Mexico and reestablished a Hispanic presence, but with a new respect for the Pueblos.

The Pueblo uprising also turned the interest of Spaniards toward Texas. But the story of the exploration of Texas has to be told within the context of the colonization of the large province of Coahuila, of which Texas was an extension. The first newcomers were prospectors searching for precious metals, and indeed some silver mines were opened in Monclova, Coahuila, such as the Santa Rosa. But the diggings were sparse and most of the attention was soon turned to agriculture and livestock. Motivated by the need to provide foodstuffs and livestock to the rich mining regions to the south, in 1689 the first royal *mercedes* (land grants) were granted to Spaniards in the fertile valleys of Monclova, just south of the present border.

Like Oñate, the Spaniards in the northeast also brought Tlaxcalan Indians to provide labor for their haciendas. Many of these enterprising natives established themselves as artisans in Saltillo and acquired a reputation as excellent weavers and silversmiths. Many of the modern inhabitants of Coahuila and immigrants to Texas from this area are descendants of the Tlaxcalans. Saltillo acquired great importance because it served as an entrepôt between the livestock-raising areas to the north and the silver and mercantile communities to the south. In the eighteenth century, a new dynasty of Spanish kings, the Bourbons, initiated reforms that led to a revitalization of the silver industry. As a consequence, by 1767 Saltillo had become a prosperous commercial hub with a population of over two thousand, and as new settlers arrived to colonize the northeast, they filtered through this beautiful colonial city.

Large, sprawling haciendas with huge herds of cattle and sheep characterized the economy and societal life of the northeast by 1800. The biggest landholding belonged to the Sánchez-Navarro family. It was sixteen million acres in size. This latifundia was so immense that it took in almost half of the province, and its mainstay was sheep raising. Peonage was the lot of many of the lower classes, as that was the only method by which *hacendados* (landowners) could deter their workers from going off to work in mines. But hindering the effectiveness of the haciendas were constant depredations by the Comanche, who had learned that raiding the livestock regions was more prosperous than hunting the buffalo. This provoked the Spanish government to establish buffer zones across the Rio Grande, or the Rio Bravo, as it is known in Mexico.

Besides the adversity posed by the Comanche, Spanish officials recognized another threat. While explorations north of the Rio Grande were motivated by the time-honored traditions of prospecting for precious metals and converting the Indians, now defense of the frontier began to acquire more importance. In the 1680s, the French sailed down the Mississippi from the Great Lakes and established a fort in the western extreme of Louisiana, precipitously close to Spanish Texas. The news traveled fast and in 1686 Alonso de León set out to look for the fort and found it destroyed by Indians. Still, the French threat remained, and a Spanish *presidio* (fort) was established near Nacogdoches, Texas. By the early eighteenth century, French Biloxi (established in 1699) and New Orleans (1718) served as junctions for the burgeoning Mississippi trade. The main trading activity of the French with the Indians was in fur pelts. If the Indians did not know how to trap, the French would teach them, provoking the natives to abandon other ways of life and become ever more dependent on trapping. A mission was also established in Nacogdoches in tandem with the fort, a policy that the Spaniards emulated in other parts of their frontier. The Indians, however, did not take to the Christian religion, and in 1700 the mission was abandoned. In the beginning, the Spaniards found little desirable in Texas territory.

Nonetheless, at the turn of the century, a persistent priest named Francisco Hidalgo, from his base of San Juan Bautista, a settlement on the Rio Grande about 150 miles west of Laredo, zealously set out to work among the Indians north of the river. Initially his requests for support were ignored by Spanish officials, so he sought help from the French, which prompted the Spaniards to act, because they recognized the threat France would pose if her colonists made inroads with the natives. Domingo Ramón in 1717 was sent to colonize along the Nueces River and to build missions. In 1718, the San Antonio de Béjar and de Valero churches were built where the city of San Antonio is located today. The chapel in the de Béjar mission was called El Alamo. The efforts to colonize Texas remained very difficult because of the nomadic, warlike character of the tribes. Therefore,

REGLAMENTO,
E INSTRUCCION
PARA LOS PRESIDIOS
QUE SE HAN DE FORMAR
EN LA LINEA DE FRONTERA
de la Nueva España.
RESUELTO POR EL REY N. S.
en Cedula de 10. de Septiembre
de 1772.

DE ORDEN DE SU MAGESTAD.

MADRID: Por Juan de San Martin, Impresor de la Secretaria del Despacho Universal de Indias.
Año de 1772.

Rules that were issued by the King of Spain regarding the founding and governance of presidios on the frontier.

instead of spreading the gospel, the Spaniards spent most of their time pacifying the resistant natives.

The French remained a threat, however. To thwart Spanish efforts to colonize and settle Texas, the French supplied the Indians with firearms and gunpowder. Nonetheless, colonization remained a priority on the Spanish colonial agenda. In 1760, after the Seven Years' War, which united France and Spain against Britain, France ceded claims to all lands west of the Mississippi in order not to give them to the victorious British. Overnight, New Spain's territory expanded dramatically. Then, in the American Revolution of 1776, the Spaniards, because of their alliance with France, were able to obtain lands all the way to Florida. Basically all of that territory had few Hispanic settlers, however. In Texas, most of the Hispanic settlers lived in clusters of villages along the lower Rio Grande Valley. By 1749, 8,993 Hispanics and 3,413 Indians lived in what came to be known as Nuevo Santander. Laredo was on the north bank of the river and Meier, Camargo, and Reynosa were on the south bank. Some Anglo settlers came in the last few decades of the eighteenth century; thus, some south Texas Mexicans have English and Scottish names that can be traced to this era.

Also during this same period, colonists were pushing north and establishing ranches in the Nueces River Valley. The Crown encouraged the settlement of this region in order to create a buffer zone against all intruders, such as the Comanche and the French. By 1835, three million head of livestock, cattle, and sheep roamed the region between the Nueces River and the Rio Grande, and about five thousand persons inhabited the region. The biggest town in the vast Nuevo Santander province, Reynosa, was larger than Philadelphia in 1776. Most border people did not inhabit the towns, however. Instead, they lived on ranches as tight-knit family groups and clans on land granted by the Spanish Crown. Having to withstand the depredations of the Comanche promoted even tighter cohesion and class cooperation than was true on the larger haciendas farther south to the interior of Mexico.

Arizona was the next area of the northernmost frontier to be explored and settled. The region was part of the province of Sonora, but it acquired a distinct geographical name, Pimería Alta, because of the numerous Pima Indians that inhabited southern Arizona and northern Sonora. Its settlement, then, was simply an extension of the colonization of Sonora. The first Europeans in Sonora were Jesuit missionaries who in 1591 introduced a new religion, European crops, and livestock to Yaqui and Mayo in southern Sonora. The natives were more receptive to the latter offerings than to the former, but they were receptive, nonetheless. When the first Hispanic colonists arrived some fifty years later, they found wheat and other European crops abundantly planted by Indians on mission lands.

Pedro de Perea, a miner from Zacatecas, was allowed the first *entrada* (Spanish Crown colonization sanction) into Sonora in 1640 and he arrived with forty soldiers in 1641. Because of problems with local leaders in Sinaloa and Jesuit missionaries in Sonora, he went to New Mexico, where he recruited twelve families and five Franciscan priests. The local Jesuits objected to the viceroy in Mexico City, and eventually the Franciscans went back, but the families stayed. Then a series of silver discoveries led to more settlement along the Sonoran River valleys by colonists who came directly from Zacatecas, Durango, and Sinaloa.

By the 1680s, most settlers dedicated their efforts to mining, but many others raised crops and livestock to supply the mines. Farmers and miners lived in the same towns, which usually contained a store for goods not available locally. The Hispanics introduced tools, livestock, and crops never before seen in Sonora. These communities became the focus for the Hispanicization of the Indians, and the Mexicans here evolved a unique cultural system known today in Mexico as *sonorense* (sonoran). It is characterized by an intrepid that was shaped by the necessity of learning to survive in the most challenging environment of the Spanish Empire. As a consequence of Europeanization, basically the same food was eaten by the Hispanics and the mission Indians, a food way relationship that existed between natives and Hispanic colonists throughout Mexico. Meat sustenance consisted of mutton, chicken, pork, and beef. The latter was the mainstay of the poorer people. But weddings, baptisms, funerals, and the Christian holidays were occasion for celebrations, and meat other than beef was consumed by everyone on these special days. The missions and the colonists grew corn, wheat, and, to a lesser degree, barley, beans, chile, sweet potatoes, squash, and some fruits, such as figs, peaches, watermelons, cantaloupes, and citrus fruits.

The influence of the Indian culture on the Mexicans, especially the lower classes, most of whom were mestizos, was inordinate, however. The Hispanic colonists had already acquired a tradition of supplementing their diet with wild plants in the interior of New Spain. These included such staples as *quelites* (wild amaranth) and cactus fruits from the *nopales* (prickly pear) and *pitayas* (organ pipe), but in Sonora they added some of the wild plants gathered by the local Indians, such as the fruit of the saguaro cactus, which grows only in the northern part of the desert.

But it was in the struggle to find water that the

native knowledge was the most advantageous. Indians could survey the lay of the land and pinpoint water sources a mile or more away by using vegetation as reference points. The Mexicans would then gratefully name their settlements after the water: Agua Prieta (Dark Water), Agua Linda (Pretty Water), Agua Fría (Cold Water), and so forth. There is no other area in the United States where place-names in honor of water are as numerous.

Mining was of course the focal point of life and engaged both Indian and Hispanic labor. Many Indians entered into the Hispanic economy as workers, drawn by material inducement. Thus, acculturation, which occurred whenever there was any kind of contact between the two groups, intensified in the mining towns. Life for the majority of the miners was wretched because of poor working conditions. Pulmonary ailments, shaft cave-ins, and agonizing work-related aches and pains were common. Faced with such an array of ailments and a lack of doctors, Hispanics continued to use Spanish folk-healing traditions and herbal medicine acquired from Indian Mexico before they moved north to Sonora. Inevitably, the Sonoran indigenous traditions, such as the use of jojoba and aloe vera plants enriched the repertoire of healing techniques and increased medicinal options.

Intense dependence on mining made the Sonoran communities very unstable, because when production of the local mine played out, the community dispersed. Also, mercury, which was indispensable to the amalgamation of silver, was a monopoly of the Spanish Crown. In the seventeenth century, prices were hiked up so high that it was impossible to operate the mines profitably. As happened elsewhere in New Spain when mining opportunity waned at the end of the century, more and more Mexican settlers engaged in subsistence agriculture rather than mining. But also, as elsewhere in New Spain, the eighteenth-century Bourbon reforms precipitated in Sonora a growing and booming economy. More Hispanics came in from the other provinces of New Spain and from Spain itself. Consequently, the indigenous population declined in proportion. In 1765, only 30 percent of the population was considered Hispanic, while by 1800 that figure had changed to 66 percent.

In the Santa Cruz Valley, Pimas and Tohono O'odom (known as Pápagos by Spaniards) predominated in the northern half near Tucson, and Hispanic settlers occupied the southern part. The missionaries, however, preceded the settlers, pacifying the Indians and making the area safer for colonization. This impetus surged the line of Hispanic settlement even farther north in Sonora to Pimería Alta (northern Sonora and southern Arizona), theretofore the

domain of Jesuit missions. In 1691, Father Eusebio Kino, an untiring Jesuit missionary, made the first inroads into Arizona and established a mission in 1700 at San Xavier del Bac, near present-day Tucson, and in 1702 founded another mission some thirty miles south in Tumacácori. In 1706, a presidio was established next to that complex, in Tubac, complementing the mission in much the same way as the haciendas did the reales.

By the 1730s, Hispanic settlers were in what is now the Santa Cruz Valley of the Sonoran Desert, mining silver at Arizonac just south of the present-day border. The name "Arizonac" was Pima for "land of few springs" and is how the state of Arizona derived its name. To deal with disturbances like the uprisings instigated by the Pima in the 1750s or the incursion by the Apache in the 1730s, the Hispanics built presidios and Mexican settlers manned these military garrisons, extending their influence even farther north. Basically, the same pattern of missions and presidio life as in the earlier settlements was established along the Altar and Santa Cruz valley of Pimería Alta in the eighteenth century. Ironically, the farther north Hispanics moved, the more they relied on wheat rather than maize as a staple. This was even true among the Indians. The Tohono O'odom, for example, had taken to making what we know today as "Indian fried bread" and wheat flour tortillas.

Because Jesuit influence in the Spanish Empire had become so pervasive, in 1767 the Bourbons expelled them from the realm, and the Hispanic communities throughout Sonora were forced to undergo significant alterations. After the expulsion, the mission system declined despite the Franciscans' replacing the Jesuit order. Former mission farms were put to livestock raising, and because foodstuffs from the missions were scarce, the Hispanics had to engage in more extended agricultural activity. As a result, Mexican settlements proliferated in the river valleys of the Sonoran Desert. Small villages existed everywhere, and the new arrivals assumed the way of life forged by the earlier settlers. Between the 1790s and 1820s, the Apache threat subsided because of successful military tactics and negotiations on the part of local leaders, and Hispanic settlements began to thrive in Pimería Alta. At one point as many as one thousand Hispanics lived in the Santa Cruz Valley. But with the independence of Mexico, the Spanish Crown abandoned its fortifications and the Apache lost no time in taking advantage of the opportunity. Overrunning Pimería Alta, they forced Hispanic settlers to the southern part of the desert.

As in Arizona, the establishment of colonies in California was an extension of the Spanish drive into northwestern New Spain. In addition, defense was the utmost consideration in the decision to go farther into the frontier. Like other world powers, the Russians were drawn to the prosperity of eighteenth-century New Spain. They threatened from their outposts in Alaska, compelling the Spaniards to try to halt their southward advance. In 1769, José de Gálvez, an aggressive representative of the Bourbons in New Spain, gave orders to settle Alta California from Baja California, and the same year a tired expedition led by the Franciscan Fray Junípero Serra founded the San Diego mission. A year later another mission was built in Monterey. During this period of flux, Juan Bautista de Anza, the Sonoran-born son of a Spanish official who himself became an officer, and Pedro de Garcés, a Spanish Franciscan missionary, founded the first overland route to California in 1774.

For the Franciscans, converting numerous California Indians became the main incentive in the drive northward. The first exploration of Juan Bautista de Anza resulted in the reinforcement of a mission along the beautiful Pacific coast in Monterey and the additional building of a presidio. Two years later, de Anza lead another expedition and founded San Francisco, where the presidio is still a landmark.

In a few years, familiar religious and military institutions, the mission and the presidio, dotted the California coastline all the way from San Diego to San Francisco. Soldiers of various racial mixtures, missionaries, and Indians made up the demographic profile of the coast. The soldiers were encouraged to go as settlers and to take their families, as was the tradition in other frontier regions of New Spain. Those who did not have mates found suitable partners among the Indian women, to the chagrin of the missionaries, who considered the mestizo soldiers a bad influence on the Indian communities. As time went by, many of the soldiers became landowners, especially after 1831, when mission property was confiscated by the now independent Mexican government. Some of these former soldiers acquired thousands of acres, laying the foundation for some of the old California families.

Soldier at the Monterey presidio in 1786. (Courtesy of the Bancroft Library, University of California.)

✸ANGLO ENCROACHMENT INTO THE MEXICAN NORTH

While Spain attempted to hold off encroachment into the northern regions of New Spain by other European imperialists, a series of events took place that changed the relationship between the Hispanic and Anglo areas of North America. In 1776, Anglo-Americans declared their independence from England, and thirty-four years later Hispanics proclaimed their independence from Spain. In both areas new nations were formed. The thirteen former British colonies came to be known as the United States of America in 1781, and the newly independent people of New Spain named their nation the Republic of Mexico.

Both areas had immense problems as they experimented with new forms of government and attempted to get their economies afloat. Mexico, however, had the most difficult time. Anglo-Americans had a preexisting political structure and economy, which allowed them to make a relatively smoother transition into independent status. While the thirteen colonies had been under the colonial tutelage of England, they had enjoyed more freedom than the colonists in the Spanish realms. Spain ruled and controlled the domains with an iron hand and had imposed a rigid economic and social caste system on its colonial subjects, which allowed the Catholic church to have inordinate influence on their everyday lives. As a consequence, the Mexicans were not as well prepared for the democratic ideals to which they aspired in the

A *patrón* in early California. (Courtesy of the Bancroft Library, University of California.)

1824 constitution. The result was years of confusion and interminable internal strife, which greatly weakened the economy and made the new nation vulnerable to outside powers.

The area of greatest weakness was in the far northern frontier. As has been indicated, Spain had difficulty in peopling its vast territory in New Spain. This condition made the area even more vulnerable to outside powers. To augment its forces in the interior of New Spain, which were busy squelching the independence movement that had started on September 16, 1810, with the insurrection of Father Miguel Hidalgo y Costilla, the Spaniards withdrew their troops from the frontier presidios. This further weakened the lines of defense in the north, inviting incursions from the newly independent but aggressive North Americans.

The danger of Yankee encroachment was apparent to the Spaniards much earlier. In 1803, a powerful France under Napoleon Bonaparte acquired from Spain the Louisiana Territory, which she had ceded during the Seven Years' War in the previous century. Napoleon, who was vying for dominance in Europe and needed revenue quickly, sold the vast territory to

Wife of a presidio soldier in Monterey, 1786. (Courtesy of the Bancroft Library, University of California.)

Presidio and pueblo of Santa Barbara in 1829. (From a lithograph by G. & W. Endicott. Courtesy of the Bancroft Library, University of California.)

the United States, and then the borders of the expanding infant nation connected directly with New Spain.

Anglo-Americans lost no time in determining what the new acquisition meant for the fledgling country. To the consternation of Spain, President Thomas Jefferson funded the historical expedition of Lewis and Clark in 1804. Spain was obviously worried that the exploration was a prelude to the settlement of the territory by Anglos. Then in 1806, Zebulon Pike, an army officer searching for the headwaters of the Red River in Arkansas, entered Spanish territory in Colorado, built a fort, and raised the colors of the United States. Spanish officials found and destroyed the fortification and arrested Pike and his men. Taken to Santa Fe and then to Chihuahua City farther south, Pike saw more of New Spain than most anybody else who was not a Spanish subject. In the memoirs of his adventure, Pike recognized the potential for trade with Mexico. This peaked the interest of many of his fellow Anglo-Americans.

A series of other events demonstrated that Anglo-Americans were anxious to fulfill what they considered their Manifest Destiny to settle areas even beyond their sovereign realm. In 1820, Stephen Long led a revolt, ostensibly as part of the independence movement against the Spanish, but obviously he was acting as a filibusterer for his countrymen. Spain finally entered into deliberations with Moses Austin, a Catholic from Missouri, to settle Anglo-Catholic families in Texas. The rationale for this seemingly paradoxical policy was to people the region between the more populated portions of New Spain and the United States with persons who owed a loyalty to Spain, even if they were not Hispanic. Initially, the Austin colony was made up of three hundred families in east Texas who were given generous empresario land grants. The stipulation was that they had to be Catholic, become subjects of the Crown, and abide by Spanish law. Moses died during the process and so the contract was concluded with Stephen, his son. These negotiations were concluded in 1821, right before Mexico acquired its independence under the leadership of Augustine Iturbide, a former Spanish officer who wanted to lead the newly independent nation down the path of monarchy. But Mexico honored the agreements that were established by Spain.

Iturbide was overthrown in 1823 and a more liberal constitutional government was established in 1824.

The new constitution called for a president, a congress, nineteen states with their own legislatures, and four territories. That same year, Erasmo Seguín, a delegate to the national congress from Texas, persuaded a willing congress to pass a colonization act designed to bring even more Anglo settlers to Texas. Between 1824 and 1830, thousands of Anglo families entered east Texas, acquiring hundreds of thousands of free acres and also buying land much cheaper than they could have in the United States. By 1830, Texas had eighteen thousand Anglo inhabitants and their African slaves, who numbered over two thousand.

Anglo-Americans found it difficult to live under Mexican rule from the outset. They had an aversion to the Spanish language and the Mexican laws and legal system (in particular, the nonexistence of juries). In 1824, Texas was joined with Coahuila into a gigantic state, with most of the population residing in the Coahuila portion of the entity. Anglo-Texans rankled at the remoteness of the seat of government in faraway Saltillo in Coahuila, and exacerbating this sentiment was the inability of the Mexican government to provide adequate protection from the marauding Comanche. Anglos also feared the threat to the institution of slavery on which they were so dependent. Indeed, in 1829 the Mexican government abolished slavery during the liberal administration of Vicente Guerrero, the second president under the constitution. The uproar in Texas was so intense that Guerrero decided not to enforce the law. Nonetheless, slaveholders in Texas knew that their days were numbered.

Perhaps the most vexing development for Texans was the Immigration Law of 1830. In 1827, Manuel Mier y Terán, a military officer charged with assessing the general conditions in Texas, concluded that Anglos posed a threat to the sovereignty of Mexico. Then in 1830, a coup d'état by Guerrero's vice president, Anastasio Bustamante, installed a conservative government that was intent on closing off the borders of Mexico to outsiders. The result was the law that forbade any new immigration into Texas, an act that greatly concerned Anglos, who wanted to expand the economy and their culture by emigration from the United States.

All in all, the sentiment for independence from Mexico was on the increase in Texas. In 1832, General Antonio López de Santa Anna ousted Bustamante and was elected president the following year. But he allowed his liberal vice president, Valentín Gómez Farías, to institute some anticlerical reforms against the Catholic church. This provoked powerful Mexican conservatives to act decisively. Somehow, General Santa Anna was persuaded in 1835 to oust his own vice president and to dissolve congress and institute a more closed system than even Bustamante had attempted a few years earlier. One of the first steps taken by Santa Anna under his centralized conservative constitution of *Las Siete Leyes* (The Seven Laws) was to dismantle the state legislatures and dismiss the governors and replace them with military officials. In Texas, Mexican troops were sent to enforce restrictive customs along the Gulf Coast, leading to a skirmish with Anglos, who did not want their trade with the United States disrupted.

To the disgruntled Texans, all seemed lost. The rumblings for independence increased. Late in 1835, Santa Anna sent General Martín Perfecto de Cos to San Antonio to administer the new federal laws, but he was repelled by Anglo-Texans and Mexican Texans who were determined to resist. The Anglos fortified themselves in the mission of El Alamo and awaited the inevitable retribution. Santa Anna decided then to take matters into his own hands and, mustering a large force, descended on San Antonio. Mexican-Texan scouts warned of the impending attack, but Anglo defenders under Colonel Travis did not believe the first messages. When it was obvious that the threat was real, the Anglos prepared for

Ferdinand VII, King of Spain, 1814-1833. (From Manuel Rivera Cambas, *Los gobernantes*, 1872.)

battle. Instead of attacking immediately, the Mexican army laid siege to the fortified mission, which lasted two weeks. The long Kentucky rifles of the defenders had a much longer range than Santa Anna's artillery and muskets and the Texans were able to pick off some of the Mexicans. Travis and his men, who included such legendary heroes as Davey Crockett and Jim Bowie, with their superior weaponry took many Mexican lives in the process. Santa Anna ordered a *degüello* attack, which means taking no prisoners, and all the vastly outnumbered defenders were killed, even after they surrendered.

After the massive defeat at the Alamo, the Texas army, led by General Sam Houston, fled eastward with Santa Anna's troops in hot pursuit. At Goliad, a town east of San Antonio, the Mexicans decisively defeated the Texans, and, as at the Alamo, they took no prisoners. These defeats served to galvanize Texan resistance, and eventually Santa Anna committed a military blunder that led to the defeat of his army and his capture at San Jacinto, located near present-day Houston. The Texans declared their independence and wrested from a reluctant Santa Anna terms of surrender that included Texas's independence. Mexican officials never accepted the agreement reached with Santa Anna, but Texas remained independent, nonetheless, until 1845, when it was annexed to the United States.

The Texas rebellion caused hard feelings between Mexico and the United States, and the rift eventually grew to proportions of war in 1846. In 1836 Mexico had charged the United States with backing the rebels, an allegation denied vehemently by U.S. officials. That the United States immediately recognized the Texas republic was proof enough for the Mexicans, however, and they warned that annexation of Texas by the United States would mean war. Another cause of discord between the two uneasy neighbors was two million dollars in damage done to Anglo-American properties in Mexico as a consequence of revolutionary violence in Mexico.

Then in February 1845, the United States voted for the annexation of Texas, and Mexico broke off relations but stopped short of declaring war. Apparently, Mexico at this point was about to recognize Texas's independence and did not want any border problems. Still, the issue that eventually brought the two nations into warfare was the matter of the boundary. When Texans declared their independence in 1836, they claimed the lower Rio Grande as their southern border. The Mexicans insisted that the Nueces River, a few hundred miles to the north, was the border. With the annexation, the United States accepted the Texas version of the boundary dispute.

It was no secret that many Anglo-Americans wanted to fulfill their Manifest Destiny of expanding their country all the way to the Pacific coast. At the very moment of annexation, U.S. officials under President James K. Polk continued trying to buy vast areas of Mexico's northernmost territories, including California. In the fall of 1845, the American president sent John Slidell to Mexico with an offer of twenty-five million dollars for California, but Mexican officials refused to even see him. General Zachary Taylor was then sent across the Nueces River to set up a blockade of the Rio Grande at its mouth on Port Isabel, and Mexicans retaliated by attacking the U.S. troops on April 25, 1845. Casualties ensued. President Polk immediately went to Congress and obtained a declaration of war against Mexico. There was some opposition, however. Abraham Lincoln, then a congressman from Illinois, and some other colleagues opposed the declaration, but they were in the minority.

Two years of war followed. That it took so long was somewhat surprising, considering Mexico's weak political situation. From the time that Texas was annexed until the war ended in 1847, six different presidents attempted to make foreign policy, quite often at odds with each other. Nonetheless, the Mexican will to resist was underestimated, and it was difficult for an inexperienced U.S. Army to fight on foreign soil. The U.S. invasion took place from four different directions. Troops under General Taylor crossed north across the Rio Grande, while General Stephen Watts Kearny took an army overland to New Mexico and then to California. There he encountered considerable resistance from the Californios (Mexican Californians) at the Battle of San Pascual before reaching Los Angeles. California was also assaulted by sea by Commodore John C. Fremont. But the most decisive drive was by General Winfield Scott, who bombarded Vera Cruz and then proceeded with the most sizable force all the way to Mexico City, with the Mexicans offering the greatest resistance at Churubusco (part of present-day Mexico City).

Not all Americans supported the war. Newspapers carried reports that General Scott had admitted that his men had committed horrible atrocities. By September, his troops occupied Mexico City. General Santa Anna had been president since December of 1846, but his attempts to fend off the American invasion were hopeless and in November he resigned in disgrace. The Mexicans refused to come to the bargaining table until they were thoroughly routed. Finally, in February 1848, they signed the Treaty of Guadalupe Hidalgo, which brought the war officially to an end.

The treaty provided fifteen million dollars for the vast territories of New Mexico, Arizona, and Califor-

Pío Pico (1801-1894) was the last governor of California under Mexican rule. (Courtesy of the California Historical Society.)

nia and parts of Nevada, Utah, and Colorado. The most important provisions of the treaty as far as understanding the history of Mexican Americans had to do with the Mexicans who remained in the territory acquired by the United States. They had a year to retreat into Mexico's shrunken border or they automatically would become citizens of the United States. They would then acquire all the rights of citizens. In addition, the treaty assured southwest Mexicans that their property would be protected and they would have the right to maintain religious and cultural integrity. These provisions, which the Mexican negotiators at the town of Guadalupe Hidalgo had insisted on, seemed protective of the former Mexican citizens, but these stipulations were only as good as the ability and desire to uphold the promises.

✳MEXICANS UNDER U.S. RULE

The Supreme Court ruled in 1855 that the Treaty of Guadalupe Hidalgo did not apply to Texas, but Mexicans in Texas were supposedly protected under the 1836 constitution of the Republic of Texas, which was modified to become a state constitution in 1845. The territorial acquisition delineated in the Treaty of Guadalupe Hidalgo did not include southern Arizona and southern New Mexico. That region, which included the area from present- day Yuma along the Gila River (twenty-five miles south of Phoenix) all the way to the Mesilla Valley, where Las Cruces, New Mexico, is located, was sold to the United States by General Santa Anna the year that he returned to power in 1853. Ironically, hundreds of Mexicans who in 1848 had moved south into the Mesilla Valley or the Santa Cruz Valley in southern Arizona found themselves in the United States again. The provisions in the Gadsden Treaty regarding Mexicans in the newly annexed territory were similar to those in the Treaty of Guadalupe Hidalgo. Few Mexicans had any faith that any of the provisions protecting Mexicans would be honored, and many were embittered because they felt betrayed by Mexico. But the Mexican government did attempt to attract Mexicans from the southwestern United States into what became the most northernmost Mexican region in the present-day border states. Of the 80,000 or so Mexicans living in the ceded territories, only a few thousand took up the offer.

The promise that the remaining Mexicans would receive all the rights accrued to U.S. citizens did not really materialize. New Mexico, with the largest number of Hispanics, perhaps 60,000, was able to achieve some political self-determination for its citizens. But there and everywhere else in what was now the southwestern United States, the newly minted U.S. citizens were systematically discriminated against. Except in New Mexico, Anglo immigration overwhelmed Mexicans in the newly acquired territories almost from the beginning. In Texas, for example, the population increased from 30,000 in 1836 to 140,000 in 1846. While there was migration from Mexico, this rapid increase in population was mainly due to the influx of Anglos from the United States. Mexicans were outnumbered six to one.

The 1836 Texas constitution stipulated that all residents living in Texas at the time of the rebellion would acquire all the rights of citizens of the new republic, but if they had been disloyal, these rights were forfeited. Numerically superior Anglos, embittered with Mexicans during the rebellion, retaliated by mistreating or forcing Mexicans off their property. Many Mexicans simply crossed the border and went to Mexico. In 1857, Anglo businessmen attempted to run off Mexican teamsters, who had dominated the transport of goods in south Texas since the colonial period, by hiring thugs to strongarm the carters off the trails. The attempt was not wholly successful, but it demonstrated the increasing antipathy toward Mexicans and a continuing violation of the guarantees offered by the Treaty of Guadalupe Hidalgo.

When Texas joined the union in 1845, only one Mexican Texan was a delegate to the convention that framed the new state constitution. And in the convention itself, there were many who felt that Mexicans should not be allowed to vote. But in the end, they were not denied suffrage. In spite of this victory, Mexican Texans were intimidated into not voting, and the result was that few politicians were Mexicans. During the era of the republic, 1836-1845, only a few rich Mexicans living in the San Antonio area acquired political power. Juan Seguín, for example, became mayor of the city only to be forced out after Anglos arrived in larger numbers. After Texas became a state, even fewer Mexicans participated in politics. In 1850, of the sixty-four members in the state legislature, none were born in Texas or Mexico. Whenever Mexicans did vote, their power was diminished because they were dominated by political bosses who were able to buy in mass the votes of Mexicans. In addition, there were white-only primaries from which Mexicans were barred, and since the Democratic party dominated in Texas, the elections were really decided in these primaries. Poll taxes, that is, taxes levied for voting, also served to deter from voting those with few economic resources; this included most Mexicans.

In California, while Mexican and Anglos did not have the same legacy of conflict that characterized racial relations in Texas, many of the newcomers were from the U.S. South, where prejudice against racial minorities was the rule. Political participation of Californios was also minimal in the state, although in the beginning their integration was more evident than in Texas. For example, out of forty-eight delegates, eight Mexican Californians were selected to

Confederate officers from Laredo, Texas: Refugio Benavides, Atanacio Vidaurri, Cristóbal Benavides and John Z. Leyendecker. (Courtesy of the Laredo Public Library.)

participate in the state constitutional convention of 1849 when California joined the Union.

The constitutional convention was the last major political event in which Mexicans participated. The gold rush of 1849 attracted thousands of Anglos, which resulted in an even more imbalanced ratio of Mexicans to Anglos. In 1850, Mexicans were 15 percent of the population, but twenty years later that figure dropped to only 4 percent. Political and economic influence declined first in the north, the area that attracted the majority of Anglos, because of the goldfields. The lack of political influence led to legislation contrary to Californio interests. For example, in 1851 the six southern counties where most Mexicans resided were taxed five times the rate of other local entities. In 1855, so-called greaser laws were passed that prohibited bearbaiting, bullfights and cockfights, clearly aimed at prohibiting the customs of the Californios. Vagrancy laws were passed, also aimed at Mexicans, because when a community wanted to force Mexicans out, these laws were applied selectively. One of the most onerous laws was the Foreign Miners tax of 1850, which levied a charge for anyone who was not a U.S. citizen. While some miners were French, Australian, or Irish, most "foreigners" were Mexicans or South Americans, who possessed superior mining skills. There can be no doubt that the tax was designed to eliminate this competition from the gold diggings.

In New Mexico, Mexicans participated more fully in both the economy and in politics than in any other region. A major reason for this was that Hispanic New Mexicans remained a numerical majority until the turn of the century. Anglos came to quickly dominate the southeastern part of the state, but New Mexican Hispanics maintained control in the north around Santa Fe and Albuquerque. From 1850 to 1911, Hispanics dominated most key political slots and controlled the territorial legislature until the 1890s. Ironically, one reason it took so long for the New Mexican territory to become a state was a reluctance among Anglo politicians in Washington, D.C., to allow a new state dominated by Mexicans.

In Arizona, which was part of the New Mexican territory until 1863, Mexicans maintained some political power in the area that was purchased under the Gadsden Treaty in 1853. This was especially true in and around Tucson, which became the territorial capital after Arizona separated from New Mexico. Political and economic cooperation was more evident between Anglos and Mexicans in this area because economic activity depended greatly on trade through the state of Sonora. With the coming of the railroads in the 1880s, however, the relationship between both groups became more strained as a new

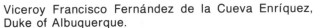

Viceroy Francisco Fernández de la Cueva Enríquez, Duke of Albuquerque.

General Manuel Mier y Terán, Laredo, 1928.

influx of Anglos who did not need to cooperate with Mexicans overwhelmed the older Anglo population. Politically, this demographic shift translated into lack of political power. The territorial seat was removed to Prescott, away from Mexicans, and eventually to Phoenix when Arizona became a state. Mexicans in southern Arizona retained a modicum of political power, and the few Hispanic legislators in Arizona until the 1950s all came from that section.

Lack of protection for Mexicans in the Southwest was most obvious in the violation of property rights. While the Treaty of Guadalupe Hidalgo was vague regarding property, it did constitute the most definite commitment in the document. As more Anglos entered the Southwest and the area became more economically developed, land values rose and the thirst for land became more apparent. The system of keeping records of property claims differed between Mexico and the United States. As a consequence, proof of title became an immediate burden for Mexicans throughout the newly acquired territories.

To address the issue of property ownership, Congress passed the California Land Act of 1851 to facilitate legalization of land belonging to Californios

prior to the takeover. Instead of helping the Californios resolve their property problems quickly, however, official procedures sometimes took years, forcing the ranchers to turn over huge tracts of land to the very lawyers who were adjudicating their cases. Then in 1862, the Homestead Act was passed in Congress, allowing squatters in the West to settle and claim vacant lands. In California, thousands converged on lands claimed by Mexicans, creating legal entanglements that were many times settled in favor of the squatters. Many of the homesteaders were front men for speculators who took these free lands and held them for future use or sale.

In the New Mexico territory, an even slower system, the surveyor of general claims office, was established in 1854. It took that office fifty years to settle just a few claims, and in the meantime many Mexicans in New Mexico were also defrauded of their land in grabs similar to those in California. During the 1890s, for example, as the Santa Fe Railroad was built from Kansas through the northern part of the territory, land speculators known as the Santa Fe Ring concocted ruses that divested hundreds of Hispanic landowners of their farms and ranches. In response, the Mexicans organized into Las Gorras Blancas (The White Caps), bands of hooded night riders who tore down fences and tried to derail trains in the hope of intimidating Anglo land developers and railroad companies into abandoning New Mexico. Then, the establishment of state parks during the early twentieth century contributed to even further erosion of Mexican landholdings in New Mexico.

All in all, New Mexicans did not suffer the same degree of land usurpation as in other parts of the Southwest, but the acreage held by Hispanics prior to the Mexican-American War declined considerably. In the final analysis, while the Treaty of Guadalupe Hidalgo did not precisely define the rights of Mexicans, it is clear that most of the guarantees were not upheld and Mexicans in the Southwest declined considerably, economically and politically, during their experience with Anglo domination. But by the 1890s, considerable immigration from Mexico resulted in the swelling of Mexican communities throughout the Southwest, changing the character of Mexican life in the United States.

✴AFRICA AND THE MAKING OF SOCIETY IN CUBA AND PUERTO RICO

While New Spain evolved a society made up primarily of an Indian-Spanish race mixture, Africans and Europeans commingled with the few Indian survivors to form the Spanish Caribbean community. Sugarcane transformed the Caribbean region into a lucrative source of wealth for the Spaniards. But because the natives were too few, another adequate source of labor was found in Africa. The slave trade had been started by the Portuguese in the fifteenth century, but it did not become profitable until the great plantation system developed in such American regions as Brazil, the British colonies in North America, and, of course, the Caribbean islands.

The source of slaves in Africa was the western coast between the Senegal River to the north and Angola to the south. They were captured and sold to European traders, usually Portuguese, by slave hunters who many times were also Africans. Varying forms of slavery already existed among these ethnic groups where workers toiled in large-scale agricultural systems. Slaves were sought in this area, rather than in other African areas, because the people there already had some experience with systematic work demands.

The slaving expeditions in West Africa brought untold anguish to the black Africans who were affected by the raids. Families were broken up as the young males (the most sought after) were torn from their roots. That was only the beginning of the suffer-

ing, however. In preparation for the odious voyage, captured Africans were first housed in overcrowded slave castles called *barranconas*, where thousands perished. In the trip across the Atlantic, thousands more died in the crowded hulls of the slave ships making their way either to the Caribbean islands or Brazil, where these human beings were auctioned off and sold like cattle in huge markets.

In the Caribbean islands, this human chattel was sent to work the hundreds of plantations developed by colonists from the major European imperial powers. Not all slaves wound up on the plantation fields, however, as they were also sold to artisans as helpers or to the huge households of rich merchants within the plantations themselves. Although males were preferred as slaves, hundreds of thousands of females also entered the market. Women worked just as hard, and it was not lost on slave owners that by coupling slaves of the opposite sex, even by promoting a family structure based on the new conditions encountered in the Caribbean, they could ensure that the offspring of the slaves would be born into slavery. This perpetuated a valuable commodity within their own domain.

Black slaves also found their way to Mexico, especially to the coastal areas of Vera Cruz and Guerrero, where they were concentrated around the port of Acapulco. Their labor was required for sugar plantations as well, although these enterprises were not as extensive as in the Caribbean. Slavery in Mexico was abolished in 1829 by the new republican government that emerged after independence. In Cuba and Puerto Rico, under Spanish rule until the end of the nineteenth century, slavery was legal until late into the nineteenth century. But the growth of slavery everywhere in the Caribbean New World was intimately linked to the fortunes of sugarcane production. However, a large-scale sugar plantation system did not emerge in either Cuba or Puerto Rico until the end of the eighteenth century. Up to that point, independent peasant farmers, squatters that relied little on African slaves, and peons on large haciendas predominated. The development of slavery was slow as a consequence. Between 1550 and 1650, the slave population only increased from 1,000 to 5,000. Nonetheless, in Cuba before the nineteenth century, free Africans were more proportionally numerous than anywhere else in the Western Hemisphere, because the sugar economy was never as ensconced there as in other colonies, such as those of the British. These freedmen engaged in all kinds of trades and activities, creating a class of African-Cubans that enjoyed a status of independence not as attainable to blacks in the British colonies. The ramifications of this more relaxed relationship, at least as it existed before the nineteenth century, is crucial to the persistence of African culture in Cuba.

But that does not mean that life was in any way promising for slaves. Whenever they could, *cimarrones* (runaway slaves) ran away to Orient province, creating scores of fortified communities called *palenques*. Indicative of the discontent of the Africans in Cuba was the persistence of the feared slave rebellions. For example, 300 rebelled on one plantation in 1727, killing practically all of the whites, and one year later all the copper mines were closed off in Santiago because of uprisings in that province.

In the late eighteenth century, the African population began to rise rapidly. Following thirty years of warfare between the European imperial powers, the British occupied Cuba in 1763, ushering in an intensive period of economic development; thus, sugarcane production expanded dramatically. From the time the first African slave stepped foot on Cuba to 1770, 60,000 were introduced to the island. Then between 1770 and 1790 there was a striking increase in slave traffic. At least 50,000 Africans arrived in those years alone. At the end of the century, a unique opportunity arose for investors in Cuban sugar production—the collapse of the Haitian sugar industry

after rebels had ravaged that country in the 1790s— leading to an even larger number of slaves on the island. During this time, 30,000 French émigrés and their slaves entered Cuba from Santo Domingo during a time of rising prosperity in sugar and coffee.

The slave population continued to grow into the early nineteenth century, and by 1827, African slaves accounted for about 40 percent of the Cuban population, which was over 700,000. By midcentury, the percentage of African-born slaves expanded to about 70 percent of the slave population and, for the first time, blacks outnumbered whites. In the 1850s, the combination of free Afro-Cubans and slaves made the black population over 56 percent. According to one study, 550,000 slaves were imported into Cuba between 1812 and 1865 in spite of the worldwide ban on the slave trade that was instituted by the British in the 1820s.

A remarkable expansion in Cuban sugar production accounted for the growth of slave traffic in the nineteenth century. While many slaves toiled on coffee *fincas* or haciendas or tobacco *vegas*, most worked on sugar *ingenios*. The percentage of blacks, which throughout the colonial period had been among the smallest in the Caribbean, was now larger

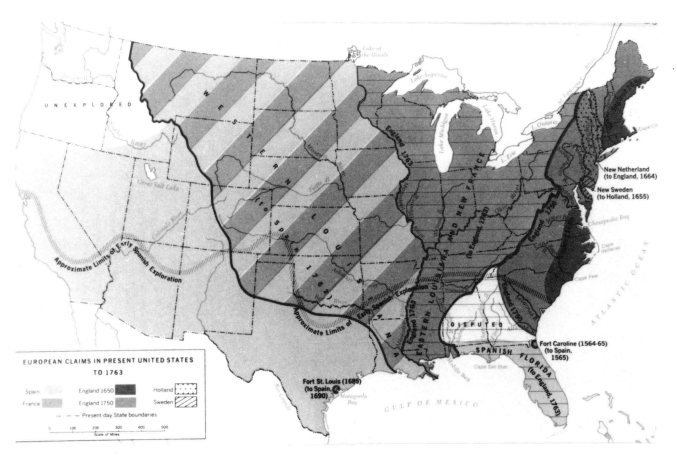

(Courtesy of the U.S. Department of the Interior and the National Park Service.)

than anywhere else. Quite predictably, during the nineteenth century, slave rebellions became more common. In these, whites were often killed, and retribution was quick and brutal. Suppression of the uprisings was often consummated by the indiscriminate execution of slaves, regardless of their involvement. Rebellions increased because of the larger number of newly arrived slaves from Africa with immediate memories of their lost freedom; they were resentful and less accepting of their lot.

Independence sentiment was retarded in Cuba because of this reliance on slavery by whites. Lacking was the diversity of dissatisfied classes that characterized other colonies in New Spain whose independence struggles started early in the nineteenth century. Island society reflected the dichotomy of the black and white races more than ever. The Haitian example, where the independence movement was unleashed by the pent-up emotions of slaves, struck a familiar chord of fear among the white planter class.

But the world was changing as industrialization and technological innovation required new markets and the use of more diverse amounts of raw materials. Cuba could not remain out of step for long in its use of outmoded methods in the production of sugar. In the second half of the nineteenth century, some Cuban and Spanish capitalists realized that Cuba's success in the impending order required diversified production and the use of wage labor that was cheaper and more efficient than slavery. As a consequence, the sugar industry was modernized, made more competitive, and expanded. Foreign capital from the United States was largely responsible for the innovations, and the colonial economy passed increasingly into the hands of North Americans.

To meet the wage-labor demands, 125,000 Chinese were brought to Cuba between 1840 and 1870 to work as cane cutters, to build railroads in rural areas, and to serve as domestics in the cities. Also, the influx of European immigrants, primarily from Spain, increased during that period. Newly arrived Spaniards became concentrated in the retail trades and operated small general stores called *bodegas*. In the 1880s, slavery was abolished by Spain in a gradual program that took eight years. The influx of new people in this period made Cuba more heterogeneous, leading to the social diversity that is so apparent today. Immigration to the United States before the revolution of 1959 was more reflective of this racial variety. But as Cubans fled communism in recent years, the outflow came more from the descendants of European emigrants.

In Puerto Rico, although African slaves were brought over almost immediately after the settlement of the island by Spaniards, they never quite acquired the numerical importance that they had in Cuba. In fact, the proportion of slaves in Puerto Rico never exceeded 14 percent. In 1775, for example, out of a total Puerto Rican population of 70,250, only 6,467 were slaves. As a result, one hundred years later when slavery was abolished, the transition to wage labor was easier than in Cuba.

In the nineteenth century the slave traffic did increase, but it was not as important in establishing a rural culture as was the case in Cuba. In many regions of Puerto Rico, a large class of rural poor whites and persons with a mixed European, African, and Indian heritage dominated. Their way of life was strictly preindustrial. Country folk eked out a living as peasants, tenants on subsistence farms, or craftsmen in the towns and villages. This group came to be known as *jíbaros* (a South American word for "highlander" or "rustic") and remain to this day an identifiable group in both Puerto Rico and on the U.S. mainland.

As happened in Cuba in the first half of the 1800s, the importation of slaves increased because of an expansion in sugar plantations. At the same time, however, foreign investment and immigration grew, and the mixed classes who comprised the rural peasants and working people were marginalized by an empowered planter class and a large-scale export agricultural system. But the influx of slaves during the nineteenth century was larger than ever and African culture achieved a greater voice at the folk level, albeit mixing with a still strong jíbaro expression.

In Puerto Rico there has not been an upheaval such as the Mexican Revolution of 1910 or the Cuban Revolution of 1959 that would have provoked large-scale immigration of the middle and upper classes to the United States. As a consequence, the character of Puerto Rican society in the United States is more reflective of Puerto Rico's diversity. Unlike the case of Cubans in Florida, in New York and other cities where Puerto Ricans have gone in large numbers, the fine blend of jíbaro/mestizo, African, and European cultures is evenly dispersed. In Mexican-American society, on the other hand, the impact of the upper classes has been greatly mitigated by their wholesale return to Mexico after the revolution in the 1920s and during the Great Depression. Moreover, since the 1940s, the amplified immigrant stream that continues to arrive to this day is largely working class.

But regardless of the makeup of the Hispanic society in the United States, there is no doubt that African culture brought from both the Spanish Caribbean islands and Mexico has greatly influenced American culture. This phenomenon is especially evident in music. The so-called tropical sound that permeates all of this region with such colorful appellations as salsa, *merengue, mambo, rhumba,* and *jarocho,* has deep roots in the percussion-rich expression of Africa. To see this, all one has to do is observe a *conjunto* (band) playing a variation of this music. The percussion requirements alone mean that individual players are needed for congas, bongos, timbales, and maracas. The religions of Africa have also greatly influenced, in a syncretic fashion, the Catholicism brought over from Spain, producing an array of observances known popularly as *santerismo.* And, of course, the food owes much to Africa, as does the Spanish language.

The most evident African vestige, however, is genetic. Everywhere in the Caribbean and Mexico where slavery was prominent, the Negro features of Africa are evident. A racial consciousness in Hispanic culture is also part of this heritage and has manifested itself in racism and self-hate. Fortunately, in recent years the Caribbean and Mexican people of African descent have undergone a cathartic effort to combat the debilitating effects of racism coming from their own Hispanic compatriots.

✳ INDEPENDENCE OF CUBA AND PUERTO RICO

As is the case with Mexico, independence from Spain and the eventual subordination of the island economies to U.S. interests provide the foundation for understanding migration from Cuba and Puerto Rico. Along with the Philippines, Cuba and Puerto Rico remained the only major Spanish colonies that did not secede during the massive struggles that wracked the entire Spanish Empire in the early nineteenth century. In the second half of the century, both these Caribbean holdings experienced conspiracies and rebellions, although efforts to finally obtain independence were not successful until 1898. In Cuba, a nationalist movement was vitalized in the latter part of the century as Spain's treatment of the colony became increasingly arbitrary. A crosscut of the Cuban classes became more and more resentful as the inept and corrupt colonial government imposed heavier taxes and, through censorship, restricted their freedom.

But much of the sentiment for liberty came from the sizable class of middle-class farmers and merchants who opposed slavery and desired to be free of the Spanish colonial tie. On the first issue, Madrid waffled, and although total freedom was eventually granted to the slaves, it came very slowly. In October 1868, a group of Cuban rebels led by Carlos Manuel de Céspedes, a black general, took advantage of revolutionary fomentation in Spain itself and declared independence at Yara in the eastern portion of the island.

This region had few slaves and was a hotbed of emancipation activity.

A provincial government headed by de Céspedes was established in Orient province, where Yara is located, and from there the movement obtained widespread support. A bloody war known as the Ten Years' War, ensued, in which Spanish attempts to evict the rebels from the eastern half of Cuba were unsuccessful. Guerrilla tactics used by the rebels stymied the efforts of Spanish troops, but neither side could really win a clear victory. The war came to an end when both rebels and Spaniards signed the Pact of El Zajón in 1878. The document promised amnesty for the insurgents and home rule; it also provided freedom for the slaves that fought on the side of the rebels.

Eventually, slavery was abolished, but Spain's failure to provide political reform provoked the Cubans to reconsider independence. In 1895, the poet and patriot José Martí opened the final battle for independence. Much of the planning for this insurrection was done in New York, where Martí had obtained Yankee support. But looming darkly behind the whole liberation cause were North American economic and political interests. Because of its proximity, Cuba had strategic value for the United States, but as long as it was under Spain, many Americans thought that it would not fall into the wrong hands. Before the Civil War, Southerners wanted to annex Cuba in order to expand the territory under slavery, but antislavery interests in the United States thwarted any such plans. In the nineteenth century, Americans tried to buy the island from Spain on several occasions. In 1869, taking advantage of the chaos of the Ten Years War, the United States offered $100 million for the island but was rejected. So it was not surprising, when independence seemed more likely at the end of the nineteenth century, that U.S. officials pressed to influence the unfolding process.

The trajectory toward independence in Puerto Rico was not as conspicuous as in Cuba, but a strong sentiment for freedom emerged, nonetheless. Puerto Rican nationalism was influenced by the same conditions that provoked the feeling in Cuba. While the planter classes expressed a wish for political autonomy from the mother country, they also wanted to maintain an economy based on slavery and peonage. Equivocal and confused about their desires, the criollo elites vacillated and were reluctant to assume the lead toward acquiring independence.

The nationalist movement was directed more by activists from the urban middle class and small farmers. This was especially true after 1850, when the Madrid government assumed a more mercantilistic stance. But in spite of high-tariff barriers that were

Albizu Campos, leader of the Puerto Rican independence movement, at a press conference on December 16, 1947.

exile known sympathizers of independence. Among these was Ramón Emeterio Betances, who fled to New York, where he joined other like-minded Puerto Ricans and Cubans. On September 23, 1868, this group declared an abortive insurrection known as El Grito de Lares. Members of the *criollo* middle class and free Afro-Cubans who lived in the coffee-growing region of Lares were the main supporters of the effort. The poorly planned attempt was doomed from the outset, and Spain easily defeated the insurrectionists.

But the movement did not die with the failure of the Lares revolt. As in Cuba, Puerto Ricans remained dissatisfied with the mother country's feeble attempts to redress their accumulating grievances. Later in the century, such patriots as the intellectual José Julián Acosta and the young and untiring newspaper editor Luis Muñoz-Rivera were responsible for forcing major concessions from Spain. A covenant was signed in 1897 that granted to both Cuba and Puerto Rico autonomy and home rule.

But much of the movement for complete independence was already set in motion, and these gestures from Spain were too little, too late. Increasingly, a

designed to force Puerto Ricans to pay more for American-made goods, so that Spanish merchandise would be cheaper, Spain's hold over the Spanish Caribbean steadily declined as it lost control over the sugar trade to the Americans. By 1870, 68 percent of Puerto Rican sugar products were marketed in the United States and only 1 percent were sent to Spain. Exerting its imperial power, Madrid, by the time of independence, managed to regain 35 percent of the market and continued to provide the Caribbean colonies with some finished products. Still, U.S. merchants were buying 61 percent of all Puerto Rican exports, while providing the lion's share of all industrial machinery necessary for processing sugar cane. Eventually, it became evident to the Puerto Ricans, as it did to the Cubans, that the link to the mother country was both intrusive and unnecessary.

The earliest indication of a strong united Puerto Rican nationalism goes back to 1867. On April 27, a mutiny among Spanish troops stationed on the island provoked the colonial governor, who was uneasy over the possibility of freedom movements, to not only execute the mutineers but also round up and

Luis Muñoz-Rivera, patriot of Puerto Rican independence.

vital core of Puerto Rican conspirators joined their Cuban co-colonialists in a movement for freedom. But every leap toward freedom from Spain threw the revolutionaries into the American sphere of influence. When José Martí initiated the final battles for independence in 1895 in Cuba, much of his preparation was done in the United States. Martí had started his proindependence party, the Cuban Revolutionary party (PRC) in Tampa, Florida. Many of the patriots, such as Tomás Estrada Palma, the first president of independent Cuba, acquired U.S. citizenship while in exile and then returned to the island to join the insurgency. Tragically, the valiant efforts of these patriots involved them with the United States to such a degree that the final price was costly. In the end, Cuba and Puerto Rico traded one master for another.

Spain's retaliation was characteristically harsh. José Martí was killed four months after the struggle began. One year after the insurrection started, Madrid sent General Valeriano Weyler, a hardened veteran who launched the brutal "war with war" campaign to wipe out the rebel movement. In a highly successful campaign, Cuban propagandists in the United States worked hand in hand with the English-language press to evoke sympathy for the Cuban cause against Spain. General Weyler was then pulled out of Cuba to quell the intensity of world public opinion, which had turned against Spain, especially among Americans.

But American support quickly turned into outright confiscation of the Cuban and Puerto Rican rebel cause. When the American battleship the USS *Maine* blew up mysteriously in Havana Harbor in April 1898, "yellow press" newspapers in the United States clamored for war against Spain. President William McKinley, reflecting an American longing for a maritime empire, seized the opportunity and declared war against Spain on April 28. Five months later Spain capitulated and signed the Treaty of Paris, transferring Cuba, Puerto Rico, and the Philippines to the United States. President McKinley quickly achieved the overseas realm that he wanted.

Cuba, unlike Puerto Rico, was allowed to become independent and promulgate a constitution, but hopes for true Cuban sovereignty were quickly dashed when Cuban politicians were pressured into including the Platt Amendment in their founding document. The provision allowed the United States to intervene militarily in Cuban affairs. The two neighboring Caribbean islands had much in common but had evolved separate cultural and ethnic identities. Overnight, both began an intimate, albeit antagonistic, relationship with the United States. Out of such closeness, migration to the mainland ensued.

✳EARLY MEXICAN IMMIGRATION TO THE UNITED STATES

Mexican immigration by the beginning of the twentieth century can roughly be placed in three categories. The first is migrants who were left outside the borders of a shrinking Mexico after 1836, 1848, and 1853 and the natives who, although not really migrants, were considered foreigners in their native land. The second category consists of migrants who continued entering and leaving the U.S. Southwest in a preestablished pattern that preceded the takeover. The third and most important group, in terms of the bigger picture of immigration, are Mexicans who arrived in response to the dramatically expanding need for laborers after the 1880s.

Three significant events occurred in Anglo-Mexican relations that set the stage for this immigration pattern. The Texas Rebellion (1836), the Mexican War (1848), and the Gadsden Purchase (1853) severed immense territorial lands from Mexico and the eighty thousand or so Mexicans that were living on them. These Spanish-speaking settlers were dispersed in sparsely settled areas throughout the lost territories. In less than forty years, they had been subjects of Spain and citizens of Mexico and were now entering a new phase. The inhabitants were descendants of the Spanish-Mexican settlers who had migrated from the interior of Mexico and in many areas had pushed aside or conquered the indigenous groups that occupied the land before them.

Now they found themselves conquered and colonized, separated from their political and cultural roots by an invisible and, for a time, unpatrolled boundary line. Initially, they resisted the North American invasion and occupation as best they could. Some retreated within the shrunken borders of Mexico rather than remain under U.S. domination. Many of the Spanish-speaking inhabitants living in the conquered territories had been born on the southern side of what was now the border, in villages like Camargo in Tamaulipas, Ojinaga in Chihuahua, or Tubutama in Sonora. Their present circumstances, brought on by the drama of war and conquest, had originally been dictated by a less dramatic decision to move north within what they considered their home areas. Moving from Tubutama to Tubac, Arizona, for example, was a matter of some sixty miles. The migrant might have had property interests and family kinships in Tubac, so close were relationships between the Altar Valley in northern Sonora and the Santa Cruz Valley of southern Arizona.

To a lesser degree, Mexican areas in northern New Mexico and California shared similar characteristics with the Mexican territories that the new boundary lines now designated as the northernmost outpost.

Still, a century of relatively close economic and social relationships between Chihuahua and New Mexico, for example, dictated that the two provinces evolve along similar lines. Until Yankee traders penetrated Santa Fe in the late eighteenth century, Chihuahua was the only link that New Mexican settlements had to civilization, probably being the only source of cultural progression within the realm of larger Spanish society.

In California, a society also evolved that was separated from the areas that make up the present border regions. A fanciful myth regarding the pure Spanish origins of these Californios and their link to Spain has been perpetuated by romantic writers and Hollywood lore. In reality, the closest ties this society had to Spain were Acapulco, San Blas, and Guaymas, the main sources of supply and trade for this region until Yankee traders rounded the Strait of Magellan in their ships. Like the other frontier outposts, California was sparsely settled and devoid of the comforts and cultural attributes found in such colonial centers as Guanajuato and San Luis Potosí. Moreover, California was populated by colonists whose earlier roots were established in Sonora, and for a long time California was considered an appendage of this northern province.

Thus, when the United States took over these territories, it acquired a Mexican population that was for all intents and purposes a continuation of Mexico's frontier north. The inhabitants during the Mexican period had migrated freely back and forth across what was later to become a border. Movement made by parents, grandparents, brothers, uncles, and kin of all types meant that an extensive network of family ties existed in the region that was now politically divided. In southern Arizona, for example, thousands of Mexicans had abandoned their lands for Sonora during the independence period in the early nineteenth century, mostly because of a menacing increase in Indian depredations.

In spite of the changed political status, migration within the border region continued during the early occupation period, and immigrants were, for the most part, oblivious to the geopolitical distinctions that national governments made so carefully. Various factors stimulated this migration. In some cases economic inducements, such as the discovery of gold in California, provoked a massive outpouring of miners from Sonora and other parts of Mexico. They arrived before the influx of the Anglo forty-niners, and mining techniques introduced by these northern Mexican miners prevailed in the numerous mining centers of California during the heyday of the gold rush. After 1836, thousands of peons fled the large

haciendas of northeast Mexico, seeking their freedom in south Texas; the border was much closer now.

In general, before 1870 there were only minimal economic inducements to Mexican immigration to the United States. Anglos who came after 1836 and 1848 interacted within the native Mexican economy through raising stock and some mining. Markets for southwestern products did expand during the early years of the Anglo takeover, as population growth throughout the territories demanded more foodstuffs. Mexicans in Texas, New Mexico, and California, however, had been trading with American interests in the East before the Texas rebellion and the Mexican border campaign. With the changeover to American rule, trade patterns were little changed, except that markets in the East for cattle hides, tallow, wool, and other stock-raising products widened and diversified. Furthermore, in New Mexico and Arizona a flourishing trade developed as the U.S. Army increased its efforts to subdue and destroy the nomadic Indian tribes. Provisions for troops and Indian reservations were channeled through private merchant houses in Santa Fe, Albuquerque, and Tucson.

Trade with Mexico, which before the nineteenth century had been the main source of external activity in all of the Southwest, continued after 1848, and many Mexicans entered the Southwest as transport workers or to act as agents for merchant houses in Monterrey. During the American Civil War, when southern ports were blocked off by the Union Navy, cotton was transported through Texas to such Mexican ports as Tampico in order to ship the product to European markets. Moreover, Arizona ports of entry to Mexico served California exporters and importers as a gateway to the Mexican ports of Guaymas and Mazatlan for shipping to the United States east around the Cape of Good Hope and over the Isthmus of Panama.

Initially, the labor needs of this slowly expanding economy were met by the resident population. Some immigration from Mexico, Europe, and the eastern United States provided the rest. Except for some cotton in Texas and gold and silver mining in other southwestern areas, there was little requirement for intensive labor use. After 1880, because of the railroad, dramatic changes in the southwestern economy stimulated Mexican immigration tremendously. During the two decades before 1900, 127,000 Mexicans entered the United States from Mexico, one and one-third times as many as the native Mexican population in 1848. Radical economic transformations that occurred not only in the Southwest but in Mexico as well dictated this later trend. By 1900, a railroad network integrated Texas, New Mexico, Arizona, and California with northern Mexico and parts of central and southern Mexico. The economic impact of the railroads soon drew Mexicans into the United States in a movement that dwarfed the influx of previous years. After the 1880s, then, the strong ties that previous *norteño* (northern) immigrants had to the Southwest and its native peoples diminished as railroads induced the migration of Mexicans whose roots were farther and farther from the border.

In northern Mexico, similar railroad building took place during the same years. The new railroads were financed by American interests, and, as in the American Southwest, the northern Mexican economy became linked to the crucial markets of the U.S. industrial basin in the Midwest and the Northeast. In northern Mexico, an economic transformation resulted, and adjacent areas along both sides of the U.S.-Mexican border supported similar agriculture and mining interests that depended completely on the same railroad network to market their products.

The Southwest was still sparsely populated during this period of rapid economic growth. Thousands of Anglos and Europeans had come in before the railroad era, and even more came after trains revolutionized transportation. Initially, many were induced by the discovery of gold and silver, but more consistently they came as farmers, small-scale merchants, and clerks and to work in other middle-sector positions. Many of them were squatters who slowly drew away the lands of the old Mexican elites. But a great many were middle-class entrepreneurs and agents of eastern companies who during the railroad era forcibly acquired millions of acres that had once belonged to wealthy Mexicans. It was these entrepreneurs who were responsible for the huge agribusiness and mining development in the Southwest. In the process it was discovered that the resident Mexican population was not sufficient to meet the growing labor needs. The poorer classes of Anglos did not compete with Mexicans because of the low wages offered in agriculture or because of the menial type of labor involved. Besides, many of the poorer Anglos were involved in their own endeavors on small farms and ranches.

In California, Chinese labor continued to be used after the building of the transcontinental railways from northern California during the 1860s and the development of southern California after the 1870s. In the 1880s, the first Chinese exclusion acts were passed by Congress in response to nativist pressures, but surreptitious entry continued into the twentieth century. In other parts of the Southwest, a dependence on Mexican labor remained the only alternative. Since railroad building in most of Mexico had resulted from the same thrust that built the lines in the Southwest, workers from Mexico were used in the construction, and the same reserves were utilized within both political zones. European laborers were also used in the West, but only a small number filtered southwest of industrialized cities like Chicago and Kansas City.

From Mexico, railroad building in the 1880s tapped labor resources according to a geographic pattern. American companies built extensions of the southwest network south from Nogales, El Paso, and Laredo. The southward penetration of these lines provided access to the United States from the interior of the northern states, and the movement back and forth was no longer restricted to the immediate border area. But as railroads spurred other areas of the economy, the competition for Mexican labor became greater, and populations in the Southwest and northern Mexico did not suffice. Late in the 1880s, railway construction reached into the more populated but landlocked areas of Mexico, south of Zacatecas. Now, many of the men from such states as Aguascalientes, Guanajuato, San Luis Potosí, Jalisco, and Michoacán served as seasonal laborers in construction and maintenance of way.

Population pressures in central Mexico were creating a clear surplus of workers by this time. Seasonal workers on large haciendas and small farmers whose inherited plot was too small to support a family were attracted to the railroads nearby, leaving home during the growing seasons and returning for planting and harvesting. Eventually these agricultural workers from central Mexico were induced, with the aid of the government of President Porfirio Díaz, to travel farther north to the sparsely populated regions of Chihuahua and other northern areas where labor was scarce. Becoming accustomed to a money economy, many severed their attachment to agricultural pursuits. Although they maintained their ties to their farms, villages, and haciendas, by the end of the nineteenth century many west-central Mexicans were depending almost exclusively on work in northern Mexico and the U.S. Southwest. By the early 1900s, railroads had penetrated deep into the very populous Bajío and west to the region surrounding Lake Chapala (west-central Mexico), reaching many small towns and ensuring that Mexican labor to the north was plentiful.

Once Mexican immigrants were in the United States, they could, in many ways, identify with the Southwest, which at the turn of the century was still very Mexican. Nevertheless, the Mexican was an immigrant in every sense of the word. Unable to speak or understand English, the dominant language, they were subject to immigration laws and regulations and forced to adapt to a foreign pattern of racism and discrimination. The native Mexican American, while faced with similar problems, was able after lengthy exposure to the gringo to make the adaptations necessary for survival and to participate more within the system. In New Mexico, for example, which contained the largest native population of Mexicans after the 1848 takeover, many of the old elites made the transition into the new economic and political structure, which was increasingly dominated by Anglos. In essence, the native was more equipped for survival than the immigrant.

Among the immigrants themselves, adaptation and the difficulty of life in the United States varied. Much depended on their economic conditions when crossing the border, the ability to transport families, the type of labor they performed, the distance between origins in Mexico and ultimate destination in the United States, and the type of community they lived in once in the United States. Before the Mexican Revolution of 1910, because practically all immigrants came from the lower classes, poverty was an endemic problem. The only commodity that such immigrants could trade was their labor.

Proximity to their homes in Mexico, once in the United States, made a difference in their ability to adapt. Northern Mexicans by 1900, like their cousins across the border, had been influenced by Anglo society. Anglo-Americans of all types farmed, operated mines, and ran communications systems and the railroads in northern Mexico, just as they did in the Southwest. Northern Mexico was integrated into the greater U.S. economy in much the same way as the Southwest. The northern Mexicans were immigrants almost before they crossed the border. Besides, they were close to their homes once they crossed, and most took their families with them.

Farther south, away from the border, the U.S. influence was not as pervasive. This was especially true in west-central Mexico (Jalisco, Guanajuato, and Michoacán), where the economy was more independently Mexican, being based on subsistence agricultural and artisan activity. Thus, workers and their families from this part of Mexico, who by 1900 began to comprise a significant proportion of all immigration to the United States, can be considered somewhat distinct from the northern Mexicans and Southwest natives who shared similar characteristics.

The food, Spanish usage, wearing apparel, and music of the central Mexican immigrants all combined to make a contribution to Mexican culture in the United States. These newer immigrants tended to cluster around existing Mexican communities, and their cultures competed with and then mingled with the older norteño-Southwest societies. Distinctions were made among the Mexicans themselves, when-

ever the three groups were thrown together, and often a social order existed, with the central Mexican at the bottom.

Rapid economic expansion in the Southwest also meant that the settlement of Mexicans shifted beyond the original native Hispanic centers. Anglos and Mexicans were attracted to the numerous new communities that sprang up along the length of the railway lines in new agricultural sections and in the emerging mining districts. Here the Mexican *colonias* (Mexican colonies) were all new, made up of displaced Southwest natives and Mexican immigrants. Such communities were formed in cotton-based towns in Texas during the early 1900s, and the same was true of the countless communities in the sugarbeet-growing regions of Colorado and California and in the mines of Arizona and New Mexico.

While the west-central Mexican male lived and worked side by side with his compatriots in all the areas requiring Mexican labor, in the long run he was more mobile. The exigencies of distance and meager resources forced him to travel without his wife and children, and once he was in the United States, one thousand miles or so separated him from his home and family. As the railroads required temporary section gangs farther and farther north in the United States, the central Mexican immigrant responded more readily than his coworkers from the American Southwest and northern Mexico. The other immigrants were more reluctant; they preferred to work closer to home within the agricultural sectors where they were initially recruited. Thus, northeastern Mexicans traveled by wagon to the cotton fields of Texas and Oklahoma in the early 1900s, but no farther. Then they returned to their homes in south Texas or northeast Mexico as soon as possible.

By 1915, Mexicans could be found as far north as Chicago and Kansas City. Most were from west-central Mexico. Thus, when the United States demanded a greater amount of labor during World War I, it was the inhabitants of the cities and villages along the railroad lines in Mexico, who already had exposure to the American North, particularly those from the Bajío region of Mexico, who were recruited. During the fifteen years or so following the start of the Mexican Revolution in 1910, a massive outpouring from Mexico greatly changed the demographic profile of Mexicans in the United States.

✳THE MEXICAN REVOLUTION AND IMMIGRATION TO THE UNITED STATES

The Mexican Revolution entailed a tremendous exodus of human beings fleeing political persecution, military impressment, depressed economic conditions, and simply the cross fire of violent events. The hard-fought struggles and their aftermath bred new social and economic conditions that drastically altered and disrupted Mexican society to the point that many, who would not have emigrated under their previous circumstances, flocked to the United States in large numbers.

Nonetheless, immigration to the United States was curtailed during the early years of the struggles when many Mexicans, from the same classes providing the bulk of emigration during this period, remained in Mexico and fought for the revolutionary cause. The appeal of the revolution was mixed in different parts of Mexico. In the north, thousands of urban workers, miners, middle-class professionals, small-scale landowners, cowboys, and even *hacendados* (hacienda owners) who supplied their peons as soldiers responded to the composite ideological appeals of the early phases of the revolution. In the south, around the state of Mexico, followers of Emiliano Zapata responded to the appeal to regain land usurped by speculators and hacendados during the reign of Porfirio Díaz. West-central Mexico was not as affected by the destabilizing events of the Díaz regime, but as the revolutionary tide swept to the south, most of the battles were fought in that region.

It is not surprising, then, that the revolution had distinct regional origins when Francisco I. Madero issued the Plan de San Luis Potosí in 1910. The soldiers in the rebel armies reflected these origins. Eventually, hardly any region of Mexico was left untouched by the struggle; almost every citizen and foreigner in the republic was affected. All in all, Mexicans endured twenty years of bloodshed. Many were caught up in the struggle because they believed the revolution was for the best. Others did not want the revolution, because it was not in their interest. The majority simply did not understand it or could not relate to its limited goals. Many of the disaffected, finding their Mexico torn asunder, left. For the first time, large numbers of middle-class Mexicans joined the emigrant streams. They composed a group that was critical to the formation of Mexican expatriate culture in the United States.

Initially, the exodus to the United States was a northern phenomenon, where much of the revolutionary activity originated after 1910. Indeed, in the southern areas that were not accessible to the United States, those uprooted by the peasant struggles sought safety in Mexico City or nearby areas not as affected by the revolution. In general, however, the displacement of people from their homes, in the city and in the countryside, followed the revolutionary tide southward. Many of those fortunate enough to be near the border or near a railroad station attempted to get to the United States.

Most refugees were from the lower and middle classes, but families like the Creels and the Terrazas of Chihuahua, and other wealthy *norteños*, lived comfortably while in the United States, accompanied by their liquid assets, which were deposited in American banks along the border. It was not until 1915 that the flight of large numbers of refugees assumed massive proportions in the Bajío and its environs, during a time when not only the direct destruction of the battles, but also the economic side effects of war, served to expel people from Mexico. During the struggles in Mexico, World War I spurred growth in every sector of the U.S. economy, owing primarily to the nation's position as a supplier to warring factions in Europe. Labor requirements had never been so great, yet disruption in trans-Atlantic transportation during the war and utilization of potential European emigrants in opposing armies were beginning to hinder the influx of workers from traditional European sources. When the United States became directly involved, American laborers were drafted, and a vacuum was created in industry, agriculture, mining, and transportation. These sectors looked south of the border to meet demands for expanding labor requirements during a time when Mexico was experiencing one of its worst economic crises.

Obtaining easy access to Mexican labor during this time of duress in Mexico and labor scarcity in the Southwest proved to be more difficult than had been the case in previous years, however. In February, Congress, in response to nativist pressures, enacted the Immigration Act of 1917, imposing a literacy requirement and an eight-dollar head tax on all individual immigrants. The act was passed before the United States entered the war, apparently without considering the manpower shortages that the wartime economy could create. The bill was designed to curb an "undesirable" influx from southern and eastern Europe, an immigrant group characterized by immigration officials as being two-thirds illiterate. Nevertheless, the act ultimately inhibited immigration to the United States from Mexico. Some of the Mexican states, such as Michoacán, a source of large numbers of emigrants, had illiteracy rates as high as 85 percent. In addition, the eight-dollar head tax was prohibitive for most migrants, many of whom arrived at the border destitute. Legal immigration of Mexicans suffered a temporary setback that year.

Surreptitious entry continued, but initially the interests that needed Mexican labor wanted legal, free, and easy access to this valuable reserve to the south. As the summer harvests approached, agriculturists and related interest groups became desperate, and they pressured Congress to waiver implementation of immigration laws in the case of Mexicans. During June, Congress complied, but the waiver was applicable only to agricultural workers, and there was so much red tape involved in meeting waiver requirements that eventually both the employers and Mexican workers preferred illegal entry. In essence, the general requirement of the 1917 act stimulated clandestine immigration. Unauthorized immigration intensified in later years after another act, in 1924, required that Mexicans add a ten-dollar visa fee to the already existing head tax, thus increasing the total that every immigrant paid to eighteen dollars. A lucrative trade emerged after 1917 in smuggling illegal aliens across the Rio Grande. It consisted mainly of ferrying large groups of Mexican laborers on rafts to the U.S. side.

If the 1917 act proved to be an obstacle to legal entry, agriculturalists and other interest groups were more frustrated by what seemed a worse threat to their steady supply of labor. In May 1917, the Selective Service Act became law. While Mexican citizens were not eligible for the draft in the United States, unless they applied for their first naturalization papers, they were obliged to register with the local draft board, a requirement that Mexicans were loathe to comply with for fear of being drafted. Besides, during this era, first-generation Mexican Americans were indistinguishable from many Mexican-born citizens. Consequently, nationals from Mexico were mistakenly drafted anyway.

The conscription problem was eventually resolved and Mexican immigration resumed a normal flow. Mexicans by 1915 were also beginning to enter California in larger numbers. Oriental labor had been heavily relied on in the past, but the southern California agricultural sector had expanded tremendously since 1915, and Chinese workers no longer sufficed. Secretary of Labor William Wilson suggested in June 1917 that the waiver be extended to nonagricultural sectors, such as transportation. The years of rapid economic expansion brought about by U.S. involvement in World War I resulted in Mexican migration to geographic regions that they previously never worked in, in such sectors as oil fields, munitions factories, meat-packing plants, and steel mills. Hundreds of colonias expanded or were established anew in cities such as Los Angeles, Kansas City, Chicago, Phoenix, and Houston. Ironically, few Mexican immigrants settled where traditional southwestern Hispanic culture was strong, such as in northern New Mexico and southern Colorado. Mexicans migrated to work, and work was more plentiful in areas where there were fewer Hispanics, in new agricultural towns, or in industrial cities that were built by Anglos, such as Chicago or Houston.

A lamentable side effect of the struggle was an increase in anti-Mexican prejudice. Americans resented and feared the revolution, which many times was brought to their doorstep at the border. The revolutionary Pancho Villa and his followers, for example, raided into American territory to obtain supplies, and on some occasions Americans were killed in these incursions. In 1914, President Woodrow Wilson ordered the invasion of Vera Cruz in an effort to depose Victoriano Huerta, a general who assassinated President Francisco Madero, the founder of the revolutionary movement, and took over Mexico. To get support from the American people for the invasion, however, Mexicans were cast as undisciplined and violent. By the 1920s, Anglo-American opinion of Mexicans was lower than before the revolution, and these emotions were taken out on Mexicans living in the United States. Americans failed to see that brutality is part of any war, not just a trait manifested by Mexicans during this era. Indeed, strong parallels exist between the behavior of soldiers, both Union and Confederate, during the American Civil War.

✳ THE "MEXICO LINDO" GENERATION

In the 1920s, economic expansion continued, owing to commercial agriculture and large-scale mining activity. But in addition, the United States was experiencing an all-time-high economic expansion in manufacturing. Increasingly, Mexican labor was used in cities. At the same time, immigration increased to floodtide proportions, coming from farther south in central Mexico, including Jalisco, Guanajuato, Michoacán, and San Luis Potosí. With the new infusion of immigrants from areas so remote from the Southwest, Mexicans found few familiar surroundings in agricultural or mining towns and in cities like Houston, Dallas, and Chicago. Also in this period, the vast majority of persons living in the United States who were considered of Mexican origin were either born in Mexico or the children of immigrants; the original Mexican residents of the United States were considered "Americans."

Like many other newcomers to the United States in the late nineteenth and early twentieth centuries, Mexicans came from a peasant or an agricultural village background and were from a country that was only then acquiring a sense of nationhood. An extensive *patria chica* (homeland region) identity existed among the majority of the immigrants as they arrived in the United States. For example, some people identified themselves as Tapatíos, people of northeastern Jalisco and western Guanajuato, while others were

Huastecos from southern Tamaulipas, eastern San Luis Potosí, or northern Veracruz. The state of Sonora, cut off in the south by the vastness of the Yaqui and Mayo settlements, to the east by the Sierra Madres, and to the north by U.S. expansion, acquired a strong sense of identity known as *Sonorense*. The bond of each area was forged by common economic activity, distinctive food ways, music, and even phenotypology (physical features).

Mexicans had this provincialism in common with other "new immigrants," such as Italians and eastern Europeans, who tended to have weak national allegiances and strong regional identities. In the initial immigrant settlements, friends and relatives from the same village or province in the old country lived and socialized together, forming parochial clusters within the larger enclave. Often, the immigrants physically segregated themselves in sections with names such as El Michoacanito (Little Michoacán) or Chihuahita (Little Chihuahua). The mining town near Ray, Arizona, was called Sonora, possibly because of the great number of Sonorenses that worked there. In addition, some of the ethnic organizations had a preponderance of members who originated in the same province in Mexico. Divisions based on regional origins were further complicated by significant class differences. Although the vast majority of the Mexicans in the United States were from the lower classes, many upper- and middle-class refugees escaping the violence of the revolution joined them in the immigrant colonias.

The majority of the Mexicans entering the United States between 1910 and 1930 were seeking work and intended to return home. Indeed, many did. But even those who remained harbored a dream of someday going back. Another characteristic of this emerging identity was an exaggerated loyalty to Mexico, coupled with a dutiful celebration of the Mexican patriotic holidays (*fiestas patrias*). Scholar Paul Schuster Taylor, in studying the colonias in the late 1920s noted, "First there is a strong emotional attachment to Mexico and patriotism is heightened, as the Mexicans themselves sometimes note, by their expatriation" (1932, pp. 117-118). The formation of this "México Lindo" (Pretty Mexico) identity became a full-fledged phenomenon in the nation's immigrant colonias.

During the Mexican Revolution, a sizable portion of the Mexican urban middle classes and elites, who were the critical core in Mexico imbued with nationalistic feelings, immigrated to the United States. They were the most important source of nationalism, in addition to being the carriers of *indigenismo* (pride in the Indian heritage of Mexico) and other forms of patriotism.

Obviously, the maintenance of Mexican culture and the Spanish language was seen as the most necessary nationalist statement. The names given to their mutual aid societies, such as La Sociedad Benito Juárez, México Bello, Sociedad Cuauhtemoc, to name a few, demonstrate the close allegiance to Mexico. During this time the self-identifier was Mexicano/a in Spanish and Mexican in English. Even the names given to their barrios had a strong nostalgic ring. In Phoenix, one neighborhood was known as Cuatro Milpas. Its name was derived from a famous musical lament that was immensely popular among Mexicans throughout the United States. Called simply "Las cuatro milpas," the song relates the story of a peasant who returns to his farm after a long absence only to find it in ruin; obviously the farmer's sojourn was interpreted by the immigrants as their stay in the United States. The musical consumption of Mexican immigrants, in its various forms, is an incisive vehicle for understanding the Mexican colonias in this country. In tandem with other kinds of live entertainment, such as Mexican vaudeville and drama, the musical production of Mexicans was just as important as their religious, political, and economic institutions. All these combined to give the immigrant community the cohesion necessary to be able to defend its interests. Many of the immigrants were successful in their new surroundings, but most were probably disenchanted by discrimination, poverty, inadequate housing, segregation, and the prospect of menial labor. Music had a greater ability to promote cultural reaffirmation in this harsh immigrant milieu, invoking a nostalgia for what they considered a simpler and happier past. The invention of the wax record increased the power of music to reach Mexican farm workers and miners living in tents, far from centers of live entertainment. As a consequence, the phonograph was indispensable, and for vendors selling both items, it became another lucrative opportunity.

Theater productions and other forms of live entertainment, like their musical counterparts, also ranked in importance with the church and other immigrant institutions, and because the troupes were mobile, the medium was taken into the most remote areas where Mexicans lived and worked. Companies like those owned by the renowned actress Virginia Fábregas preferred the large houses of Los Angeles, San Antonio, and Chicago. In agricultural communities and mining towns, smaller tent-show ensembles, called *carpas*, were more common. These entertainment groups were made up of family members who put on skits or performed simple circus-type acts, such as tightrope walking. Larger circuses, such as Circo Escalante, with a full array of acts, often went to larger towns and cities and became the joy of the whole population, not just Mexicans.

Not singing and dancing, but finding work, setting up homes, building churches, and coping with a hostile reception from Anglos dominated the lives of Mexicans in the colonias. Segregation, police brutality, and general rejection drove home the need to coalesce and embrace unity. The badge of inferiority imposed by the Anglo provoked the immigrants to dispel negative stigma by forcefully demonstrating that Mexicans engaged in positive cultural activities. They believed that Mexican artistic and cultural contributions were as good or better than those in Anglo America.

Another strong component of immigrant identity was a form of indigenismo, or the proud recognition of Mexico's pre-Columbian Indian ancestry. This ideology was deeply rooted in Mexican history and given profound expression by Mexican intellectuals and writers in the colonial period and throughout most of the nineteenth century. Understandably, the sentiment was carried to the colonias in the United States by immigrant leaders who deliberately maintained and projected this image. In this respect, reverence to Our Lady of Guadalupe, the Virgin Mother, who is considered to be an Indian, and the homage paid to Benito Juárez, also an Indian, is part of this tradition. Every major colonia in the United States had an organization named after Juárez and a Catholic church named Our Lady of Guadalupe. Religion served to provide more than a spiritual focus. It served to give a sense of purpose to the community, because it was the immigrants themselves who built and maintained the churches.

But in this early era the immigrants had to contend with intense police brutality, segregation, abuse in the workplace, and general rejection from the mainstream community. In the early part of the century El Congreso Mexicanista (The Mexican Congress) was held in Texas in order to implement a strategic plan to stem the tide of legal abuses and violence against Mexicans. The meeting was attended by representatives from Mexican communities across Texas, and although the lack of political power limited its success, the effort demonstrated that Mexicans were willing to defend themselves. It also served as model for later political mobilization. In later years, many other organizations also strived to end abuses against Mexicans in the justice system, such as the Asamblea Mexicana, organized in Houston in 1925. Perhaps the most distressing abuse was the disproportionate execution of Mexicans in prisons throughout the United States; Mexicans spent much of their collective energy attempting to save condemned men. In many parts of the United States,

Mexicans formed organizations, usually called La Liga Protectora Mexicana (The Mexican Protective League), that served to protect the legal rights of Mexicans. On several occasions, Mexican consuls met with the state governor or the board of pardons and paroles, usually accompanied by members of Mexican organizations that had collected petitions with thousands of signatures pressing for clemency.

In 1921, a depression caused severe destitution among Mexicans who suddenly found themselves unemployed. The Mexican government, working through its consulate service, formed *comisiones honoríficas* (honorary commissions) to protect the rights of hundreds of thousands Mexicans who found themselves stranded in many communities and unable to return home after prices for mining and agricultural products had collapsed. Thousands were repatriated with money provided by the Mexican government, but those that remained found themselves destitute until the economy recovered.

Recovery from the 1921 crisis was quick, and economic expansion throughout the 1920s went beyond the boom conditions precipitated by World War I. Mexicans were again in demand, and during this decade their influx dwarfed previous entries. Resistance to Mexican immigration was intense, however. The larger their numbers became in the United States, the more nativists thought Mexicans were a threat to cultural and racial integrity. But employers would not countenance any restriction of a valuable labor supply. Indeed, when the National Origins Quota Act was passed in 1924 to curtail immigration, lobbyists representing agricultural and mining interests managed to persuade Congress not to include the Western Hemisphere. This ensured that the Mexican labor source would be protected. Nativists, such as Representative John C. Box of Texas, wanted to stop immigration from Mexico completely, but in the spirit of the prosperous decade, the desires of the powerful employers who needed Mexican labor were not overcome.

During this period, a product of the heavy inflow was the appearance of many new colonias with familiar México Lindo institutions. The leadership promoted cohesion and unity more successfully when practically everyone was newly arrived, was segregated from the rest of the society, and was working and bringing in some money. They expected their stay in the United States to be temporary, although most stayed until their death. As the American-born children of those who remained grew older, slowly the elders' influence waned as younger family members began to adopt American ways and identify with the United States as their permanent home.

*DEPRESSION, REPATRIATION, AND ACCULTURATION

The Great Depression altered the lives of everyone, and it also dramatically changed the evolution of the Mexican colonias. Mexicans who had been so desirable as workers in the previous decade became unwanted throughout the United States in the 1930s. From throughout, thousands of Mexicans left, many times pressured by community authorities. But those that resisted repatriation were more rooted and, in most cases, had families with growing children. Indeed, during the decade, a generation grew up that had no memories of Mexico. Their only home had been the barrios in their immigrant communities.

A cultural shift became apparent in the early 1930s. The dominant immigrant posture of the 1920s gave way to "Mexican American" adaptation, which was characterized by assimilation of U.S. values and a less faithful adherence to Mexican culture. By the mid-1930s it was apparent that a fusion of cultures was evolving. Cultural expression of Mexican Americans in this period was obviously influenced by Anglo society. Immigrant symbolism did not disappear in the 1930s, but the reinforcing influence from Mexico declined with the depression-related hiatus in immigration. Ostensibly pure Mexican traditions were barely kept alive by the aging immigrants, who also were losing their influence over younger Mexican Americans born in the United States.

The México Lindo source of identity, then, however virulent it seemed in the initial colonia-building stage, did not survive the massive repatriation of Mexicans that had been provoked by the Great Depression. Repatriation, especially from the large cities, was massive and highly organized. This was especially true in Los Angeles and industrial cities in the Midwest, but thousands left from more rural communities as well. For those remaining in the United States, Americanization was seized upon by the new leadership through organizations such as the Latin American Club in cities like Phoenix and Houston and the Mexican American Political Club in East Chicago. These groups, of course, were intent on achieving political clout. Even the word "Mexican" seemed to be abandoned in this period, as the term "Latin American" attests. The League of United Latin American Citizens (LULAC), initially very strong in Texas, eventually spread to other parts of the United States. Besides, the leaders of these organizations were no longer immigrants who intended to return to Mexico. They consisted of a new and younger generation that was either born in the United States or very young upon arriving. Overall in the decade, significant alterations took place for the second-generation Mexican Americans that had been

born or raised in the United States. Increasingly more graduated from high school, and their expectations from the larger society were more extensive. The depression of the 1930s subsided because of wartime spending, and by the end of the decade, thousands of young Mexican Americans had grown up in this country exposed to the greater Anglo society through such New Deal agencies as the Civilian Conservation Corps and National Youth Administration, both designed to enroll young people and keep them off the streets during this era of massive unemployment.

*WORLD WAR II AND THE MEXICAN-AMERICAN GENERATION

When the United States declared war in 1941, Mexican Americans responded to the war effort enthusiastically. In spite of continuing discrimination, patriotism among Mexican Americans was intense, as they felt like part of the United States. Unlike their parents, they had no direct ties to Mexico. Thousands joined their white and black counterparts in all branches of the armed forces. Most Mexican women stayed behind, but many moved to California and other industrial areas in the boom years of the war and worked in places where Mexicans had never been allowed. The League of United Latin American Citizens (LULAC) spread throughout the United States in the 1940s, and thousands of Mexicans not serving in the military engaged in many "home front" efforts, such as bond drives. After the war, Mexican Americans strove to achieve political power by making good use of their war record. Many Mexican-American war veterans were motivated by the continued discrimination that greeted them after the war. In 1947, the American G.I. Forum was organized by Mexican-American veterans in response to the denial of a funeral home in Three Rivers, Texas, to bury a Mexican American killed in the Pacific. The organization went on to become a leading advocate for civil rights. In addition, many American Legion posts for Mexican Americans were founded by these same veterans.

Immigration to the United States greatly decreased during the Great Depression, during which time a generation of Mexican Americans was greatly influenced by Anglo culture. Because few new immigrants came, much cultural reinforcement from Mexico was lost. When the war ended, Mexican-American GIs came back by the thousands to their barrios in cities and small towns alike. Many young people who had postponed wedding plans during the years of strife now married and had babies. These Mexican-American soldiers came back more assertive, ready to take their place in a society that, by any reckoning, they had fought to preserve. After the war, hundreds of young married Mexican-American couples moved to the growing suburbs and were further acculturated.

Mexican culture in the United States did not subside in spite of acculturation, however. The Bracero Program was instrumental in reviving immigration to the United States during the war years, reinstating the crucial link to Mexico. The program, in which U.S. labor agents actually went to Mexico and recruited thousands of workers, was prompted by the wartime need for labor. The experienced *braceros* (manual laborers) inspired many others to immigrate on their own. Many of these contract laborers worked primarily in agricultural communities and in railroad camps until the program ended in 1965; however, some of them stayed, or returned after they were delivered back to Mexico. Ever since then, the renewal of immigration has continued unabated. The Mexican movie industry, which came into its own in the 1940s, by the 1950s dominated the Spanish-speaking market on a worldwide basis and also ensured that Mexican culture entered with a new vigor into Mexican-American communities. It was logical that Mexican movies found a large market in the United States, where so many of Mexico's people were living and where no other medium equaled it as a vibrant exponent of Mexican culture. Only the record industry had as pervasive a Mexicanizing impact on Mexican-American culture.

But in spite of the resurgence of Mexican immigration and the persistence of Mexican cultural modes, Mexican Americans could not help but become Americanized in the milieu of the 1950s and 1960s, when more and more acquired educations in Anglo systems, lived in integrated suburbs, and were subjected to Anglo-American mass media, especially when television came into its own. It is difficult to measure just how pervasive Americanization was at that time, however. Certainly, the culture of Mexican Americans, fused as it was with mainstream society in the United States, was more acceptable. But prejudice and rejection persisted. Nonetheless, Mexican Americans, more integrated into society, were more effective than ever in their efforts to break down obstacles to economic and social mobility. For example, in the 1950s and early 1960s segregation was abolished in Texas, Arizona, and many other communities, largely through the efforts of LULAC and the Alianza Hispano Americana (Hispanic American Alliance), another civil rights organization in the Southwest.

✳ FROM CHICANOS TO HISPANICS

The late 1960s and early 1970s was a time of intellectual foment and rebellion in the United States. Caught up in the mood, young Mexican Americans throughout the country sought a new identity while struggling for the same civil rights objectives of previous generations. This struggle became known as the Chicano movement. The word "Chicano" was elevated from its pejorative usage in the 1920s to denote lower-class Mexican immigrants and from its slang usage of the 1940s and 1950s to substitute for Mexicano. It now symbolized the realization of a new-found and unique identity. Proudly, Chicanos proclaimed an Indo-Hispanic heritage, and accused older Mexican Americans of pathologically denying their racial and ethnic reality because of an inferiority complex.

In the movement, an attempt was made to use some of the same symbols of their immigrant grandfathers, but with a few added touches. Tapping several intellectual traditions, movement leaders attempted to define true ethnic character. Allusions were made to factual and mythical pasts used so often by *indigenistas* (indigenists). For example, the concept of Aztlán, the mythical place of origin of the Aztec, became the Chicano movement name for the Southwest. In addition, participants in the movement differed from the previous Mexican-American generation in that they did not care whether they were accepted and they rejected assimilation. Many of the images they construed reflected their alienation as they blended pachuco cultural modes, *pinto* (ex-convict) savvy, pre-Columbian motifs, and myth with a burning conviction that Chicanos were deliberately subordinated by a racist American society. Chicano student organizations sprang up throughout the nation, as did barrio groups such as the Brown Berets. Thousands of young Chicanos pledged their loyalty and time to such groups as the United Farmworkers Organizing Committee, which, under Cesar Chávez, had been a great inspiration for Chicanos throughout the nation. An offshoot of both impulses, the farm worker and the student movement, was La Raza Unida party in Texas, an organization formed in 1968 to obtain control of community governments where Chicanos were in the majority.

In the 1980s, the term "Hispanic," which has considerable longevity, took a special generic meaning referring to any person living in the United States who is of Spanish ancestry. In the Mexican-American community, the term has been eagerly accepted, and only vestiges remain of the virulent nationalism of Chicano movement days evoked to forge an identity. The United Farmworkers Organization and La Raza Unida party, the latter still existing in various communities, are direct heirs of the movement, but they do not seem to have prospered in recent years. Use of "Hispanic" represents a rejection by the Mexican American leadership of both cultural nationalism and radical postures.

In essence, the "Hispanic Generation" is the latest synthesis of radicalism and nationalism. Those Chicanos that identify with "Hispanic" are more nationalistic than the GI generation, while rivaling Chicano movement activists in their fervor for civil rights. They also accept a nonwhite racial identity, paying lip service to the concept of Aztlán. But the new upbeat, sophisticated, "professional" image that the term conjures is alluring to the new generation.

The fiestas patrias celebrations have continued down to this date. Unlike those in the 1920s organized by the México Lindo leaders, the historical reasons for celebration do not figure in a very precise fashion. For example, during the Cinco de Mayo celebration, very little is said about the 1862 Battle of Puebla. Instead, the day seems to have been converted into a celebration of the Hispanic presence in the United States.

Today, immigration from Mexico and Latin America continues unabated, a condition that has to be taken into account as we trace the continuing development of Mexican communities throughout the United States. Since the 1960s, a massive influx of Hispanic immigrants has reinforced Hispanic culture in the United States. All in all, the culture and identity of Mexican Americans will continue to change, reflecting both inevitable generational fusion with Anglo society and the continuing influence of immigrants, not only from Mexico, but from throughout Latin America.

✴ MIGRATION TO THE UNITED STATES FROM PUERTO RICO

Most of the two million Puerto Ricans who have trekked to the U.S. mainland in this century are World War II or postwar-era entries. And unlike the immigrant experience of Mexicans, or Cubans before 1959, the vast majority of Puerto Ricans entered with little or no red tape. After 1920, the passage of the Jones Act granted Puerto Ricans citizenship, even if they were born on the island. Migration out of Puerto Rico was a defined trend quite a few years before the Spanish-American War, however, establishing a pattern that would be repeated and accelerated in the twentieth century.

The first migrant wave was stimulated by escalating economic relations between Puerto Rico and the United States. Exchange between both areas actually began in the eighteenth century but did not achieve large proportions until the second half of the nineteenth century. Still a colony of Spain, however, the island was subjected to the mother country's mercantilistic hold, thus trade was clandestine. For Puerto Rican planters and Yankee merchants, the exchange of sugar and molasses produced on the island for American goods that were cheaper than those from Spain was mutually satisfying. The chain of smuggling activity that led to the first Anglo incursions into Texas and California was, significantly, part of this very same process. The economic contact with North Americans eventually resulted in the divestment of Texas, New Mexico, and California from Mexico. A similar fate was in store for Puerto Rico and Cuba.

In the early nineteenth century the economic relationship was sufficiently mature for Cuban and Puerto Rican traders to found a benevolent society in New York to serve merchants and their families from both island colonies. But economic ties were not the only attraction in the United States for Puerto Ricans and Cubas. Many also found in the northern colossus a haven for plotting against Spain. From the time of El Grito de Lares, an insurrection in 1868, to the time Puerto Rican exiles formed part of the Cuban Revolutionary party's governing board at the end of the century, hundreds traveled to the mainland. Staying for years, some sent for families and found employment to sustain themselves. While most of the first exiles were from the criollo middle classes, eventually skilled artisans and laborers, all dissatisfied with Spain's rule, joined their compatriots in New York.

Large-scale immigration, however, is linked more to structural changes in the Puerto Rican economy during the course of the latter nineteenth century than any other condition. The freeing of slaves in the 1870s and the rise of coffee as a significant competitor of sugar created new land-tenure systems and more fluid labor conditions. As in Mexico during the regime of Porfirio Díaz, such radical changes disrupted the fabric of rural life, forcing Puerto Ricans into day agricultural labor or into the urban centers like San Juan. The population also increased dramatically in the course of the nineteenth century, from 583,000 in 1860, to 1,000,000 in 1900. Meanwhile the labor market was not developing at the same rate. As a consequence, many of the unemployed decided to cast their lot with contractors who sought agricultural workers in other regions of the Caribbean. Eventually others found their way to the United States.

But hastening the process of migration to the United States was the acquisition of Puerto Rico after the Spanish-American War. In May 1898, Spanish fortifications in San Juan were bombarded by the U.S. Navy while U.S. Army troops invaded the rest of the island to ferret out the Spaniards. Cheering crowds, longing for their independence, enthusiastically welcomed the U.S. forces entering Ponce under General Nelson Miles. Little did they know that soon they would trade the sovereignty of Spain for the tutelage of the United States. Quickly, a military government was established for Puerto Rico under General Guy V. Henry. But the transition was negotiated not with Spain, but with Puerto Ricans led by Luis Muñoz-Rivera. Muñoz had assumed the leadership of the home-rule government granted by the Spanish Crown just before the occupation by the United States, and now he had to deal with another foreign interloper.

A quasi republic under U.S. dominance was established by the Foraker Act in 1900. It created a lower house with thirty-five members, but the highest-ranking officials had to be appointed by the president of the United States. In essence, there would have been more self-direction under the autonomy agreement reached with Spain right before the American takeover. Muñoz-Rivera continued to serve his people as a politician, however, as an organizer of the Federalist party and as commissioner to the United States Congress from the protectorate. To the dismay of Puerto Ricans, this position did not carry very much power.

Then in 1917, the Jones Act, a proviso more to the liking of Puerto Ricans, was enacted. Skillful diplomacy by island politicians resulted in the passage of this congressional bill that created two Puerto Rican houses of legislature whose representatives were more properly elected by the people. More important, in terms of how it would affect future immigration, the act conceded U.S. citizenship to Puerto Ricans.

In spite of this victory, Puerto Rico was quickly deluged by American economic interests. Absentee landlords built large, modern sugar plantations that wiped out even more preindustrial subsistence farming than was the case during the last years of the Spanish period. Even coffee production, in which thousands of workers had been employed, declined as the capital-intensive sugar plantations and refineries covered much of the island. In the towns and cities, artisans such as independent shoemakers, carpenters, and other craftsmen found their livelihoods abolished by manufactured commodities produced in the United States.

To be sure, as a result of the American intervention, schools, hospitals, and public projects were built. This development, designed to improve life on the island, also paved the way for the new American

investors and hastened the end of a way of life on which most Puerto Ricans depended for survival. Additionally, jobs that employed many women in tobacco factories and domestic service all declined. As the twentieth century progressed, island workers were marginalized and reduced to part-time miscellaneous work, which in Puerto Rico is known as *chiripeo*. Unemployment and underemployment created even greater pressure to leave Puerto Rico.

In the early part of the century, Hawaii's sugar industry was in need of experienced workers, and a few thousand Puerto Ricans were recruited. First they were shipped to New Orleans by ship, then by train to San Francisco, and then by water again for the last leg of the journey. Small colonias emerged in both San Francisco and New Orleans because some workers decided not to make the full trip and remained at these debarkation points. Most of the island people migrated to the eastern seaboard of the United States, however. In 1910, according to census figures, 1,513 Puerto Ricans were living on the mainland, two thirds in New York. Like Mexicans, their fellow Hispanics in the Southwest, Puerto Ricans continued to arrive during World War I and the prosperous 1920s when jobs were plentiful.

U.S. immigration policy also influenced the pattern of migration from Puerto Rico. Two national origin quota acts designed to curtail immigration from eastern and southern Europe and Asia were passed in 1921 and 1924. With fewer workers coming in from these areas, a labor shortage ensued. The Western Hemisphere was not included in the quota policy, however, and so employers turned there for labor. Mexico became a major of source of workers, as did Puerto Rico. It was easier for recruiters to target Puerto Ricans because they could travel freely to the mainland as citizens. By 1930, there were approximately fifty-three thousand living in various North American communities, although most were in New York City. There, they concentrated in Brooklyn, the Bronx, and East Harlem. As their numbers increased in later years, these barrios remained the core areas of first arrival.

✳EARLY SETTLEMENT OF PUERTO RICANS IN THE UNITED STATES

The establishment of Puerto Rican colonias was similar to that of the Mexican immigrant colonias, characterized earlier as the México Lindo phase of the Mexican-American experience. As Puerto Ricans first arrived on the mainland, they looked back to their island origins for identity. Although Puerto Rico, unlike Mexico, was not an independent nation, the vital nationalism pervading the island during the rise of independent sentiment was tapped by newcomers to the United States looking for a source of ethnic consciousness. In the quest for roots during the Puerto Rican struggle for independence from Spain, the pre-Hispanic name of the island, Borinquen, was revived. Immigrants, in their new environment, used Borinquen *querido* (beloved Borinquen) to refer to a homeland to which they felt closer once they had left it. When the United States took over the island, love and identification with their roots increased even more, and many Puerto Ricans felt the U.S. occupation was as a continuation of the colonial experience.

This feeling was exacerbated even more when they encountered rejection in this country. In the so-called Harlem Riots, in July 1926, Puerto Ricans were attacked by non-Hispanics as their numbers were becoming larger in Manhattan neighborhoods. As the Puerto Ricans united to defend themselves, symbols of the homeland common to all, regardless of regional origin, became a powerful bond. The Spanish language, perpetuated through a barrage of newspapers, music, and theater, also solidified Borinquen kindredness and allowed Puerto Ricans to identify with other Hispanics in New York, such as Cubans and Spaniards.

The Catholic religion also served as a cohesive ingredient. As it did for Mexicans in Mexico, Catholicism in Puerto Rico took a unique shape according to the exigencies of local island society. On the mainland, the particular features of Puerto Rican worship served as an additional focus, bringing the islanders together in a common ceremony. Still, it was mainly in New York where Catholic churches existed that catered primarily to Puerto Ricans, albeit other Spanish-speakers also attended. Significantly, language affinity was perpetuated in these religious institutions as well.

Formal multipurpose organizations and clubs were probably the most important vehicle for cohesion, and they also served to make Puerto Rican settlement more visible in the city. The most common associations were the *hermandades* (brotherhoods). These societies, which could be traced to emancipation groups in the nineteenth century, provided mutual aid and intensified ethnic nationalism. Attending to primordial needs of the community, the brotherhoods appeared very quickly after the arrival of Puerto Ricans on the mainland. Additionally, merchant organizations and groups associated with labor unions also proliferated.

Political activity was also apparent during the initial building stages of the colonias. Associated with the desire for independence back home, such

groups as the Club Borinquen had as their main agenda through such periodical organs as *El Porvenir* (The Future) and *La Revolución* (The Revolution), freedom from colonial rule. But because throughout most of this century Puerto Ricans were citizens before they set out from their homeland, they were able to participate much more than Mexican immigrants in American electoral politics. Usually associating with the Democratic party, but not always, they organized political groups and joined the ethnic machines prevalent in eastern cities as early as 1918. This of course was one year after the Jones Act granted Puerto Ricans citizenship. In the 1920s, La Liga Puertorriquena (The Puerto Rican League), an organization made up primarily of community associations, became an unabashed supporter of the Democratic party.

As was the case in the Mexican colonias in the United States, Puerto Rican businessmen perpetuated ethnic bonds by providing Caribbean food, barbershops, religious relics, and, very important, Latin records, and the phonographs to play them. Music and theater were two of the most important exponents of Puerto Rican solidarity, and by the 1930s such theaters as El Teatro Hispano in New York featured not only Spanish-language drama but also musical groups. Puerto Ricans pursued their penchant for music at the family level, as well. Practically every gathering, whether it was a baptism, wedding, or coming-out party, had the obligatory singing trio of two guitar players and a maraca player. The music itself intensified the link with the homeland and defined Puerto Ricans' experience as immigrants. Rafael Hernández, a trained composer and owner of a music store in New York, wrote numerous songs that embodied the spirit of this genre. Hernández's most famous piece is "Lamento Borincano" (Borinquen Lament). The song, like the Mexican "Canción Mixteca" (Mixteca Song), was a poignant but romantic reminder of the beauty and rural simplicity of the homeland.

As happened with Mexican immigrants during the Great Depression, there was a reverse migration. Between 1930 and 1934, probably 20 percent of the Puerto Ricans living in the United States went back to the island, although they were not coerced to the same degree as Mexicans to return home. Those who could hang on to their jobs, primarily in service sectors of New York and other eastern cities, became acculturated more to life in the United States. Moreover, the U.S. cities in which Puerto Ricans lived had a vital urban life that exerted a strong influence on growing families.

✳ THE GREAT MIGRATION

Post World War II Puerto Ricans in the United States

The most massive migration of Puerto Ricans, almost two million, occurred after World War II. While the wartime Bracero Program brought over 100,000 Mexicans to work in the labor-scarce economy of the war period, Puerto Ricans did not start immigrating in large numbers until the postwar boom era. They came in response to a classical push-pull phenomenon. Simply put, wages were higher and employment was more plentiful than on the island. Operation Boot Strap, a strategy designed to develop Puerto Rico economically, resulted in altering the employment structure, as had the modernization of the sugar industry earlier in the century. The project was the brainchild of the popular governor Luis Muñoz Marín, the son of nationalist patriot Luis Muñoz-Rivera. The plan emphasized investment, primarily American, in light industry and manufacturing. To a large degree, the process did provide more technical employment for some Puerto Ricans. But as investors turned away from sugar production, agricultural employment declined, and Operation Boot Strap did not adequately provide replacement jobs. Then in the 1960s, petrochemical plants and refineries, activities that required even less labor than light industry, pervaded much of the economy. The net result was as inevitable: more migration.

As their numbers increased on the mainland, Puerto Ricans transcended their New York home, moving to textile mill towns in Rhode Island and Connecticut, factories in Chicago, and the steel mills of Pennsylvania, Ohio, and Indiana. The most remarkable feature of the new immigration was that it was airbound. The large volume of passengers leaving Puerto Rico soon drove the price of fares down and gave opportunity to new airlines, which pressed surplus World War II cargo planes into service. By 1947, over twenty airlines provided service between San Juan and Miami and San Juan and New York. In the 1950s, Puerto Ricans were also landing in New Jersey cities and paid, on average, forty dollars for a one-way ticket.

The newer arrivals, like their Mexican counterparts in Los Angeles and Chicago, crowded into large barrios in New York and other eastern cities. The cold weather in the Northeast was inhospitable and almost unbearable for the hundreds of thousands who had left their warm tropical island. Adaptation in this environment was very difficult, indeed. What is abundantly clear, and here there are some very close parallels to the Mexican-American experience during the postwar period, is that early Puerto Rican

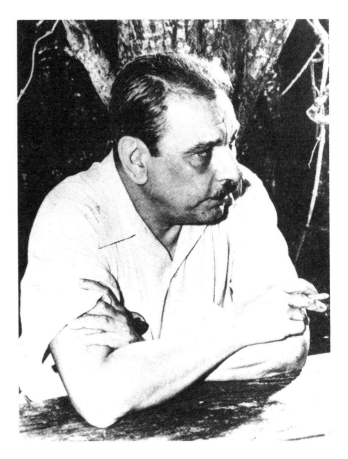

Luis Muñoz Marín, architect of the present commonwealth status of Puerto Rico.

immigrants built a foundation of organizations and institutions that made life more bearable for later arrivals.

Many second-generation Puerto Ricans acquired some social mobility within the society to which their parents had migrated before the war, and in some cases these first-generation parents were already professionals upon arriving. Basically, however, prewar communities that cushioned the shock for the immigrants were strongly working-class in structure, very much like Mexican Americans. Unlike Mexican Americans, second-generation Puerto Ricans in the 1930s did not coalesce into organizations like the League of United Latin American Citizens, which was started in Texas in 1929 by frustrated Mexican Americans who found practically every avenue to opportunity in the United States blocked. Perhaps for Puerto Ricans in the United States before the 1950s, segregation was not as intense as it was for Mexicans in the Southwest, a problem that was particularly acute in Texas.

Interethnic hostility, however, especially when Puerto Ricans arrived in very large numbers in Italian-American or Irish-American neighborhoods, peaked into severe hostile rivalries in many northern cities. Much of this hostility was fought out in the streets by gangs of youth who called themselves by colorful names. These rivalries, for better or worse, inspired the famous "West Side Story" by Leonard Bernstein. But the reality of these clashes was not as romantic as those portrayed in the musical between the Sharks and the Jets.

The second-largest concentration of Puerto Ricans outside the New York City area sprang up in the Chicago area. The birth of the Chicago colonias dates to World War II. Today, approximately 200,000 live in the city proper, and many thousands more in Gary and East Chicago, Indiana, and Milwaukee. One of the most important organizations in the early formation of the colonias was the Caballeros de San Juan (Knights of St. John). Its main function was to provide leadership and religious values in the Puerto Rican community. Other groups known as hermandades emerged in the 1950s and 1960s and were similar to the ones formed in New York in the early 1900s. Religion continued to serve as a focal point of the community, and Puerto Ricans identified strongly with the folk level of worship, as did Mexican immigrants. In fact, they shared, in an amicable arrangement, Our Lady of Guadalupe churches in both South Chicago and in East Chicago with Mexicans.

As more and more Puerto Ricans committed to remaining on the mainland during the 1950s and 1960s, they encountered a great amount of rejection, but at the same time they demonstrated a growing concern for social and economic mobility. Their early employment pattern consisted of menial jobs in the service sector of the Chicago economy and in light factory work—in essence low- paying work. And because of housing discrimination, Puerto Ricans were relegated to low-rent but overcrowded housing. Exacerbating these grievances were inequities in the courts and a persistent pattern of police brutality in the barrio.

To face that challenge they resorted, as did Mexican Americans during this same period, to self-help and civil rights organizations. Like Mexican Americans, thousands of Puerto Ricans served in World War II and the Korean conflict. Because many of these soldiers left directly from the island, before they could speak English, the military became an educational experience. Upon being discharged, many opted to remain on the mainland, where economic opportunity seemed to beckon. But even for former soldiers, there were still many obstacles that had to be overcome to achieve any kind of equality.

The emergence of the Puerto Rican Forum in New York in the mid fifties demonstrated a clear departure from the Borinquen querido organizations of the 1930s and 1940s that defined their identity in terms of political and cultural links to the island. The forum proposed an agenda to eliminate problems associated with urban poverty. In 1961, Aspira (Aspire) was founded to promote the education of youth by raising public and private sector funds. Clearly, both of these organizations were similar to the Mexican American organizations in the Southwest during the same period. Aspira, more than the Puerto Rican Forum, acquired a national following, serving Puerto Ricans wherever they lived in large numbers.

But when these organizations did not seem to alleviate the frustrations and despair that was common in many barrios, the politics of passion broke out. In 1966, hundreds of Chicago Puerto Rican youths went on a rampage, breaking windows and burning down many of the businesses in their neighborhoods. Ostensibly, the riots were in response to an incident of police brutality, but the underlying causes were broader, linked to the urban blight that characterized their life in Chicago. During this time, the rise of militant organizations that rejected the orientation of earlier groups emerged. As the Chicano and black pride movements pervaded the consciousness of their respective communities, a similar voice was heard in the Puerto Rican barrios throughout the country. Foremost among the new militants were the Young Lords, a grass roots youth group that was similar to the Black Panthers in the black community and the Brown Berets in the Chicano. They promoted Borinquen pride and put forth an agenda to change poverty-stricken neighborhoods. In both New York and Chicago, the Young Lords promoted neighborhood improvements using tactics such as sit-ins in service agencies and churches.

Today, Puerto Rican immigration is not as intensive as in past years, nor does it compare to the continuing and massive immigration from Mexico. But Puerto Ricans continue the movement back and forth, and such proximity keeps the fervor of their identity alive. Puerto Rico's status vis-á-vis the United States is still uncertain. In 1953, the island's capacity was upgraded from its protectorate status to commonwealth, a change that had the support of many Puerto Ricans. Today the island is divided, however, over the issue of what the island's relationship should be with the United States. Some would like to see Puerto Rico become a state, while others want independence. Independence, however unlikely, would eliminate the ability of Puerto Ricans to enter and leave the mainland freely. Probably for that reason alone, many who have families scattered on both the island and the mainland oppose such a status.

Puerto Ricans are, next to Mexican Americans, the largest Hispanic group in the United States and will continue to play an important role in the evolution of the rubric Hispanic ethnicity that emerged in the 1980s and is pervading the United States at the present time. Whatever the future brings in terms of the mainland-island political link, the millions of Puerto Ricans who came in the course of the last two centuries have already left their mark.

But the third-largest group, influential beyond their numbers in the formation of "Hispanidad," as the poet Octavio Paz termed the identity of Hispanics in the United States, are the Cuban Americans.

✳EARLY CUBAN IMMIGRATION TO THE UNITED STATES

Large-scale Cuban immigration to the United States occurred much more recently than that from either Puerto Rico or Mexico. In fact, over one million Cubans have entered the country since the Cuban Revolution of 1959. But like those of Puerto Ricans, Cuban communities in the United States can be traced back to the nineteenth century. From the outset, Florida, because of its proximity to the island and its Hispanic past, has been the destination of practically all Cubans. Each wave, starting with the first one in the 1860s, has many similar characteristics. A feature that distinguishes Cuban immigration from Mexican and Puerto Rican immigration is that Cubans have come in similar proportions from the middle class and the working class. As has been indicated, most immigrants from Mexico and Puerto Rico have been from the working class.

As early as the first major independence attempt, in 1868, Cubans left for Europe and the United States in sizable numbers. At least 100,000 had left by 1869, both as political refugees and in quest of better economic conditions. The wealthier émigrés fled to Europe to live in relative luxury, but middle-class merchants and professionals went to cities on the U.S. East Coast, such as New York. But the majority were workers who crossed the ninety miles or so to Florida. Cuban cigar manufacturers in Florida that had been operating in Key West since the 1830s eagerly welcomed the new arrivals for their factories. Key West was ideal for cigar-making because of its access to the tobacco plantations of Cuba. But more important, Cuban cigar-makers, such as the Spaniard Vicente Martínez Ybor, abandoned their Cuban operations and relocated to Florida, where they would not be as affected by Spanish mercantilistic policies. By the 1870s, Key West had become practically a Cuban town.

The Cuban community in the Florida town soon manifested strong ethnic solidarity, made even stronger by the affinity they felt for the Cubans fighting for independence back in their island home. Revolutionary clubs were formed to raise funds for the cause and to help such exiles as Carlos Manuel de Céspedes, who were organizing support in New York in the 1860s. A few years before he launched the 1895 independence bid, Jose Martí visited Key West often and considered the Florida town's Cuban community a key source of support for the cause of independence. Once they established a base, Cubans became involved in local American politics. By 1875, there were over one thousand Cubans registered to vote in Monroe County, where Key West is located. The city's first mayor, who had the same given name as his father, was the son of Carlos Manuel de Céspedes, the hero of the Ten Years' War. In 1885, following labor problems in Key West, the manufacturer Martínez Ybor moved his operations to an area east of Tampa. The new development was named Ybor City, and soon other cigar manufactures located in the new complex. Countless cigar workers followed, and Tampa became the center of cigar-making in Florida. As in Key West, ethnic solidarity was bonded by the commitment to Cuban independence. Consequently, class differences were blurred as both wealthy owners and workers saw themselves supporting the same sacred cause. Other Cuban communities in Florida, smaller than the Key West and Tampa enclaves, also supported the independence movement, providing the exile aggregation with strong intraethnic links throughout the state. Racial differences between the white and black Cubans tested the ability to bond, however. The tension became worse in Florida when Jim Crow laws separated the races and Cuban blacks were forced to form their own institutions.

When Cuba was free of Spain, many exiles went back, but for many who had set roots in their respective émigré communities and who had children growing up in the United States, returning was difficult. Significantly, the Cuban presence in Florida during the last half of the nineteenth century was marked by many accomplishments. The first labor movements were Cuban, many businesses were operated and owned by Cubans, bilingual education received an impetus in the state, and, in cities like Key West and Tampa, Cubans were responsible for many improvements in city services and civic culture.

As Cuban political and economic influence increased in the nineteenth century, the Cubans played an increasingly more important role in U.S. policy toward the Spanish colonies in the Caribbean. But while helping the cause of independence, U.S. politicians also wanted to control a Cuba that one day would be free of Spanish dominance. Just as the struggle for Cuban independence had resulted in chaotic conditions leading to emigration, domination by Americans in the twentieth century fostered economic and political tensions that also provoked exile and emigration.

The Florida enclaves, established by earlier immigrants, served the Cubans who continued to arrive in Florida during the first fifty years of this century. Many left Cuba because of continued political turmoil on the island. In the 1920s, for example, a small number of young intellectuals moved to Miami to escape the repressive policies of Gerardo Machado and to plot against him. A dictator who ruled Cuba with the blessing of the United States, Machado was finally overthrown by a worker and student coalition in 1933. His demise was precipitated by the collapse of the U.S. economy, on which Cuba was completely dependent. He and his cronies, then, like countless others before them, also sought asylum in Florida. Since Cuba did not really achieve political peace after Machado's ouster, Miami, as well as other Florida communities, continued to be a refuge for Cubans who were not welcome in Cuba by the politicians in power.

✳ THE REVOLUTION OF FIDEL CASTRO AND CUBAN IMMIGRATION

It was for political reasons as well that the most dramatic exodus out of Cuba began after 1959. That year, Fidel Castro made his triumphant entry into Havana after he and his revolutionaries had defeated the brutal and repressive regime of Fulgencio Batista, a dictator who had been deeply involved in Cuban politics since the 1930s. Batista was only an army sergeant when in 1935 he led a barracks revolt that overthrew a president installed by the military to replace the banished dictator Antonio Machado. Then the next year, Batista overthrew the government that he himself had helped come to power, and in 1940, after a series of machinations, he was elected the first president under a new constitution promulgated that same year. Batista had become perhaps the most astute opportunist in the history of Cuba, and he returned Cuba to levels of corruption not seen since the Machado years. But at least in this period, he seemed content to allow democracy to take its course by allowing elections. Two irresolute and corrupt administrations followed Batista's in 1944 and 1948, dashing any hopes that these new leaders would bring political stability and honesty to the troubled island republic. Consequently, many Cubans became disillusioned with the promises of democracy. Then in 1952, Batista seized power again, this time as an arrogant dictator. Batista then took Cuba to new heights of repression and corruption.

For much of this time, Batista had the support of the United States. Ever since Cuba's independence, Americans had remained ever-vigilant about political events on the island. While policy toward Cuba followed the distinct requirements of the various U.S. administrations, both Republican and Democrat, the main course of foreign policy was to protect the extensive investments held by Americans in Cuba. The Platt Amendment allowed for intervention in Cuba whenever it seemed necessary to an American president. Indeed, before the 1920s, U.S. troops were sent three times to Cuba to intervene in internal affairs.

In the opinion of many Cubans, the United States had blatantly held Cuba as an economic and political colony. Even though the hated Platt Amendment was abrogated in 1934, it was apparent that Americans, during Batista's last rule in the 1950s, controlled most of the economy and much of the political process. By the time a young lawyer named Fidel Castro initiated guerrilla warfare against Batista, the former sergeant's feral methods of running his country began to alienate even the most cynical of American

Fidel Castro.

supporters. Thus, when Castro came to power in February 1959, his 26th of July Movement did not meet too much resistance from the United States, and at home he acquired a wide and popular following.

To Washington officials during the presidency of Dwight D. Eisenhower, Castro turned out to be more than what they bargained for, however. The young revolutionary exhibited an eclectic ideology, but it was clear that the new government was no longer going to permit American dominance, a stance which quickly alienated the Eisenhower administration. Another position, soon embraced by Castro, involved extensive land reform and radical restructuring of the economy. Very quickly, many of those affected, such as landowners and other members of the upper classes, turned against the revolution. Castro, to protect his fledgling movement, repressed those who resisted, and soon thousands of the disaffected left for the United States in a time-honored tradition established during the many previous shake-ups.

Increasingly, Castro adopted socialistic ideas and turned to the Cuban Communist party for support, but not before the Eisenhower administration broke off relations with his revolutionary government. Eventually, the Soviet Union pledged its support to Castro, while the American government initiated a plan to welcome refugees. Eisenhower's motives to allow disaffected Cubans to enter the United States unencumbered were largely political. The 1950s were characterized by a cold-war mentality in which the Soviet Union and the United States waged an intense propaganda campaign for world prominence and acceptance. The flight of refugees was correctly anticipated by American officials to be middle class and essential to Cuba's economic well-being. Thus, their escape would deprive Cuba of technical and professional skills, serve as a propaganda victory against communism, and, by extension, deliver a blow to the Soviet Union's world prestige. But the Eisenhower administration projected another role for the exiles. Considering the history of discontented Cubans using the United States as a mustering point for insurgency against governments on the island, American officials foresaw the potential for a repetition with the latest wave of arrivals.

A curious element of the refugee project was a children's program designed to bring over thousands of young Cubans, supposedly to escape forced indoctrination by Castro's government. Wild rumors, abetted by American officials, circulated in Cuba and the refugee community in the United States that children were forcibly taken from their homes and sent to the Soviet Union to receive a Communist education. Within three years, 14,048 mostly male children left Cuba and were fostered in this country

by various groups, including the Catholic church. Most of these youngsters were scions of the middle and upper classes, and because many were nurtured further in this country, they became fairly well educated. As a consequence, today there are countless middle-aged Cuban professionals who were not rejoined with parents and other family members until their adult years, if at all.

With the election of John F. Kennedy to the presidency, relations between the two countries did not improve. President Eisenhower had encouraged Cuban refugees to prepare an invasion of Cuba to topple Castro, and in the cold-war atmosphere of the early 1960s, Kennedy subsumed this policy. In April 1961, Cuban exiles who were trained and armed by the United States but who did not receive direct military support in their invasion attempted a foray into Cuba that was doomed from the beginning. The failure of the infamous Bay of Pigs invasion embittered the thousands of Cubans who were in exile, but Castro's position at home was strengthened. To many observers throughout the world, especially in the Third World, the United States was clearly taking the side of the usurpers, who attempted to overthrow a legitimately based government.

With the Bay of Pigs fiasco behind him, Kennedy continued to welcome Cuban refugees and to provide more structured military training for Cubans, most of whom still desired another attempt at overthrowing Cuba's Communist government. But in 1962, Kennedy redeemed himself from the Bay of Pigs disgrace by backing down the Soviet Union on a Russian plan to establish missile bases in Cuba. After this, the more viable of the two courses inherited from the Eisenhower years was to expand the refugee program.

Increasingly, welcoming refugees became more important to the U.S. policy of destabilizing the Cuban revolutionary government than armed insurrection or outright invasion. Such a course deprived Cuba of the merchants, technicians, and professionals so necessary to the island's struggling economy. In the ten years after the disastrous Bay of Pigs invasion, almost 500,000 Cubans left the island. Because of the heavy influx, a special program was initiated to settle the refugees outside of Florida. Although the majority of the fleeing Cubans stayed in Florida, thousands more went to other regions of the United States, especially to California, New York, and Chicago, areas that already had large populations of Hispanics. An elaborate project ensued that included numerous prerogatives for incoming Cubans. Refugee emergency housing, English-language training, federal educational funds for Cuban children, and medical care became part of a package that facilitated the immigration process.

When Lyndon B. Johnson became president after Kennedy's assassination, he also vowed to embrace Cubans who wished to leave the island. Cubans then qualified for immigration status under special immigration provisions for refugees fleeing repressive governments. But Fidel Castro himself announced as early as 1965 that Cubans could leave Cuba if they had relatives in the United States. Castro stipulated, however, that Cubans already in Florida had to come and get them at Camarioca Bay. Nautical crafts of all types systematically left Miami to Camioraca, returning laden with anxious Cubans eager to rejoin their families on the mainland. The spectacle of the motley fleet of boats converging on Miami docks was dramatic, but the trip was also dangerous for the thousands of fleeing Cubans. Many of the boats were not seaworthy and capsized. An airlift was then organized with a great deal of publicity and fanfare. Thousands more arrived in the United States before the flights ended in 1973.

Castro also tapped the refugee issue so that he could gain moral backing from the rest of Latin America and from the millions of Cubans living on the island who still supported him. He charged those who wanted to leave the island with betrayal, branding the emigrants with the epithet *gusano* (worm), which rhymes with *cubano* and is a derogatory name. In addition, he constantly reminded the world that, while Americans welcomed Cubans as displaced persons fleeing political persecution, they would not allow the same considerations to Chileans, Haitians, and other Latin Americans escaping repressive governments.

The final and most dramatic influx of Cubans came in the early 1980s. By that time much of the hard antipathy that Cubans felt toward Castro had become as much ritualistic as real. A generation had grown up in the United States that did not have the same sentiments as their parents. In addition, President Jimmy Carter, determined to depart from the cold-war policies of his predecessors, made advances toward Castro, urging reconciliation with the Cubans in the United States. Remarkably, moderate elements within that community responded and advocated harmonizing relations with the aging Castro. In 1977, a group of young Cuban exiles called the Antonio Maceo Brigade traveled to Cuba to participate in service work and to achieve a degree of rapprochement with the Cuban government. Back in Florida, many of the exiles branded these young envoys as traitors, and a clear message was sent out to rest of the Cuban community that any sympathizers would have to face their wrath.

The first flight of American citizens repatriated from Cuba on December 19, 1966. (Courtesy of the *Texas Catholic Herald*.)

Nonetheless, Castro's overtures to the exiled Cubans escalated and they were met with some positive response. His offer was the more attractive because he promised to release political prisoners as well, most whom had relatives in the United States. Cuban-American adherence to reconciliation with Castro and his government continued to provoke intense opposition from conservative members of the exile community, however. Indeed, some of the advocates of a dialogue with the Communist leader were assassinated by armed paramilitary Cubans, but in spite of the opposition, relations between the exile community and Castro improved during the Carter years. They improved so much, in fact, that the earlier tact of using the refugee issue for propaganda purposes was lost as the tension abated between Castro and Cubans in the United States.

In April 1980, however, a dramatic incident received worldwide attention: a bus carrying a load of discontented Cubans crashed through the gates of the Peruvian embassy in Havana and the passengers received political asylum from Peru. When it became apparent that what the gate-crashers really wanted was to leave Cuba, Castro began to revise his policy of gradually allowing Cubans to leave. In a calculated move, the Castro government announced that whoever wanted to leave Cuba should go to the Peruvian embassy. Immediately, ten thousand people crowded in. The Cuban government then processed and gave exit documents to those who came forth. Cuban exiles who happened to be on the island at the time of the embassy gate-crashing, upon their return to Miami, organized a flotilla of forty-two boats. With Castro's blessing, they began the round-the-clock evacuation of the "Havana Ten Thousand," and Carter, as did presidents before him, decided to welcome the new influx of Cuban exiles.

Since the flotilla converged at Mariel Harbor to pick up passengers, which totaled over 125,000 by the time the boat-lifts ended at the end of 1980, the refugees became known as the Marielitos. The explanation given by Castro for this whole phenomenon was rather simplistic. He charged that his policy of allowing exiles to visit the island had contaminated many erstwhile revolutionaries with the glitter of consumerism. It is probably true that travelers from the United States to the island did tempt Cubans with their abundance of consumer products, convincing

many that life in a capitalist society was easier than life in Cuba. Nonetheless, Castro had to accept that socialism was at this point experiencing many difficulties and not delivering on many of the promises made some twenty years earlier.

The new refugees differed significantly from the earlier waves of displaced Cubans. Few were from the middle and upper classes of pre-Castro Cuba, as were most exiles then living in the United States, and there were also some racial differences. The new arrivals were more reflective of the general racial composition of Cuba; many blacks and mulattoes were in the Marielito ranks. Furthermore, in a crafty move, Castro deliberately cast out many political and social misfits during the boat-lift, an act that unfairly stigmatized the majority of 1980 émigrés, who were in the main normal, hardworking Cubans.

During the Marielito exit, Fidel Castro and President Carter became entangled in a now familiar struggle over which country would get more political capital from the refugee issue. Thousands of new arrivals crowded into processing centers, living in tent cities and even a football stadium in Miami! Many of the refugees became frustrated over the delay in being able to leave the camps. For many the

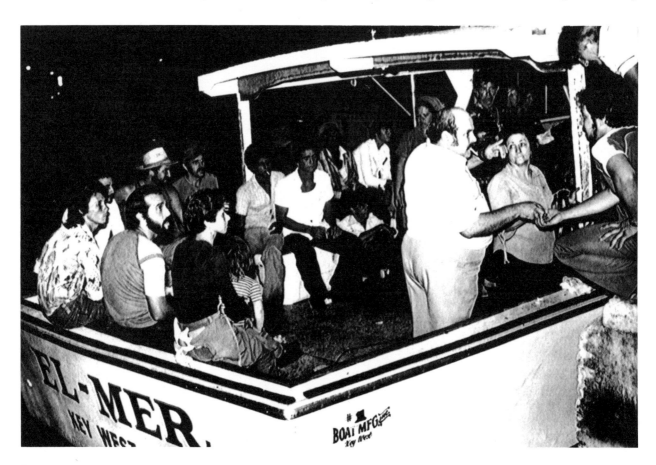

Cubans arriving in Miami during the Mariel boat-lift.

stay in these "temporary camps" stretched out into months, even years. The Castro government was quick to imply that the United States was not really that anxious to provide refuge to Cubans who were poor, uneducated, and racially not as white as the previous influx.

While these charges probably had some validity, the truth was more complex. Unlike previous émigrés, most of the Marielitos did not have families in Florida or elsewhere in the United States, and receiving a discharge from a camp required having an American sponsor. At first Cuban Americans and other Americans were anxious to provide this service, but as the excitement and newness of the boatlift wore off, sponsors became harder to come by. The stigma suffered by Marielitos also led to difficulties once they were released. To be sure, a hard-core criminal element was dispersed among the new arrivals, but Marielitos were no different than the millions of immigrants who had preceded them to American shores in previous years. They sought to work and to find opportunities in their new environment. After all, that was the reason they had come.

The Cuban community has now acquired such deep roots in the United States that the term "exile" for many is no longer applicable. The post-Castro refugees and their children, along with descendants of Cubans who came to the United States earlier in the century, are now just another ethnic group in this country. They are part of the larger aggregate of Hispanics in the United States, which, of course, includes the Mexican Americans and Puerto Ricans already discussed.

As did Mexicans and Puerto Ricans, Cubans before the Castro era immigrated to the United States to work, to flee violence and repression, and, in general, to make a new life for themselves. Consequently, to survive, they forged fraternal organizations and looked to their homeland and culture to provide them with the necessary identity to build strong ethnic solidarity. In this respect Cuban Americans differ little from Mexican Americans and Puerto Ricans.

The vast, overwhelming majority, however, arrived in this country during the past thirty years. To be sure, fewer Cubans than Mexicans have immigrated to the United States in this same period, but the influx of the latter is part of a very long history of massive working-class immigration across the bor-

A legally immigrating Cuban woman is reunited with her granddaughter in Miami in 1980. (Courtesy of the *Texas Catholic Herald*.)

der. Cubans, because of the political conditions that provoked them to leave, were primarily from the more privileged classes. As a consequence, advantages of education, wealth, and racial acceptance allowed them to succeed in the United States at a faster pace than Mexicans and Puerto Ricans. In addition, because it was politically convenient, Cubans received an inordinate amount of assistance from U.S. administrations, from Eisenhower to Reagan, which helped their effort to settle and adapt. This has provoked invidious comparisons and charges that the cards were stacked in their favor. Much of this sentiment has some foundation in fact, but it also has to be recognized that Cuban Americans have demonstrated a great amount of their own native initiative and drive, a fact that accounts for a large part of their success.

✱HISPANIC IDENTITY IN THE UNITED STATES

Today an uneasy ethnic solidarity exists among Hispanics in the United States. At the political level there is much rhetoric that attempts to bring them all under one rubric, and, indeed, the term "Hispanic" has been fostered as an agent of this process. While Cubans are conservative on issues dealing with Cuba and communism, they share the same ideology with Mexican Americans and Puerto Ricans when it comes to cultural maintenance and resistance to what many consider debasing American values. Another bond is language, an issue that has been forced into the political arena by the "English only" movement. All Hispanics resent the onus placed on them because they speak Spanish, a language that is despised in many quarters of the Anglo-American community.

The development of a rubric hispanidad has been facilitated by three Spanish-language television networks and hundreds of radio stations that indirectly pound the message of ethnic bonding into millions of Hispanic homes. Variety entertainment programs, soap operas, and talk shows that air nationally are many times crafted to bring a balanced appeal to the variegated Spanish-speaking peoples taking their turn at the American opportunity structure. A plethora of slick-cover magazines have appeared in the last ten years aimed at all the Hispanic groups. Some use English, others Spanish, or they contain bilingual renditions. This process alone, perhaps unwittingly, is bound to evolve a pan-Hispanicism unique to the United States.

In large cities such as Los Angeles, Chicago, Houston, and Miami, Hispanics of all kinds are thrown together and many times common ties result in an affinity and some mingling. Where they have been together for a longer time, as in Chicago, Mexicans and Puerto Ricans, who have lived together since the 1940s, have merged into political coalitions, and interethnic marriages have produced thousands of Mexican-Puerto Rican offspring. The melding of Salvadorans, Puerto Ricans, Mexicans, and Spaniards in San Francisco has also been transpiring for a long time, and there, during the heady sixties movements, a strong Latino consciousness emerged in such barrios as the Mission District. In Los Angeles and Houston, entrepreneurs have tapped the Hispanic market, creating chains of enormous food stores called El Tíanguis and Fiesta, respectively. These outlets cater to the food tastes of every imaginable Hispanic group.

Another possible scenario is that differences will make for a separate evolution in the respective communities. As each Hispanic group evolves in the United States, with separate identities, they may become ensconced and comfortable in their own elaborated ethnicity. Indeed, this is true of the older and larger Hispanic groupings, who see themselves as Mexican Americans, Cuban Americans, and mainland Puerto Ricans. Hispanos in northern New Mexico, who are for all intents and purposes Mexican Americans, at times even remain insular from this group. So what can be expected from them when it comes to identifying with a larger national denomination?

Furthermore, interethnic prejudices still persist at the community level between Hispanics. For example, at times Latin Americans or Spaniards living in the United States distance themselves from Mexican Americans or Puerto Ricans so that they will not be mistaken for them by non-Hispanics who hold prejudices against those groups. They may buy into Anglo-American prejudices and unwarranted stereotypes against certain groups in an unconscious effort to ingratiate themselves with the mainstream population. This is true even if back home they might have never dreamed of having these misgivings toward fellow Latins.

Another common source of inter-Hispanic antipathy is based on class origin. If the majority of one group is working class, as is the case with Mexicans, Puerto Ricans, and Central Americans, middle-class immigrants who come from South America often find it difficult to relate to what they consider a lower-class culture. They also demonstrate this orientation, of course, toward the working class back in their homelands. That phenomenon is also borne out among some upper-class Mexicans in the United States who look with disdain at compatriots who come from the *clases populares*.

There is even opposition to amalgamation among some Hispanic intellectuals who see the whole trend toward Hispanicization as a tool of consumerism. Obviously, it would be easier to aim at a large market rather than at disparate groups. There is also a residue of resentment within some in the Hispanic community toward Cuban exiles because of that group's persistent support of a conservative foreign policy toward Latin America. But the ultimate fear is that a bland, malleable ethnic group will emerge.

Regardless, the process is going to find its own level. Despite the destructive prejudices that exist between Hispanic groups or the well-intended admonitions of intellectuals, common roots exist between Hispanics regardless of national or class origin. These will eventually make crucial links that no one can foresee. Rather than resist, Hispanics would be better off trying to shape this irresistible force into a positive ideal of brotherhood and humanity so that they can take their rightful place in the American mosaic, and even become a remarkably potent political power.

References

Acuña, Rudolfo. *Occupied America: A History of Chicanos.* New York: Harper & Row, 1981.

Bannon, John Francis. *The Journey of Alvar Nuñez Cabeza de Vaca.* Chicago: Río Grande Press, 1964.

Bolton, Herbert. *Spanish Exploration in the Southwest 1542-1706.* New York: Barnes and Noble, 1946.

Cabral del Hoyo, Humberto. *The Thumbnail History of Mexico.* Ciudad Méxíco. Comité Norteamericano Pro-Mexíco, 1960.

Claypole, William, and John Robottom. *Caribbean Story.* White Plains, N.Y.: Longman, 1986.

De Leon, Arnoldo. *The Tejano Community.* Albuquerque: University of New Mexico Press, 1982.

García, Mario T. *Mexican Americans.* New Haven: Yale University Press, 1989.

Morales, Julio. *Puerto Rican Poverty and Migration: We Just Had to Try Elsewhere.* New York: Praeger, 1986.

Taylor, Paul Schuster, *Mexican Labor in the United States: Chicago and the Calumet Region.* Berkeley: University of California Press, 1932.

Suchlicki, Jaime. *Cuba: From Columbus to Castro.* Washington: Pergammon, 1986.

Weber, David J. *The Mexican Frontier, 1821-1846: The American Southwest under Mexico.* Albuquerque: University of New Mexico Press, 1982.

F. Arturo Rosales

②

Spanish Explorers and Colonizers

❋ Native American Cultures ❋ The Age of Exploration: The Caribbean, Mexico, and Florida ❋ Spanish Expeditions to Florida ❋ Spanish Exploration and Colonization of the Southwest ❋ Spanish Explorations to California

No one is sure when pre-Columbian inhabitants of the Western Hemisphere first appeared, although scholars generally agree that they originated in Asia. Presumably, they crossed the land bridge that existed between what is now the Soviet Union and Alaska and moved southward. Traveling a few miles per generation, some settled around Canada and the Mississippi Valley, while others migrated to what is today the Southwest, Mexico, Central America, the Caribbean, and all the way down to Cape Horn. By 1492, the native American population of the Western Hemisphere may have reached between thirty-five to forty-five million.

Over the vast area that is now Canada and the United States—with a few exceptions—the pre-Columbian inhabitants never advanced much beyond hunting, fishing, and subsistence farming. By contrast, those who lived on the Mexican plateau, as well as those who lived in Central America and in the Andean sierras, had demonstrated a high degree of cultural achievement. The great discoveries that they made in science, as well as the great works of art that they created, still affect our lives.

❋ NATIVE AMERICAN CULTURES

The Mayan Civilization

Agriculture had its beginnings around 7000 B.C. when a native American group known as the Otomí discovered a plant they called *teozintle* that produced edible grain. The Otomí of the southern Mexican plateau apparently perfected the cultivation of teozintle over the years until it produced corn. The development of corn allowed these native Americans to abandon their nomadic ways, and they began to build permanent dwellings. By 5000 B.C. the Otomíes

were cultivating a variety of crops, such as corn, squash, beans, and chile, as well as weaving garments from vegetable fibers. Eventually, they acquired skills in the making of pottery and utensils. Perhaps from the Otomí sprang the Mayan civilization of Central America and southern Mexico.

Mayan civilization can be divided into three periods: the Preclassic, from about 800 B.C. to about A.D. 300; the Classic, from about A.D. 300 to 1000; and the Postclassic, from about A.D. 1000 A.D. to 1500. Of these three periods, the Classic and the Post classic were the most important.

The Classic period was centered in the southern jungles of the Yucatán Peninsula, the present-day Mexican states of Chiapas and Tabasco, and the present-day nations of Guatemala, Belize, and Honduras. Among the great Mayan cultural centers of the Classic period were Tikal in Guatemala, Copán in Honduras, and Palenque in Mexico. The Classic period ended shortly before A.D. 1000. No one is sure what caused the Maya to abandon the sites. Some think that it was soil exhaustion, while others believe that it was a civil war.

The Postclassic period began around A.D. 1000. Apparently, ruling nobles toward the end of the Classic period moved to Mayan outposts in northern Yucatán and began to transform them into city-states. Among the great city-states of the Postclassic period were Mayapan, Chichén Itzá, and Uxmal, all of them located on the Yucatán Peninsula.

Thanks to the work of archaeologists and the accuracy of Mayan records, we know more about the Maya than any other native Americans. Unlike the Aztec or Inca, the Maya never built a centralized empire. At the peak of their civilization, the Maya occupied an area of approximately 200,000 square miles. In that vast area were sovereign city-states sharing in language, culture, and religion. While the Mayan governmental structure could be characterized as a simple one—a hereditary ruler aided by priests and nobles presided over each city-state—Mayan cultural achievement could not. During both the Classic and the Postclassic periods, the Maya reached a very high state of cultural development, which was reflected in their dress, customs, buildings, and arts.

Mayan intellectual achievements included carved hieroglyphics and watercolor pictographs on fiber paper. Still preserved is the *Popol-Vuh*, the sacred book of the Maya, which traces the creation of man prior to 3151 B.C., and the book of Chilam Balam, known as the masterpiece of Mayan literature. The Maya excelled in chronology; their year was composed of twenty months of eighteen days each, to which they added five extra days. The Maya were also accomplished mathematicians. As the late Mayanist Sylvanus Morley wrote, "for the first time in the history of the human race, they had devised a system of numeration by position involving the concept and use of the mathematical quantity of zero" (Herring, 40).

Mayan architecture was both original and outstanding. The material used by the Maya in building their cities and pyramids consisted of burnt limestone. Their cities were a collection of temples and monuments embellished with carvings and wall paintings. Mayan architecture was characterized by use of the corbeled roof or false arch as well as the vault.

When the Spaniards first arrived in Yucatán in 1511, the Mayan civilization was in a decadent state as a result of civil wars. Soon the conquerors began the process of destroying the few Mayan cities that were left standing and began building Catholic churches on top of Mayan temples. Ironically, the descendants of the once proud Maya live today in misery and exploitation.

The Aztec

Undoubtedly, the most famous native Americans, who inhabited Mexico when Hernán Cortés landed on the coast of Veracruz in 1519, were the Aztec. Around A.D. 1200, when the city of Atzcapotzalco ruled the Central Valley of Mexico, there arrived a tribe of nomads who called themselves Aztec and who said they came from Aztlán (Place of the Herons). Legend has it that the Aztec were moving southward from northern Mexico because one of their gods, Huitzilopochtli, had ordered them to settle where they saw an eagle poised on a cactus and with a snake in its mouth. After wandering from one place to the other, the Aztec supposedly saw the sign on the shores of Lake Texcoco, east of present-day Mexico City. Atzcapotzalco's rulers allowed the Aztec to settle on the lake's shores in exchange for a tribute, and in 1325 the Aztec began to build their capital, Tenochtitlán, in honor of Tenoch.

In 1428, the Aztec launched a surprise attack on Atzcapotzalco, and Aztec armies began to conquer the Central Valley. By the early sixteenth century, Aztec dominance extended from the Central Valley of Mexico to parts of Guatemala. An estimated twenty million people lived in that empire.

The Aztec governmental structure was theoretically a democratic one, with each tribe practicing a certain degree of autonomy. In addition, each tribe appointed a delegate to the Supreme Council, which elected the emperor. In practice, as the Aztec nobility acquired more power, the Aztec Empire became a theocratic oligarchy.

Aztec religion was less spiritual than Mayan religion, and it was certainly a bloodthirsty one. Because their ferocious war-god, Huitzilopochtli, demanded human sacrifices, Aztec warriors were educated from childhood to seek prisoners of war to be offered as sacrifices. In 1487, for example, the Aztec inaugurated the temple of Huitzilopochtli by sacrificing more than twenty-five thousand captives. In short, the Aztecs waged war just to placate their war-god.

The Aztec capital of Tenochtitlán was a magnificent city. It had an estimated population of 200,000. Connected by a system of causeways and canals, the city had its own aqueduct. The giant market of Tlatelolco exhibited fresh produce from *chinampas* (floating gardens). In the center of the city there was the magnificent temple of Tenochtitlán, attended by five thousand priests. Tenochtitlán, in sum, was a city of beauty and pageantry.

Like their predecessors, the Aztec had outstanding knowledge of the medicinal properties of plants, and they were able potters and weavers. Intellectually, however, the Aztec were not original. Their pyramids were merely copies of Toltec architecture, and their sculptures never quite matched those of the Maya. Their writing never went beyond simple pictographs painted on cloth, skin, and magúey paper. They made no contribution to mathematics or astronomy, and their calendar was a copy of the Toltec calendar. In spite of its lack of originality, the Aztec civilization was a splendid one.

The Aztec Empire might have been a prosperous one, but it had a very serious weakness. This flaw was the hostility of the conquered tribes who supplied the victims for the bloodthirsty Huitzilopochtli. Any powerful savior who would curb or destroy the power of the hated Aztecs would certainly find allies among the conquered tribes. In 1519, the subjugated tribes were expecting the scheduled visit of the blond Toltec deity Quetzalcoatl, who was going to bring justice and punish the evil ones. Instead of Quetzalcoatl, a blond-haired, blue-eyed Spaniard named Hernán Cortés landed in Veracruz and quickly moved northward to conquer the Aztec Empire. Cortés and his fellow Spaniards leveled Tenochtitlán in 1521 and built Mexico City on the same site. Ironically, the "liberators" would become masters for three centuries.

The Pueblo Culture of the Southwest

The most magnificent archaeological sites and the best-preserved pre-Columbian cultures in the United States are found in the Southwest. There were many native American cultures in the Southwest, some nomadic, some sedentary. Perhaps the most important was the Pueblo culture.

Descendants of the prehistoric Anasazi people, the Pueblos lived in western New Mexico and the upper Rio Grande area of that state. In addition, there were Pueblo villages in northeastern Arizona. Among the Pueblo peoples at the time of the Spanish arrival were the Zuni, Hopi, Keres, and Tano.

It is speculated that the Pueblos were sedentary people whose life primarily depended on agriculture. At the time of Coronado's expedition to the Southwest in the 1540s, there were an estimated sixty-six Pueblo villages in the area of New Mexico, growing such crops as corn, beans, squash, and cotton. Chile pepper, a trademark of the Southwest, was apparently not known to the Pueblos. Since water was essential to the arid region where the Pueblos lived, they had a system of irrigation, which consisted of using the runoff from rains. Each Pueblo village also had a cistern. Although the Pueblos lacked the plow, they nevertheless made good use of the digging stick.

Because the Pueblos were extremely concerned with their security, most of their dwellings were built on barren hilltops away from their fertile patches of land. Their houses were made out of stone or adobe and were strong enough to withstand an enemy attack. In pre-Columbian times, Pueblo houses had neither doors nor windows—a security measure—and the only entrance was by means of portable ladders through hatches in the roofs. Essential to the Pueblo village was the *kiva*, a secret underground ceremonial chamber that served both as a ceremonial center and a meeting place. Only males were allowed in the kiva.

Pueblo governmental organization was simple. The Pueblos never achieved any unity beyond the village, for each village was politically autonomous. Land belonged to the community, and each village was ruled by a council of elders varying from ten to thirty members.

The Pueblos were religious people who worshiped the sun and the elements. It is estimated that they devoted half their time to religious activities. Foremost among their ceremonies were the communal dances combining drama, dance, music, and poetry.

Being a sedentary people, the Pueblos had time to create works of art. Pueblo artistic expression showed itself in basketry, weaving, and pottery. Pueblo basketry was known for its geometric design and symmetry. Although the Pueblos did not learn weaving until A.D. 700, they perfected this art through the use of transverse colored patterns and a technique called tie-dyeing. The Pueblos lacked the potter's wheel, but their pottery was carefully crafted by hand and showed gradual changes in design, color, and symbols.

In spite of more than 450 years of contact with the white man, the remnants of the pre-Columbian Pueblo of the Southwest have survived to the present.

The Natives of Florida

When Ponce de León landed on the shores of Florida in 1513, there were an estimated 100,000 native Americans living there. They were divided among six major groups: the Timucua, the Tocobaga, the Apalachee, the Ais and Jeagas, the Tequesta, and the Calusa.

The Timucua, who occupied a diagonal region from northeast Florida to the Tampa Bay area, were mostly hunters but also practiced subsistence farming. About forty thousand strong, they were the most numerous of the Florida natives. The Tocobaga, who lived around the Tampa Bay area, numbered around seven thousand. They were mostly fishermen but also cultivated corn, beans, and squash. The Apalachee population of Florida, which existed in the panhandle area, numbered about twenty-five thousand. The Apalachee depended on corn and vegetables for their living, but when these ran out they would turn to hunting and fishing. The Ais and Jeagas, who numbered only around three thousand, were the most primitive. Living on the eastern coast of Florida, they never learned agriculture and were principally fishermen and gatherers. South of the Ais and Jeagas, there were some five thousand Tequesta, who knew no agriculture but were excellent fishermen. Finally, there were the twenty-five thousand fierce Calusas living in an area that extended from Cape Sable to the Tampa Bay area. Nonagricultural, the Calusa lived on shellfish.

Although the Florida natives had no system of writing and made no contribution to the advancement of knowledge, they nevertheless developed organized governments with real authority and were skilled at making pottery. To label all of them primitive would be erroneous.

The Pre-Columbian Inhabitants of the Caribbean

Although anthropologists have evidence of the culture of the people who inhabited the Caribbean islands, there is no reliable estimate as to their numbers. Figures have ranged from as low as sixty thousand people to as high as seven million. Knowledge regarding their origins is also rather sketchy. The most plausible theory indicates that they originated on the Venezuelan mainland and migrated to the islands more than one thousand years before the arrival of Columbus. When Columbus discovered the New World, there were four major cultures in the Caribbean: the Guanahatabey, the Ciboney, the Arawak, and the Carib.

The Guanahatabey were the oldest culture group. They were concentrated in the Guanahacabibes Peninsula of western Cuba. The Guanahatabey were extremely primitive and seemed to depend on shellfish for their existence. They had no dwellings and possessed no organizational skills.

The Ciboney was a Stone Age culture. Although remains of the Ciboney have been found in some of the Bahama islands and in areas of Jamaica, they primarily inhabited western Cuba and the southwestern peninsula of the island of Hispaniola. Characterized by their kindness and gentle manners, the Ciboneyes developed a crude form of subsistence agriculture, but fishing was more important to them.

While some of the Ciboney lived in caves, the majority lived in *bajareques* (primitive thatched huts). Ciboney governmental organization was very simple, and its symbol of authority was the *cacique* (village chieftain). Although the Ciboney lacked artistic ability, they had knowledge of the medicinal property of various herbs and plants. Because of their lack of military skills, some of the Ciboney had been subjugated by the Arawak when Columbus first arrived in Cuba.

The Arawak probably originated in Venezuela and spread across the Greater Antilles and the Bahamas. There were two major groups: the Lucayo, who occupied the Bahamas, and the Taino, who inhabited central and eastern Cuba, as well as Hispaniola, Jamaica, and Puerto Rico.

Arawakan settlements ranged from a few *bohíos* (thatched-roofed huts) to villages of more than five thousand people. Although matrilineal inheritance characterized Arawakan society, political organization was male-dominated. Each Arawak village was headed by a cacique. Although the cacique was not an all-powerful ruler, he nevertheless was the final authority in all village matters. Cacique leadership was hereditary. When the cacique died, he was replaced by his son. If there was no male heir, the eldest son of the cacique's sister became the new cacique. The cacique was aided by his *nitaínos* (principal advisers). The nitaínos were usually in charge of the labor force, and they were mostly the oldest males in the village. Since Arawak religion was highly organized, the *behique* (priest) occupied an important part in Arawak society. The behique interpreted the signs of the *zemíes* (gods) and was also a medicine man. Each village had a zemí house, where *areítos* (ceremonies) were performed. Finally, there were the *naboríes* (commoners).

Research on Arawak villages seems to indicate that they were located in areas that were conducive to agriculture. Although the Arawak harvested corn, yams, beans, and peanuts, their principal staple was *yuca* (manioc). From the yuca plant they made a type of unleavened bread called *cassava*. Tobacco was also grown by the Arawak and used by the behique in religious ceremonies in order to attract the spirits. The Arawak supplemented their diet with fish, mollusks, turtle eggs, snakes, bats, and iguanas.

The Arawak had few metallurgical skills. Arawak pottery, on the other hand, showed a degree of sophistication. The Arawak were excellent basket weavers; they made basket fish traps and there is evidence they used a type of basket for carrying water. Another area in which they excelled was wood carving. The Arawak constructed canoes without the help of metal tools, making it possible for them to conduct an intensive island trade. In addition, the Arawak carved out wooden zemí figures and were known for the *macana* (a wooden club used as a weapon). Since cotton was grown on the islands, the Arawak weaved it into hammocks, nets, and bags.

A few years before Columbus's arrival in the New World, Arawak hegemony in the Caribbean was being challenged by the Carib. Little is known about this group, for they were merely island raiders. The Carib were the last of the native Americans that entered the Caribbean. By 1492, they occupied most of the Lesser Antilles, and Carib warriors had already terrorized the Arawak population of Cuba, Puerto Rico, and Hispaniola.

Knowledge of Carib social and political organization, economic development, and way of life is sketchy at best. They practiced subsistence farming. Unlike the Arawak, they grew crops for dietary purposes only and not for trade. Their religion lacked the zemíes of the Arawak, as well as the ceremonial rituals. Carib political organization was even simpler than that of the Arawak. The Carib cacique busied himself planning raids rather than solving village problems. The Carib raided islands for the dual purpose of finding female slaves and male prisoners. The male Arawak they captured were ritualistically cooked and eaten. (The word *Carib* means cannibal in Arawak.)

According to William Claypole and John Robottom (1986, p.6), the Carib were decorative people. They applied flower petals and gold dust to their body paint before it dried. They also wore chains of stone and coral around their arms, wrists, and legs. They pierced their nose, lips, and ears to hold ornaments made from fish spines and plates of turtle shells.

As one might expect, the Carib excelled in the area of weaponry. Their arsenal included bows, spears, and *macanas* (wooden clubs). The Carib *piragua* (a narrow, high-prowed canoe) was the fastest and swiftest canoe in the Caribbean, and it was capable of traveling great distances. Carib expansion in the Caribbean was checked only by the arrival of the Spaniards, and later, the British, French, and Dutch.

The year 1492 marked the beginning of the end for the native Americans of the Caribbean. The Ciboney and Arawak, whom Columbus described as gentle people of great simplicity, disappeared from the cultural scene as a result of diseases and exploitation. A little over a century after Columbus's arrival, the Carib succumbed to British, French, and Dutch firepower.

✳THE AGE OF EXPLORATION: THE CARIBBEAN, MEXICO, AND FLORIDA

It was near the end of the fifteenth century when the nations of Europe set in motion the discovery and exploration of the New World. The glory of the discovery, exploration, and colonization of this vast mass of land for more than a century and a half fell to practically one nation—Spain.

Spain's discovery and conquest of the New World came at a fortuitous time, for it was after the union of the Crowns of Aragón and Castile and the expulsion of the Moors from their bastion in Granada that Spain could supply manpower. Thus, with men trained in the profession of arms and eager to seek glory under one monarch, one religion, one empire, and one sword, Spain was able to make her greatest contribution to the Renaissance—discovery and colonization of the New World.

The Voyages of Christopher Columbus

Christopher Columbus was not the first European to step foot on the New World. Research has shown that the Scandinavian Leif Eriksson had earned that honor some five hundred years before Columbus. Yet, if Columbus was not the first European to step onto American soil, he certainly had the good fortune of being the first one to keep a record of his voyage and thus establish a permanent presence in the New World.

Christopher Columbus was probably born in Genoa in 1451 and became a sailor at an early age. An intuitive man, Columbus collected and studied maps. From his studies, he gathered that the world was round and that the East could be reached by sailing west. Although he was persistent, Columbus failed to persuade several European monarchs to finance his proposed voyage to the rich island of Cipango (Japan) and the mainland of Cathay (China), where the Great Khan lived. Finally, after a series of pleas, Columbus convinced Queen Isabella of Castile to support his quest. He not only obtained financial backing but also managed to get Isabella to appoint him admiral in the Spanish navy and governor of any land he should discover.

On August 3, 1492, Columbus sailed from the Spanish port of Palos de Moguer with three ships: the Pinta, the Niña, and the Santa María, his flagship. On October 12, 1492, the Spaniards landed on an island called San Salvador—either present-day Watling Island or Samana Cay in the eastern Bahamas. On October 27, they landed on northeastern Cuba. Convinced that it was either Cipango or Cathay, Columbus sent representatives to the Great Khan and his gold-domed cities, only to find impoverished Arawak living in *bohíos* (huts).

Columbus then sailed eastward to an island he named La Española—Hispaniola—which today is shared by Haiti and the Dominican Republic. On the treacherous coast of La Española, Columbus lost his flagship. With what remained of the Santa María, he made a makeshift fort, which he called La Navidad, and set sail for Spain. He reached Palos de Moguer on March 15, 1493.

Columbus was convinced that he had reached the Far East, and the queen responded by granting him a fleet of seventeen ships and twelve hundred men for a second voyage. Choosing a southerly course, Columbus discovered the Virgin Islands and Puerto Rico before reaching La Española in November 1493. There, he found La Navidad destroyed and no trace of his men. Apparently, the gentle Arawak of La Española could no longer tolerate the abuses of the Spanish garrison and had killed them.

After establishing Isabella, the first permanent European settlement in the New World, Columbus set sail from La Española and discovered Jamaica in the summer of 1494. Obsessed with finding the Great

Queen Isabella la Católica.

Khan, he sailed for Cuba and back to La Española. Finally, he returned to Spain in 1496.

Although he had little but complaints to show for his efforts, Columbus still remained in the good graces of the Spanish queen and had a positive response from her to his request for a third voyage. On this voyage, in 1498, he sailed south of La Española and on July 31 discovered the island of Trinidad. He then sighted the Venezuelan coast and discovered the mouth of the Orinoco River. He concluded that the Venezuelan coast was Cathay and the Orinoco one of the four rivers of Paradise. But Columbus found no paradise when he returned to La Española. A settlers' revolt had taken place against his brother Bartholomew, whom he had left in charge after his second voyage. The flow of complaints against the Columbus brothers reached Isabella, and she dispatched her chief justice and royal inspector, Francisco de Bobadilla, to investigate. In 1500, a year after his arrival in La Española, Bobadilla ordered Columbus's arrest and sent him in chains to Spain.

Isabella stripped Columbus of his titles, but was willing to give him one more chance—a fourth voyage. With four ships and 150 men, he sailed from Spain in May 1502. After discovering the island of

Martinique, he made a few brief stops in the Lesser Antilles and Puerto Rico. He then headed for La Española, where he was denied permission to land by the Spanish authorities on the island. After being rebuffed, he sailed west and cruised the coast of Central America.

After an eight-month search for the Great Khan, Columbus headed for La Española, only to be shipwrecked off Jamaica. Finally, in 1503, rescuers from La Española arrived. In November 1504, reached Spain. Two years later he died a dishearted Columbus in the Spanish city of Valladolid.

Shortly after Columbus's death, Spain was firmly entrenched in the New World, thanks to his efforts and to those of the Spanish conquistadors who followed.

The Conquest of Puerto Rico

After the expulsion of the Moors from Granada, a great number of men trained in the profession of arms found themselves idle. Since it was difficult for them to adapt to this new way of life, they swarmed over the New World, prepared to conquer land for their king

Frontispiece from the original 1493 edition of Cristóbal Colón's letter to the Catholic Kings describing his discoveries

and garner glory for themselves. One such man was Juan Ponce de León, a native of the village of Santervás de Campos, kingdom of León.

Ponce de León was born in 1460. He was a member of one of the oldest families of Spain, the Ponces, and a relative of Rodrigo Ponce, also called the "second Cid Campeador" for his actions against the Moors. The surname León had been acquired by the marriage of one of the Ponces to doña Aldonza de León, sister of Fernando III, conqueror of Seville and father of Alfonso el Sabio.

Ponce de León spent his boyhood serving as page to Pedro Núñez de Guzmán, a powerful nobleman who later became tutor to Prince Ferdinand, brother of Charles V. During his adolescence, Ponce de León entered the profession of arms. He served faithfully and bravely in the struggle to capture Granada from the Moors, and in 1493 he qualified to go with Columbus on his second voyage to the New World.

After his voyage with Columbus, Ponce de León returned to Spain. In 1502, however, he was recalled by the governor of La Española, Nicolás de Ovando, to crush a revolt in Higuey (now Haiti), on the eastern part of the island. He was so successful in extinguishing the revolt that he was appointed second in command by Ovando in 1504. While performing his military duties in the village of Salvaleón, Ponce de León had news that there was gold on the nearby island of Borinquen (Puerto Rico) and obtained a license from Ovando to explore the island and search for it. In 1508, he sailed in a small caravel for Puerto Rico, where he established friendly relations with the native chieftain, Agueibana, who presented him with gold, which was later sent to Ovando.

When Ponce de León returned to La Española from Puerto Rico, he learned that Ovando had been replaced as governor by Diego Columbus, who in turn had appointed Juan Cerón governor of Puerto Rico. Instead of revolting, Ponce de León accepted the situation philosophically. When Ovando reached Spain in 1509, the situation changed drastically, for he persuaded the king to appoint Ponce de León governor of Puerto Rico. So great was the success of Ovando's talk with the king that Ponce de León's appointment as governor of Puerto Rico disregarded the rights of Diego Columbus.

Ponce de León proceeded immediately to establish his supremacy as governor of Puerto Rico by arresting Cerón and enslaving the natives who refused to submit. Perhaps his closest ally in pacifying the natives was Becerrillo, his greyhound. According to the colonial chronicler Gonzalo Fernández de Oviedo, Becerrillo's fierceness proved of such great value to the Spaniards that it led to the coining of a new word in the language—*aperrear*—(to cast to dogs).

While Ponce de León was busy pacifying the natives, the king, perceiving the injustice done to Diego Columbus, deposed Ponce de León as governor and appointed Juan Cerón to the post in 1511. Ponce de León's dismissal did not change the overall picture; the Spanish conquest of Puerto Rico had been completed.

The Conquest of Cuba

Two years after Columbus's death, the Spanish Crown became interested in colonizing Cuba. In 1508, Sebastián de Ocampo sailed around the island and began to spread tales that there was gold and silver in Cuba. The governor of La Española, Nicolás de Ovando, chose his most trusted lieutenant, Diego Velázquez, to carry out the task of colonization. A native of Cuéllar, Spain, Velázquez had accompanied Columbus during his second voyage to the New World and later had served in La Española. Velázquez had gained both fame and fortune on that island, and in late 1510 he departed with over three hundred men to conquer Cuba.

Velázquez landed at Puerto Escondido, close to where the present-day American naval base of Guantánamo is located. There he met the resistance of Hatuey, an expatriate Arawak from La Española who conducted deadly guerrilla raids against the Spaniards. Hatuey's fighters, however, succumbed to Spanish firepower. Hatuey was captured by Velázquez and condemned to be burned at the stake. He is remembered in Cuban history as the first island hero and a symbol of Cuba's resistance against the foreigners.

After subjugating the Arawak population of the area, Velázquez proceeded to establish the town of Nuestra Señora de la Asunción de Baracoa in 1512. Thus, Baracoa became Cuba's first permanent settlement. By 1517, Velázquez had conquered the entire island.

While there was little gold in Cuba, La Española, and Puerto Rico, the islands nevertheless became the laboratories of the Spanish Empire. It was there where the *repartimiento* (the practice of parceling native Americans) was carried out by the Spaniards. Eventually, the repartimiento was replaced by the *encomienda* system, which granted a predetermined number of native Americans and a predetermined amount of land to a deserving Spaniard, known as the encomendero. He, in turn, was entitled to free labor from the native Americans in exchange for protecting them. The system, however, failed, for the encomenderos exploited the native Americans mercilessly. It was in the Antilles where the mixing of the races first occurred and where the missions to convert the native population were first established. The islands also served as havens to launch expeditions to other parts of the New World.

✳SPANISH EXPEDITIONS TO FLORIDA

After the discovery of the New World by Columbus, the nations of western Europe extended their radius of exploration. In May 1497 the British sent a Venetian sailor, Sebastian Cabot, to explore the coast of North America. Sailing from Bristol, Cabot supposedly ran down the Atlantic coast from Cape Breton as far south as thirty-eight degrees north latitude. Scarcity of provisions compelled him to abandon his project and return to England.

It is difficult to calculate how far Cabot might have sailed in his southward trek along the eastern coast of North America before he was forced to direct his course toward England. It is equally difficult to determine how much of the southern portion of North America at that time bore the name Florida. We learn from Brinton's *Notes on the Floridian Peninsula* that Florida then included an indefinite extent of territory north and west of present Florida (14); and in Williams's *The Territory of Florida* (1837), it is said that "the name of Florida was at one period applied to all the tract of country which extends from Canada to the Rio del Norte" along the U.S.-Mexican border (7). Whatever might have been the southernmost point reached by Cabot in coasting America, it is certain that he did not land in present-day Florida.

During the same month of the same year as Cabot's voyage (May 1497), Amerigo Vespucci, who had been occupied in providing naval equipment for the Spanish monarchs, sailed from the Spanish port of Cádiz on a voyage of exploration to the New World. The possibility that Vespucci had explored the Florida coast was accepted until the 1930s, when discrepancies in the Vespucci documents were discovered by scholars.

Obviously, unidentified mariners had visited the coasts of Florida, but probably not until after 1493. It was in May of that year that Pope Alexander VI issued a Bull of Demarcation for the purpose of dividing the newly discovered lands between Portugal and Spain. Some historians are of the opinion that this Bull of Demarcation is the reason unknown mariners who had explored the Atlantic coast as far down as Florida had judged it expedient to leave their discoveries and exploration unrecorded. As proof of their point, they often offer the fact that Ponce de León and those who followed him found the Florida Indians suspicious and hostile. Although this is evidence of prior discovery, the official credit for discovering Florida goes to Ponce de León, because his voyage in 1513 was made under official Spanish auspices, recorded, and recognized.

Legend tells us that while Ponce de León was in Puerto Rico, he heard of an island called Bimini, lying north of La Española, called Bimini, reputedly famous for a spring that restored youth to all who drank its waters. This legend has been used often by some as a reason for Ponce de León's expedition. Historians agree, however, that this was not the prime reason for Ponce de León's voyage. It seems ridiculous that Ponce de León, a robust adventurer who had spent many years fighting the Indians in Puerto Rico and La Española, would have been influenced by such a tale to the extent of expending most of his fortune in outfitting an expedition in order to verify it.

Using the influence he had at court, Ponce de León obtained from Ferdinand a patent in February 1512 allowing him to discover and settle the island of Bimini and granting him the title *adelantado* (advance representative of the king). The patent specified that he was to equip the expedition at his own cost and prohibited him from trespassing on any lands belonging to the Portuguese sovereign. It also provided that the natives found on the island were to be divided among the members of the expeditionary force as slaves. The king also reserved the right to keep one-tenth of all riches that were found. Finally, it provided that a report on the conditions found on the island was to be sent to the king. There is no mention in this patent of the Fountain of Youth, and furthermore there is a complete absence of any provision for Christianizing the native Americans; it is therefore also surprising that this document was countersigned by the bishop of Palencia.

Armed with this royal grant, the veteran man of arms purchased a vessel in order to go to Spain and make preparations for the conquest of Bimini. Meanwhile, the king, finding Ponce de León's services necessary in Puerto Rico, sent orders to the Council of the Indies to postpone the expedition to Bimini and placed Ponce de León in command of a fort in Puerto Rico.

Thus delayed in the royal service, Ponce de León was unable to obtain supplies until the following year. On March 3, 1513, he set sail from the Puerto Rican port of San Germán with three caravels (the Santiago, the Santa María de la Consolación, and the San Cristóbal), taking along as pilot a native of Palos de Moguer named Antón de Alaminos, who had as a boy accompanied Columbus and whose name would long be associated with explorations around the Gulf of Mexico. Sailing northwest by north, they landed on the fourteenth of that month in San Salvador, the island where Columbus probably had first landed on his first voyage to the New World. After refitting at San Salvador, Ponce de León navigated on a north-westerly course, and on Easter Sunday, the twenty-seventh of March, he sighted the Florida mainland, along which he sailed until the second of April, when he anchored. On some day between the second and eighth of April, Ponce de León went ashore to take possession of this newly discovered land. Some historians believe that Ponce de León was so impressed with the beauty of this land that he named it La Florida. Others are of the opinion that he named the land *La Florida* because it was discovered on Easter Sunday, which in Spanish is called *Pascua Florida*. Although there is no record of the landing place, many historians believe that it was the coastal area between the Saint Johns River and Saint Augustine; others affirm that it was Cape Sable.

Of the landing ceremony there is no record. There could have been no celebration of mass, for there were no priests in the expedition. There was probably no proclamation to the natives to convert to Christianity, for the patent under which Ponce de León was sailing did not require it.

Leaving his first anchorage, Ponce de León started up the coast, but for an unknown reason he turned back and headed in a south-southeasterly course parallel to the coastline. In thus maneuvering, he missed a most important discovery, for had he sailed a little to the north, he would have seen the Saint Johns River; and judging from its size, he would have recognized that what he had discovered was a mainland and not an island, as he imagined Florida to be throughout the voyage. The vessels continued southward until the twentieth of the month when they ran into the Gulf Stream and were forced to anchor.

The following day Ponce de León went ashore and found the natives so hostile that he was obliged to repel the attack by force. In the skirmish with the Indians, two of his men were wounded, and he was forced to retreat to a river that he named Río de la Cruz. Here, seventy natives attacked them, and one was taken prisoner by the Spaniards to give information about the coast and country. On Sunday, May 8, they rounded a cape which Ponce de León named Cabo de las Corrientes, and anchored near a village called Abayoa. After this, they cruised along various islands, which he named Los Mártires.

The Spaniards continued to follow the coast southward, rounding the southern end of the peninsula and following up the western shores. On the twenty-third of May, they returned southward, and the following day discovered several islands off the coast, on one of which they repaired the San Cristóbal. They remained there until the third of June when the natives descended upon them with a shower of arrows. The Spaniards retaliated by going ashore, capturing four Indian women and breaking two canoes.

On Friday, June 4, while they were preparing to go in search of the cacique (chieftain) Carlos, there came to the ship a canoe with a native who understood Spanish. Some historians cite this incident as proof that the natives had come in contact with Spaniards prior to the voyage of Ponce de León. Others do not consider this incident as sufficient proof, for it is possible that this native was from Cuba or La Española and had been living with the Spaniards for some time. The native informed the Spaniards that the cacique was to send gold as a gift to them. Because of their greed, the Spaniards fell into the trap and waited. Suddenly, there were twenty canoes surrounding them. A sloop was lowered from one of the vessels, which put the natives on the run. The Spaniards captured four of them; two of these were released and sent to the cacique with a message for peace.

The following day, a sloop was sent out to explore the harbor. The crew were met by some natives who informed them that the cacique would come the next day to trade. As it turned out, the message was nothing more than a plan on the part of Carlos to gain time in order to attack, for at eleven o'clock, eighty canoes attacked one of the ships. The fight lasted until sunset, with no harm to the Spaniards, for the natives were kept at a distance by the Spaniards' artillery. When the natives retreated, Ponce de León decided to leave that hostile land and return to La Española and Puerto Rico.

On the fourteenth of June, they lifted anchor and retraced part of their former course through the Florida Keys. On the twenty-first, they came upon some small islands, which Ponce de León named Tortugas (turtles), for he had captured 170 turtles there. They sailed back and forth until the twenty-third of September, when Ponce de León sent Antón de Alaminos as pilot of one of his vessels in search of the island of Bimini, while he returned to Puerto Rico, arriving on October 10, 1513. He was joined there four months later by Alaminos, who had discovered the island but not the famous fountain reported to be there.

Thus ended the first of a series of unsuccessful ventures by the Spaniards to control the coast of North America. Ponce de León had obtained neither gold nor youth, only hard blows. Yet these blows were not enough to destroy the high spirits of the old soldier, for like a true Spanish hidalgo, he was to come back again, roaring like a lion.

Diego Miruelo

In 1516, three years after Ponce de León's first expedition to Florida, a small brigantine under the command of pilot Diego Miruelo sailed from Cuba and reached the coast of Florida. After trading mirrors and other small objects with the natives, Miruelo returned to Cuba. Upon his return, he enlarged the report of the wealth of Florida, and many Spaniards were lured by the desire to enjoy these riches. The irony of his voyage is that Miruelo, although a pilot, failed to note the latitude of the places he visited. Miruelo's reason for not giving the latitude of the places visited in Florida was probably that he wanted to organize a larger expedition to Florida under royal auspices and was fearful that someone would anticipate this and disclose the location of the places to the governors of Cuba and La Española.

Francisco Hernández de Córdova

In 1517, a year after the voyage of Miruelo, Francisco Hernández de Córdova, a wealthy nobleman who resided in Cuba, sailed with three ships and 110 seasoned men with the object of capturing Bahamian natives and selling them as slaves. Among the men in this expedition was Bernal Díaz del Castillo, destined to become the chronicler of Hernán Cortes's conquest of the Aztec Empire. Hernández de Córdova sailed westward, but his purpose was frustrated by storms, and he landed on the peninsula of Yucatán. The natives of Yucatán must have been as hostile as the weather he had encountered, for Henández de Córdova, after several battles with the Indians, in which he lost nearly fifty of his men, decided to sail back to Cuba.

Again misfortune pursued him, and on his return trip he encountered such a stout north wind that it drove his vessels from their course. The chief pilot, Antón de Alaminos, who had been the pilot of Ponce de León in his first expedition to Florida, persuaded Hernández de Córdova to cross over to Florida to take refuge from the weather and chart a shorter, safer passage to Cuba. Alaminos drove the ships to the bay previously visited by Ponce de León (Charlotte Harbor), where they anchored to make repairs.

Twenty soldiers, including Bernal Díaz del Castillo and Antón de Alaminos, went ashore. While digging for water, a cascade of arrows descended on the unfortunate Spaniards, wounding six of them, including Bernal Díaz. Simultaneously, the Indians attacked the vessels, inflicting several casualties among the Spaniards. Ashore, the Spanish, fighting in water up to their belts, repelled the natives and captured three of the attackers. In this engagement, all of the Spaniards, including Alaminos, Bernal

Díaz, and Hernández de Córdova were wounded. There was also a Spaniard missing in action, a soldier named Berrio, who was acting as sentry on shore; he presumably fell into the hands of the natives.

After this incident, the battered Spaniards sailed for Havana. Upon arrival, Hernández de Córdova sent word of their expedition to Diego Velázquez, governor of Cuba, who welcomed them and rewarded their captain with a feast. Hernández de Córdova died ten days later of the wounds received in his encounter with the Indians of Florida.

Alonzo Alvarez de Pineda

In 1519, two years after the ill-fated expedition of Hernández de Córdova, Antón de Alaminos gave a detailed account of the coast of Florida to the governor of Jamaica, Francisco de Garay, a powerful and ambitious man. Impressed by the report, and determined to conquer a province for himself, Garay outfitted four vessels under the command of his most trusted lieutenant, Alonzo Alvarez de Pineda, to search for a passage dividing the mainland.

Alvarez de Pineda sailed around the northern boundary of the Gulf of Mexico and coasted the western shore of Florida. Unable because of the currents to round the Cape of Florida, he retraced his course, made notes of rivers and bays, and landed at several places and took possession in the name of Charles V. Then, after coasting nearly three hundred leagues, he reached the province of Pánuco (Tampico), where he encountered none other than Hernán Cortés.

Sailing eastward again, Alvarez de Pineda reached the mouth of a great river, the Mississippi. There he found a sizable town and remained forty days trading with the natives and repairing his vessels. Pineda reported the land to be rich in gold, since the natives wore gold ornaments in their nose and ears. He also told of tribes of giants and pygmies, but declared these natives to be friendly.

Pineda continued to follow the coast for nine months and returned to Garay in 1520 with the news of this newly discovered province of Amichel. Although he failed to find a strait, the voyage of Alvarez de Pineda settled the question of Florida's geography. He proved that Florida was no longer to be regarded as an island, but part of a vast continent.

Fired by Alvarez de Pineda's account, Garay applied for a patent authorizing him to conquer and settle this new province, which extended from some point near Pensacola Bay to Cabo Rojo in Mexico. A royal patent was indeed issued to Garay in 1521, but in his haste to occupy his new territory, he ignored the final approval and sent four vessels under Diego de Camargo to occupy some posts near Pánuco. The expedition was doomed from the start, for one of the vessels ran into a settlement already established by Cortés and was captured. Cortés, in turn, learned of Camargo's plan.

Alarmed by the news of Camargo's failure, Garay equipped a powerful force to settle Amichel in 1523. Instead of reaching Amichel, Garay landed in the town of San Esteban, Mexico, which Cortés had already founded. He surrendered to Cortés, and with his surrender his dream of conquering Amichel expired.

The Slave Raider Gordillo

In December 1520, Lucas Vázquez de Ayllón, a wealthy judge of the audiencia of Santo Domingo, eager for the glory of discovering a new land, secured the necessary permission and dispatched a vessel to "La Florida" under Francisco Gordillo.

While Gordillo was sailing through the Bahamas, he recognized another vessel commanded by Pedro de Quexos. This vessel was returning from a slave-raiding expedition through the islands. Quexos and Gordillo agreed to sail together, and after nine days they reached the coast near the mouth of a large river, which they named the San Juan Bautista, because they had arrived on June 24, the feast day of the man who had baptized Christ.

Although Ayllón had instructed Gordillo to explore and establish friendly relations with the natives of any new land he might discover, Quexos influenced Gordillo to aid in capturing some seventy natives, with whom they sailed away without exploring the coast.

Upon Gordillo's arrival in Santo Domingo, Ayllón punished him and brought the matter to Diego Columbus. The governor declared the Indians to be free, but many of the group had already died from the treatment received by Quexos and Gordillo.

A Lion Returns to Florida

After his discovery of Florida in 1513, Ponce de León sailed to Spain to ask the king for a patent to colonize Florida and Bimini. The patent, which was granted on September 27, 1514, empowered him to colonize the island of Bimini and the "island" of Florida, which he had discovered. It also had the provision that the natives submit to the Catholic faith and the authority of Spain; they were not to be captured nor enslaved if they submitted. Provision was also made as to the revenues from the lands, and orders were sent to Diego Columbus to aid with the expedition.

The grant also specified that prior to launching the expedition, Ponce de León was required to wage war against the Carib. Juan Ponce de León sailed to pacify the Carib; after he reached the island of Guadalupe, they ambushed his soldiers and dealt them a severe blow. Forced to retreat to Puerto Rico, Ponce de León remained on the island and apparently abandoned the idea of colonizing Florida. But since the discoverer of Florida was a typical conquistador, the idea of giving up Florida never took root in his mind. So when he heard that the fame of Cortés in Mexico was rivaling his own, he decided to return and settle the land he had discovered.

Although the patent issued in 1514 was good for three years, Ponce de León used his influence at court so that his term was to date from the day he set sail for his new province, since he had been employed in the king's service fighting the Carib. Thus, in 1521, Ponce de León sent a letter to Charles V, dated February 10, asking him for permission to settle Florida. He outfitted two vessels with two hundred men, fifty horses, and many domestic animals. There were also several priests to spread the Catholic faith among the natives and render service to the needs of the Spaniards. The expedition departed from the port of San Germán, Puerto Rico, in February 1521.

The exact landing place of his second voyage to the Florida coast is not precisely known, but historians believe it was in the vicinity of Charlotte Harbor, where on his first voyage he had heard of gold. Immediately after they landed, Ponce de León and his men were attacked by the natives. Although wounded by an arrow, Ponce de León bravely led his men against the natives. When the natives attacked again, the "old lion," who by this time lacked the strength of his glory days, ordered his men on board and sailed for Cuba. Within a few days of his return, the fierce conquistador yielded to death. His body was shipped to his beloved island of Puerto Rico.

The old warrior died with his ambition thwarted and without really knowing Florida was part of a continent. But the voyage produced a number of "firsts" for the history of the United States: the first attempt to plant a self-sustaining colony, the first attempt to implant the Catholic religion among the natives, and the first assigned residence for priests.

Lucas Vázquez de Ayllón

Although el Inca Garcilaso de la Vega (p. 15) states that Lucas Vázquez de Ayllón was the leader of the 1521 slave-raiding expedition to Florida, historians believe that el Inca Garcilaso probably confused the role of Vázquez de Ayllón, who sponsored an expedition of exploration of Florida, with that of Gordillo, the man who actually commanded the expedition and was later reprimanded for disobeying Ayllón's orders. Ayllón was never in Florida prior to his 1526 expedition.

After settling the matter of the surviving native slaves brought back by the Gordillo expedition, Lucas Vázquez de Ayllón sailed to Spain to request a patent for discovery. Charles V not only accepted Vázquez de Ayllón's request but also bestowed upon him the habit of Santiago, making him a member of a prestigious lay order. On June 12, 1513, a patent was conferred on Ayllón. By it, Vázquez de Ayllón was given the title of *Adelantado* (commander) and was empowered to discover and navigate the coast for a distance of eight hundred leagues. The patent also granted Vázquez de Ayllón rights to fisheries and prisoners of war held by the natives. It also provided for the conversion of natives to the Catholic faith and subsidy for the Dominican missionaries who were to accompany this expedition.

After years of preparation, Vázquez de Ayllón was able to sail from the port of La Plata on the northern coast of Santo Domingo in 1526. His expedition consisted of 500 men and women and 89 horses. There were also three Dominican missionaries and several black slaves. Thus, this was the first attempt in the history of the United States to introduce black slaves to the country.

Vázquez de Ayllón landed not at the mouth of the Saint Johns, but at the mouth of a river he named the Jordán (near Cape Fear, North Carolina). Dissatisfied with the locality, Vázquez de Ayllón sent scouts into the country. Upon their reports, he sailed northward and founded the settlement of San Miguel de Guadalupe (Jamestown). The colony was fated not to prosper, for winter came on; sickness broke out among the Spaniards and many died. Vázquez de Ayllón succumbed to death in October 1526. The Spaniards decided to sail back to Santo Domingo, and of the 500 who sailed with Vázquez de Ayllón, only 150 returned.

The Expedition of Pánfilo de Narváez

Although the expedition of Paufilo de Narváez was one of the most disastrous in the annals of Spanish history, it was one of the expeditions that contributed the most to the history of the southern section of the United States, for one of its members, a stout Spaniard named Àlvar Núñez Cabeza de Vaca, made a major contribution to the world's knowledge in his own time by writing *La relación* (*The Account*), an eyewitness account of the ill-fated expedition.

Pánfilo de Narváez was born in Valladolid, Spain, in 1470. When, in 1511, Diego Velázquez was named governor of Cuba, he appointed Narváez, who had a reputation as a tough Indian fighter in Jamaica, as his lieutenant in charge of "pacifying" the natives of

The title page of Cabeza de Vaca's *La relación* (*The Account of His Trip*), 1542.

Cuba. Narváez distinguished himself from the beginning, and Velázquez entrusted to him the conquest of the rest of the island. In a few years, the faithful servant of Velázquez won the island for his governor. His most famous deed during this contest was the massacre of 500 defenseless natives in the town of Caonao, which brought a strong protest from Fray Bartolomé de las Casas; thus, Narváez was probably the one who initiated the feud between the conquistadors and the missionaries.

Narváez retired to his encomienda but was called back by his friend Velázquez to command an expedition to discipline Hernán Cortés, who with a small group of men had conquered the Aztec Empire. With an impressive force of some 900 soldiers, Don Pánfilo landed in San Juan de Ulúa, Mexico, in 1520. His first decision after he landed was to arrest Lucas Vázquez de Ayllón, who had been sent by the audiencia in Santo Domingo to prevent a clash between Cortés and Narváez. This decision proved costly for Narváez, because when Ayllón was released, he informed the audiencia of Narváez's conduct.

Another of his decisions was to send three envoys to Cortés and ask for his surrender. Cortés, in turn, showered the men with gifts and gold, and they later returned to the headquarters of Narváez unharmed. By this maneuver, the skillful conqueror of Mexico gained information about the strength of Narváez and also created a "fifth column" (secret sympathizers) in the latter's camp, for many men lured by the tales of gold deserted Narváez.

On May 27, 1520, a force of 250 men commanded by Hernán Cortés launched an attack on Narváez's headquarters in Cempoala. Don Pánfilo not only was humiliated but also lost an eye in the battle and was sent to Veracruz, where he was imprisoned until Cortés released him in 1522. Narváez stayed in Cuba, and since he was so impressed with all the gold and jewelry that he had seen in Mexico, sailed to Spain with the illusion that Charles V would reward his services with an appointment as ruler of rich domains.

Don Pánfilo must have had strong connections at court, for he was awarded the governorship of Florida, which had been vacant since the death of Juan Ponce de León. On November 17, 1526, Charles V issued a patent to Pánfilo de Narváez that granted him the right to discover, conquer, and settle the territory from the Río de las Palmas to the "island" of Florida. The grant also stipulated that Narváez was to build three forts and two settlements. It also granted him the titles of governor and captain-general for life, along with a private estate of ten square leagues and an annual salary of 250,000 *maravedíes*. In addition, he was given 4 percent of the tax levies and had the authority to make slaves of rebellious natives.

The most significant aspect of this document was that for the first time, guidelines were set for the treatment of the natives of "La Florida." Any act of brutality on the part of an officer was to be investigated by the Council of the Indies. The natives were to be treated as free men, and priests were to accompany the expedition in order to protect the natives from mistreatment at the hands of civil or military authorities. The natives were not to be forced to work in mines and were to be paid for their labor. Only with the consent of the priests could a native be assigned to an encomienda.

The 600-man expedition left the Spanish port of San Lúcar de Barrameda on June 27, 1527. The expedition seemed to have been doomed from the start. One hundred and forty men deserted when they arrived at La Española, and two ships were wrecked by a hurricane near Trinidad, Cuba. After spending the winter in Cuba, the expedition sailed from the Cuban port of Cienfuegos on February 20, 1528. It carried only 400 men.

After hitting a number of sandbars off the Cuban coast, the expedition anchored in the neighborhood of Tampa Bay on April 12, 1528. A few days later, Narváez landed and took possession in the name of the king. Immediately after the landing, Narváez approached a nearby village and asked the natives if there was gold. They indicated by signs that there were great quantities of that precious metal in a province that they called Apalachee—present-day Tallahassee. The natives, of course, wanted the Spaniards to leave their village and, undoubtedly, invented the story.

Lured by the tales of gold and riches, Narváez decided to march inland with the bulk of his expedition. On May 1, 1528, 300 men with meager rations, which amounted to one-half pound of bacon and two pounds of bread per man, marched northward in the direction of the reputedly gold-laden Apalachee. On the twenty-fifth of June, after a 56-day march, the tired Spaniards arrived in Apalachee. Narváez and his men soon realized that Apalachee contained neither palaces nor gold, but fierce natives. Since there was very little food in the area, the Spaniards began to frantically search for it. An Apalachee captive informed Narváez that to the south there was a village called Aute—present-day Saint Marks or Apalachicola—where there was an abundance of food. It was located near the sea.

The Spaniards arrived in Aute nine days after their departure from Apalachee, only to find that the natives had turned to a scorched-earth policy. Tired, hungry, and constantly harassed by the natives, the Spaniards decided to build barges and leave by sea to Mexico, which they estimated to be nearby. It was an incredible task, for they lacked tools and proper knowledge of shipbuilding. The Spaniards sawed down trees with their swords and pikes and made them into planks, transformed their horseshoes into nails, ripped their shirts and made them into sails, and converted the hides of their horses into water skins. Finally, on September 22, 1528, the five barges carrying 242 men set sail.

The makeshift armada sailed close to the Gulf Coast of present-day Florida, Alabama, Mississippi, and Louisiana for more than a month. Narváez's barge abandoned the rest of the barges and was never seen again. As they were approaching the Texas coast, the remaining barges were caught in a hurricane. Eighty men managed to survive by reaching present-day Galveston Island. They named the island Isla de Malhado (Badluck Island).

The natives of Malhado took the Spaniards captive once they landed. A bitter winter descended upon the Spaniards and natives alike, bringing cold, hunger, and disease. The Spaniards even resorted to cannibalism in order to survive. Of the eighty men who reached Malhado, only fifteen survived the winter. While in Malhado, some of the Spaniards were forced by the natives to act as medicine men. Àlvar Núñez Cabeza de Vaca built a reputation as a medicine man among the natives by simply making the sign of the cross and reciting a Hail Mary and the Lord's Prayer.

In April 1529, the fifteen survivors were transported to the Texas mainland by their captors. While on the mainland, twelve of them managed to escape. Cabeza de Vaca and two companions, Jerónimo de Aláñiz and Lope de Oviedo, were left behind because they were too sick. Aláñiz died, but Lope de Oviedo and Cabeza de Vaca were later transferred to Malhado. After some twenty-two months of traveling back and forth, Cabeza de Vaca and Lope de Oviedo began their journey to freedom. They crossed a number of inlets and arrived at a large bay—present-day Matagorda Bay—where, on the shore, they met several natives. The natives informed them that there were three other men like themselves in the possession of their tribe farther inland. These three were the only survivors of the original twelve escapees (the other nine had died from cold and hunger).

Frightened by the rough treatment he had received at the hands of the natives, Lope de Oviedo deserted Cabeza de Vaca and departed for the island of Malhado. He was never seen again. Two days after Lope de Oviedo's departure, the rest of the tribe arrived near Matagorda Bay with their three other prisoners. Àlvar Núñez Cabeza de Vaca, Andrés Dorantes, Alonso del Castillo, and the black slave Estevanico were reunited for the first time in more than three years. The four of them spent the winter of 1532-33 together, and in August 1533 they moved with the natives to the tuna (prickly pear) thickets south of the present-day region of San Antonio. The natives separated the four, but before they were separated they agreed on an escape plan.

Cabeza de Vaca lived with a native tribal group until September 13, 1534. A day later he was met by Castillo, Dorantes, and Estevanico. On September 15, 1534, two days after all of them had been reunited, they began the most daring, difficult, and remarkable escape in the history of the New World.

Wandering from tribe to tribe as medicine men, Cabeza de Vaca, Castillo, Dorantes, and Estevanico traveled thousands of miles through present-day Texas, New Mexico, and Arizona. Traveling naked and barefooted over the treacherous terrain of the Southwest, the three Spaniards and Estevanico learned to conquer the freezing winds of winter and the blistering sun of summer. They had stoically adapted themselves to eat spiders, salamanders, lizards, worms, and prickly pears.

Finally, in February 1536, they found a company of Spanish soldiers thirty leagues from the Spanish settlement of San Miguel in northern Mexico. A few days later, they arrived in San Miguel. Their ordeal was now over. They had survived because they had worked as a unit and had kept their faith. On May 15, 1536, the four of them departed San Miguel. They arrived in Mexico City on June 24, 1536.

Of the four survivors, Alonso del Castillo returned to Spain and was later given an encomienda in Tehuacán, Mexico. Andrés Dorantes joined Viceroy Antonio de Mendoza's conquest of Jalisco, Mexico, and spent the rest of his life in Mexico. Estevanico joined the expedition of Fray Marcos de Niza to New Mexico as a guide and was killed by the natives in 1539 at Hawikuh. As to Àvar Núñez Cabeza de Vaca, he returned to Spain in 1537 and spent some three years writing *La relación*, an account of his wanderings in the North American continent. Published in 1542, *La relación* is a document of inestimable value because of the many first descriptions about the flora, fauna, and inhabitants of what later was to become part of the United States.

In 1540, Àlvar Núñez Cabeza de Vaca was appointed governor of the Río de la Plata. He arrived in Asunción, Paraguay, in March 1542. Cabeza de Vaca's tenure as governor was characterized by his good treatment of the native population and his reform program. Because of his reforms on behalf of the natives, Cabeza de Vaca became the victim of a coup carried out by other conquistadors on April 25, 1544. He arrived in Seville in chains and was condemned to serve a prison sentence.

After seven years of trials and tribulations, Àlvar Núñez Cabeza de Vaca emerged from prison. Disheartened and ill, he busied himself writing the second edition of *La relación*, which was published in 1555 and which also contains the narrative of his days as governor of the Río de la Plata. In 1556, Àlvar Núñez Cabeza de Vaca, the most humane and farsighted of the conquistadors and America's first chronicler, died in Spain.

The Expedition of Hernando de Soto

Hernando de Soto was born in 1500 in the Spanish town of Jerez de Badajoz. When he was in his teens he went to Central America and later joined Francisco Pizarro in his conquest of Peru. After remaining in Peru for a few years, de Soto returned to Spain in 1536. Shortly after his return to Spain, the wealthy hidalgo sought out Alvar Núñez Cabeza de Vaca, who had recently returned returned from his eight-year odyssey across the North American continent. Cabeza de Vaca's reticence during this meeting did nothing more than fire de Soto's imagination and greed, for he was convinced that Florida was covered with gold.

On April 20, 1537, King Charles V granted de Soto a patent naming him governor of Cuba and captain-general of Florida. On April 7, 1538, Hernando de Soto sailed for Cuba. After making provisions for governing the island, he left Havana for Florida on May 18, 1539. De Soto's expedition consisted of 650 men and a large herd of pigs and other livestock.

On May 30, 1539, they arrived at Tampa Bay. Shortly after their landing, they met Juan Ortiz, a member of the Narváez expedition who had been saved by the daughter of the cacique Hirrihigua. Thus, Spanish Florida had its romance story some sixty-eight years prior to that of John Smith and Pocahontas.

Unable to find gold in the neighborhood of Tampa Bay, de Soto, accompanied by more than 550 men, marched north along the coast to Apalachee, where they wintered. It was there that the first Thanksgiving was celebrated.

Harassed by the natives, de Soto and his expeditionaries departed Apalachee on March 3, 1540, in

A portrayal of Hernando de Soto by an unknown eighteenth-century artist. (Courtesy of the U.S. Department of the Interior and the National Park Service.)

search of gold. They took a northeasterly route and reached present-day Georgia.

According to the most recent research, de Soto's route is as follows. In April his troupe crossed the Savannah River and entered South Carolina. After a fruitless search for gold, they headed north and arrived at Xuala—present-day Marion, North Carolina. They then crossed the Great Smoky Mountains into Tennessee. From the mountains, they headed southwest through Georgia and Alabama.

On October 18, 1540, they reached the village of Mauvilla, near Mobile Bay. At Mauvilla, de Soto and his men were attacked by the native chief, Tascaluza, and his allies. Although the Spaniards managed to kill about 3,000 natives, they lost 22 men and 148 were wounded. De Soto was to meet Diego de Maldonado, whom he had sent to Havana to gather supplies, in present-day Pensacola, Florida, sometime in 1540. But he never went to see Maldonado because he did not want to reveal to him that he had failed to find gold. In addition, he had already lost 102 men since his landing at Tampa Bay. The Spaniards were in Mauvilla for about a month and then moved northwest to present-day Mississippi. They spent the 1540-41 winter at Chicasa in northern Mississippi.

On March 4, 1541, as de Soto was about to depart Chicasa, he was attacked by natives. Twelve Spaniards, fifty-nine horses, and three hundred pigs were killed in the attack as the Indians managed to set the Spanish camp on fire. The Spaniards retreated to a nearby village and proceeded in a northwesterly direction. On May 9, they saw a great river, the Mississippi. They spent more than a month building barges for the river crossing.

After crossing the mighty river on June 19, 1541, de Soto and his men found themselves in the neighborhood of present-day Horseshoe Lake, Arkansas. Lured by tales of gold and silver from the natives, de Soto moved into the Plains Indians' territory, only to find buffalo skins. On September 13, they saw the Arkansas River. The Spaniards continued to march west but decided to turn back to the southeast as winter was approaching. They spent the winter of 1541-42 at Autiamque—present-day Redfield, Arkansas. It was a harsh winter and by then the expedition had lost 250 men. On March 6, 1542, the expedition set out toward the south, trying to find a way out of their misery. After hearing negative reports concerning the countryside, de Soto became depressed and fell ill. On May 21, 1542, he died in Guachoya—present-day McArthur, Arkansas.

Luis de Moscoso quickly took command of the expedition and ordered the burial of de Soto. The Spaniards buried him outside Guachoya, but since de Soto had pointed out to the natives that he was immortal, Moscoso ordered that the body be dug up. The Spaniards exhumed de Soto's body, wrapped it in a mantle weighted with sand, and then proceeded to carry it in a canoe out into the Mississippi River. Somewhere in the Mississippi, they cast the body of the golden conquistador. When the natives asked where de Soto was, Moscoso replied that the governor had gone to heaven, from where he would shortly return.

Moscoso thought that the best way to reach Mexico was to go overland, so they proceeded on a southwesterly course as far as present-day Texas. Lack of food and constant Indian attacks forced them to turn back to the Mississippi River, where they knew there was food. The Spaniards wintered near the Mississippi. Early in 1543, they began to build seven boats. They also killed their horses and pigs and dried the meat. On July 2, 1543, they sailed down the river. Two weeks later, they reached its mouth. Finally, on September 10, 1543, they arrived at Tampico, Mexico. Three hundred and eleven men out of 650 had walked and sailed more than thirty-five hundred miles and had survived an incredible journey.

Although the de Soto expedition was a failure for Spain, it nevertheless was one of the most remarkable in the history of North America. Furthermore, it provided valuable insights into the life-styles of the natives of the Southeast and their interaction with the Spaniards. As the anthropologist Charles Hudson (1990, p. 20) states, "the de Soto expedition was the historical context in which these two cultures met. It was the historical moment in which our forgotten European forebears came into conflict with the likewise forgotten native lords of the Southeast. It constitutes one of the great episodes in the age of European exploration."

The De Luna Fiasco

The disastrous results of Hernando de Soto's expedition put a temporary halt to Spain's interest in colonizing Florida. In 1558, however, King Philip II ordered Viceroy Luis de Velasco to settle Florida. The peninsula's strategic location and the possibility of rival European encroachments in the area prompted the Spanish monarch to take this action.

On June 11, 1559, fifteen hundred would-be colonists sailed from Veracruz under the command of Tristán de Luna. They arrived in Pensacola on August 18, 1554. The expedition was a disaster from the start. Reconnaissance proved that the area was not conducive to agriculture. On September 19, a hurricane sank twelve of the thirteen ships in the harbor, causing great loss of men and cargo. A cold winter followed and lack of provisions forced the settlers to eat nothing but acorns boiled in salt water.

In the spring of 1560, De Luna decided to move his settlers inland, hoping to find food in the neighborhood of present-day Coosa County, Alabama. The hardships, continued, however, and De Luna had no alternative but to retreat to Pensacola. Dissension against De Luna broke out among the settlers during the winter of 1560-61. Many of them refused to carry out his orders. Worried about the colony's fate, the authorities in Havana decided to replace De Luna.

In April 1561, Angel de Villafañe arrived at Pensacola with orders to replace De Luna, evacuate the colonists to Cuba, and settle Santa Elena—present-day Port Royal, South Carolina Villafañe arrived at Santa Elena in May 1561 and continued to explore the coast as far north as Cape Hatteras. Finding the area unsuitable for colonization, Villafañe left for La Española. Thus, another attempt to settle La Florida had ended in disappointment.

The Conquest of Florida by Pedro Menéndez de Avilés

In 1564, Philip II's fears of a possible rival occupation of Florida materialized when a group of French Huguenots, led by Rene de Laudonniére, settled Fort Caroline on the mouth of Florida's Saint Johns River. Laudonniére, however, would shortly be replaced by Jean Ribault. Exasperated by the news of the French settlement, the Spanish monarch instructed Pedro Menéndez de Avilés to drive the French out of Florida.

Menéndez, considered to be one of the ablest commanders in the Spanish army, carefully laid out his strategy. On June 29, 1565, he set sail from the Spanish port of Cádiz for Puerto Rico. On the fifteenth of August, he sailed from San Juan carrying 800 soldiers and colonists. The expedition arrived in Florida on the twenty-eighth of August. Menéndez named the area Saint Augustine in honor of the saint's feast day.

After scouting the area, Menéndez learned from the natives that the French were some twenty leagues to the north. On September 4, 1565, Menéndez set sail to the north and sighted four French vessels. The French exchanged gunfire with the Spanish vessels and then fled. Menéndez abandoned the attempt to capture them and sailed south toward Saint Augustine.

On September 6, 1565, a Spanish contingent arrived at Saint Augustine and in two days built a crude fort. Two days later Menéndez himself landed and took possession in the name of King Philip II. Thus, Saint Augustine became the first permanent European settlement in what was to become the United States.

Concerned over the possible invasion of Saint Augustine by the French Huguenots, Menéndez decided

Pedro Menéndez de Avilés.

massacre took place still bears the name Matanzas (Place of Slaughter). The week after the slaughter, the natives informed Menéndez that there were still some 170 Frenchmen south of Saint Augustine in the neighborhood of present-day Cape Canaveral. On November 26, 1565, Menéndez captured them. This time, however, he spared their lives and gave orders to return them to France.

When news of Menéndez's actions reached France, Charles IX, the French monarch, not only protested but also demanded reparations. Philip II, on the other hand, turned a deaf ear to the French protests and even commended Menéndez for driving the French out of La Florida.

Menéndez was a dreamer who wanted to create a large Spanish colony from Florida all the way north to Canada. The dream, however, would never become a reality. On February 20, 1574, Menéndez was recalled to Spain and given command of Philip II's Spanish Armada, whose purpose was to invade England. But Menéndez, fell ill and died on September 17, 1574.

Menéndez's death halted operations until 1588.

to attack Fort Caroline by land. Menéndez was right, for Ribault had already sailed with 600 men on September 10, 1565, to attack Saint Augustine. A storm, struck the vessels, however, and the French became shipwrecked on the Florida coast. Unaware of the French calamity, Menéndez marched inland on September 16. After a rough four-day march through the Florida marshes, Menéndez caught the French garrison at Fort Caroline by surprise and inflicted over 130 casualties. After sparing the lives of women and children, Menéndez set out for Saint Augustine.

On September 24, Menéndez arrived at Saint Augustine and learned of the French disaster. A few days later, he and 50 men marched in search of the shipwrecked French. The search netted 208 of Ribault's men. With the exception of 10 of them, who proved to be Catholics, the French were put to death by Menéndez.

On October 10, 1565, Menéndez received news that Ribault and 150 of his men were in the neighborhood of the site where he had previously executed their countrymen. Menéndez quickly set out to capture them. After extensive negotiations, the French surrendered. Once they surrendered, Menéndez executed Ribault and 134 of his men. The site where the

Drawing of the type of free black militia that were stationed in Spanish colonies in Florida and elsewhere (1795).

The disaster of the Spanish Armada in that year put an end to Spanish supremacy. No one knows if the outcome would have been different had Menéndez lived. In spite of the armada's disaster, Florida was firmly in Spanish hands. It remained a Spanish colony until 1763, when Spain was forced to cede Florida to the British. Twenty years later, in 1783, Spain regained Florida. The sun finally set on Spanish Florida in July 1821, when Florida was purchased by the United States for five million dollars.

✻SPANISH EXPLORATION AND COLONIZATION OF THE SOUTHWEST

Fray Marcos de Niza and the Seven Cities of Cíbola

Cabeza de Vaca's return to Mexico in 1536 indirectly involved Spain in exploring and colonizing what became the American Southwest. Rumors were started in Mexico City that Cabeza de Vaca and his companions had discovered cities laden with gold and silver, and suddenly the legend of the Seven Cities was revived. The legend started sometime during the Muslim invasion of the Iberian Peninsula. While the Muslims were conquering Portugal, seven Portuguese bishops purportedly crossed the Atlantic and founded the Seven Cities of Antilla, rich in gold and silver.

Convinced that Cabeza de Vaca and his companions had sighted the Seven Cities, Spanish Viceroy Antonio de Mendoza entrusted Fray Marcos de Niza to explore the mysterious land to the north. Mendoza chose Fray Marcos because he was an experienced traveler. The friar had been part of Pedro de Alvarado's conquest of Guatemala and had also participated in the Spanish conquest of Peru.

On March 7, 1539, Fray Marcos left the northern Mexican village of Culiacán with an expedition. He took with him Estevanico, the black slave who had been one of the survivors of the ill-fated Narváez expedition. On March 21, they crossed the Río Mayo. Fray Marcos decided to send Estevanico and a few of his Indian guides as scouts. Estevanico was to mark each "city" that he found with a cross. The larger the cross, the bigger the settlement.

For two months, the friar and his party followed a route marked with crosses. The crosses kept getting larger and the friar thought that he was getting nearer the Seven Cities. Messengers sent by Estevanico informed Fray Marcos that he had seen seven great cities, which the natives called Cíbola. Convinced that they were the Seven Cities, Fray Marcos pushed northward up the Sonora valley and into southeastern Arizona.

In late May, however, Fray Marcos received the stunning news that Estevanico had been killed by the natives as he was approaching the first city—present-day Hawikuh, New Mexico. Undeterred, Fray Marcos pressed on toward the first city of Cíbola. As he approached the city, the friar wrote: "I proceeded on my journey until coming within sight of Cíbola, which is situated in a plain at the base of a round hill. . . . The city is larger than that of Mexico. . . . The chieftains told me that it was the smallest of the seven cities" (Blacker, 265).

Fray Marcos, however, did not want to risk his life and did not enter the city. After taking possession in the name of the king and erecting a cross, Fray Marcos and his expedition started their return to Mexico. They arrived in Mexico City in September 1539. While in Mexico City, Fray Marcos wrote the following report to Viceroy Mendoza: "I was told that there is much gold there and the natives make it into vessels and jewels for their ears, and into little blades with which they wipe away their sweat" (Daniels, 29) If Fray Marcos was not a liar, he certainly wrote what Mendoza wanted to hear.

The Expedition of Francisco Vázquez de Coronado

Lured by Fray Marcos's report, Viceroy Mendoza commissioned the governor of the northern Mexican province of Nueva Galicia, Don Francisco Vázquez de Coronado to undertake an expedition to the Seven Cities. Born in Salamanca, Spain, in 1510, Francisco Vázquez de Coronado was a loyal supporter of Mendoza and had helped him put down a native revolt in Mexico in 1537.

The expedition, composed of three hundred Spaniards and eight hundred natives, left Compostela, Nueva Galicia, on February 23, 1540. Fray Marcos was also part of the expedition. By April 1, 1540, the expedition had covered 350 miles from Compostela to Sinaloa. Disgusted with the slow progress of the expedition, Coronado decided to push ahead with one hundred men and left Tristán de Arellano in charge of the main force.

With Fray Marcos serving as guide, Coronado and his men marched through the Sonora valley and into southwestern Arizona. Then they veered eastward. On July 7, 1540, after a 1,000-mile journey, they arrived at the first of the Seven Cities—Hawikuh. The Zuñi town did not have the gold that Fray Marcos had described in his report. Instead, hostile natives awaited the Spaniards.

After several scouting forays, Coronado wrote to Mendoza on August 3, 1540: "It now remains for me to tell about the city and kingdom and province of which Fray Marcos gave your Lordship an account. In brief,

I can assure you that he has not told the truth in a single thing that he said, except the name of the city and the large stone house. . . . The Seven Cities are seven little villages, all having the kind of houses I have described" (Blacker 285). Coronado may have saved Fray Marcos from being hacked to pieces by his angered men when he ordered him to carry his report to Viceroy Mendoza.

While waiting for the bulk of his expedition to arrive in Cíbola, Coronado sent scouting parties in hopes of finding gold. One of these parties went into the Hopi villages of northeastern Arizona, but reported that there was no gold in the area. Another one, led by Captain López de Cárdenas, discovered the Grand Canyon, but no precious metals. A third group, led by Hernando de Alvarado, went off to explore a province that the natives called Tiguex—present-day Albuquerque. They then traveled to Cicuye on the upper Rio Grande and then swung eastward along the Pecos River. A Pawnee guide whom the Spaniards called El Turco (the Turk) informed the conquistadors of a rich land called Quivira, but De Alvarado decided to return to Tiguex to await Coronado.

When the bulk of his army reached Cíbola, Coronado decided to follow Alvarado's recommendation and encamped at Tiguex to spend the winter of 1540-41. The Spaniards angered the once friendly Pueblo natives of Tiguex as a result of their outrageous requisitions. The Pueblos revolted and Coronado spent the winter battling them. In one instance, Coronado ordered two hundred Pueblo prisoners to be burned at the stake.

On April 23, 1541, Coronado set out to reach Quivira. With "the Turk" leading the way, the Spaniards reached the border of present-day Oklahoma. Informed by the natives that Quivira lay far to the north, Coronado decided to leave the army in the panhandle and set out for Quivira with thirty men on June 1, 1531. After a five-week march, Coronado reached Quivira on July 6. There was no great city, but only a settlement of seminomadic natives. Coronado and his men explored the area for more than a month. The soil was fertile, but there was no gold. While in the area of present-day Wichita, Kansas, the Spaniards discovered that "the Turk" was urging the local natives not to help them. After torturing him, they found out that he had been lying all along about the riches of Quivira. Once he confessed, "the Turk" was condemned to die by garrote.

The disgruntled Spaniards left Quivira in late August and spent the 1541-42 winter in Tiguex. In the spring of 1542, Coronado decided to return to Mexico City. Several Franciscan friars who had accompanied Coronado decided to stay to preach the gospel to the natives. As soon as the soldiers left, they were killed by the natives.

In July 1542, Coronado returned to Mexico City with fewer than one hundred of the three hundred Spaniards that once formed part of "the most brilliant company ever assembled in search of new lands" (Daniels, 34). Brokenhearted and with his fortune decimated in his quest for Cíbola and Quivira, Coronado died in Mexico City in 1544.

The Rodríguez-Chamuscado Expedition

Coronado's failure only put a temporary halt to Spain's interest in the Southwest. In June 1581, Fray Agustín Rodríguez and Captain Francisco Sánchez Chamuscado left the northern Mexican town of Santa Bárbara in hopes of finding another Mexico. The expedition went into the Conchos-Rio Grande area and continued upstream to the Rio Grande. On August 25, 1581, they reached the first Pueblo villages of New Mexico—the present-day Bernalillo area. The expedition explored the Pueblo country of New Mexico as far north as Queres and as far west as Acoma and Zuñi. Fray Agustín Rodríguez and another Franciscan, Fray Francisco López, decided to stay at Puaray—opposite Bernalillo—to convert the natives. Sánchez Chamuscado, on the other hand, decided to return to Santa Bárbara. He never made it to his destination, for he fell ill and died. The rest of his party, however, arrived at Santa Bárbara on April 15, 1582.

The Espejo-Beltrán Expedition

Concern over the fate of the two friars in the Rodríguez-Chamuscado expedition prompted the Franciscan community to send a rescue expedition led by the hidalgo Antonio de Espejo and Fray Bernardino Beltrán.

The expedition set out from Santa Bárbara in November of 1582, basically following the Rodríguez-Chamuscado route. Once the Spaniards arrived in Pueblo country, they were told by the natives that the friars had been killed. Probably because he was the main financial backer of the expedition, Espejo decided to continue exploring the area. In May 1583, Beltrán and a few of the men left for Mexico, but Espejo continued exploring the area. He, along with nine other men, marched west in search of La Laguna del Oro (the Lake of Gold). After traveling nearly fifty leagues, he entered western Arizona. In view of the natives' hostility, Espejo decided to return to Mexico.

Espejo and his men arrived in to Mexico on September 10, 1583, claiming that they had discovered La

Laguna del Oro. Once again, another tale of riches would lure the Spanish to the Southwest.

Castaño de Sosa and Juan Morlete

The prospect of finding gold mines in Pueblo country prompted Gaspar Castaño de Sosa to organize an unauthorized expedition in 1589. Castaño de Sosa went as far north as Santo Domingo, New Mexico. While Castaño de Sosa was in the Santo Domingo area, the Spanish viceroy of Mexico, Don Luis de Velasco, ordered Captain Juan Morlete to arrest Castaño de Sosa. Following the route of previous expeditions, Morlete reached Santo Domingo in April 1591. He promptly arrested Castaño de Sosa and dispatched him to Mexico City. Morlete kept on exploring the area, but, finding no riches, he returned to Mexico in November 1591.

Francisco Leyva de Bonilla and Antonio Gutiérrez de Humaña

Castano de Sosa's fiasco did not deter two Spaniards, Francisco Leyva de Bonilla and Antonio Gutiérrez de Humaña, from trying their luck. In 1593, they departed Santa Barbara on an unauthorized expedition to Quivira. They traveled to the Santa Fe area and then eastward into Kansas. When they reached a place called the Great Settlement—present-day Wichita, Kansas—an argument ensued between the two leaders. Humaña butchered Leyva de Bonilla, and the Plains Indians later killed Humaña and the rest of the Spaniards on their way back. Only one member of the expedition, Jusepe Gutiérrez, survived to tell the story.

Oñate Settles New Mexico

In spite of the failures of previous authorized and unauthorized expeditions to the Southwest, Mexican Viceroy Luis de Velasco had a keen interest in settling the area. In 1595, he granted a patent in the name of the king to Juan de Oñate to colonize New Mexico.

The choice of Juan de Oñate as adelantado seemed like a good one. A wealthy man, Juan de Oñate was the son of Cristóbal de Oñate, one of the conquerors of Nueva Galicia. He was also married to the great-granddaughter of Aztec emperor Moctezuma. Despite these connections, Oñate was delayed for three years by the monstrous Spanish bureaucracy and the new viceroy, Don Gaspar de Zúñiga.

Finally, on February 7, 1598, the Oñate expedition left Santa Bárbara with 400 men, of whom 130 brought their families. As the expedition approached the San Pedro River, a group of ten Franciscans joined it. On the nineteenth of April, the expedition

reached the sand dunes south of El Paso, and on the fourth of May they arrived at El Paso. They moved upstream along the Rio Grande into the Pueblo country of New Mexico. On the eleventh of July, they arrived at Caypa. Onate renamed it San Juan de los Caballeros and established a settlement there.

Oñate and his men began to establish contact with the natives of the area, and the Franciscan missionaries began to preach the gospel. After building a church in San Juan de los Caballeros, Oñate sent his nephew, Captain Vicente de Zaldívar, to explore the plains to the northeast and bring herds of buffalo. Zaldívar failed to bring the herds, but brought back plenty of hides and beef.

While awaiting Zaldívar, Oñate sent scouting parties to the Jumano Pueblos and the Zuni. In November 1598, Vicente Zaldívar's brother, Juan, was ambushed by the Acoma Pueblos while on a scouting mission. Saddened by the loss of his nephew, Oñate sent Vicente on a punitive expedition against the Acoma on January 15, 1599. In spite of the natives' fierce resistance, the Spaniards laid waste to Acoma, taking with them more than six hundred prisoners.

Attempts by Oñate's men to reach the South Sea—the Gulf of California—had failed, so in June 1601, Oñate led an expedition in the opposite direction toward Quivira. The five-month journey to Quivira failed to bring riches.

When Oñate returned to San Juan de los Caballeros, he found the settlement in a chaotic state. Dissatisfied with the lack of economic progress, a group of colonists returned to Santa Bárbara and started a campaign to discredit Oñate and New Mexico. The rumors even reached the Spanish Crown, and the king was even contemplating the withdrawal of the Spaniards from New Mexico. Luckily for Oñate, the Spanish viceroy supported him.

In spite of his troubles, Oñate was persistent in reaching the South Sea. In October 1604, he left San Juan de los Caballeros with thirty-five men. They went through the Zuñi and Hopi country, down to the Colorado River. They then moved downstream past the Gila River and reached the Gulf of California. They returned to New Mexico on April 25, 1605. Once more, the Spaniards had failed to find riches.

After two years of trials and tribulations, Oñate resigned from his enterprise. He had spent his entire fortune in colonizing New Mexico and was now in debt. Luis de Velasco, who was once again the Spanish viceroy of New Spain, appealed directly to the king to hold New Mexico. In 1608, the Royal and Supreme Council of the Indies made New Mexico an official province of the viceroyalty of New Spain and appointed Pedro de Peralta governor of New Mexico.

Despite the vicissitudes, including several native

uprisings, New Mexico was in Spanish hands until 1680. That year, the native Pueblo leader Popé led a revolt of the Pueblos and pushed the Spanish settlers all the way down to El Paso. It took a dozen years for Spanish forces to reconquer New Mexico. After 1692, however, New Mexico was be in Spanish control until 1821, when Mexico gained its independence, and with it, New Mexico.

The Settlement of Texas

The land we now call Texas was not unknown to the Spaniards. In 1519, Alonso Alvarez de Pineda claimed it for Spain. A few years later Alvar Núñez Cabeza de Vaca started his remarkable adventure in Texas. Spanish conquistadors also used Texas as a waystation in their many expeditions. Yet, Spain paid little attention to Texas because it simply lacked the logistical capabilities to settle it.

Fear of French intrusion into Texas prompted the Spanish authorities in Mexico to send five expeditions commanded by Antonio de León. In 1686, De León left Monterrey and reached the Rio Grande. He then followed the river to the gulf and explored the coast. The following year, in his next expedition, he crossed the Rio Grande but had to return to Mexico. In 1688, while on yet another expedition, he crossed the Rio Grande and took a Frenchman named Jean Jarri prisoner.

Spanish fears were confirmed when in 1689 De León discovered the ruins of a French settlement near Garcitas Creek during his fourth expedition. Apparently, the natives had killed the French intruders. During this expedition, De León entered into friendly relations with the Caddo natives. He observed that the Caddo constantly used the word *tayshas* (friends) to refer to the Spaniards. From then on, the Spaniards referred to the territory as "Tejasl."

In May 1690, De León set out on a fifth expedition and established the first permanent Spanish settlement in Texas, San Francisco de los Tejas, near the Neches River.

Despite the fact that Texas was made a separate Spanish province in 1691, with Don Domingo de Terán as its governor, the Spanish Crown ordered its abandonment in 1693. Fear of Indian uprisings was the reason given by the Spanish authorities. The Spanish withdrawal from Texas was not a permanent one. Continued concerns over possible French encroachment into Texas prompted the Spaniards to reoccupy Texas in 1716 by establishing a series of missions to serve two purposes: convert the natives to Catholicism and ward off the French. Of these missions, San Antonio, founded in 1718, was the most important and most prosperous.

On January 9, 1717, war broke out between Spain and France. Reports of a French invasion from Louisiana panicked the Spanish settlers of East Texas, who sought refuge in San Antonio. The invasion force, however, consisted of only seven men who attacked the Spanish settlement of San Miguel, which consisted of one Franciscan brother and one soldier! The invasion, nevertheless, prompted the governor of Coahuila, the marquis of Aguayo, to march into Texas with a rescue expedition. On April 10, 1721, the marquis of Aguayo arrived in San Antonio. After resupplying San Antonio, he marched through the interior, looking for French soldiers but found none. His job done, the marquis returned to Coahuila in 1722, leaving behind a string of missions and presidios.

After the marquis of Aguayo's departure, the viceroy of New Spain appointed Don Fernando Pérez de Almazán governor of Texas. Pérez de Almazán consolidated Spanish rule over the province. Despite the lack of settlers and the frequency of Comanche raids, Spain was able to maintain its presence in Texas until 1821.

✳SPANISH EXPLORATIONS TO CALIFORNIA

California owes its name to a mythical island that appeared in the Spanish chivalric novel *Las sergas de Esplandián* (*The Deeds of Esplandian*).

Hernán Cortés, the conqueror of the Aztec Empire, became interested in finding a northwest passage and sent several expeditions to what today is the Mexican state of Baja California.

In 1542, Viceroy Antonio de Mendoza commissioned Juan Rodríguez de Cabrillo, a Portuguese sailor, to sail north of the west coast of Mexico in search of treasures. On September 28, 1542, Cabrillo entered what he described to be an excellent port — San Diego. He then sailed northward. As the ships went along the coast, they found no treasures. Cabrillo died on January 3, 1545. After the death of Cabrillo, Bartholomé Ferrelo took over the expedition and sailed all the way north to the Oregon coast. Disease broke out among the crew, and Ferrelo was forced to return to Mexico. The expedition arrived at the Mexican port of La Navidad on April 14, 1543.

The Expeditions of De Gali, Rodrigues Cermenho, and Vizcaíno

Interest in exploring California waned after the Cabrillo-Ferrelo expedition, but when the Spanish developed a profitable trade between their Philippine colony and Mexico, interest rekindled. Spanish authorities not only saw the need to secure ports in California as possible repair ports for their fleet, but also feared the presence of British pirates in the area. In 1579, Sir Francis Drake had even claimed the California coast for the British.

In 1584, Francisco de Gali was instructed to scout the Alta California coast. In 1595, the Portuguese sailor Sebastiao Rodrigues Cermenho was ordered by Viceroy Luis de Velasco to explore the California coast on his return from the Philippines. Following Gali's course, Rodrigues Cermenho ventured closer to the coast and discovered Monterey Bay in December 1595. He arrived at the Mexican port of La Navidad in January 1596.

The new Spanish viceroy, Monterey, continued Luis de Velasco's policy of finding possible repair ports in California and in May 1602 sent the experienced sailor Sebastián Vizcaíno to scout the area.

Although Vizcaíno's detailed exploration, which lasted eleven months, succeeded in finding the entrance to Monterey Bay, the expedition returned to Acapulco, Mexico, with only one-quarter of its original members. The rest had died of malnutrition. Exploration of Alta California was proving to be costly.

California: The Last Frontier

Russia's announced intentions, rather than the quest for treasures and riches, was largely responsible for Spain's colonization of California. As a reply to the Russian menace, Inspector General Don José de Gálvez decided that the settling of Alta California was essential. He commissioned the governor of Baja California, Don Gaspar de Portolá, to lead an expedition to Alta California. Father Junípero de Serra, the recently arrived Franciscan superior of Baja California, was also part of this expedition.

In January and February 1769, two ships carrying supplies left for San Diego. They were to rendezvous with Portolá's land expedition, which was divided into two parties. One party, commanded by Fernando Rivera Moncada, left Velicatá in Baja California on March 22, 1769. The other party, commanded by Portolá and with Serra as its chaplain, left Loreto in Baja California on May 15, 1769.

After traveling hundreds of miles through treacherous terrain, the two groups joined with the ships in San Diego on July 1, 1769. Two days later Father Serra planted a cross on a San Diego hill, and the construction of the first mission of Alta California followed. San Diego was the first of twenty-one missions that the Franciscans built in California.

An impatient man, Portolá departed by land to find Monterey. He arrived in Monterey in October, but unconvinced that the harbor he had seen was Monte-

rey, he pushed northward. Days later, he arrived at a large bay. Portolá knew it was not Monterey Bay, so he called it San Francisco. Portolá wanted to continue the search for Monterey, but his tired men refused and he had no option but to return to San Diego. They arrived at San Diego on January 24, 1770.

The restless Portolá was obsessed with finding Monterey, and on May 31, 1770, he and Father Serra boarded the *San Antonio* in search of Monterey. Three days later, they finally reached the elusive harbor. A few days after that, they landed in Monterey, and Father Serra had his second Alta California mission. Portolá returned to Mexico. Spain now had two presidios to guard its empire in Alta California: Monterey to the north and San Diego to the south.

The new Spanish viceroy in Mexico, Don Antonio María Bucareli, wanted to establish another presidio in California. In 1773, he summoned Captain Juan Bautista de Anza, commander of the Tubac presidio in northern Mexico, to establish a route between Monterey and Sonora. In January 1774, De Anza set out on a probing expedition. At the junction of the Gila and Colorado rivers, De Anza established good relations with the cacique Palma and his Yuma natives. He then forded the river and wandered through the desert. On March 22, 1774, he reached Mission San Gabriel near present-day Los Angeles and then continued to Monterey. Anza returned to Tubac and then proceeded to Mexico City to report to the viceroy. Both of them concluded that a presidio should be established in San Francisco.

In October 1775, De Anza's expedition, consisting of 240 settlers and enough provisions to make San Francisco self-sustaining, departed Tubac. As the expedition reached Yuma country, they were welcomed by chief Palma. On January 2, 1776, they reached San Gabriel. In March, they arrived at Monterey. Finally, on September 17, 1766, the presidio of San Francisco was founded. Spain's northernmost frontier outpost was now a reality. His mission accomplished, De Anza returned to Mexico City. He was later appointed governor of New Mexico.

The California provinces, however, showed little progress. The Yuma became impatient with the Spaniards, and in 1781 they revolted. The Spaniards were able to suppress the uprising, but California remained an isolated province of the Spanish Empire, lacking in colonists and resources. In 1821, Spain's northernmost frontier became part of independent Mexico.

The Missionary Trails

Ferdinand and Isabella, as well as the other Spanish monarchs that succeeded them, thought it was their duty to convert the natives of the New World to the Catholic faith. Although priests were sent to convert the natives, the missions did not begin until 1512. That year, the Jeronymite Fathers in La Española decided to save the decimated Arawak population by gathering them into missions. Soon, missions spread like wildfire throughout the Spanish Empire.

Spain's purpose in adopting the mission system was not only to save the souls of the natives but also to assimilate them. The natives were persuaded to join the mission in order to be taught the Catholic faith, the Spanish language, the Spanish way of life, and various skills. Missions were staffed by members of a religious order and were financially supported by the Spanish Crown. The mission system was really a system of paternalistic theocracy working for Spain and the salvation of souls.

Missions in "La Florida"

In 1573, the Franciscan order arrived in Florida to establish missions. A century after their arrival, they had established a trail of missions along the east coast of North America from Saint Augustine to North Carolina. The Franciscans also established a string of missions from Saint Augustine westward to present-day Tallahassee. Franciscan missions were even founded in the interior of Georgia and Alabama.

Florida and the Southeast were not the only places where missions were established. Missions went side by side with the Spanish colonization of Texas, the Southwest, and California. In many instances, missions assumed the character of political and military outposts against Spain's rivals. In short, they became the most important Spanish colonial institution in what was to become the United States.

Eusebio Kino: The Padre on Horseback

Among the many missionaries that came to the Spanish Empire in North America was Eusebio Kino. A Tyrolean by birth, Eusebio Kino was born in 1644 and studied at the Universities of Freiburg and Ingolstadt. While at Ingolstadt, Kino contracted a serious disease and commended himself to Saint Francis Xavier, the patron saint of the Indies. He then joined the Jesuit order and became a missionary.

Father Kino wanted to go as a missionary to the Philippines, but in 1678 his superiors ordered him to go to Mexico. He arrived in Mexico in 1680. From 1683 until 1686, Kino participated as a missionary in an unsuccessful attempt at settling Baja California.

The enterprise's failure did not deter Father Kino from pursuing his goal as a missionary. In 1687, he got his wish when his superior entrusted him with the missionary effort in the Pimería Alta. It was not an

easy task, for the Pimería Alta encompassed a large area—present-day Upper Sonora, Mexico, and southwestern Arizona. The "padre on horseback," as Kino was called, ventured into the arid and hostile country of the Pimería Alta with only his faith and zeal. In less than a year, he founded his first mission, Nuestra Señora de los Dolores, in Sonora, about one hundred miles from present-day Tucson.

By the early 1700s Father Kino had established several missions in Sonora and five missions in Arizona. Among his Arizona missions were Nuestra Señora de los Dolores, Santa Gertrudis de Saric, San José de Imuris, Nuestra Señora de los Remedios, San Cayetano de Tumacácori, and San Javier del Bac.

An accomplished farmer and stockman, Father Kino taught the natives new techniques and even encouraged them to plant wheat. In addition to his agricultural endeavors, Father Kino was an excellent cosmographer, astronomer, and mathematician. It was Father Kino who proved that Baja California was not an island but a peninsula.

Father Eusebio Kino died in 1711, at age 66. In his twenty-four years as a missionary, he had built a trail of twenty-four missions stretching from Sonora to southern Arizona. It can be stated that Arizona was practically settled by one man, Father Eusebio Kino, "the padre on horseback."

Fray Junípero de Serra and the California Mission Trail

In 1767, King Charles III expelled the Jesuits from the Spanish Empire. This event opened the door for the Franciscan conquest of California. This conquest would never have been accomplished without Fray Junípero de Serra. Miguel José de Serra was born on November 24, 1713, in Petra, Majorca. He entered the Franciscan friary when he was sixteen. After completing his vows, he took the name Junípero in honor of Brother Junípero, one of Saint Francis of Assisi's companions who was known for his compassion and humility.

Father Serra first arrived in the New World in 1749 with a group of Franciscan missionaries. He began preaching in Mexico City and later served as a missionary with the natives of eastern Mexico. Known for his energy and zeal, Father Serra was sent over to supervise the missionary efforts in Baja California in 1768.

Even though Father Serra was called to supervise the establishments of Franciscan missions in Baja California, he had another goal—to establish other missions in Alta California. This he did, for his order eventually established twenty-one missions in Alta California. Father Serra's missions in turn became the foundation of the Spanish colonization of California.

Father Serra founded his first mission, San Diego de Alcalá, on July 3, 1769. When he died on August 28, 1784, Father Serra had founded nine missions, traveled more than ten thousand miles, and converted close to sixty-eight hundred natives.

Father Serra's death did not stop missionary activity in California. His fellow Franciscans established another twelve missions. Thus, by 1823, the famous mission trail of California included the following missions: San Diego de Alcalá (1769), San Carlos de Monterey (1770), San Antonio de Padua (1771), San Gabriel Arcángel (1771), San Luis Obispo de Tolosa (1772), San Francisco de Asís (1776), San Juan Capistrano (1776), Santa Clara de Asís (1777), San Buenaventura (1782), Santa Bárbara (1786), La Purísima Concepción (1787), Santa Cruz (1791), San José de Guadalupe (1797), San Juan Bautista (1797), San Miguel Arcángel (1797), San Fernando Rey (1797), San Luis Rey (1798), Santa Inés (1804), San Rafael Arcángel (1817), and San Francisco Solano (1823).

Father Serra remains a controversial figure today. His admirers consider him a holy man worthy of canonization. They often refer to his missions as havens of peace and tranquility, where the padres taught the natives to be useful Spanish citizens. Detractors, on the other hand, classify Serra as a ruthless man who never respected the rights of the natives to be free and to live as they wanted. They often have compared the missions to penal institutions and claim their purpose was to enslave and exploit the natives. In spite of the controversy, Serra's name still remains an integral part of California's history, and the mission system is essential to an understanding of the Spanish Empire in the New World.

References

Bailey, Helen Miller, and Abraham P. Nasatir. *Latin America: The Development of Its Civilization*. Englewood Cliffs, N.J.: Prentice Hall, 1973.

Bandelier, Fanny. *The Journey of Alvar Nuñez Cabeza de Vaca*. Chicago: Río Grande Press, 1964.

Bannon, John Francis. *The Spanish Borderlands Frontier 1513-1821*. New York: Holt, Rinehart and Winston, 1970.

Blacker, Irwin R. *The Golden Conquistadors*. Indianapolis, Ind: Bobbs-Merrill, 1960.

Bolton, Herbert. *Spanish Exploration in the Southwest 1542-1706*. New York: Barnes and Noble, 1946.

———. *The Spanish Borderlands: A Chronicle of Old Florida and the Southwest*. New Haven, Conn.: Yale University Press, 1921.

Claypole, William, and John Robottom. *Caribbean Story*. White Plains, N.Y.: Longman, 1986.

Clissold, Stephen. *The Seven Cities of Cibola*. New York: Clarkson N. Potter, 1962.

Daniels, George. *The Spanish West*. New York: Time-Life Books, 1976.

Davis, Frederick. "History of Juan Ponce de Leon's Voyages to Florida." *Florida Historical Quarterly* 14 (July 1935): 7-66.

De Grazia, Ettore. *De Grazia and Padre Kino*. Tucson, Ariz.: De Grazia Gallery in the Sun, 1979.

De la Vega, Garcilaso. *La Florida del Inca*. México: Fondo de Cultura Económica, 1956.

De Nevi, Don, and Francis Moholy. *Junipero Serra*. New York: Harper and Row, 1985.

Driver, Harold E. *Indians of North America*. Chicago: University of Chicago Press, 1961.

Favata, Martin, and José B. Fernández. *La relación o naufraugios de Alvar Núñez Cabeza de Vaca*. Potomac, Md.: Scripta Humanis-tica, 1986.

Fernández, José B. *Alvar Núñez Cabeza de Vaca*. Miami, Fla.: Ediciones Universal, 1975.

Fernández-Flores, Darío. *Drama y aventura de los españoles en Florida*. Madrid: Ediciones Cultura Hispánica, 1963.

Fernández de Navarrete, Martín. *Colección de los viajes y descubrimientos que hicieron por mar los españoles desde fines del siglo XV*. Buenos Aires: Editorial Guarania, 1945.

Fernández de Oviedo, Gonzalo. *Historia general y natural de las Indias*. Madrid: Ediciones Atlas, 1959.

García Mercadal, José. *Lo que España llevó a América*. Madrid: Taurus, 1959.

Gónzalez de Barcia, Andrés. *Ensayo cronológico para la historia de la Florida*. Gainesville: University of Florida Press, 1951.

Grove Day, A. *Coronado's Quest*. Berkeley: University of California Press, 1964.

Hallenbeck, Cleve. *Journey and Route of Alvar Nuñez Cabeza de Vaca*. Glendale: The Arthur H. Clark Company, 1940.

Herring, Hubert. *A History of Latin America*. New York: Alfred A. Knopf, 1967.

Hudson, Charles. "A Synopsis of the Hernando de Soto Expedition, 1539-1543." In *De Soto Trail*. Washington, D.C.: National Park Service, 1990.

James, George W. *The Old Franciscan Missions of California*. Boston: Longwood Press, 1978.

Keen, Benjamin, and Mark Wasserman. *A History of Latin America*. Boston: Houghton Mifflin, 1988.

Knight, Franklin W. *The Caribbean*. New York: Oxford University Press, 1990.

Lowery, Woodbury. *The Spanish Settlements Within the Present Limits of the United States, 1531-1561*. New York: Russell and Russell, 1959.

Masó, Calixto. *Historia de Cuba*. Miami, Fla.: Ediciones Universal, 1976.

McGann, Thomas F. "The Ordeal of Cabeza de Vaca." *American Heritage* (December 1960): 78-82.

Murga Sanz, Vicente. *Juan Ponce de León*. San Juan: Ediciones de la Universidad de Puerto Rico, 1959.

Rolle, Andrew. *California: A History*. New York: Thomas Y. Crowell, 1969.

Spencer, Robert, ed. *The Native Americans*. New York: Harper and Row, 1965.

Suchlicki, Jaime. *Cuba: From Columbus to Castro*. Washington, D.C.: Pergammon, 1986.

Tebeau, Charlton W. *A History of Florida*. Coral Gables: University of Miami Press, 1971.

———, and Ruby L. Carson. *Florida from Indian Trail to Space Age*. Delray Beach, Fla.: Southern Publishing Company, 1965.

Te Paske, John. "Funerals and Fiestas in Early Eighteenth Century St. Augustine." *Florida Historical Quarterly* (January 1973): 97-104.

Terrell, John Upton. *Journey into Darkness*. New York: William Morrow and Company, 1962.

Thomas, David Hurst, ed. *Columbian Consequences*. Washington, D.C.: Smithsonian Institution Press, 1989.

Williams, John L. *The Territory of Florida*. New York: A. T. Goodrich, 1837.

José Fernández

3

Significant Documents

✹ CESSION OF LOUISIANA

Treaty Between the United States of America and the French Republic

The President of the United States of America and the First Consul of the French Republic in the name of the French People desiring to remove all Source of misunderstanding relative to objects of discussion mentioned in the Second and fifth articles of the Convention of the 8th Vendemiaire and 9/30 September 1800 relative to the rights claimed by the United States in virtue of the Treaty concluded at Madrid the 27 of October 1795, between His Catholic Majesty, & the Said United States, & willing to Strengthen the union and friendship which at the time of the Said Convention was happily reestablished between the two nations have respectively named their Plenipotentiaries to wit The President of the United States, by and with the advice and consent of the Senate of Said States; Robert P. Livingston Minister Plenipotentiary of the United States and James Monroe Minister Plenipotentiary and Envoy extraordinary of the Said States near the Government of the French Republic; And the First Consul in the name of the French people, Citizen Francis Barbe Marbois Minister of the public treasury who after having respectively exchanged their full powers have agreed to the following Articles.

Article I

Whereas by the Article the third of the Treaty concluded at St. Idelfonso the 9th Vendemiaire and 9/1 October 1800 between the First Consul of the French Republic and his Catholic Majesty it was agreed as follows.

"His Catholic Majesty promises and engages on his part to cede to the French Republic six months after the full and entire execution of the conditions and Stipulations herein relative to his Royal Highness the Duke of Parma, the Colony or Province of Louisiana with the Same extent that it now has in the hands of Spain, & that it had when France possessed it; and Such as it Should be after the Treaties subsequently entered into between Spain and other States."

And whereas in pursuance of the Treaty and particularly of the third article the French Republic has an incontestible title to the domain and to the possession of the said Territory—The First Consul of the French Republic desiring to give to the United States a strong proof of his friendship doth hereby cede to the said United States in the name of the French Republic for ever and in full Sovereignty the said territory with all its rights and appurtenances as fully and in the Same manner as they have been acquired by the French Republic in virtue of the above mentioned Treaty concluded with his Catholic Majesty.

Article II

In the cession made by the preceding article are included the adjacent Islands belonging to Louisiana, all public lots and Squares, vacant lands and all public buildings, fortifications, barracks and other edifices which are not private property. The Archives, papers & documents relative to the domain and Sovereignty of Louisiana and it dependencies will be left in the possession of the Commissaries of the United States, and copies will be afterwards given in due form to the Magistrates and Municipal officers of Such of the said papers and documents as may be necessary to them.

Article III

The inhabitants of the ceded territory shall be incorporated in the Union of the United States and admitted as soon as possible according to the principles of the federal Constitution to the enjoyment of all the rights, advantages and immunities of citizens of the United States, and in the mean time they shall be maintained and protected in the free enjoyment of their liberty, property and the Religion which they profess.

Article IV

There Shall be Sent by the Government of France a Commissary to Louisiana to the end that he do every act necessary as well to receive from the Officers of his Catholic Majesty the Said country and its dependencies in the name of the French Republic if it has not been already done as to transmit it in the name of the French Republic to the Commissary or agent of the United States.

Article V

Immediately after the ratification of the present Treaty by the President of the United States and in case that of the first Consul's shall have been previously obtained, the Commissary of the French Republic shall remit all military posts of New Orleans and other parts of the ceded territory to the Commissary or Commissaries named by the President to take possession—the troops whether of France or Spain who may be there shall cease to occupy any military post from the time of taking possession and shall be embarked as soon as possible in the course of three months after the ratification of this treaty.

Article VI

The United States promise to execute Such treaties and articles as may have been agreed between Spain and the tribes and nations of Indians until by mutual consent of the United States and the said tribes or nations other Suitable articles Shall have been agreed upon.

Article VII

As it is reciprocally advantageous to the commerce of France and the United States to encourage the communication of both nations for a limited time in the country ceded by the present treaty until general arrangements relative to the commerce of both nations may be agreed on, it has been agreed between the contracting parties that the French Ships coming directly from France or any of her colonies loaded only with the produce and manufactures of France or her Said Colonies; and the Ships of Spain coming directly from Spain or any of her colonies loaded only with the produce or manufactures of Spain or her Colonies Shall be admitted during the Space of twelve years in the Port of New Orleans and in all other legal ports-of-entry within the ceded territory in the Same manner as the Ships of the United States coming directly from France or Spain or any of their Colonies without being Subject to any other or greater duty on merchandise or other or greater tonnage than that paid by the citizens of the United States. During the Space of time above mentioned no other nation Shall have a right to the Same privileges in the Ports of the ceded territory—the twelve years Shall commence three months after the exchange of ratifications if it Shall take place in France or three months after it Shall have been notified at Paris to the French Government if it Shall take place in the United States; It is however well understood that the object of the above article is to favor the manufactures, Commerce, freight and navigation of France and of Spain So far as relates to the importations that the French and Spanish Shall make into the Said Ports of the United States without in any Sort affecting the regulations that the United States may make concerning the exportation of produce and merchandize of the United States, or any right they may have to make Such regulations.

Article VIII

In future and for ever after the expiration of the twelve years, the Ships of France shall be treated upon the footing of the most favored nations in the ports above mentioned.

Article IX

The particular Convention Signed this day by the respective Ministers having for its object to provide for the payment of debts due to the Citizens of the United States by the French Republic prior to the

30th Sept. 1800 (8 Vendemiaire an 9) is approved and to have its execution in the Same manner as if it had been inserted in this present treaty and it Shall be ratified in the Same form and in the Same time So that the one Shall not be ratified distinct from the other.

Another particular Convention Signed at the Same date as the present treaty relative to a definitive rule between the contracting parties is in the like manner approved and will be ratified in the Same form, and in the Same time and jointly.

Article X

The present treaty Shall be ratified in good and due form and the ratifications Shall be exchanged in the Space of Six months after the date of the Signature by the Ministers Plenipotentiary or Sooner if possible.

In faith whereof the respective Plenipotentiaries have Signed these articles in the French and English languages; declaring nevertheless that the present Treaty was originally agreed to in the French language; and have thereunto affixed their Seals. Done at Paris the tenth day of Floreal in the eleventh year of the French Republic; and the 30th of April 1803.
ROB. R. LIVINGSTON
J.A. MONROE
BARBE MARBOIS

✳CESSION OF LOUISIANA: FINANCIAL ARRANGEMENT

A Convention Between the United States of America and French Republic

The President of the United States of America and the First Consul of the French Republic in the name of the French people, in consequence of the treaty of cession of Louisiana which has been Signed this day; wishing to regulate definitively every thing which has relation to the Said cession have authorized to this effect the Plenipotentiaries that is to say: the President of the United States has, by and with the advice and consent of the Senate of the Said States nominated for their Plenipotentiaries, Robert R. Livingston Minister Plenipotentiary of the United States and James Monroe Minister Plenipotentiary and Envoy-Extraordinary of the Said United States near the Government of the French Republic; and the First Consul of the French Republic in the name of the French People has named as Plenipotentiary of the Said Republic the citizen Francis Barb-Marbois: who in virtue of their full powers, which have been exchanged this day have agreed to the following articles:

Article: 1

The Government of the United States engages to pay to the French Government in the manner Specified in the following article the Sum of Sixty millions of francs independent of the Sum which Shall be fixed by another Convention for the payment of the debts due by France to citizens of the United States.

Article: 2

For the payment of the Sum of Sixty millions of francs mentioned in the preceding article the United States Shall create a Stock of eleven millions, two hundred and fifty thousand Dollars bearing an interest of Six per cent: per annum payable half yearly in London, Amsterdam or Paris amounting by the half year to three hundred and thirty Seven thousand five hundred Dollars according to the proportions which Shall be determined by the French Government to be paid at either place: The principal of the Said Stock to be reimbursed at the treasury of the United States in annual payments of not less than three millions of Dollars each; of which the first payment Shall commence fifteen years after the date of the exchange of ratifications—this Stock Shall be transferred to the Government of France or to Such person or persons as Shall be authorized to receive it in three months at most after the exchange of the ratifications of this treaty and after Louisiana Shall be taken possession of in the name of the Government of the United States.

It is further agreed that if the French Government Should be desirous of disposing of the Said Stock to receive the capital in Europe at Shorter terms that its measures for that purpose Shall be taken So as to favor in the greatest degree possible the credit of the United States and to raise to the highest price the Said Stock.

Article: 3

It is agreed that the Dollar of the United States Specified in the present Convention Shall be fixed at five francs 3333/10000 or five livres eight Sous tournois.

The present Convention Shall be ratified in good and due form, and the ratifications Shall be exchanged in the Space of Six months to date from this day or Sooner if possible.

In faith of which the respective Plenipotentiaries have Signed the above articles both in the French and English languages, declaring nevertheless that the present treaty has been originally agreed on and written in the French language; to which they have hereunto affixed their Seals.

Done at Paris the tenth of Floreal eleventh year of the French Republic (30th April 1803.)

Rob. R. Livingston
J.A. Monroe
Barbe Marbois

✳THE MONROE DOCTRINE

ANNUAL MESSAGE from President James Monroe to the United States Congress, Containing the "Monroe Doctrine," December 2, 1823

John Bassett Moore, *A Digest of International Law, VI,* 401

AT THE PROPOSAL of the Russian Imperial Government, made through the minister of the Emperor residing here, a full power and instructions have been transmitted to the minister of the United States at St. Petersburg, to arrange, by amicable negotiation, the respective rights and interests of the two nations on the northwest coast of this continent. A similar proposal has been made by his Imperial Majesty to the Government of Great Britain, which has likewise been acceded to. The Government of the United States has been desirous, by the friendly proceeding, of manifesting the great value which they have invariably attached to the friendship of the Emperor, and their solicitude to cultivate the best understanding with his Government. In the discussions to which this interest has given rise, and in the arrangements by which they may terminate, the occasion has been judged proper for asserting as a principle in which the rights and interests of the United States are involved, that the American continents, by the free and independent condition which they have assumed and maintain, are henceforth not to be considered as subjects for future colonization by any European powers.

It was stated at the commencement of the last session that a great effort was then making in Spain and Portugal to improve the condition of the people of those countries, and that it appeared to be conducted with extraordinary moderation. It need scarcely be remarked that the result has been, so far, very different from what was then anticipated. Of events in that quarter of the globe with which we have so much intercourse, and from which we derive our origin, we have always been anxious and interested spectators. The citizens of the United States cherish sentiments the most friendly in favor of the liberty and happiness of their fellow-men on that side of the Atlantic. In the wars of the European powers in matters relating to themselves we have never taken any part, nor does it comport with our policy so to do. It is only when our rights are invaded or seriously menaced that we resent injuries or make preparation

for our defense. With the movements in this hemisphere we are, of necessity, more immediately connected, and by causes which must be obvious to all enlightened and impartial observers. The political system of the allied powers is essentially different in this respect from that of America. This difference proceeds from that which exists in their respective Governments. And to the defense of our own, which has been achieved by the loss of so much blood and treasure, and matured by the wisdom of their most enlightened citizens, and under which we have enjoyed unexampled felicity, this whole nation is devoted. We owe it, therefore, to candor, and to the amicable relations existing between the United States and those powers, to declare that we should consider any attempt on their part to extend their system to any portion of this hemisphere as dangerous to our peace and safety. With the existing colonies or dependencies of any European power we have not interfered and shall not interfere. But with the governments who have declared their independence and maintained it, and whose independence we have, on great consideration and on just principles, acknowledged, we could not view any interposition for the purpose of oppressing them, or controlling in any other manner their destiny, by any European power, in any other light than as the manifestation of an unfriendly disposition toward the United States. In the war between these new governments and Spain we declared our neutrality at the time of their recognition, and to this we have adhered and shall continue to adhere, provided no change shall occur which, in the judgment of the competent authorities of this Government, shall make a corresponding change on the part of the United States indispensable to their security.

The late events in Spain and Portugal show that Europe is still unsettled. Of this important fact no stronger proof can be adduced than that the allied powers should have thought it proper, on any principle satisfactory to themselves, to have interposed by force, in the internal concerns of Spain. To what extent such interposition may be carried, on the same principle, is a question in which all independent powers whose governments differ from theirs are interested, even those most remote, and surely none more so than the United States. Our policy in regard to Europe, which was adopted at an early stage of the wars which have so long agitated that quarter of the globe, nevertheless remains the same, which is, not to interfere in the internal concerns of government for us; to cultivate friendly relations with it, and to any of its powers; to consider the government de facto as the legitimate preserve those relations by a frank, firm, and manly policy, meeting, in all instances, the just claims of every power, submitting to injuries from none. But in regard to these continents, circumstances are eminently and conspicuously different. It is impossible that the allied powers should extend their political system to any portion of either continent without endangering our peace and happiness; nor can anyone believe that our southern brethren, if left to themselves, would adopt it of their own accord. It is equally impossible, therefore, that we should behold such interposition, in any form, with indifference. If we look to the comparative strength and resources of Spain and those new governments, and their distance from each other, it must be obvious that she can never subdue them. It is still the true policy of the United States to leave the parties to themselves, in the hope that other powers will pursue the same course.

The Monroe doctrine finds its recognition in those principles of international law which are based upon the theory that every nation shall have its rights protected and its just claims enforced.

Of course this Government is entirely confident that under the sanction of this doctrine we have clear rights and undoubted claims. Nor is this ignored in the British reply. The prime minister, while not admitting that the Monroe doctrine is applicable to present conditions, states: "In declaring that the United States would resist any such enterprise if it was contemplated, President Monroe adopted a policy which received the entire sympathy of the English Government of that date." He further declares: "Though the language of President Monroe is directed to the attainment of objects which most Englishmen would agree to be salutary, it is impossible to admit that they have been inscribed by any adequate authority in the code of international law." Again he says: "They (Her Majesty's Government) fully concur with the view which President Monroe apparently entertained, that any disturbance of the existing territorial distribution in the hemisphere by any fresh acquisitions on the part of any European state, would be a highly inexpedient change."

In the belief that the doctrine for which we contend was clear and definite, that it was founded upon substantial considerations and involved our safety and welfare, that it was fully applicable to our present conditions and to the state of the world's progress and that it was directly related to the pending controversy and without any conviction as to the final merits of the dispute, but anxious to learn in a satisfactory and conclusive manner whether Great Britain sought, under a claim of boundary, to extend her possessions on this continent without right, or whether she merely sought possession of territory fairly included within her lines of ownership, this Government proposed to the Government of Great Britain a resort to arbitration as the proper means of settling the question to the end that a vexatious boundary dispute between the two contestants might be determined and our exact standing and relation in respect to the controversy might be made clear.

It will be seen from the correspondence herewith submitted that this proposition has been declined by the British Government, upon grounds which in the circumstances seem to me to be far from satisfactory. It is deeply disappointing that such an appeal actuated by the most friendly feelings towards both nations directly concerned, addressed to the sense of justice and to the magnanimity of one of the great powers of the world and touching its relations to one comparatively weak and small, should have produced no better results.

The course to be pursued by this Government in view of the present condition does not appear to admit of serious doubt. Having labored faithfully for many years to induce Great Britain to submit this dispute to impartial arbitration, and having been now finally apprized of her refusal to do so, nothing remains but to accept the situation, to recognize its plain requirements and deal with it accordingly. Great Britain's present proposition has never thus far been regarded as admissible by Venezuela, though any adjustment of the boundary which that country may deem for her advantage and may enter into of her own free will can not of course be objected to by the United States.

Assuming, however, that the attitude of Venezuela will remain unchanged, the dispute has reached such a stage as to make it now incumbent upon the United States to take measures to determine with sufficient certainty for its justification what is the true divisional line between the Republic of Venezuela and British Guiana. The inquiry to that end should of course be conducted carefully and judicially and due weight should be given to all available evidence records and facts in support of the claims of both parties.

In order that such an examination should be prosecuted in a thorough and satisfactory manner I suggest that the Congress make an adequate appropriation for the expenses of a commission, to be appointed by the Executive, who shall make the necessary investigation and report upon the matter with the least possible delay. When such report is made and accepted it will in my opinion be the duty of the United States to resist by every means in its power as a willful aggression upon its rights and interests the appropriation by Great Britain of any lands or the exercise of governmental jurisdiction over any territory which after investigation we have determined of right belongs to Venezuela.

In making these recommendations I am fully alive to the responsibility incurred, and keenly realize all the consequences that may follow.

I am nevertheless firm in my conviction that while it is a grievous thing to contemplate the two great English-speaking peoples of the world as being otherwise than friendly competitors in the onward march of civilization, and strenuous and worthy rivals in all the arts of peace, there is no calamity which a great nation can invite which equals that which follows a supine submission to wrong and injustice and the consequent loss of national self-respect and honor beneath which are shielded and defended a people's safety and greatness.

Period of the "Roosevelt Corollary"

ANNUAL MESSAGE from President Theodore Roosevelt to the United States Congress, December 3, 1901:

. . .MORE AND MORE the civilized peoples are realizing the wicked folly of war and are attaining that condition of just and intelligent regard for the rights of others which will in the end, as we hope and believe, make world-wide peace possible. The peace conference at The Hague gave definite expression to this hope and belief and marked a stride toward their attainment.

This same peace conference acquiesced in our statement of the Monroe doctrine as compatible with the purposes and aims of the conference.

The Monroe doctrine should be the cardinal feature of the foreign policy of all the nations of the two Americas, as it is of the United States. Just seventy-eight years have passed since President Monroe in his Annual Message announced that "The American continents are henceforth not to be considered as subjects for future colonization by any European power." In other words, the Monroe doctrine is a declaration that there must be no territorial aggrandizement by any non-American power at the expense of any American power or American soil. It is in no wise intended as hostile to any nation in the Old World. Still less is it intended to give cover to any aggression by one New World power at the expense of any other. It is simply a step, and a long step, toward assuring the universal peace of the world by securing the possibility of permanent peace on this hemisphere.

During the past century other influences have established the permanence and independence of the smaller states of Europe. Through the Monroe doctrine we hope to be able to safeguard like independence and secure like permanence for the lesser among the New World nations.

This doctrine has nothing to do with the commercial relations of any American power, save that it in truth allows each of them to form such as it desires. In other words, it is really a guaranty of the commercial independence of the Americans. We do not ask under this doctrine for any exclusive commercial dealings with any other American state. We do not guarantee any state against punishment if it misconducts itself, provided that punishment does not take the form of the acquisition of territory by any non-American power.

Our attitude in Cuba is a sufficient guaranty of our own good faith. We have not the slightest desire to secure any territory at the expense of any of our neighbors. We wish to work with them hand in hand, so that all of us may be uplifted together, and we rejoice over the good fortune of any of them, we gladly hail their material prosperity and political stability, and are concerned and alarmed if any of them fall into industrial or political chaos. We do not wish to see any Old World military power grow up on this continent, or to be compelled to become a military power ourselves. The peoples of the Americas can prosper best if left to work out their own salvation in their own way.

Our people intend to abide by the Monroe doctrine and to insist upon it as the one sure means of securing peace of the Western Hemisphere. The Navy offers us the only means of making our insistence upon the Monroe doctrine anything but a subject of derision to whatever nation chooses to disregard it. We desire the peace which comes as of right to the just man armed; not the peace granted-on terms of ignominy to the craven and the weakling. . . .

ANNUAL MESSAGE from President Theodore Roosevelt to the United States Congress, December 2, 1902:

. . .THE CANAL Will be of great benefit to America, and of importance to all the world. It will be of advantage to us industrially and also as improving our military position. It will be of advantage to the countries of tropical America. It is earnestly to be hoped that all of these countries will do as some of them have already done with signal success, and will invite to their shores commerce and improve their material condition by recognizing that stability and order are the prerequisites of our successful development. No independent nation in America need have the slightest fear of aggression from the United States. It behooves each one to maintain order within its own borders and to discharge its just obligations to foreigners. When this is done, they can rest assured that, be they strong or weak, they have nothing to dread from outside interference. More and more the increasing interdependence and complexity of international political and economic relations render it incumbent on all civilized and orderly powers to insist on the proper policing of the world. . . .

ADDRESS by President Theodore Roosevelt at Chicago, April 2, 1903:

I BELIEVE in the Monroe Doctrine with all my heart and soul; I am convinced that the immense majority of our fellow-countrymen so believe in it; but I would infinitely prefer to see us abandon it than to see us put it forward and bluster about it, and yet fail to build up the efficient fighting strength which in the last resort can alone make it respected by any strong foreign power whose interest it may ever happen to be to violate it.

There is a homely old adage which runs: "Speak softly and carry a big stick; you will go far." If the American nation will speak softly and yet build and keep at a pitch of the highest training a thoroughly efficient navy the Monroe Doctrine will go far.

ANNUAL MESSAGE from President Theodore Roosevelt to the United States Congress, December 6, 1904:

IT IS NOT TRUE that the United States feels any land hunger or entertains any projects as regards the other nations of the Western Hemisphere save such as are for their welfare. All that this country desires is to see the neighboring countries stable, orderly, and prosperous. Any country whose people conduct themselves well can count upon our hearty friendship. If a nation shows that it knows how to act with reasonable efficiency and decency in social and political matters, if it keeps order and pays its obligations, it need fear no interference from the United States. Chronic wrongdoing, or an impotence which results in a general loosening of the ties of civilized society, may in America, as elsewhere, ultimately require intervention by some civilized nation, and in the Western Hemisphere the adherence of the United States to the Monroe Doctrine may force the United States, however reluctantly, in flagrant cases of such wrongdoing or impotence, to the exercise of an international police power. If every country washed by the Caribbean Sea would show the progress in stable and just civilization which with the aid of the Platt amendment Cuba has shown since our troops left the island, and which so many of the republics in both Americas are constantly and brilliantly showing, all question of interference by this Nation with their affairs would be at an end. Our interests and those of our southern neighbors are in reality identical. They have great natural riches, and if within their borders the reign of law and justice obtains, prosperity is sure

to come to them. While they thus obey the primary laws of civilized society they may rest assured that they will be treated by us in a spirit of cordial and helpful sympathy. We would interfere with them only in the last resort, and then only if it became evident that their inability or unwillingness to do justice at home and abroad had violated the rights of the United States or had invited foreign aggression to the detriment of the entire body of American nations. It is a mere truism to say that every nation, whether in America or anywhere else, which desires to maintain its freedom, its independence, must ultimately realize that the right of such independence can not be separated from the responsibility of making good use of it.

In asserting the Monroe Doctrine, in taking such steps as we have taken in regard to Cuba, Venezuela, and Panama, and in endeavoring to circumscribe the theater of war in the Far East, and to secure the open door in China, we have acted in our own interest as well as in the interest of humanity at large.

ANNUAL MESSAGE from President Theodore Roosevelt to the United States Congress, December 5, 1905:

ONE OF THE MOST effective instruments for peace is the Monroe Doctrine as it has been and is being gradually developed by this Nation and accepted by other nations. No other policy could have been as efficient in promoting peace in the Western Hemisphere and in giving to each nation thereon the chance to develop along its own lines. If we had refused to apply the Doctrine to changing conditions it would now be completely outworn, would not meet any of the needs of the present day, and indeed would probably by this time have sunk into complete oblivion. It is useful at home, and is meeting with recognition abroad, because we have adapted our application of it to meet the growing and changing needs of the Hemisphere. When we announce a policy, such as the Monroe Doctrine, we thereby commit ourselves to the consequences of the policy, and those consequences from time to time alter. It is out of the question to claim a right and yet shirk the responsibility for its exercise. Not only we, but all American Republics who are benefitted by the existence of the Doctrine, must recognize the obligations each nation is under as regards foreign peoples no less than its duty to insist upon its own rights.

That our rights and interests are deeply concerned in the maintenance of the Doctrine is so clear as hardly to need argument. This is especially true in view of the construction of the Panama Canal. As a mere matter of self-defense we must exercise a close watch over the approaches to this canal; and this means that we must be thoroughly alive to our interests in the Caribbean Sea.

There are certain essential points which must never be forgotten as regards the Monroe Doctrine. In the first place we must as a nation make it evident that we do not intend to treat it in any shape or way as an excuse for aggrandizement on our part at the expense of the republics to the south. We must recognize the fact that in some South American countries there has been much suspicion lest we should interpret the Monroe Doctrine as in some way inimical to their interests, and we must try to convince all the other nations of this continent once and for all that no just and orderly government has anything to fear from us. There are certain republics to the south of us which have already reached such a point of stability, order, and prosperity that they themselves, though as yet hardly consciously, are among the guarantors of this Doctrine. These republics we now meet not only on a basis of entire equality, but in a spirit of frank and respectful friendship which we hope is mutual. If all of the republics to the south of us will only grow as those to which I allude have already grown, all need for us to be the especial champions of the Doctrine will disappear, for no stable and growing American Republic wishes to see some great non-American military power acquire territory in its neighborhood. All that this country desires is that the other republics on this Continent shall be happy and prosperous; and they can not be happy and prosperous unless they maintain order within their boundaries and behave with a just regard for their obligations toward outsiders. It must be understood that under no circumstances will the United States use the Monroe Doctrine as a cloak for territorial aggression. We desire peace with all the world, but perhaps most of all with the other peoples of the American Continent. There are of course limits to the wrongs which any self-respecting nation can endure. It is always possible that wrong actions toward this Nation, or toward citizens of this Nation, in some State unable to keep order among its own people, unable to secure justice from outsiders, and unwilling to do justice to those outsiders who treat it well, may result in our having to take action to protect our rights; but such action will not be taken with a view to territorial aggression, and it will be taken at all only with extreme reluctance and when it has become evident that every other resource has been exhausted.

Moreover, we must make it evident that we do not intend to permit the Monroe Doctrine to be used by any nation on this Continent as a shield to protect it from the consequences of its own misdeeds against foreign nations. If a republic to the south of us commits a tort against a foreign nation, such as an outrage against a citizen of that nation, then the Monroe Doctrine does not force us to interfere to prevent punishment of the tort, save to see that the punishment does not assume the form of territorial occupation in any shape. The case is more difficult when it refers to a contractual obligation. Our own Government has always refused to enforce such contractual obligations on behalf of its citizens by an appeal to arms. It is much to be wished that all foreign governments would take the same view. But they do not; and in consequence we are liable at any time to be brought face to face with disagreeable alternatives. On the one hand, this country would certainly decline to go to war to prevent a foreign government from collecting a just debt; on the other hand, it is very inadvisable to permit any foreign power to take possession, even temporarily, of the customhouses of an American Republic in order to enforce the payment of its obligations; for such temporary occupation might turn into a permanent occupation. The only escape from these alternatives may at any time be that we must ourselves undertake to bring about some arrangement by which so much as possible of a just obligation shall be paid. It is far better that this country should put through such an arrangement, rather than allow any foreign country to undertake it. To do so insures the defaulting republic from having to pay debts of an improper character under duress, while it also insures honest creditors of the republic from being passed by in the interest of dishonest or grasping creditors. Moreover, for the United States to take such a position offers the only possible way of insuring us against a clash with some foreign power. The position is, therefore, in the interest of peace as well as in the interest of justice. It is of benefit to our people; it is of benefit to foreign peoples; and most of all it is really of benefit to the people of the country concerned.

This brings me to what should be one of the fundamental objects of the Monroe Doctrine. We must ourselves in good faith try to help upward toward peace and order those of our sister republics which need such help. Just as there has been a gradual growth of the ethical element in the relations of one individual to another, so we are, even though slowly, more and more coming to recognize the duty of bearing one another's burdens, not only as among individuals, but also as among nations.

ANNUAL MESSAGE from President Theodore Roosevelt to the United States Congress, December 3, 1906:

. . .LAST AUGUST an insurrection broke out in Cuba which it speedily grew evident that the existing Cuban Government was powerless to quell. This Government was repeatedly asked by the then Cuban Government to intervene, and finally was notified by the President of Cuba that he intended to resign; that his decision was irrevocable; that none of the other constitutional officers would consent to carry on the Government, and that he was powerless to maintain order. It was evident that chaos was impending, and there was every probability that if steps were not immediately taken by this Government to try to restore order, the representatives of various European nations in the island would apply to their respective governments for armed intervention in order to protect the lives and property of their citizens. Thanks to the preparedness of our Navy, I was able immediatry of War and the Assistant Secretary of State, in order that they becoming hopeless; and I furthermore dispatched to Cuba the Secreately to send enough ships to Cuba to prevent the situation from might grapple with the situation on the ground. All efforts to secure an agreement between the contending factions, by which they should themselves come to an amicable understanding and settle upon some modus vivendi-some provisional government of their own-failed. Finally the President of the Republic resigned. The quorum of Congress assembled failed by deliberate purpose of its members, so that there was no power to act on his resignation, and the Government came to a halt. In accordance with the so-called Platt amendment, which was embodied in the constitution of Cuba, I thereupon proclaimed a provisional government for the island, the Secretary of War acting as provisional governor until he could be replaced by Mr. Magoon, the late minister to Panama and governor of the Canal Zone on the Isthmus; troops were sent to support them and to relieve the Navy, the expedition being handled with most satisfactory speed and efficiency. The insurgent chiefs immediately agreed that their troops should lay down their arms and disband; and the agreement was carried out. The provisional government has left the personnel of the old government and the old laws, so far as might be, unchanged, and will thus administer the island for a few months until tranquillity can be restored, a new election properly held, and a new government inaugurated. Peace has come in the island; and the harvesting of the sugar-cane crop, the great crop of the Island, is about to proceed.

When the election has been held and the new government inaugurated in peaceful and orderly fashion the provisional government will come to an end. I take this opportunity of expressing upon behalf of the American people, with all possible solemnity, our most earnest hope that the people of Cuba will realize the imperative need of preserving justice and keeping order in the Island. The United States wishes nothing of Cuba except that it shall prosper morally and materially, and wishes nothing of the Cubans save that they shall be able to preserve order among themselves and therefore to preserve their independence. If the elections become a farce, and if the insurrectionary habit becomes confirmed in the Island, it is absolutely out of the question that the Island should continue independent; and the United States, which has assumed the sponsorship before the civilized world for Cuba's career as a nation, would again have to intervene and to see that the government was managed in such orderly fashion as to secure the safety of life and property. The path to be trodden by those who exercise self-government is always hard, and we should have every charity and patience with the Cubans as they tread this difficult path. I have the utmost sympathy with, and regard for, them; but I most earnestly adjure them solemnly to weigh their responsibilities and to see that when their new government is started it shall run smoothly, and with freedom from flagrant denial of right on the one hand, and from insurrectionary disturbances on the other. . . .

ADDRESS by President Woodrow Wilson at San Francisco, September 17, 1919:

. . .I WANT TO SAY again that Article X is the very heart of the Covenant of the League, because all the great wrongs of the world have had their root in the seizure of territory or the control of the political independence of other peoples. I believe that I speak the feeling of the people of the United States when I say that, having seen one great wrong like that attempted and having prevented it, we are ready to prevent it again.

Those are the two principal criticisms, that we did not do the impossible with regard to Shantung and that we may be advised to go to war. That is all there is in either of those. But they say, "We want the Monroe Doctrine more distinctly acknowledged." Well, if I could have found language that was more distinct than that used, I should have been very happy to suggest it, but it says in so many words that nothing in that document shall be construed as affecting the validity of the Monroe Doctrine. I do not see what more it could say, but, as I say, if the clear can be clarified, I have no objection to its being clarified. The meaning is too obvious to admit of discussion, and I want you to realize how extraordinary that provision is. Every nation in the world had been jealous of the Monroe Doctrine, had studiously avoided doing or saying anything that would admit its validity, and here all the great nations of the world sign a document which admits its validity. That constitutes nothing less than a moral revolution in the attitude of the rest of the world toward America.

What does the Monroe Doctrine mean in that Covenant? It means that with regard to aggressions upon the Western Hemisphere we are at liberty to act without waiting for other nations to act. That is the Monroe Doctrine. The Monroe Doctrine says that if anybody tries to interfere with affairs in the Western Hemisphere it will be regarded as an unfriendly act to the United States-not to the rest of the world-and that means that the United States will look after it, and will not ask anybody's permission to look after it. The document says that nothing in this document must be construed as interfering with that. . . .

✸PEACE, FRIENDSHIP, LIMITS, AND SETTLEMENT: TREATY OF GUADALUPE HIDALGO 1848

In the name of Almighty God:

The United States of America and the United Mexican States, animated by a sincere desire to put an end to the calamities of the war which unhappily exists between the two Republics, and to establish upon a solid basis relations of peace and friendship, which shall confer reciprocal benefits upon the citizens of both, and assure the concord, harmony and mutual confidence, wherein the two Peoples should live, as good Neighbors, have for that purpose appointed their respective Plenipotentiaries: that is to say, the President of the United States has appointed Nicholas P. Trist, a citizen of the United States, and the President of the Mexican Republic has appointed Don Luis Gonzaga Cuevas, Don Bernardo Couto, and Don Miguel Atristain, citizens of the said Republic; who, after a reciprocal communication of their respective full powers, have, under the protection of Almighty God, the author of Peace, arranged, agreed upon, and signed the following TREATY OF PEACE, FRIENDSHIP, LIMITS AND SETTLEMENT BETWEEN THE UNITED STATES OF AMERICA AND THE MEXICAN REPUBLIC

Article I

There shall be firm and universal peace between the United States of America and the Mexican Republic, and between their respective Countries, territories, cities, towns and people, without exception of places or persons.

Article II

Immediately upon the signature of this Treaty, a convention shall be entered into between a Commissioner or Commissioners appointed by the General in Chief of the forces of the United States, and such as may be appointed by the Mexican Government, to the end that a provisional suspension of hostilities shall take place, and that, in the places occupied by the said forces, constitutional order may be reestablished, as regards the political, administrative and judicial branches, so far as this shall be permitted by the circumstances of military occupation.

Article III

Immediately upon the ratification of the present treaty by the Government of the United States, orders shall be transmitted to the Commanders of their land and naval forces, requiring the latter, (provided this Treaty shall then have been ratified by the Government of the Mexican Republic and the ratifications exchanged) immediately to desist from blockading any Mexican ports; and requiring the former (under the same condition) to commence at the earliest moment practicable, withdrawing all troops of the United States then in the interior of the Mexican Republic, to points, that shall be selected by common agreement, at a distance from the sea-ports, not exceeding thirty leagues; and such evacuation of the interior of the Republic shall be completed with the least possible delay: the Mexican Government hereby binding itself to afford every facility in its power for rendering the same convenient to the troops, on their march and in their new positions, and for promoting a good understanding between them and the inhabitants. In like manner, orders shall be despatched to the persons in charge of the custom houses at all ports occupied by the forces of the United States, requiring them (under the same condition) immediately to deliver possession of the same to the persons authorized by the Mexican Government to receive it, together with all bonds and evidences of debt for duties on importations and on exportations, not yet fallen due. Moreover, a faithful and exact account shall be made out, showing the entire amount of all duties on imports and on exports, collected at such Custom Houses, or elsewhere in Mexico, by authority of the United States, from and after the day of ratification of this Treaty by the Government of the Mexican Republic; and also an account of the cost of collection; and such entire amount, deducting only the cost of collection, shall be delivered to the Mexican Government, at the City of Mexico, within three months after the exchange of ratifications.

The evacuation of the Capital of the Mexican Republic by the troops of the United States, in virtue of the above stipulation, shall be completed in one month after the orders there stipulated for shall have been received by the commander of said troops, or sooner if possible.

Article IV

Immediately after the exchange of ratifications of the present treaty, all castles, forts, territories, places and possessions, which have been taken or occupied by the forces of the United States during the present war, within the limits of the Mexican Republic, as about to he established by the following Article, shall be definitively restored to the said Republic, together with all the artillery, arms, apparatus of war, munitions, and other public property, which were in the said castles and forts when captured, and which shall remain there at the time when this treaty shall be duly ratified by the Government of the Mexican Republic. To this end, immediately upon the signature of this treaty, orders shall be despatched to the American officers commanding such castles and forts, securing against the removal or destruction of any such artillery, arms, apparatus of war, munitions, or other public property. The city of Mexico, within the inner line of entrenchments surrounding the said city, is comprehended in the above stipulations, as regards the restoration of artillery, apparatus of war, &c. The final evacuation of the territory of the Mexican Republic, by the forces of the United States, shall he completed in three months from the said exchange of ratifications, or sooner, if possible: the Mexican Government hereby engaging, as in the foregoing Article, to use all means in its power for facilitating such evacuation, and rendering it convenient to the troops, and for promoting a good understanding between them and the inhabitants.

If, however, the ratification of this treaty by both parties should not take place in time to allow the embarkation of the troops of the United States to be completed before the commencement of the sickly season, at the Mexican ports on the Gulf of Mexico; in such case a friendly arrangement shall be entered into between the General in Chief of the said troops and the Mexican Government, whereby healthy and otherwise suitable places at a distance from the ports not exceeding thirty leagues shall be designated for the residence of such troops as may not yet have embarked, until the return of the healthy season. And the space of time here referred to, as comprehending the sickly season, shall be understood to extend from the first day of May to the first day of November.

All prisoners of war taken on either side, on land or on sea, shall be restored as soon as practicable after the exchange of ratifications of this treaty. It is also agreed that if any Mexicans should now be held as captives by any savage tribe within the limits of the United States, as about to be established by the following Article, the Government of the said United States will exact the release of such captives, and cause them to be restored to their country.

Article V

The Boundary line between the two Republics shall commence in the Gulf of Mexico, three leagues from land, opposite the mouth of the Rio Grande, otherwise called Rio Bravo del Norte, or opposite the mouth of it's deepest branch, if it should have more than one branch emptying directly into the sea; from thence, up the middle of that river, following the deepest channel, where it has more than one to the point where it strikes the Southern boundary of New Mexico; thence, westwardly along the whole Southern Boundary of New Mexico (which runs north of the town called Paso) to it's western termination; thence, northward, along the western line of New Mexico, until it intersects the first branch of the river Gila; (or if it should not intersect any branch of that river, then, to the point on the said line nearest to such branch, and thence in a direct line to the same;) thence down the middle of the said branch and of the said river, until it empties into the Rio Colorado; thence, across the Rio Colorado, following the division line between Upper and Lower California, to the Pacific Ocean.

The southern and western limits of New Mexico, mentioned in this Article, are those laid down in the Map, entitled "Map of the United Mexican States, as organized and defined by various acts of the Congress of said Republic, and constructed according to the best authorities. Revised edition. Published at New York in 1847 by J. Disturnell:" Of which Map a Copy is added to this Treaty, bearing the signatures and seals of the Undersigned Plenipotentiaries. And, in order to preclude all difficulty in tracing upon the ground the limit separating Upper from Lower California, it is agreed that the said limit shall consist of a straight line, drawn from the middle of the Rio Gila, where it unites with the Colorado, to a point on the Coast of the Pacific Ocean, distant one marine league due south of the southernmost point of the Port of San Diego, according to the plan of said port, made in the year 1782, by Don Juan Pantoja, second sailing-master of the Spanish fleet, and published at Madrid in the year 1802, in the Atlas to the voyage of the schooners *Sutil* and *Mexicana*: of which plan a Copy is hereunto added, signed and sealed by the respective Plenipotentiaries.

In order to designate the Boundary line with due precision, upon authoritative maps, and to establish upon the ground landmarks which shall show the limits of both Republics, as described in the present Article, the two Governments shall each appoint a Commissioner and a Surveyor, who, before the expiration of one year from the date of the exchange of ratifications of this treaty, shall meet at the Port of San Diego, and proceed to run and mark the said

Boundary in its whole course to the mouth of the Rio Bravo del Norte. They shall keep journals and make out plans of their operations; and the result, agreed upon by them, shall be deemed a part of this treaty, and shall have the same force as if it were inserted therein. The two Governments will amicably agree regarding what may be necessary to these persons, and also as to their respective escorts, should such be necessary.

The Boundary line established by this Article shall be religiously respected by each of the two Republics, and no change shall ever be made therein, except by the express and free consent of both nations, lawfully given by the General Government of each, in conformity with its own constitution.

Article VI

The vessels and citizens of the United States shall, in all time, have a free and uninterrupted passage by the Gulf of California, and by the river Colorado below its confluence with the Gila, to and from their possessions situated north of the Boundary line defined in the preceding Article: it being understood that this passage is to be by navigating the Gulf of California and the river Colorado, and not by land, without the express consent of the Mexican Government.

If, by the examinations which may be made, it should be ascertained to be practicable and advantageous to construct a road, canal or railway, which should, in whole or in part, run upon the river Gila, or upon its right or its left bank, within the space of one marine league from either margin of the river, the Governments of both Republics will form an agreement regarding its construction, in order that it may serve equally for the use and advantage of both countries.

Article VII

The river Gila, and the part of the Rio Bravo del Norte lying below the southern boundary of New Mexico, being, agreeably to the fifth Article, divided in the middle between the two Republics, the navigation of the Gila and of the Bravo below said boundary shall be free and common to the vessels and citizens of both countries; and neither shall, without the consent of the other, construct any work that may impede or interrupt, in whole or in part, the exercise of this right: not even for the purpose of favoring new methods of navigation. Nor shall any tax or contribution, under any denomination or title, be levied upon vessels or persons navigating the same, or upon merchandise or effects transported thereon, except in the case of landing upon one of their shores. If, for the purpose of making the said rivers navigable, or for maintaining them in such state, it should be necessary or advantageous to establish any tax or contribution, this shall not be done without the consent of both Governments.

The stipulations contained in the present Article shall not impair the territorial rights of either Republic, within its established limits.

Article VIII

Mexicans now established in territories previously belonging to Mexico, and which remain for the future within the limits of the United States, as defined by the present Treaty, shall be free to continue where they now reside or to remove at any time to the Mexican Republic, retaining the property which they possess in the said territories, or disposing thereof and removing the proceeds wherever they please; without their being subjected, on the account, to any contribution, tax or charge whatever.

Those who shall prefer to remain in the said territories, may either retain the title and rights of Mexican citizens, or acquire those of citizens of the United States. But, they shall be under the obligation to make their election within one year from the date of the exchange of ratifications of this treaty: and those who shall remain in the said territories, after the expiration of that year, without having declared their intention to retain the character of Mexicans, shall be considered to have elected to become citizens of the United States.

In the said territories, property of every kind, now belonging to Mexicans not established there, shall be inviolably respected. The present owners, the heirs of these, and all Mexicans who may hereafter acquire said property by contract, shall enjoy with respect to it, guaranties equally ample as if the same belonged to citizens of the United States.

Article IX

The Mexicans who, in the territories aforesaid, shall not preserve the character of citizens of the Mexican Republic, conformably with what is stipulated in the preceding article, shall be incorporated into the Union of the United States and be admitted, at the proper time (to be judged of by the Congress of the United States) to the enjoyment of all the rights of citizens of the United States according to the principles of the Constitution; and in the mean time shall be maintained and protected in the free enjoyment of their liberty and property, and secured in the free exercise of their religion without restriction.

Article X

All grants of land made by the Mexican Government or by the competent authorities, in territories previously appertaining to Mexico, and remaining for the future within the limits of the United States, shall be respected as valid, to the same extent that the same grants would be valid, if the said territories had remained within the limits of Mexico. But the grantees of lands in Texas, put in possession thereof, who, by reason of the circumstances of the country since the beginning of the troubles between Texas and the Mexican Government, may have been prevented from fulfilling all the conditions of their grants, shall be under the obligation to fulfill the said conditions within the periods limited in the same respectively; such periods to be now counted from the date of the exchange of ratifications of this treaty: in default of which the said grants shall not be obligatory upon the State of Texas, in virtue of the stipulations contained in this Article.

The foregoing stipulation in regard to grantees of land in Texas, is extended to all grantees of land in the territories aforesaid, elsewhere than in Texas, put in possession under such grants; and, in default of the fulfillment of the conditions of any such grant, within the new period, which as is above stipulated, begins with the day of the exchange of ratifications of this treaty, the same shall be null and void.

The Mexican Government declares that no grant whatever of lands in Texas has been made since the second day of March one thousand eight hundred and thirty six; and that no grant whatever of lands in any of the territories aforesaid has been made since the thirteenth day of May one thousand eight hundred and forty-six.

Article XI

Considering that a great part of the territories which by the present treaty are to be comprehended for the future within the limits of the United States, is now occupied by savage tribes, who will hereafter be under the exclusive control of the Government of the United States, and whose incursions within the territory of Mexico would be prejudicial in the extreme; it is solemnly agreed that all such incursions shall be forcibly restrained by the Government of the United States, whensoever this may be necessary; and that when they cannot be prevented, they shall be punished by the said Government, and satisfaction for the same shall be exacted: all in the same way, and with equal diligence and energy, as if the same incursions were meditated or committed within its own territory against its own citizens.

It shall not be lawful, under any pretext whatever, for any inhabitant of the United States, to purchase or acquire any Mexican or any foreigner residing in Mexico, who may have been captured by Indians inhabiting the territory of either of the two Republics; nor to purchase or acquire horses, mules, cattle or property of any kind, stolen within Mexican territory by such Indians;

And, in the event of any person or persons, captured within Mexican territory by Indians, being carried into the territory of the United States, the Government of the latter engages and binds itself, in the most solemn manner, so soon as it shall know of such captives being within its territory, and shall be able so to do, through the faithful exercise of its influence and power, to rescue them, and return them to their country, or deliver them to the agent or representative of the Mexican Government. The Mexican Authorities will, as far as practicable, give to the Government of the United States notice of such captures; and its agent shall pay the expenses incurred in the maintenance and transmission of the rescued captives; who, in the mean time, shall be treated with the utmost hospitality by the American Authorities at the place where they may be. But if the Government of the United States, before receiving such notice from Mexico, should obtain intelligence through any other channel, of the existence of Mexican captives within its territory, it will proceed forthwith to effect their release and delivery to the Mexican agent, as above stipulated.

For the purpose of giving to these stipulations the fullest possible efficacy, thereby affording the security and redress demanded by their true spirit and intent, the Government of the United States will now and hereafter pass, without unnecessary delay, and always vigilantly enforce, such laws as the nature of the subject may require. And finally, the sacredness of this obligation shall never be lost sight of by the said Government, when providing for the removal of the Indians from any portion of the said territories, or for its being settled by citizens of the United States; but on the contrary, special care shall then be taken not to place its Indian occupants under the necessity of seeking new homes, by committing those invasions which the United States have solemnly obliged themselves to restrain.

Article XII

In consideration of the extension acquired by the boundaries of the United States, as defined in the fifth Article of the present treaty, the Government of the United States engages to pay to that of the Mexican Republic the sum of fifteen Millions of Dollars.

Immediately after this Treaty shall have been duly ratified by the Government of the Mexican Republic, the sum of three Millions of Dollars shall be paid to the said Government by that of the United States at the City of Mexico, in the gold or silver coin of Mexico. The remaining twelve millions of dollars shall be paid at the same place, and in the same coin, in annual installments of three Millions of Dollars each, together with interest on the same at the rate of six per centrum per annum. This interest shall begin to run upon the whole sum of twelve millions, from the day of the ratification of the present treaty by the Mexican Government, and the first of the installments shall be paid at the expiration of one year from the same day. Together with each annual instalment, as it falls due, the whole interest accruing on such instalment from the beginning shall also be paid.

Article XIII

The United States engage moreover, to assume and pay to the claimants all the amounts now due them, and those hereafter to become due, by reason of the claims already liquidated and decided against the Mexican Republic, under the conventions between the two Republics, severally concluded on the eleventh day of April eighteen hundred and thirty nine, and on the thirtieth day of January eighteen hundred and forty three: so that the Mexican Republic shall be absolutely exempt for the future, from all expense whatever old account of the said claims.

Article XIV

The United States do furthermore discharge the Mexican Republic from all claims of citizens of the United States, not heretofore decided against the Mexican Government, which may have arisen previously to the date of the signature of this treaty: which discharge shall be final and perpetual, whether the said claims be rejected or be allowed by the Board of Commissioners provided for in the following Article, and whatever shall be the total amount of those allowed.

Article XV

The United States, exonerating Mexico from all demands on account of the claims of their citizens mentioned in the preceding Article, and considering them entirely and forever canceled, whatever their amount may be, undertake to make satisfaction for the same, to an amount not exceeding three and one quarter millions of dollars. To ascertain the validity and amount of those claims, a Board of Commissioners shall be established by the Government of the United States, whose awards shall be final and conclusive: provided that in deciding upon the validity of each claim, the board shall be guided and governed by the principles and rules of decision described by the first and fifth Articles of the unratified convention, concluded at the city of Mexico on the twentieth day of November one thousand eight hundred and forty-three; and in no case shall an award be made in favor of any claim not embraced by these principles and rules.

If, in the opinion of the said Board of Commissioners, or of the claimants, any books, records or documents in the possession or power of the Government of the Mexican Republic, shall be deemed necessary to the just decision of any claim, the Commissioners or the claimants, through them, shall, within such period as Congress may designate, make an application in writing for the same, addressed to the Mexican Minister for Foreign Affairs, to be transmitted by the Secretary of State of the United States; and the Mexican Government engages, at the earliest possible moment after the receipt of such demand, to cause any of the books, records or documents, so specified, which shall be in their possession or power, (or authenticated copies or extracts of the same) to be transmitted to the said Secretary of State, who shall immediately deliver them over to the said Board of Commissioners: *Provided* That no such application shall be made, by, or at the instance of, any claimant, until the facts which it is expected to prove by such books, records or documents, shall have been stated under oath or affirmation.

Article XVI

Each of the contracting parties reserves to itself the entire right to fortify whatever point within its territory, it may judge proper so to fortify, for its security.

Article XVII

The Treaty of Amity, Commerce and Navigation, concluded at the City of Mexico on the fifth day of April A.D. 1831, between the United States of America and the United Mexican States, except the additional Article, and except so far as the stipulations of the said treaty may be incompatible with any stipulation contained in the present treaty, is hereby revived for the period of eight years from the day of the exchange of ratifications of this treaty, with the same force and virtue as if incorporated therein; it being understood that each of the contracting parties reserves to itself the right, at any time after the said period of eight years shall have expired, to terminate the same by giving one year's notice of such intention to the other party.

Article XVIII

All supplies whatever for troops of the United States in Mexico, arriving at ports in the occupation of such troops, previous to the final evacuation thereof, although subsequently to the restoration of the Custom Houses at such ports, shall be entirely exempt from duties and charges of any kind: the Government of the United States hereby engaging and pledging its faith to establish and vigilantly to enforce, all possible guards for securing the revenue of Mexico, by preventing the importation, under cover of this stipulation, of any articles, other than such, both in kind and in quantity, as shall really be wanted for the use and consumption of the forces of the United States during the time they may remain in Mexico. To this end, it shall be the duty of all officers and agents of the United States to denounce to the Mexican Authorities at the respective ports, any attempts at a fraudulent abuse of this stipulation, which they may know of or may have reason to suspect, and to give to such Authorities all the aid in their power with regard thereto: and every such attempt, when duly proved and established by sentence of a competent tribunal, shall be punished by the confiscation of the property so attempted to be fraudulently introduced.

Article XIX

With respect to all merchandise, effects and property whatsoever, imported into ports of Mexico, whilst in the occupation of the forces of the United States, whether by citizens of either republic, or by citizens or subjects of any neutral nation, the following rules shall be observed:

I. All such merchandise, effects and property, if imported previously to the restoration of the Custom Houses to the Mexican Authorities, as stipulated for in the third Article of this treaty, shall be exempt from confiscation, although the importation of the same be prohibited by the Mexican tariff.

II. The same perfect exemption shall be enjoyed by all such merchandise, effects and property, imported subsequently to the restoration of the Custom Houses, and previously to the sixty days fixed in the following Article for the coming into force of the Mexican tariff at such ports respectively: the said merchandise, effects and property being, however, at the time of their importation, subject to the payment of duties as provided for in the said following Article.

III. All merchandise, effects and property, described in the two rules foregoing, shall, during their continuance at the place of importation, and upon their leaving such place for the interior, be exempt from all duty, tax or impost of every kind, under whatsoever title or denomination. Nor shall they be there subjected to any charge whatsoever upon the sale thereof.

IV. All merchandise, effects and property, described in the first and second rules, which shall have been removed to any place in the interior, whilst such place was in the occupation of the forces of the United States, shall, during their continuance therein, be exempt from all tax upon the sale or consumption thereof, and from every kind of impost or contribution, under whatsoever title or denomination.

V. But if any merchandise, effects or property, described in the first and second rules, shall be removed to any place not occupied at the time by the forces of the United States, they shall, upon their introduction into such place, or upon their sale or consumption there, be subject to the same duties which, under the Mexican laws, they would be required to pay in such cases, if they had been imported in time of peace through the Maritime Custom Houses, and had there paid the duties, conformably with the Mexican tariff.

VI. The owners of all merchandise, effects or property, described in the first and second rules, and existing in any port of Mexico, shall have the right to reship the same, exempt from all tax, impost or contribution whatever.

With respect to the metals, or other property, exported from any Mexican port, whilst in the occupation of the forces of the United States, and previously to the restoration of the Custom House at such port, no person shall be required by the Mexican Authorities, whether General or State, to pay any tax, duty or contribution upon any such exportation, or in any manner to account for the same to the said Authorities.

Article XX

Through consideration for the interests of commerce generally, it is agreed, that if less than sixty days should elapse between the date of the signature of this treaty and the restoration of the Custom Houses, conformably with the stipulation in the third Article, in such case, all merchandise, effects and property whatsoever, arriving at the Mexican ports after the restoration of the said Custom Houses, and previously to the expiration of sixty days after the day of the signature of this treaty, shall be admitted to entry; and no other duties shall be levied thereon than the duties established by the tariff found in force at such Custom Houses at the time of the restoration of the same. And to all such merchandise, effects and property, the rules established by the preceding Article shall apply.

Article XXI

If unhappily any disagreement should hereafter arise between the Governments of the two Republics, whether with respect to the interpretation of any stipulation in this treaty, or with respect to any other particular concerning the political or commercial relations of the two Nations, the said Governments, in the name of those Nations, do promise to each other, that they will endeavor, in the most sincere and earnest manner, to settle the differences so arising, and to preserve the state of peace and friendship, in which the two countries are now placing themselves: using, for this end, mutual representations and pacific negotiations. And if, by these means, they should not be enabled to come to an agreement, a resort shall not, on this account, be had to reprisals, aggression or hostility of any kind, by the one Republic against the other, until the Government of that which deems itself aggrieved, shall have maturely considered, in the spirit of peace and good neighborship, whether it would not be better that such difference should be settled by the arbitration of Commissioners appointed on each side, or by that of a friendly nation. And should such course be proposed by either party, it shall be acceded to by the other, unless deemed by it altogether incompatible with the nature of the difference, or the circumstances of the case.

Article XXII

If (which is not to be expected, and which God forbid!) war should unhappily break out between the two Republics, they do now, with a view to such calamity, solemnly pledge themselves to each other and to the world, to observe the following rules: absolutely, where the nature of the subject permits, and as closely as possible in all cases where such absolute observance shall be impossible.

I. The merchants of either Republic, then residing in the other, shall be allowed to remain twelve months (for those dwelling in the interior) and six months (for those dwelling at the sea-ports) to collect their debts and settle their affairs; during which periods they shall enjoy the same protection, and be on the same footing, in all respects, as the citizens or subjects of the most friendly nations; and, at the expiration thereof, or at any time before, they shall have full liberty to depart, carrying off all their effects, without molestation or hinderance: conforming therein to the same laws, which the citizens or subjects of the most friendly nations are required to conform to. Upon the entrance of the armies of either nation into the territories of the other, women and children, ecclesiastics, scholars of every faculty, cultivators of the earth, merchants, artisans, manufac-turers, and fishermen, unarmed and inhabiting unfortified towns, villages or places, and in general all persons whose occupations are for the common subsistence and benefit of mankind, shall be allowed to continue their respective employments, unmolested in their persons. Nor shall their houses or goods be burnt, or otherwise destroyed; nor their cattle taken, nor their fields wasted, by the armed force, into whose power, by the events of war, they may happen to fall; but if the necessity arise to take anything from them for the use of such armed force, the same shall be paid for at an equitable price. All churches, hospitals, schools, colleges, libraries, and other establishments for charitable and beneficent purposes, shall be respected, and all persons connected with the same protected in the discharge of their duties and the pursuit of their vocations.

II. In order that the fate of prisoners of war may be alleviated, all such practices as those of sending them into distant, inclement or unwholesome districts, or crowding them into close and noxious places, shall be studiously avoided. They shall not be confined in dungeons, prison-ships, or prisons; nor be put in irons, or bound, or otherwise restrained in the use of their limbs. The officers shall enjoy liberty on their paroles, within convenient districts, and have comfortable quarters; and the common soldier shall be disposed in cantonments, open and extensive enough for air and exercise, and lodged in barracks as roomy and good as are provided by the party in whose power they are for its own troops. But, if any officer shall break his parole by leaving the district so assigned him, or any other prisoner shall escape from the limits of his cantonment, after they shall have been designated to him, such individual, officer or other prisoner, shall forfeit so much of the benefit of this article as provides for his liberty on parole or in cantonment. And if any officer so breaking his parole, or any common soldier so escaping from the limits assigned him, shall afterwards be found in arms, previously to his being regularly exchanged, the person so offending shall be dealt with according to the established laws of war. The officers shall be daily furnished by the party in whose power they are, with as many rations, and of the same articles as are allowed either in kind or by commutation, to officers of equal rank in its own army; and all others shall be daily furnished with such ration as is allowed to a common soldier in its own service: the value of all which supplies shall, at the close of the war, or at periods to be agreed upon between the respective commanders, be paid by the other party on a mutual adjustment of accounts for the subsistence of prisoners; and such accounts shall not be mingled with or set off against any others, nor the balance due on them be withheld, as a compensation or reprisal for any cause whatever, real or pretended. Each party shall be allowed to keep a commissary of prisoners, appointed by itself, with every cantonment of prisoners, in possession of the other: which commissary shall see the prisoners as often as he pleases; shall be allowed to receive, exempt from all duties or taxes, and to distribute whatever comforts may be sent to them by their friends; and shall be free to transmit his reports in open letters to the party by whom he is employed.

And it is declared that neither the pretence that war dissolves all treaties, nor any other whatever shall be considered as annulling or suspending the solemn covenant contained in this article. On the contrary, the state of war is precisely that for which it is provided; and during which its stipulations are to be as sacredly observed as the most acknowledged obligations under the law of nature or nations.

Article XXIII

This treaty shall be ratified by the President of the United States of America, by and with the advice and consent of the Senate thereof; and by the President of the Mexican Republic, with the previous approbation of its General Congress: and the ratifications shall be exchanged in the City of Washington, or at the seat of government of Mexico, in four months from the date of the signature hereof, or sooner if practicable.

In faith whereof, we, the respective Plenipotentiaries, have signed this Treaty of Peace, Friendship, Limits and Settlement, and have hereunto affixed our seals respectively. Done in Quintuplicate, at the City of Guadalupe Hidalgo, on the second day of February in the year of Our Lord one thousand eight hundred and forty eight.

N. P. TRIST
LUIS G. CUEVAS
BERNARDO COUTO
MIG ATRISTAIN

✳BOUNDARIES: GADSDEN TREATY 1853

In the Name of Almighty God
The Republic of Mexico and the United States of America desiring to remove every cause of disagreement, which might interfere in any manner with the friendship and intercourse between the two Countries; and especially, in respect to the true limits which should be established, when notwithstanding what was covenanted in the Treaty of Guadalupe Hidalgo in the Year 1848, opposite interpretations have been urged, which might give occasion to questions of serious moment: to avoid these, and to strengthen and more firmly maintain the peace,

which happily prevails between the two Republics, the President of the United States has for this purpose, appointed James Gadsden Envoy Extraordinary and Minister Plenipotentiary of the same near the Mexican Government, and the President of Mexico has appointed as Plenipotentiary "ad hoc" His Excellency Don Manuel Diez de Bonilla Cavalier Grand Cross of the National and Distinguished Order of Guadalupe, and Secretary of State and of the Office of Foreign Relations, and Don Jose Salazar Ylarregui and General Mariano Monterde as Scientific Commissioners invested with Full powers for this Negotiation who having communicated their respective Full powers, and finding them in due and proper form, have agreed upon the Articles following.

Article 1

The Mexican Republic agrees to designate the following as her true limits with the United States for the future; Retaining the same dividing line between the two California's, as already defined and established according to the 5th Article of the Treaty of Guadalupe Hidalgo, the limits between the Two Republics shall be as follows: Beginning in the Gulf of Mexico, three leagues from land, opposite the mouth of the Rio Grande as provided in the fifth article of the treaty of Guadalupe Hidalgo, thence as defined in the said article, up the middle of that river to the point where the parallel of 31°47' north latitude crosses the same, thence due west one hundred miles, thence south to the parallel of 31°20' north latitude, thence along the said parallel of 31°20' to the 111th meridian of longitude west of Greenwich, thence in a straight line to a point on the Colorado river twenty english miles below the junction of the Gila and Colorado rivers, thence up the middle of the said river Colorado until it intersects the present line between the United States and Mexico.

For the performance of this portion of the Treaty each of the two Governments shall nominate one Commissioner to the end that, by common consent, the two thus nominated having met in the City of Paso del Norte, three months after the exchange of the ratifications of this Treaty may proceed to survey and mark out upon the land the dividing line stipulated by this article, where it shall not have already been surveyed and established by the Mixed Commission according to the Treaty of Guadalupe keeping a Journal and making proper plans of their operations. For this purpose if they should Judge it is necessary, the contracting Parties shall be at liberty each to unite to its respective Commissioner Scientific or other assistants, such as Astronomers and Surveyors whose concurrence shall not be considered necessary for the settlement and ratification of a true line of division between the two Republics; that line shall be alone established upon which the Commissioners may fix, their consent in this particular being considered decisive and an integral part of this Treaty, without necessity of ulterior ratification or approval, and without room for interpretation of any kind by either of the Parties contracting.

The dividing line thus established shall in all time be faithfully respected by the two Governments without any variation therein, unless of the express and free consent of the two, given in conformity to the principles of the Law of Nations, and in accordance with the Constitution of each country respectively.

In consequence, the stipulation in the 5th Article of the Treaty of Guadalupe upon the Boundary line therein described is no longer of any force, wherein it may conflict with that here established, the said line being considered annulled and abolished wherever it may not coincide with the present, and in the same manner remaining in full force where in accordance with the same.

Article 2

The government of Mexico hereby releases the United States from all liability on account of the obligations contained in the eleventh article of the treaty of Guadalupe Hidalgo, and the said article and the thirty-third article of the treaty of amity, commerce and navigation between the United States of America and the United Mexican States concluded at Mexico, on the fifth day of April, 1831, are hereby abrogated.

Article 3

In consideration of the foregoing stipulations, the government of the United States agrees to pay to the government of Mexico, in the city of New York, the sum of ten millions of dollars, of which seven millions shall be paid immediately upon the exchange of the ratifications of this treaty, and the remaining three millions as soon as the boundary line shall be surveyed, marked, and established.

Article 4

The Provisions of the 6th and 7th Articles of the Treaty of Guadalupe Hidalgo having been rendered nugatory for the most part by the Cession of Territory granted in the First Article of this Treaty, the said Articles are hereby abrogated and annulled and the provisions as herein expressed substituted therefore—The Vessels and Citizens of the United States shall in all Time have free and uninterrupted passage through the Gulf of California to and from their possessions situated North of the Boundary line of the Two Countries. It being understood that this passage is to be by navigating the Gulf of California and the river Colorado, and not by land, without the express consent of the Mexican Government, and precisely the same provisions, stipulations and restrictions in all respects are hereby agreed upon and adopted and shall be scrupulously observed and enforced by the Two Contracting Governments in reference to the Rio Colorado, so far and for such distance as the middle of that River is made their common Boundary Line, by the First Article of this Treaty.

The several Provisions, Stipulations and restrictions contained in the 7th Article of the Treaty of Guadalupe Hidalgo, shall remain in force only so far as regards the Rio Bravo del Norte below the initial of the said Boundary provided in the First Article of this Treaty That is to say below the intersection of the 31°47'30' parallel of Latitude with the Boundary Line established by the late Treaty dividing said river from its mouth upwards according to the 5th Article of the Treaty of Guadalupe.

Article 5

All the provisions of the Eighth and Ninth, Sixteenth and Seventeenth Articles of the Treaty of Guadalupe Hidalgo shall apply to the Territory ceded by the Mexican Republic in the First Article of the present Treaty and to all the rights of persons and property both civil and ecclesiastical within the same, as fully and as effectually as if the said Articles were herein again recited and set forth.

Article 6

No Grants of Land within the Territory ceded by the First Article of This Treaty bearing date subsequent to the day Twenty fifth of September—when the Minister and Subscriber to this Treaty on the part of the United States proposed to the Government of Mexico to terminate the question of Boundary, will be considered valid or be recognized by the United States, or will any Grants made previously be respected or be considered as obligatory which have not been located and duly recorded in the Archives of Mexico.

Article 7

Should there at any future period (which God forbid) occur any disagreement between the two Nations which might lead to a rupture of their relations and reciprocal peace, they bind themselves in like manner to procure by every possible method the adjustment of every difference, and should they still in this manner not succeed, never will they proceed to a declaration of War, without having previously paid attention to what has been set forth in Article 21 of the Treaty of Guadalupe for similar cases; which Article as well as the 22nd is here re-affirmed.

Article 8

The Mexican government having on the 5th of February 1853 authorized the early construction of a plank and railroad across the Isthmus of Tehuantepec, and to secure the stable benefits of said transit way to the persons and merchandise of the citizens of Mexico and the United States, it is stipulated that neither government will interpose any obstacle to the transit of persons and merchandise of both nations; and at no time shall higher charges be made on the transit of persons and property of citizens of the United States than may be made on the persons and property of other foreign nations, nor shall any interest in said transit way, nor in the proceeds thereof, be transferred to any foreign government.

The United States by its Agents shall have the right to transport across the Isthmus, in closed bags, the mails of the United States not intended for distribution along the line of communication; also the effects of the United States government and its citizens, which may be intended for transit, and not for distribution on the Isthmus, free of custom-house or other charges by the Mexican government. Neither passports nor letters of security will be required of persons crossing the Isthmus and not remaining in the country.

When the construction of the railroad shall be completed, the Mexican government agrees to open a port of entry in addition to the port of Vera Cruz, at or near the terminus of said road on the Gulf of Mexico. The two governments will enter into arrangements for the prompt transit of troops and munitions of the United States, which that government may have occasion to send from one part of its territory to another, lying on opposite sides of the continent. The Mexican government having agreed to protect with its whole power the prosecution, preservation and security of the work, the United States may extend its protection as it shall judge wise to it when it may feel sanctioned and warranted by the public or international law.

Article 9

This Treaty shall be ratified, and the respective ratifications shall be exchanged at the City of Washington, within the exact period of six months from the date of its signature or sooner if possible.

In testimony whereof, We the Plenipotentiaries of the contracting parties have hereunto affixed our hands and seals at Mexico the—Thirtieth (30th)—day of December in the Year of Our Lord one thousand eight hundred and fifty three, in the thirty third year of the Independence of the Mexican Republic, and the seventy eighth of that of the United States

JAMES GADSDEN
MANUEL DIEZ DE BONILLA
JOSE SALAZAR YLARREGUI
J. MARIANO MONTERDE

✳OUR AMERICA BY JOSÉ MARTÍ

Following is Cuban patriot José Martí's famous analysis of the political and governmental problems confronting Spanish America and his perception of the threat of United States imperialism. Published in New York's La revista ilustrada (The Illustrated Review) on January 10, 1891, it forever fixed the idea of two Americas, that of the United States and that of the Latin American countries.

The conceited villager believes the entire world to be his village. Provided that he can be mayor, or humiliate the rival who stole his sweetheart, or add to the savings in his strong-box, he considers the universal order good, unaware of those giants with seven-league boots who can crush him underfoot, or of the strife in the heavens between comets that streak through the drowsy air-devouring worlds. What remains of the village in America must rouse itself. These are not the times for sleeping in a nightcap, but with weapons for a pillow, like the warriors of Juan de Castellanos weapons of the mind, which conquer all others. Barricades of ideas are worth more than barricades of stone.

There is no prow that can cut through a cloudbank of ideas. A powerful idea, waved before the world at the proper time, can stop a squadron of iron-clad ships, like the mystical flag of the Last Judgment. Nations that do not know one another should quickly become acquainted, as men who are to fight a common enemy. Those who shake their fists, like jealous brothers coveting the same tract of land, or like the modest cottager who envies the squire his mansion, should clasp hands and become one. Those who use the authority of a criminal tradition to lop off the lands of their defeated brother with a sword stained with his own blood, ought to return the lands to the brother already punished sufficiently, if they do not want the people to call them robbers. The honest man does not absolve himself of debts of honor with money, at so much a slap. We can no longer be a people of leaves living in the air, our foliage heavy with blooms and crackling or humming at the whim of the sun's caress, or buffeted and tossed by the storms. The trees must form ranks to keep the giant with seven-league boots from passing! It is the time of mobilization, of marching together, and we must go forward in close order, like silver in the veins of the Andes.

Only those born prematurely are lacking in courage. Those without faith in their country are seven-month weaklings. Because they have no courage, they deny it to others. Their puny arms—arms with bracelets and hands with painted nails, arms of Paris or Madrid—can hardly reach the bottom limb, and they claim the tall tree to be unclimbable. The ships should be loaded with those harmful insects that gnaw at the bone of the country that nourishes them. If they are Parisians or from Madrid, let them go to the Prado under lamplight, or to Tortoni's for a sherbet. Those carpenters' sons who are ashamed that their fathers are carpenters! Those born in America who are ashamed of the mother who reared them, because she wears an Indian apron, and who disown their sick mother, the scoundrels, abandoning her on her sickbed! Then who is a real man? He who stays with his mother and nurses her in her illness, or he who puts her to work out of sight, and lives at her expense on decadent lands, sporting fancy neckties, cursing the womb that carried him, displaying the sign of the traitor on the back of his paper frockcoat? These sons of Our America, which will be saved by its Indians and is growing better; these deserters who take up arms in the armies of a North America that drowns its Indians in blood and is growing worse! These delicate creatures who are men but are unwilling to do men's work! The Washington who made this land for them, did he not go to live with the English, to live with the English at a time when he saw them fighting against his own country? These "iconoclasts" of honor who drag that honor over foreign soil, like their counterparts in the French Revolution with their dancing, their affectations, their drawling speech!

For in what lands can men take more pride than in our long-suffering American republics, raised up from among the silent Indian masses by the bleeding arms of a hundred apostles, to the sounds of battle between the book and the processional candle? Never in history have such advanced and united nations been forged in so short a time from such disorganized elements.

The presumptuous man feels that the earth was made to serve as his pedestal because he happens to have a facile pen or colorful speech, and he accuses his native land of being worthless and beyond redemption because its virgin jungles fail to provide him with a constant means of traveling over the world, driving Persian ponies and lavishing champagne like a tycoon. The incapacity does not lie with the emerging country in quest of suitable forms and a utilitarian greatness; it lies rather with those who attempt to rule nations of a unique and violent character by means of laws inherited from four centuries of freedom in the United States and nineteen centuries of monarchy in France. A decree by Hamilton does not halt the charge of the plainsman's horse. A phrase by Sieyes does nothing to quicken the stagnant blood of the Indian race. To govern well, one must see things as they are. And the able governor in America is not the one who knows how to govern the Germans or the French; he must know the elements that compose his own country, and how to bring them together, using methods and institutions originating within the country, to reach that desirable state where each man can attain self-realization and all may enjoy the abundance that Nature has bestowed on everyone in the nation to enrich with their toil and defend with their lives. The government must originate in the country. The spirit of the government must be that of the country. Its structure must conform to rules appropriate to the country. Good government is nothing more than the balance of the country's natural elements.

That is why the imported book has been conquered in America by the natural man. Natural men have conquered learned and artificial men. The native halfbreed has conquered the exotic Creole. The struggle is not between civilization and barbarity, but between false erudition and Nature. The natural man is good, and he respects and rewards superior intelligence as long as his humility is not turned against him, or he is not offended by being disregarded—a thing the natural man never forgives, prepared as he is to forcibly regain the respect of whoever has wounded his pride or threatened his interests. It is by conforming with these disdained native elements that the tyrants of America have climbed to power, and have fallen as soon as they betrayed them. Republics have paid with oppression for their inability to recognize the true elements of their countries, to derive from them the right kind of government, and to govern accordingly. In a new nation a governor means a creator.

In nations composed of both cultured and uncultured elements, the uncultured will govern because it is their habit to attack and resolve doubts with their fists in cases where the cultured have failed in the art of governing. The uncultured masses are lazy and timid in the realm of intelligence, and they want to be governed well. But if the government hurts them, they shake it off and govern themselves. How can the universities produce governors if not a single university in America teaches the rudiments of the art of government, the analysis of elements peculiar to the peoples of America? The young go out into the world wearing Yankee or French spectacles, hoping to govern a people they do not know. In the political race entrance should be denied to those who are ignorant of the rudiments of politics. The prize in literary contests should not go for the best ode, but for the best study of the political factors of one's country. Newspapers, universities, and schools should encourage the study of the country's pertinent components. To know them is sufficient, without mincing words; for whoever brushes aside even a part of the truth, whether through intention or oversight, is doomed to fall. The truth he lacks thrives on negligence, and brings down whatever is built without it. It is easier to resolve our problem knowing its components than to resolve it without knowing them. Along comes the natural man, strong and indignant, and he topples all the justice accumulated from books because he has not been governed in accordance with the obvious needs of the country. Knowing is what counts. To know one's country and govern it with that knowledge is the only way to free it from tyranny. The European university must bow to the American university. The history of America, from the Incas to the present, must be taught in clear detail and to the letter, even if the archons of Greece are overlooked. Our Greece must take priority over the Greece which is not ours. We need it more. Nationalist statesmen must replace foreign statesmen. Let the world be grafted onto our republics, but the trunk must be our own. And let the vanquished pedant hold his tongue, for there are no lands in which a man may take greater pride than in our long-suffering American republics.

With the rosary as our guide, our heads white and our bodies mottled, both Indian and Creole, we fearlessly entered the world of nations. We set out to conquer freedom under the banner of the virgin. A priest, a few lieutenants, and a woman raised the Republic of Mexico onto the shoulders of the Indians. A few heroic students, instructed in French liberty by a Spanish cleric, made Central America rise in revolt against Spain under a Spanish general. In monarchic garb emblazoned with the sun, the Venezuelans to the north and the Argentineans to the south began building nations. When the two heroes clashed and the continent was about to rock, one of them, and not the lesser, handed the reins to the other. And since heroism in times of peace is rare because it is not as glorious as in times of war, it is easier for a man to die with honor than to think with logic. It is easier to govern when feelings are exalted and united than after a battle, when divisive, arrogant, exotic, or ambitious thinking emerges. The forces routed in the epic struggle with the feline cunning of the species, and using the weight of realities were under-mining

the new structure which comprised both the rough-and-ready, unique regions of our halfbreed America and the silk-stocking and frockcoated people of Paris beneath the flag of freedom and reason borrowed from nations skilled in the arts of government. The hierarchical constitution of the colonies resisted the democratic organization of the republics. The clavated capitals left their country boots in the vestibule. The bookworm redeemers failed to realize that the revolution succeeded because it came from the soul of the nation; they had to govern with that soul and not without it or against it. America began to suffer, and still suffers, from the tiresome task of reconciling the hostile and discordant elements it inherited from a despotic and perverse colonizer, and the imported methods and ideas which have been retarding logical government because they are lacking in local realities. Thrown out of gear for three centuries by a power which denied men the right to use their reason, the continent disregarded or closed its ears to the unlettered throngs that helped bring it to redemption, and embarked on a government based on reason—a reason belonging to all for the common good, not the university brand of reason over the peasant brand. The problem of independence did not lie in a change of forms but in a change of spirit.

It was imperative to make common cause with the oppressed, in order to secure a new system opposed to the ambitions and governing habits of the oppressors. The tiger, frightened by gunfire, returns at night to his prey. He dies with his eyes shooting flames and his claws unsheathed. He cannot be heard coming because he approaches with velvet tread. When the prey awakens, the tiger is already upon it. The colony lives on in the republic, and Our America is saving itself from its enormous mistakes the pride of its capital cities, the blind triumph of a scorned peasantry, the excessive influx of foreign ideas and formulas, the wicked and un-politic disdain for the aboriginal race because of the higher virtue, enriched with necessary blood, or a republic struggling against a colony. The tiger lurks behind every tree, lying in wait at every turn. He will die with his claws unsheathed and his eyes shooting flames.

But "these countries will be saved," as was announced by the Argentinean Rivadavia, whose only sin was being a gentleman in these rough-and-ready times. A man does not sheathe a machete in a silken scabbard, nor can he lay aside the short lance in a country won with the short lance merely because he is angered and stands at the door of Iturbide's Congress, "demanding that the fairhaired one be named Emperor." These countries will be saved because a genius for moderation, found in the serene harmony of Nature, seems to prevail on the continent of light, where there emerges a new realistic man schooled for these realistic times in the critical philosophy which in Europe has replaced the philosophy of guess-work and phalanstery that saturated the previous generation.

We were a phenomenon with the chest of an athlete, the hands of a dandy, and the brain of a child. We were a masquerader in English breeches, Parisian vest, North American jacket, and Spanish cap. The Indian hovered near us in silence, and went off to the hills to baptize his children. The Negro was seen pouring out the songs of his heart at night, alone and unrecognized among the rivers and wild animals. The peasant, the creator, turned in blind indignation against the disdainful city, against his own child. As for us, we were nothing but epaulets and professors' gowns in countries that came into the world wearing hemp sandals and headbands. It would have been the mark of genius to couple the headband and the professors' gown with the founding fathers' generosity and courage, to rescue the Indian, to make a place for the competent Negro, to fit liberty to the body of those who rebelled and conquered for it. We were left with the judge, the general, the scholar, and the sinecure. The angelic young, as if caught in the tentacles of an octopus, lunged heavenward, only to fall back, crowned with clouds, in sterile glory. The native, driven by instinct, swept away the golden staffs of office in blind triumph. Neither the European nor the Yankee could provide the key to the Spanish American riddle. Hate was attempted, and every year the countries amounted to less. Exhausted by the senseless struggle between the book and the lance, between reason and the processional candle, between the city and the country, weary of the impossible rule by rival urban cliques over the natural nation tempestuous or inert by turns, we begin almost unconsciously to try love. Nations stand up and greet one another.

"What are we?" is the mutual question, and little by little they furnish answers. When a problem arises in Cojimar, they do not seek its solution in Danzig. The frockcoats are still French, but thought begins to be American. The youth of America are rolling up their sleeves, digging their hands in the dough, and making it rise with the sweat of their brows. They realize that there is too much imitation, and that creation holds the key to salvation. "Create" is the password of this generation. The wine is made from plantain, but even if it turns sour, it is our own wine! That a country's form of government must be in keeping with its natural elements is a foregone conclusion. Absolute ideas must take relative forms if they are not to fail because of an error in form. Freedom, to be viable, has to be sincere and complete. If a republic refuses to open its arms to all, and move ahead with all, it dies. The tiger within sneaks in through the crack; so does the tiger from without. The general holds back his cavalry to a pace that suits his infantry, for if the infantry is left behind, the cavalry will be surrounded by the enemy. Politics and strategy are one. Nations should live in an atmosphere of self-criticism because criticism is healthy, but always with one heart and one mind. Stoop to the unhappy, and lift them up in your arms! Thaw out frozen America with the fire of your hearts! Make the natural blood of the nations course vigorously through their veins. The new Americans are on their feet, saluting each other from nation to nation, the eyes of the laborers shining with joy. The natural statesman arises, schooled in the direct study of Nature. He reads to apply his knowledge, not to imitate. Economists study the problems at their point of origin. Speakers begin a policy of moderation. Playwrights bring native characters to the stage. Academies discuss practical subjects. Poetry shears off its romantic locks and hangs its red vest on the glorious tree. Selective and sparkling prose is filled with ideas. In the Indian republics, the governors are learning Indian.

America is escaping all its dangers. Some of the republics are still beneath the sleeping octopus, but others, under the law of averages, are draining their lands with a sublime and furious haste, as if to make up for centuries lost. Still others, forgetting that Juarez went about in a carriage drawn by mules, hitch their carriages to the wind, their coachmen soap bubbles. Poisonous luxury, the enemy of freedom, corrupts the frivolous and opens the door to the foreigner. In others, where independence is threatened, an epic spirit heightens their manhood. Still others spawn an army capable of devouring them in voracious wars. But perhaps Our America is running another risk that does not come from itself but from the difference in origins, methods, and interests between the two halves of the continent, and the time is near at hand when an enterprising and vigorous people who scorn or ignore Our America will even so approach it and demand a close relationship. And since strong nations, self-made by law and shotgun, love strong nations, and them alone; since the time of madness and ambition from which North America may be freed by the predominance of the purest elements in its blood, or on which it may be launched by its vindictive and sordid masses, its tradition of expansion, or the ambitions of some powerful leader is not so near at hand, even to the most timorous eye, that there is no time for the test of discreet and unwavering pride that could confront and dissuade it; since its good name as a republic in the eyes of the world's perceptive nations puts upon North America a restraint that cannot be taken away by childish provocations or pompous arrogance or parricidal discords among Our American nations the pressing need of Our America is to show itself as it is, one in spirit and intent, swift conqueror of a suffocating past, stained only by the enriching blood drawn from hands that struggle to clear away the ruins, and from the scars left upon us by our masters. The scorn of our formidable neighbor who does not know us is Our America's greatest danger. And since the day of the visit is near, it is imperative that our neighbor know us, and soon, so that it will not scorn us. Through ignorance it might even come to lay hands on us. Once it does know us, it will remove its hands out of respect. One must have faith in the best in men and distrust the worst. One must allow the best to be shown so that it reveals and prevails over the worst. Nations should have a pillory for whoever stirs up useless hates, and another for whoever fails to tell them the truth in time.

There can be no racial animosity, because there are no races. The theorists and feeble thinkers string together and warm over the bookshelf races which the well-disposed observer and the fair-minded traveler vainly seek in the justice of Nature where man's universal identity springs forth from triumphant love and the turbulent hunger for life. The soul, equal and eternal, emanates from bodies of various shapes and colors. Whoever foments and spreads antagonism and hate between the races, sins against humanity.But as nations take shape among other different nations, there is a condensation of vital and individual characteristics of thought and habit, expansion and conquest, vanity and greed which could from the latent state of national concern, and in a period of internal disorder, or the rapidity with which the country's character has been accumulating be turned into a serious threat for the weak and isolated neighboring countries, declared by the strong country to be inferior and perishable. The thought is father to the deed. And one must not attribute, through a provincial antipathy, a fatal and inborn wickedness to the continent's fairskinned nation simply because it does not speak our language, or see the world as we see it, or resemble us in its political defects, so different from ours, or favorably regard the excitable, darkskinned people, or look charitably from its still uncertain eminence upon those less favored by history, who climb the road of republicanism by heroic stages. The self-evident facts of the problem should not be obscured, because the problem can be resolved, for the peace of centuries to come, by appropriate study, and by tacit and immediate unity in the continental

spirit. With a single voice the hymn is already being sung. The present generation is carrying industrious America along the road enriched by their sublime fathers; from the Rio Grande to the Straits of Magellan, the Great Sem, astride his condor, is sowing the seed of the new America through-out the Latin nations of the continent and the sorrowful islands of the sea!

✳TREATY OF PEACE (TREATY OF PARIS) 1898

The United States of America and Her Majesty the Queen Regent of Spain, in the name of her August Son Don Alfonso XIII, desiring to end the state of war now existing between the two countries, have for that purpose appointed as Plenipotentiaries: The President of the United States, William R. Day, Cushman K. Davis, William P. Frye, George Gray, and Whitelaw Reid, citizens of the United States; and Her Majesty the Queen Regent of Spain,

Don Eugenio Montero Rios, President of the Senate,

Don Buenaventura de Abarzuza, Senator of the Kingdom and ex-Minister of the Crown,

Don Jose de Garnica, Deputy to the Cortes and Associate Justice of the Supreme Court,

Don Wenceslao Ramire de Villa-Urrutia, Envoy Extraordinary and Minister Plenipotentiary at Brussels, and

Don Rafael Cerero, General of Division;

Who, having assembled in Paris, and having exchanged their full powers, which were found to be in due and proper form, have, after discussion of the matters before them, agreed upon the following articles:

Article I

Spain relinquishes all claim of sovereignty over and title to Cuba.

And as the island is, upon its evacuation by Spain, to be occupied by the United States, the United States will, so long as such occupation shall last, assume and discharge the obligations that may under international law result from the fact of its occupation, for the protection of life and property.

Article II

Spain cedes to the United States the island of Porto Rico and other islands now under Spanish sovereignty in the West Indies, and the island of Guam in the Marianas or Ladrones.

Article III

Spain cedes to the United States the archipelago known as the Philippine Islands, and comprehending the islands lying within the following line:

A line running from west to east along or near the twentieth parallel of north latitude, and through the middle of the navigable channel of Bachi, from the one hundred and eighteenth (118th) to the one hundred and twenty seventh (127th) degree meridian of longitude east of Greenwich, thence along the one hundred and twenty seventh (127th) degree meridian of longitude east of Greenwich to the parallel of four degrees and forty five minutes (4°45') north latitude to its intersection with the meridian of longitude one hundred and nineteen degrees and thirty-five minutes (119°35') east of Greenwich to the parallel of latitude seven degrees and forty minutes (7°40') north, thence along the parallel of latitude seven degrees and forty minutes (7° 40') north to its intersection with the one hundred and sixteenth (116th) degree meridian of longitude east of Greenwich, thence by a direct line to the intersection of the tenth (10th) degree parallel of north latitude with the one hundred and eighteenth (118th) degree meridian of longitude east of Greenwich, and thence along the one hundred and eighteenth (118th) degree meridian of longitude east of Greenwich to the point of beginning.

The United States will pay to Spain the sum of twenty million dollars ($20,000,000) within three months after the exchange of the ratifications of the present treaty.

Article IV

The United States will, for the term of ten years from the date of the exchange of the ratifications of the present treaty, admit Spanish ships and merchandise to the ports of the Philippine Islands on the same terms as ships and merchandise of the United States.

Article V

The United States will, upon the signature of the present treaty, send back to Spain, at its own cost, the Spanish soldiers taken as prisoners of war on the capture of Manila by the American forces. The arms of the soldiers in question shall be restored to them.

Spain will, upon the exchange of the ratifications of the present treaty, proceed to evacuate the Philippines, as well as the island of Guam, on terms similar to those agreed upon by the Commissioners appointed to arrange for the evacuation of Porto Rico and other islands in the West Indies, under the Protocol of August 12, 1898, which is to continue in force until its provisions are completely executed.

The time within which the evacuation of the Philippine Islands and Guam shall be completed shall be fixed by the two Governments. Stands of colors, uncaptured war vessels, small arms, guns of any calibres, with their carriages and accessories, powder, ammunition, livestock, and materials and supplies of all kinds, belonging to the land and naval forces of Spain in the Philippines and Guam, remain the property of Spain. Pieces of heavy ordnance, exclusive of field artillery, in the fortifications and coast defenses, shall remain in their emplacements for the term of six months, to be reckoned from the exchange of ratifications of the treaty; and the United States may, in the mean time, purchase such material from Spain, if a satisfactory agreement between the two Governments on the subject shall be reached.

Article VI

Spain will, upon the signature of the present treaty, release all prisoners of war, and all persons detained or imprisoned for political offenses, in connection with the insurrections in Cuba and the Philippines and the war with the United States. Reciprocally, the United States will release all persons made prisoners of war by the American forces, and will undertake to obtain the release of all Spanish prisoners in the hands of the insurgents in Cuba and the Philippines.

The Government of the United States will at its own cost return to Spain and the Government of Spain will at its own cost return to the United States, Cuba, Porto Rico, and the Philippines, according to the situation of their respective homes, prisoners released or caused to be released by them, respectively, under this article.

Article VII

The United States and Spain mutually relinquish all claims for indemnity, national and individual of every kind, of either Government, or of its citizens or subjects, against the other Government, that may have arisen since the beginning of the late insurrection in Cuba and prior to the exchange of ratifications of the present treaty, including all claims for indemnity for the cost of the war.

The United States will adjudicate and settle the claims of its citizens against Spain relinquished in this article.

Article VIII

In conformity with the provisions of Articles I, II, and III of this treaty, Spain relinquishes in Cuba, and cedes in Porto Rico and other islands in the West Indies, in the island of Guam, and in the Philippine Archipelago, all the buildings, wharves, barracks, forts, structures, public highways and other immovable property which, in conformity with law, belong to the public domain, and as such belong to the Crown of Spain.

And it is hereby declared that the relinquishment or cession, as the case may be, to which the preceding paragraph refers, cannot in any respect impair the property or rights which by law belong to the peaceful possession of property of all kinds, of provinces, municipalities, public or private establishments, ecclesiastical or civic bodies, or any other associations having legal capacity to acquire and possess property in the aforesaid territories renounced or ceded, or of private individuals, of whatsoever nationality such individuals may be. The aforesaid relinquishment or cession, as the case may be, includes all documents exclusively referring to the sovereignty relinquished or ceded that may exist in the archives of the Peninsula. Where any document in such archives only in part relates to said sovereignty, a copy of such part will be furnished whenever it shall be requested. Like rules shall be reciprocally observed in favor of Spain in respect of documents in the archives of the islands above referred to.

In the aforesaid relinquishment or cession, as the case may be, are also included such rights as the Crown of Spain and its authorities possess in respect of the official archives and records, executive as well as judicial, in the islands above referred to, which relate to said islands or the rights and property of their inhabitants. Such archives and records shall be carefully preserved, and private persons shall without distinction have the right to require, in accordance with law, authenticated copies of the contracts, wills and other instruments forming part of notarial protocols or files or which may he contained in the executive or judicial archives, be the latter in Spain or in the islands aforesaid.

Article IX

Spanish subjects, natives of the Peninsula, residing in the territory over which Spain by the present treaty relinquishes or cedes her sovereignty, may remain in such territory or may remove therefrom, retaining in either event all their rights of property, including the right to sell or dispose of such property or of its proceeds; and they shall also have the right to carry on their industry, commerce and professions, being subject in respect thereof to such laws as are applicable to other foreigners. In case they remain in the territory they may preserve their allegiance to the Crown of Spain by making, before a court of record, within a year from the date of the exchange of ratifications of this treaty, a declaration of their decision to preserve such allegiance; in default of which declaration they shall be held to have renounced it and to have adopted the nationality of the territory in which they may reside.

The civil rights and political status of the native inhabitants of the territories hereby ceded to the United States shall be determined by the Congress.

Article X

The inhabitants of the territories over which Spain relinquishes or cedes her sovereignty shall be secured in the free exercise of their religion.

Article XI

The Spaniards residing in the territories over which Spain by this treaty cedes or relinquishes her sovereignty shall be subject in matters civil as well as criminal to the jurisdiction of the courts of the country wherein they reside, pursuant to the ordinary laws governing the same; and they shall have the right to appear before such courts, and to pursue the same course as citizens of the country to which the courts belong.

Article XII

Judicial proceedings pending at the time of the exchange of ratifications of this treaty in the territories over which Spain relinquishes or cedes her sovereignty shall be determined according to the following rules:

1. Judgments rendered either in civil suits between private individuals, or in criminal matters, before the date mentioned, and with respect to which there is no recourse or right of review under the Spanish law, shall be deemed to be final, and shall be executed in due form by competent authority in the territory within which such judgments should be carried out.

2. Civil suits between private individuals which may on the date mentioned be undetermined shall be prosecuted to judgment before the court in which they may then be pending or in the court that may be substituted therefore.

3. Criminal actions pending on the date mentioned before the Supreme Court of Spain against citizens of the territory which by this treaty ceases to be Spanish shall continue under its jurisdiction until final judgment; but, such judgment having been rendered, the execution shall be committed to the competent authority of the place in which the case arose.

Article XIII

The rights of property secured by copyrights and patents acquired by Spaniards in the Island of Cuba, and in Porto Rico, the Philippines and other ceded territories, at the time of the exchange of the ratifications of this treaty, shall continue to be respected. Spanish scientific, literary and artistic works, not subversive of public order in the territories in question, shall continue to be admitted free of duty into such territories, for the period of ten years, to be reckoned from the date of the exchange of the ratifications of this treaty.

Article XIV

Spain shall have the power to establish consular officers in the ports and places of the territories, the

sovereignty over which has been either relinquished or ceded by the present treaty.

Article XV

The Government of each country will, for the term of ten years, accord to the merchant vessels of the other country the same treatment in respect of all port charges, including entrance and clearance dues, light dues, and tonnage duties, as it accords to its own merchant vessels, not engaged in the coastwise trade.

This article may at any time be terminated on six months' notice given by either Government to the other.

Article XVI

It is understood that any obligations assumed in this treaty by the United States with respect to Cuba are limited to the time of its occupancy thereof; but it will upon the termination of such occupancy, advise any Government established in the island to assume the same obligations.

Article XVII

The present treaty shall be ratified by the President of the United States by and with the advice and consent of the Senate thereof, and by Her Majesty the Queen Regent of Spain; and the ratifications shall be exchanged at Washington within six months from the date hereof, or earlier if possible.

In faith whereof, we, the respective Plenipotentiaries, have signed this treaty and have hereunto affixed our seals.

Done in duplicate at Paris, the tenth day of December, in the year of Our Lord one thousand eight hundred and ninety eight.

WILLIAM R. DAY
CUSHMAN K. DAVIS
WM. P. FRYE
GEO. GRAY
WHITELAW REID
EUGENIO MONTERO RIOS
B. DE ABARZUZA
J. DE GARNICA
W. R. DE VILLA URRUTIA
RAFAEL CERERO

✳ RELATIONS WITH CUBA

Whereas the Congress of the United States of America, by an Act approved March 2, 1901, provided as follows:

Provided further, That in fulfillment of the declaration contained in the joint resolution approved April twentieth, eighteen hundred and ninety-eight, entitled, "For the recognition of the independence of the people of Cuba, demanding that the Government of Spain relinquish its authority and government in the island of Cuba, and to withdraw its land and naval forces from Cuba and Cuban waters, and directing the President of the United States to use the land and naval forces of the United States to carry resolutions into effect," the President is hereby authorized to "leave the government and control of the island of Cuba to its people" so soon as a government shall have been established in said island under a constitution either as a part thereof or in an ordinance appended thereto, shall define the future relations of the United States with Cuba, substantially as follows:

"I.—That the government of Cuba shall never enter into any treaty or other compact with any foreign power or powers which will impair or tend to impair the independence of Cuba, nor in any manner authorize or permit any foreign power or powers to obtain by colonization or for military or naval purposes or otherwise, lodgement in or control over any portion of said island."

"II.—That said government shall not assume or contract any public debt, to pay the interest upon which, and to make reasonable sinking fund provision for the ultimate discharge of which, the ordinary revenues of the island, after defraying the current expenses of government shall be inadequate."

"III.—That the government of Cuba consents that the United States may exercise the right to intervene for the preservation of Cuban independence, the maintenance of a government adequate for the protection of life, property, and individual liberty, and for discharging the obligations with respect to Cuba imposed by the Treaty of Paris on the United States, now to be assumed and undertaken by the government of Cuba."

"IV.—That all Acts of the United States in Cuba during its military occupancy thereof are ratified and validated, and all lawful rights acquired thereunder shall be maintained and protected."

"V.—That the government of Cuba will execute, and as far as necessary extend, the plans already devised or other plans to be mutually agreed upon, for the sanitation of the cites of the island, to the end that a recurrence of epidemic and infectious diseases may be prevented thereby assuring protection to the people and commerce of Cuba, as well as to the commerce of the southern ports of the United States and the people residing therein."

"VI.—That the Isle of Pines shall be omitted from the proposed constitutional boundaries of Cuba, the title thereto being left to future adjustment by treaty."

"VII—That to enable the United States to maintain the independence of Cuba, and to protect the people thereof, as well as for its own defense, the government of Cuba will sell or lease to the United States lands necessary for coaling or naval stations at certain specified points to be agreed upon with the President of the United States."

"VIII.—That by way of further assurance the Government of Cuba will embody the foregoing provisions in a permanent treaty with the United States."

Whereas the Constitutional Convention of Cuba, on June twelfth, 1901, adopted a Resolution adding to the Constitution of the Republic of Cuba which was adopted on the twenty-first of February 1901, an appendix in the words and letters of the eight enumerated articles of the above cited act of the Congress of the United States;

And whereas, by the establishment of the independent and sovereign government of the Republic of Cuba, under the constitution promulgated on the 20th of May, 1902, which embraced the foregoing conditions, and by the withdrawal of the Government of the United States as an intervening power, on the same date, it becomes necessary to embody the above cited provisions in a permanent treaty between the United States of America and the Republic of Cuba;

The United States of America and the Republic of Cuba, being desirous to carry out the foregoing conditions, have for that purpose appointed as their plenipotentiaries to conclude a treaty to that end,

The President of the United States of America, Herbert G. Squiers, Envoy Extraordinary and Minister Plenipotentiary at Havana,

And the President of the Republic of Cuba, Carlos de Zaldo y Beurmann, Secretary of State and Justice,—who after communicating to each other their full powers found in good and due form, have agreed upon the following articles:

Article I

The Government of Cuba shall never enter into any treaty or other compact with any foreign power or powers which will impair or tend to impair the independence of Cuba, nor in any manner authorize or permit any foreign power or powers to obtain by colonization or for military or naval purposes, or otherwise, lodgement in or control over any portion of said island.

Article II

The Government of Cuba shall not assume or contract any public debt to pay the interest upon which, and to make reasonable sinking-fund provision for the ultimate discharge of which, the ordinary revenues of the Island of Cuba, after defraying the current expenses of the Government, shall be inadequate.

Article III

The Government of Cuba consents that the United States may exercise the right to intervene for the preservation of Cuban independence, the maintenance of a government adequate for the protection of life, property, and individual liberty, and for discharging the obligations with respect to Cuba imposed by the Treaty of Paris on the United States, now to be assumed and undertaken by the Government of Cuba.

Article IV

All acts of the United States in Cuba during its military occupancy thereof are ratified and validated, and all lawful rights acquired thereunder shall be maintained and protected.

Article V

The Government of Cuba will execute, and, as far as necessary, extend the plans already devised, or other plans to be mutually agreed upon, for the sanitation of the cities of the island, to the end that a recurrence of epidemic and infectious diseases may be prevented, thereby assuring protection to the people and commerce of Cuba, as well as to the commerce of the Southern ports of the United States and the people residing therein.

Article VI

The Island of Pines shall be omitted form the boundaries of Cuba specified in the Constitution, the title thereof being left to future adjustment by treaty.

Article VII

To enable the United States to maintain the independence of Cuba, and to protect the people thereof, as well as for its own defense, the Government of Cuba will sell or lease to the United States lands necessary for coaling or naval stations, at certain specified points, to be agreed upon with the President of the United States.

Article VIII

The present Convention shall be ratified by each party in conformity with the respective Constitutions of the two countries, and the ratifications shall be exchanged in the City of Washington within eight months form this date.

In witness whereof, we the respective Plenipoten-

tiaries, have signed the same in duplicate, in English and Spanish, and have affixed our respective seals at Havana, Cuba, this twenty-second day of May, in the year nineteen hundred and three.

H.G. SQUIERS
CARLOS DE ZALDO

✷THE "HAY-HERRAN" TREATY

Between the United States and Colombia Signed at Washington, January 22, 1903

THE UNITED STATES of America and the Republic of Colombia, being desirous to assure the construction of a ship canal to connect the Atlantic and Pacific oceans and the Congress of the United States of America having passed an Act approved June 28, 1902, in furtherance of that object, a copy of which is hereunto annexed, the high contracting parties have resolved, for that purpose, to conclude a Convention and have accordingly appointed as their plenipotentiaries,

The President of the United States of America, JOHN HAY, Secretary of State, and

The President of the Republic of Colombia, THOMAS HERRAN, Charge d'Affaires, thereunto specially empowered by said government, who, after communicating to each other their respective full powers, found in good and due form, have agreed upon and concluded the following Articles:

Article 1

The Government of Colombia authorizes the New Panama Canal Company to sell and transfer to the United States its rights, privileges, properties, and concessions, as well as the Panama Railroad and all the shares or part of the shares of that company; but the public lands situated outside of the zone hereinafter specified, now corresponding to the concessions of both said enterprises shall revert to the Republic of Colombia, except any property now owned by or in the possession of the said companies within Panama or Colon, or the ports and terminals thereof.

But it is understood that Colombia reserves all its rights to the special shares in the capital of the New Panama Canal Company to which reference is made in Article 4 of the contract of December 10, 1890, which shares shall be paid their full nominal value at least; but as such right of Colombia exists solely in its character of stockholder in said Company, no obligation under this provision is imposed upon or assumed by the United States.

The Railroad Company (and the United States as owner of the enterprise) shall be free from the obligations imposed by the railroad concession, excepting as to the payment at maturity by the Railroad Company of the outstanding bonds issued by said Railroad Company.

Article 2

The United States shall have the exclusive right for the term of one hundred years, renewable at the sole and absolute option of the United States, for periods of similar duration so long as the United States may desire, to excavate, construct, maintain, operate, control, and protect the Maritime Canal with or without locks from the Atlantic to the Pacific ocean, to and across the territory of Colombia, such canal to be of sufficient depth and capacity for vessels of the largest tonnage and greatest draft now engaged in commerce, and such as may be reasonably anticipated, and also the same rights for the construction, maintenance, operation, control, and protection of the Panama Railroad and of railway, telegraph and telephone lines, canals, dikes, dams and reservoirs, and such other auxiliary works as may be necessary and convenient for the construction, maintenance, protection and operation of the canal and railroads.

To enable the United States to exercise the rights and privileges granted by this Treaty the Republic of Colombia grants to that Government the use and control for the term of one hundred years, renewable at the sole and absolute option of the United States, for periods of similar duration so long as the United States may desire, of a zone of territory along the route of the canal to be constructed five kilometers in width on either side thereof measured from its center line including therein the necessary auxiliary canals not exceeding in any case fifteen miles from the main canal and other works, together with ten fathoms of water in the Bay of Limon in extension of the canal, and at least three marine miles from mean low water mark from each terminus of the canal into the Caribbean Sea and the Pacific Ocean respectively. So far as necessary for the construction, maintenance and operation of the canal, the United States shall have the use and occupation of the group of small islands in the Bay of Panama named Perico, Naos, Culebra and Flamenco, but the same shall not be construed as being within the zone herein defined or governed by the special provisions applicable to the same.

This grant shall in no manner invalidate the titles or rights of private land holders in the said zone of territory, nor shall it interfere with the rights of way over the public roads of the Department; provided, however, that nothing herein contained shall operate to diminish, impair or restrict the rights elsewhere herein granted to the United States. This grant shall not include the cities of Panama and Colon, except so far as lands and other property therein are now owned by or in possession of the said Canal Company or the said Railroad Company; but all the stipulations contained in Article 35 of the Treaty of 1846-48 between the contracting parties shall continue and apply in full force to the cities of Panama and Colon and to the accessory community lands and other property within the said zone, and the territory thereon shall be neutral territory, and the United States shall continue to guarantee the neutrality thereof and the sovereignty of Colombia thereover, in conformity with the above mentioned Article 35 of said Treaty.

In furtherance of this last provision there shall be created a Joint Commission by the Governments of Colombia and the United States that shall establish and enforce sanitary and police regulations.

Article 4

The rights and privileges granted to the United States by the terms of this convention shall not affect the sovereignty of the Republic of Colombia over the territory within whose boundaries such rights and privileges are to be exercised.

The United States freely acknowledges and recognizes this sovereignty and disavows any intention to impair it in any way whatever or to increase its territory at the expense of Colombia or of any of the sister republics in Central or South America, but on the contrary, it desires to strengthen the power of the republics on this continent, and to promote, develop and maintain their prosperity and independence.

Article 5

The Republic of Colombia authorizes the United States to construct and maintain at each entrance and terminus of the proposed canal a port for vessels using the same, with suitable light houses and other aids to navigation, and the United States is authorized to use and occupy within the limits of the zone fixed by this convention, such parts of the coast line and of the lands and islands adjacent thereto as are necessary for this purpose, including the construction and maintenance of breakwaters, dikes, jetties, embankments, coaling stations, docks and other appropriate works, and the United States undertakes the construction and maintenance of such works and will bear all the expense thereof. The ports when established are declared free, and their demarcations shall be clearly and definitely defined.

To give effect to this Article, the United States will give special attention and care to the maintenance of works for drainage, sanitary and healthful purposes along the line of the canal, and its dependencies, in order to prevent the invasion of epidemics or of securing their prompt suppression should they appear. With this end in view the United States will organize hospitals along the line of the canal, and will suitably supply or cause to be supplied the towns of Panama and Colon with the necessary aqueducts and drainage works, in order to prevent their becoming centers of infection on account of their proximity to the canal.

The Government of Colombia will secure for the United States or its nominees the lands and rights that may be required in the towns of Panama and Colon to effect the improvements above referred to, and the Government of the United States or its nominees shall be authorized to impose and collect equitable water rates, during fifty years for the service rendered; but on the expiration of said term the use of the water shall be free for the inhabitants of Panama and Colon, except to the extent that may be necessary for the operation and maintenance of said water system, including reservoirs, aqueducts, hydrants, supply service, drainage and other works.

Article 6

The Republic of Colombia agrees that it will not cede or lease to any foreign Government any of its islands or harbors within or adjacent to the Bay of Panama, nor on the Atlantic Coast of Colombia, between the Atrato River and the western boundary of the Department of Panama, for the purpose of establishing fortifications, naval or coaling stations, military posts, docks or other works that might interfere with the construction, maintenance, operation, protection, safety, and free use of the canal and auxiliary works. In order to enable Colombia to comply with this stipulation, the Government of the United States agrees to give Colombia the material support that may be required in order to prevent the occupation of said islands and ports, guaranteeing there the sovereignty, independence and integrity of Colombia.

Article 7

The Republic of Colombia includes in the foregoing grant the right without obstacle, cost, or impediment, to such control, consumption and general utilization in any manner found necessary by the United States to the exercise by it of the grants to, and rights conferred upon it by this Treaty, the waters of the Chagres River and other streams, lakes and lagoons, of all non-navigable waters, natural and artificial, and also to navigate all rivers, streams, lakes and other navigable water-ways, within the jurisdiction and under the domain of the Republic of Colombia, in the Department of Panama, within or without

said zone, as may be necessary or desirable for the construction, maintenance and operation of the canal and its auxiliary canals and other works, and without tolls or charges of any kind; and to raise and lower the levels of the waters, and to deflect them, and to impound any such waters, and to overflow any lands necessary for the due exercise of such grants and rights to the United States; and to rectify, construct and improve the navigation of any such rivers, streams, lakes and lagoons at the sole cost of the United States; but any such water-ways so made by the United States may be used by citizens of Colombia free of tolls or other charges. And the United States shall have the right to use without cost, any water, stone, clay, earth or other minerals belonging to Colombia on the public domain that may be needed by it.

All damages caused to private land owners by inundation or by the deviation of water courses, or in other ways, arising out of the construction or operation of the canal, shall in each case be appraised and settled by a joint commission appointed by the Governments of the United States and Colombia, but the cost of the indemnities so agreed upon shall be borne solely by the United States.

Article 8

The Government of Colombia declares free for all time the ports at either entrance of the Canal, including Panama and Colon and the waters thereof in such manner that there shall not be collected by the Government of Colombia custom house tolls, tonnage, anchorage, light-house, wharf, pilot, or quarantine dues, nor any other charges or taxes of any kind shall be levied or imposed by the Government of Colombia upon any vessel using or passing through the Canal or belonging to or employed by the United States, directly or indirectly, in connection with the construction, maintenance and operation of the main work or its auxiliaries, or upon the cargo, officers, crew, or passengers of any such vessels; it being the intent of this convention that all vessels and their cargoes, crews, and passengers, shall be permitted to use and pass through the Canal and the ports leading thereto, subject to no other demands or impositions than such tolls and charges as may be imposed by the United States for the use of the Canal and other works. It being understood that such tolls and charges shall be governed by the provisions of Article 16.

The ports leading to the Canal, including Panama and Colon, also shall be free to the commerce of the world, and no duties or taxes shall be imposed, except upon merchandise destined to be introduced for the consumption of the rest of the Republic of Colombia, or the Department of Panama, and upon vessels touching at the ports of Colon and Panama and which do not cross the Canal.

Though the said ports shall be free and open to all, the Government of Colombia may establish in them such custom houses and guards as Colombia may deem necessary to collect duties on importations destined to other portions of Colombia and to prevent contraband trade. The United States shall have the right to make use of the ports at the two extremities of the Canal including Panama and Colon as places of anchorage, in order to make repairs for loading, unloading, depositing, or transshipping cargoes either in transit or destined for the service of the Canal and other works.

Any concessions or privileges granted by Colombia for the operation of light houses at Colon and Panama shall be subject to expropriation, indemnification and payment in the same manner as is provided by Article 14 in respect to the property therein mentioned; but Colombia shall make no additional grant of any such privilege nor change the status of any existing concession.

Article 9

There shall not be imposed any taxes, national, municipal, departmental, or of any other class, upon the canal, the vessels that may use it, tugs and other vessels employed in the service of the canal, the railways and auxiliary works, store houses, work shops, offices, quarters for laborers, factories of all kinds, warehouses, wharves, machinery and other works, property, and effects appertaining to the canal or railroad or that may be necessary for the service of the canal or railroad and their dependencies, whether situated within the cities of Panama and Colon, or any other place authorized by the provisions of this convention.

Nor shall there be imposed contributions or charges of a personal character of whatever species upon officers, employees, laborers, and other individuals in the service of the canal and its dependencies.

Article 10

It is agreed that telegraph and telephone lines, when established for canal purposes, may also, under suitable regulations, be used for public and private business in connection with the systems of Colombia and the other American Republics and with the lines of cable companies authorized to enter the ports and territories of these Republics; but the official dispatches of the Government of Colombia and the authorities of the Department of Panama shall not pay for such service higher tolls than those required from the officials in the service of the United States.

Article 11

The Government of Colombia shall permit the immigration and free access to the lands and workshops of the canal and its dependencies of all employees and workmen of whatever nationality under contract to work upon or seeking employment or in any wise connected with the said canal and its dependencies, with their respective families and all such persons shall be free and exempt from the military service of the Republic of Colombia.

Article 12

The United States may import at any time into the said zone, free of customs duties, imposts, taxes, or other charges, and without any restriction, any and all vessels, dredges, engines, cars, machinery, tools, explosives, materials, supplies, and other articles necessary and convenient in the construction, maintenance and operation of the canal and auxiliary works, also all provisions, medicines, clothing, supplies and other things necessary and convenient for the officers, employees, workmen and laborers in the service and employ of the United States and for their families. If any such articles are disposed of for use without the zone excepting Panama and Colon and within the territory of the Republic, they shall be subject to the same import or other duties as like articles under the laws of Colombia or the ordinances of the Department of Panama.

Article 13

The United States shall have authority to protect and make secure the canal, as well as railways and other auxiliary works and dependencies, and to preserve order and discipline among the laborers and other persons who may congregate in that region, and to make and enforce such police and sanitary regulations as it may deem necessary to preserve order and public health thereon, and to protect navigation and commerce through and over said canal, railways and other works and dependencies from interruption or damage.

I. The Republic of Colombia may establish judicial tribunals within said zone, for the determination, according to its laws and judicial procedure, of certain controversies hereinafter mentioned. Such judicial tribunal or tribunals so established by the Republic of Colombia shall have exclusive jurisdiction in said zone of all controversies between citizens of the Republic of Colombia, or between citizens of the Republic of Colombia and citizens of any foreign nation other than the United States.

II. Subject to the general sovereignty of Colombia over said zone, the United States may establish judicial tribunals thereon, which shall have jurisdiction of certain controversies hereinafter mentioned to be determined according to the laws and judicial procedure of the United States.

Such judicial tribunal or tribunals so established by the United States shall have exclusive jurisdiction in said zone of all controversies between citizens of the United States, and between citizens of the United States and citizens of any foreign nation other than the Republic of Colombia; and of all controversies in any wise growing out of or relating to the construction, maintenance or operation of the canal, railway and other properties and works.

III. The United States and Colombia engage jointly to establish and maintain upon said zone, judicial tribunals having civil, criminal and admiralty jurisdiction, and to be composed of jurists appointed by the Governments of the United States and Colombia in a manner hereafter to be agreed upon between said Governments, and which tribunals shall have jurisdiction of certain controversies hereinafter mentioned, and of all crimes, felonies and misdemeanors committed within said zone, and of all cases arising in admiralty, according to such laws and procedures as shall be hereafter agreed upon and declared by the two Governments.

Such joint judicial tribunal shall have exclusive jurisdiction in said zone of all controversies between citizens of the United States and citizens of Colombia, and between citizens of nations other than Colombia or the United States; and also of all crimes, felonies and misdemeanors committed within said zone, and of all questions of admiralty arising therein.

IV. The two Governments hereafter, and from time to time as occasion arises, shall agree upon and establish the laws and procedures which shall govern such joint judicial tribunal and which shall be applicable to the persons and cases over which such tribunal shall have jurisdiction, and also shall likewise create the requisite officers and employees of such court and establish their powers and duties; and further shall make adequate provision by like agreement for the pursuit, capture, imprisonment, detention and delivery within said zone of persons charged with the commitment of crimes, felonies or misdemeanors without said zone; and for the pursuit, capture, imprisonment, detention and delivery without said zone of persons charged with the commitment of crimes, felonies and misdemeanors within said zone.

Article 14

The works of the canal, the railways and their auxiliaries are declared of public utility, and in consequence all areas of land and water necessary for the construction, maintenance, and operation of the ca-

nal and other specified works may be expropriated in conformity with the laws of Colombia, except that the indemnity shall be conclusively determined without appeal, by a joint commission appointed by the Governments of Colombia and the United States.

The indemnities awarded by the Commission for such expropriation shall be borne by the United States, but the appraisal of said lands and the assessment of damages shall be based upon their value before the commencement of the work upon the canal.

Article 15

The Republic of Colombia grants to the United States the use of all the ports of the Republic open to commerce as places of refuge for any vessels employed in the canal enterprise, and for all vessels in distress having the right to pass through the canal and within to anchor in said ports. Such vessels shall be exempt from anchorage and tonnage dues on the part of Colombia.

Article 16

The canal, when constructed, and the entrance thereto shall be neutral in perpetuity, and shall be opened upon the terms provided for by Section I of Article three of, and in conformity with all the stipulations of, the treaty entered into by the Governments of the United States and Great Britain on November 18, 1901.

Article 17

The Government of Colombia shall have the right to transport over the canal its vessels, troops, and munitions of war at all times without paying charges of any kind. This exemption is to be extended to the auxiliary railway for the transportation of persons in the service of the Republic of Colombia or of the Department of Panama, or of the police force charged with the preservation of public order outside of said zone, as well as to their baggage, munitions of war and supplies.

Article 18

The United States shall have full power and authority to establish and enforce regulations for the use of the canal, railways, and the entering ports and auxiliary works, and to fix rates of tolls and charges thereof, subject to the limitations stated in Article 16.

Article 19

The rights and privileges granted to the United States by this convention shall not affect the sovereignty of the Republic of Colombia over the real estate that may be acquired by the United States by reason of the transfer of the rights of the New Panama Canal Company and the Panama Railroad Company lying outside of the said canal zone.

Article 20

If by virtue of any existing treaty between the Republic of Colombia and any third power, there may be any privilege or concession relative to an interoceanic means of communication which especially favors such third power, and which in any of its terms may be incompatible with the terms of the present convention, the Republic of Colombia agrees to cancel or modify such treaty in due form, for which purpose it shall give to the said third power the requisite notification within the term of four months from the date of the present convention, and in case the existing treaty contains no clause permitting its modification or annulment, the Republic of Colombia agrees to procure its modification or annulment in such form that there shall not exist any conflict with the stipulations of the present convention.

Article 21

The rights and privileges granted by the Republic of Colombia to the United States in the preceding Articles are understood to be free of all anterior concessions or privileges to other Governments, corporations, syndicates or individuals, and consequently, if there should arise any claims on account of the present concessions and privileges or otherwise, the claimants shall resort to the Government of Colombia and not to the United States for any indemnity or compromise which may be required.

Article 22

The Republic of Colombia renounces and grants to the United States the participation to which it might be entitled in the future earnings of the canal under Article 1 of the concessionary contract with Lucien N.B. Wyse now owned by the New Panama Canal Company and any and all other rights or claims of a pecuniary nature arising under or relating to said concession, or arising under or relating to the concessions to the Panama Railroad Company or any extension or modification thereof; and it likewise renounces, confirms and grants to the United States, now and hereafter, all the rights and property reserved in the said concessions which otherwise would belong to Colombia at or before the expiration of the terms of ninety-nine years of the concessions granted to or held by the above mentioned party and companies, and all right, title and interest which it now has or may hereafter have, in and to the lands, canal, works, property and rights held by the said companies under said concessions or otherwise, and acquired or to be acquired by the United States from or through the New Panama Canal Company, including any property and rights which might or may in the future either by lapse of time, forfeiture or otherwise, revert to the Republic of Colombia under any contracts of concessions, with said Wyse, the Universal Panama Canal Company, the Panama Railroad Company and the New Panama Canal Company.

The aforesaid rights and property shall be and are free and released from any present or reversionary interest in or claims of Colombia and the title of the United States thereto upon consummation of the contemplated purchase by the United States from the New Panama Canal Company, shall be absolute, so far as concerns the Republic of Colombia, excepting always the rights of Colombia specifically secured under this treaty.

Article 23

If it should become necessary at any time to employ armed forces for the safety or protection of the canal, or of the ships that make use of the same, or the railways and other works, the Republic of Colombia agrees to provide the forces necessary for such purpose, according to the circumstances of the case, but if the Government of Colombia cannot effectively comply with this obligation, then, with the consent of or at the request of Colombia, or of her Minister at Washington, or of the local authorities, civil or military, the United States shall employ such force as may be necessary for that sole purpose; and as soon as the necessity shall have ceased will withdraw the forces so employed. Under exceptional circumstances, however, on account of unforeseen or imminent danger to said canal, railways and other works, or to the lives and property of the persons employed upon the canal, railways, and other works, the Government of the United States is authorized to act in the interest of their protection, without the necessity of obtaining the consent beforehand of the Government of Colombia; and it shall give immediate advice of the measures adopted for the purpose stated; and as soon as sufficient Colombian forces shall arrive to attend to the indicated purpose, those of the United States shall retire.

Article 24

The Government of the United States agrees to complete the construction of the preliminary works necessary, together with all the auxiliary works, in the shortest time possible; and within two years from the date of the exchange of ratification of this convention the main works of the canal proper shall be commenced, and it shall be opened to the traffic between the two oceans within twelve years after such period of two years. In case, however, that any difficulties or obstacles should arise in the construction of the canal which are at present impossible to foresee, in consideration of the good faith with which the Government of the United States shall have proceeded, and the large amount of money expended so far on the works and the nature of the difficulties which may have arisen, the Government of Colombia will prolong the terms stipulated in this Article up to twelve years more for the completion of the work of the canal.

But in case the United States should, at any time, determine to make such canal practically a sea level canal, then such period shall be extended for ten years further.

Article 25

As the price or compensation for the right to use the zone granted in this convention by Colombia to the United States for the construction of a canal, together with the proprietary right over the Panama Railroad, and for the annuity of two hundred and fifty thousand dollars gold, which Colombia ceases to receive from the said railroad, as well as in compensation for other rights, privileges and exemptions granted to the United States, and in consideration of the increase in the administrative expenses of the Department of Panama consequent upon the construction of the said canal, the Government of the United States binds itself to pay Colombia the sum of ten million dollars in gold coin of the United States on the exchange of the ratification of this convention after its approval according to the laws of the respective countries, and also an annual payment during the life of this convention of two hundred and fifty thousand dollars in like gold coin, beginning nine years after the date aforesaid.

The provisions of this Article shall be in addition to all other benefits assured to Colombia under this convention. But no delay nor difference of opinion under this Article shall affect nor interrupt the full operation and effect of this convention in all other respects.

Article 26

No change either in the Government or in the laws and treaties of Colombia, shall, without the consent of the United States, affect any right of the United States under the present convention, or under any treaty stipulation between the two countries (that now exist or may hereafter exist) touching the subject matter of this convention.

If Colombia shall hereafter enter as a constituent into any other Government or into any union or confederation of States so as to merge her sovereignty or independence in such Government, union, or confederation, the rights of the United States under this convention shall not be in any respect lessened or impaired.

Article 27

The joint commission referred to in Articles 3, 7, and 14 shall be established as follows:

The President of the United States shall nominate two persons and the President of Colombia shall nominate two persons and they shall proceed to a decision; but in case of disagreement of the Commission (by reason of their being equally divided in conclusion) an umpire shall be appointed by the two Governments, who shall render the decision. In the event of death, absence or incapacity of any Commissioner or umpire, or of his omitting, declining or ceasing to act, his place shall be filled by the appointment of another person in the manner above indicated. All decisions by a majority of the Commission or by the umpire shall be final.

Article 28

This convention when signed by the contracting parties, shall be ratified according to the laws of the respective countries and shall be exchanged at Washington within a term of eight months from this date, or earlier if possible.

In faith whereof, the respective plenipotentiaries have signed the present convention in duplicate and have hereunto affixed their respective seals.

Done at the City of Washington, the 22d day of January in the year of our Lord nineteen hundred and three.

JOHN HAY

TOMAS HERRAN

✳ THE "HAY-BUNAU-VARILLA CONVENTION"

Between the United States and Panama, Signed at Washington, November 1, 1903 Isthmian Canal Convention

THE UNITED STATES of America and the Republic of Panama being desirous to insure the construction of a ship canal across the Isthmus of Panama to connect the Atlantic and Pacific Oceans, and the Congress of the United States of America having passed an act approved June 28, 1902, in furtherance of that object, by which the President of the United States is authorized to acquire within a reasonable time the control of the necessary territory of the Republic of Colombia, and the sovereignty of such territory being actually vested in the Republic of Panama, the high contracting parties have resolved for that purpose to conclude a convention and have accordingly appointed as their plenipotentiaries,-

The President of the United States of America, JOHN HAY, Secretary of State, and

The Government of the Republic of Panama, PHILIPPE BUNAU-VARILLA, Envoy Extraordinary and Minister Plenipotentiary of the Republic of Panama, thereunto specially empowered by said government, who after communicating with each other their respective full powers, found to be in good and due form, have agreed upon and concluded the following articles:

Article I

The United States guarantees and will maintain the independence of the Republic of Panama.

Article 2

The Republic of Panama grants to the United States in perpetuity the use, occupation and control of a zone of land and land under water for the construction, maintenance, operation, sanitation and protection of said Canal of the width of ten miles extending to the distance of five miles on each side of the center line of the route of the Canal to be constructed; the said zone beginning in the Caribbean Sea three marine miles from mean low water mark and extending to and across the Isthmus of Panama into the Pacific Ocean to a distance of three marine miles from mean low water mark with the proviso that the cities of Panama and Colon and the harbors adjacent to said cities, which are included within the boundaries of the zone above described, shall not be included within this grant. The Republic of Panama further grants to the United States in perpetuity the use, occupation and control of any other lands and waters outside of the zone above described which may be necessary and convenient for the construction, maintenance, operations, sanitation and protection of the said Canal or of any auxiliary canals or other works necessary and convenient for the construction, maintenance, operation, sanitation and protection of the said enterprise, The Republic of Panama further grants in like manner to the United States in perpetuity all islands within the limits of the zone above described and in addition thereto the group of

small islands in the Bay of Panama, named Perico, Naos, Culebra and Flamenco.

Article 3

The Republic of Panama grants to the United States all the rights, power and authority within the zone mentioned and described in Article 2 of this agreement and within the limits of all auxiliary lands and waters mentioned and described in said Article 2 which the United States would possess and exercise if it were the sovereign of the territory within which said lands and waters are located to the entire exclusion of the exercise by the Republic of Panama of any such sovereign rights, power or authority.

Article 4

As rights subsidiary to the above grants the Republic of Panama grants in perpetuity to the United States the right to use the rivers, streams, lakes and other bodies of water within its limits for navigation, the supply of water or water-power or other purposes, so far as the use of said rivers, streams, lakes and bodies of water and the waters thereof may be necessary and convenient for the construction, maintenance, operation, sanitation and protection of the said Canal.

Article 5

The Republic of Panama grants to the United States in perpetuity a monopoly for the construction, maintenance and operation of any system of communication by means of canal or railroad across its territory between the Caribbean Sea and the Pacific Ocean.

Article 6

The grants herein contained shall in no manner invalidate the titles or rights of private land holders or owners of private property in the said zone or in or to any of the lands or waters granted to the United States by the provisions of any Article of this treaty, nor shall they interfere with the rights of way over the public roads passing through the said zone or over any of the said lands or waters unless said rights of way or private rights shall conflict with rights herein granted to the United States in which case the rights of the United States shall be superior. All damages caused to the owners of private lands or private property of any kind by reason of the grants contained in this treaty or by reason of the operations of the United States, its agents or employees, or by reason of the construction, maintenance, operation, sanitation and protection of the said Canal or of the works of sanitation and protection herein provided for, shall be appraised and settled by a joint commission appointed by the Governments of the United States and the Republic of Panama, whose decisions as to such damages shall be final and whose awards as to such damages shall be paid solely by the United States. No part of the work on said Canal or the Panama railroad or on any auxiliary works relating thereto and authorized by the terms of this treaty shall be prevented, delayed or impeded by or pending such proceedings to ascertain such damages. The appraisal of said private lands and private property and the assessment of damages to them shall be based upon their value before the date of this convention.

Article 7

The Republic of Panama grants to the United States within the limits of the cities of Panama and Colon and their adjacent harbors and within the territory adjacent thereto the right to acquire by purchase or by the exercise of the right of eminent domain, any lands, buildings, water rights or other properties necessary and convenient for the construction, maintenance, operation and protection of the Canal and of any works of sanitation, such as the collection and disposition of sewage and the distribution of water in the said cities of Panama and Colon, which, in the discretion of the United States may be necessary and convenient for the construction, maintenance, operation, sanitation and protection of the said Canal and railroad. All such works of sanitation, collection and disposition of sewage and distribution of water in the cities of Panama and Colon shall be made at the expense of the United States, and the Government of the United States, its agents or nominees shall be authorized to impose and collect water rates and sewerage rates which shall be sufficient to provide for the payment of interest and the amortization of the principal of the cost of said works within a period of fifty years and upon the expiration of said term of fifty years the system of sewers and water works shall revert to and become the properties of the cities of Panama and Colon respectively, and the use of the water shall be free to the inhabitants of Panama and Colon, except to the extent that water rates may be necessary for the operation and maintenance of said system of sewers and water.

The Republic of Panama agrees that the cities of Panama and Colon shall comply in perpetuity with the sanitary ordinances whether of a preventive or curative character prescribed by the United States and in case the Government of Panama is unable or fails in its duty to enforce this compliance by the cities of Panama and Colon with the sanitary ordinances of the United States the Republic of Panama grants to the United States the right and authority to enforce the same.

The same right and authority are granted to the United States for the maintenance of public order in the cities of Panama and Colon and the territories and harbors adjacent thereto in case the Republic of Panama should not be, in the judgment of the United States, able to maintain such order.

Article 8

The Republic of Panama grants to the United States all rights which it now has or hereafter may acquire to the property of the New Panama Canal Company and the Panama Railroad Company as a result of the transfer of sovereignty from the Republic of Colombia to the Republic of Panama over the Isthmus of Panama and authorizes the New Panama Canal Company to sell and transfer to the United States its rights, privileges, properties and concessions as well as the Panama Railroad and all the shares or part of the shares of that company; but the public lands situated outside of the one described in Article 2 of this treaty now included in the concessions to both said enterprises and not required in the construction or operation of the Canal shall revert to the Republic of Panama except any property now owned by or in the possession of said companies within Panama or Colon or the ports or terminals thereof.

Article 9

The United States agrees that the ports at either entrance of the Canal and the waters thereof, and the Republic of Panama agrees that the towns of Panama and Colon shall be free for all time so that there shall not be imposed or collected custom house tolls, tonnage, anchorage, lighthouse, wharf, pilot, or quarantine dues or any other charges or taxes of any kind upon any vessel using or passing through the Canal or belonging to or employed by the United States, directly or indirectly, in connection with the construction, maintenance, operation, sanitation and protection of the main Canal, or auxiliary works, or upon the cargo, officers, crew, or passengers of any such vessels, except such tolls and charges as may be imposed by the United States for the use of the Canal and other works, and except tolls and charges imposed by the Republic of Panama upon merchandise destined to be introduced for the consumption of the rest of the Republic of Panama, and upon vessels touching at the ports of Colon and Panama and which do not cross the Canal.

The Government of the Republic of Panama shall have the right to establish in such ports and in the towns of Panama and Colon such houses and guards as it may deem necessary to collect duties on importations destined to other portions of Panama and to prevent contraband trade. The United States shall have the right to make use of the towns and harbors of Panama and Colon as places of anchorage, and for making repairs, for loading, unloading, depositing, or transshipping cargoes either in transit or destined for the service of the Canal and for other works pertaining to the Canal.

Article 10

The Republic of Panama agrees that there shall not be imposed any taxes, national, municipal, departmental, or of any other class, upon the Canal, the railways and auxiliary works, tugs and other vessels employed in the service of the Canal, store houses, work shops, offices, quarters for laborers, factories of all kinds, warehouses, wharves, machinery and other works, property, and effects appertaining to the Canal or railroad and auxiliary works, or their officers or employees, situated within the cities of Panama and Colon, and that there shall not be imposed contributions or charges of a personal character of any kind upon officers, employees, laborers, and other individuals in the service of the Canal and railroad and auxiliary works.

Article 11

The United States agrees that the official dispatches of the Government of the Republic of Panama shall be transmitted over any telegraph and telephone lines established for canal purposes and used for public and private business at rates not higher than those required from officials in the service of the United States.

Article 12

The Government of the Republic of Panama shall permit the immigration and free access to the lands and workshops of the Canal and its auxiliary works of all employees and workmen of whatever nationality under contract to work upon or seeking employment upon or in any wise connected with the said Canal and its auxiliary works, with their respective families, and all such persons shall be free and exempt from the military service of the Republic of Panama.

Article 13

The United States may import at any time into the said zone and auxiliary lands, free of custom duties, imposts, taxes, or other charges, and without any restrictions, any and all vessels, dredges, engines, cars, machinery, tools, explosives, materials, supplies, and other articles necessary and convenient in the construction, maintenance, operation, sanitation and protection of the Canal and auxiliary works, and all provisions, medicines, clothing, supplies and other things necessary and convenient for the officers, employees, workmen and laborers in the service and employ of the United States and for their families. If any such articles are disposed of for use outside of the zone and auxiliary lands granted to the United States and within the territory of the Republic, they shall be subject to the same import or other duties as like articles imported under the laws of the Republic of Panama.

Article 14

As the price or compensation for the rights, powers and privileges granted in this convention by the Republic of Panama to the United States, the Government of the United States agrees to pay to the Republic of Panama the sum of ten million dollars ($10,000,000) in gold coin of the United States on the exchange of the ratification of this convention and also an annual payment during the life of this convention of two hundred and fifty thousand dollars ($250,000) in like gold coin, beginning nine years after the date aforesaid.

The provisions of this Article shall be in addition to all other benefits assured to the Republic of Panama under this convention.

But no delay or difference of opinion under this Article or any other provisions of this treaty shall affect or interrupt the full operation and effect of this convention in all other respects.

Article 15

The joint commission referred to in Article 6 shall be established as follows:

The President of the United States shall nominate two persons and the President of the Republic of Panama shall nominate two persons and they shall proceed to a decision; but in case of disagreement of the Commission (by reason of their being equally divided in conclusion) an umpire shall be appointed by the two Governments who shall render the decision. In the event of the death, absence, or incapacity of a Commissioner or Umpire, or of his omitting, declining or ceasing to act, his place shall be filled by the appointment of another person in the manner above indicated. All decisions by a majority of the Commission or by the umpire shall be final.

Article 16

The two Governments shall make adequate provision by future agreement for the pursuit, capture, imprisonment, detention and delivery within said zone and auxiliary lands to the authorities of the Republic of Panama of persons charged with the commitment of crimes, felonies or misdemeanors without said zone and for the pursuit, capture, imprisonment, detention and delivery without said zone to the authorities of the United States of persons charged with the commitment of crimes, felonies and misdemeanors within said zone and auxiliary lands.

Article 17

The Republic of Panama grants to the United States the use of all the ports of the Republic open to commerce as places of refuge for any vessels employed in the Canal enterprise, and for all vessels passing or bound to pass through the Canal which may be in distress and be driven to seek refuge in said ports. Such vessels shall be exempt from anchorage and tonnage dues on the part of the Republic of Panama.

Article 18

The Canal, when constructed, and the entrances thereto shall be neutral in perpetuity, and shall be opened upon the terms provided for by Section I of Article three of, and in conformity with all the stipulations of, the treaty entered into by the Governments of the United States and Great Britain on November 18, 1901.

Article 19

The Government of the Republic of Panama shall have the right to transport over the Canal its vessels and its troops and munitions of war in such vessels at all times without paying charges of any kind. The exemption is to be extended to the auxiliary railway for the transportation of persons in the service of the Republic of Panama, or of the police force charged with the preservation of public order outside of said zone, as well as to their baggage, munitions of war and supplies.

Article 20

If by virtue of any existing treaty in relation to the territory of the Isthmus of Panama, whereof the obligations shall descend or be assumed by the Republic of Panama, there may be any privilege or concession in favor of the Government or the citizens and subjects of a third power relative to an interoceanic means of communication which in any of its terms may be incompatible with the terms of the present convention, the Republic of Panama agrees to cancel or modify such treaty in due form, for which purpose it shall give to the said third power the requisite notification within the term of four months from the date of the present convention, and in case the existing treaty contains no clause permitting its modification or annulment, the Republic of Panama agrees to procure its modification or annulment in such form that there shall not exist any conflict with the stipulations of the present convention.

Article 21

The rights and privileges granted by the Republic of Panama to the United States in the preceding Articles are understood to be free of all anterior debts, liens, trusts, or liabilities, or concessions or privileges to other Governments, corporations, syndicates or individuals, and consequently, if there should arise any claims on account of the present concessions and privileges or otherwise, the claimants shall resort to the Government of the Republic of Panama and not to the United States for any indemnity or compromise which may be required.

Article 22

The Republic of Panama renounces and grants to the United States the participation to which it might be entitled in the future earnings of the Canal under Article 15 of the concessionary contract with Lucien N.B. Wyse now owned by the New Panama Canal Company and any and all other rights or claims of a pecuniary nature arising under or relating to said concessions, or arising under or relating to the concessions to the Panama Railroad Company or any extension or modification thereof; and it likewise renounces, confirms and grants to the United States, now and hereafter, all the rights and property reserved in the said concessions which otherwise would belong to Panama at or before the expiration of the terms of ninety-nine years of the concessions granted to or held by the above mentioned party and companies, and all right, title and interest which it now has or may hereafter have, in and to the lands, canal, works, property and rights held by the said companies under said concessions or otherwise, and acquired or to be acquired by the United States from or through the New Panama Canal Company, including any property and rights which might or may in the future either by lapse of time, forfeiture or otherwise, revert to the Republic of Panama under any contracts or concessions, with said Wyse, the Universal Panama Canal Company, the Panama Railroad Company and the New Panama Canal Company.

The aforesaid rights and property shall be and are free and released from any present or reversionary interest in or claims of Panama and the title of the United States thereto upon consummation of the contemplated purchase by the United States from the New Panama Canal Company, shall be absolute, so far as concerns the Republic of Panama, excepting always the rights of the Republic specifically secured under this treaty.

Article 23

If it should become necessary at any time to employ armed forces for the safety or protection of the Canal, or of the ships that make use of the same, or the railways and auxiliary works, the United States shall have the right, at all times and in its discretion, to use its police and its land and naval forces or to establish fortifications for these purposes.

Article 24

No change either in the Government or in the laws and treaties of the Republic of Panama shall, without the consent of the United States, affect any right of the United States under the present convention, or under any treaty stipulation between the two countries that now exists or may hereafter exist touching the subject matter of this convention.

If the Republic of Panama shall hereafter enter as a constituent into any other Government or into any union or confederation of states, so as to merge her sovereignty or independence in such Government, union or confederation, the rights of the United States under this convention shall not be in any respect lessened or impaired.

Article 25

For the better performance of the engagements of this convention and to the end of the efficient protection of the Canal and the preservation of its neutrality, the Government of the Republic of Panama will sell or lease to the United States lands adequate and necessary for naval or coaling stations on the Pacific coast and on the western Caribbean coast of the Republic at certain points to be agreed upon with the President of the United States.

Article 26

This convention when signed by the Plenipotentiaries of the Contracting Parties shall be ratified by the respective Governments and the ratifications shall be exchanged at Washington at the earliest date possible. In faith whereof the respective Plenipotentiaries have signed the present convention in du-plicate and have hereunto affixed their respective seals. Done at the City of Washington the 18th day of November in the year of our Lord nineteen hundred and three.

JON HAY

P. BUNAU VARILLA

✸TREATY OF RELATIONS BETWEEN THE UNITED STATES AND CUBA

Signed at Washington, May 29, 1934

THE UNITED STATES of America and the Republic of Cuba, being animated by the desire to fortify the relations of friendship between the two countries and to modify, with this purpose, the relations established between them by the Treaty of Relations signed at Habana, May 22, 1903, have appointed, with this intention, as their Plenipotentiaries:

[Names of Plenipotentiaries]

Who, after having communicated to each other their full powers which were found to be in good and due form, have agreed upon the following articles:

Article I

The Treaty of Relations which was concluded between the two contracting parties on May 22, 1903, shall cease to be in force, and is abrogated, from the date on which the present Treaty goes into effect.

Article II

All the acts effected in Cuba by the United States of America during its military occupation of the island, up to May 20, 1902, the date on which the Republic of Cuba was established, have been ratified and held as valid; and all the rights legally acquired by virtue of those acts shall be maintained and protected.

Article III

Until the two contracting parties agree to the modification or abrogation of the stipulations of the agreement in regard to the lease to the United States of America of lands in Cuba for coaling and naval stations signed by the President of the Republic of Cuba on February 6, 1903, and by the President of the United States of America on the 23rd day of the same month and year, the stipulations of that agreement with regard to the naval station of Guantanamo shall continue in effect. The supplementary agreement in regard to naval or coaling stations signed between the two Governments on July 2, 1903, also shall continue in effect in the same form and on the same conditions with respect to the naval station at

Guantanamo. So long as the United States of America shall not abandon the said naval station of Guantanamo or the two Governments shall not agree to a modification of its present limits, the station shall continue to have the territorial area that it now has, with the limits that it has on the date of the signature of the present Treaty.

Article IV

If at any time in the future a situation should arise that appears to point to an outbreak of contagious disease in the territory of either of the contracting parties, either of the two Governments shall for its own protection, and without its act being considered unfriendly, exercise freely and at its discretion the right to suspend communications between those of its ports that it may designate and all or part of the territory of the other party, and for the period that it may consider to be advisable.

Article V

The present Treaty shall be ratified by the contracting parties in accordance with their respective constitutional methods; and shall go into effect on the date of the exchange of their ratifications, which shall take place in the city of Washington as soon as possible.

In faith whereof, the respective Plenipotentiaries have signed the present Treaty and have affixed their seals hereto.

Done in duplicate, in the English and Spanish languages, at Washington on the twenty-ninth day of May, one thousand nine hundred and thirty-four.
CORDELL HULL
SUMNER WELLES
M. MARQUEZ STERLING

✱CONSTITUTIONAL CONVENTION OF PUERTO RICO

Hon. Antonio Fernos Isern, President
Hon. María Libertad Gómez Garriga, First Vice President
Hon. Víctor Gutiérrez Franqui, Second Vice President

Delegates	Residences
1. Manuel Acevedo Rosario	Camuy
2. Juan Alemany Silva	Guayama
3. Arcilio Alvarado Alvarado	Santurce
4. Enrique Àlvarez Vicente	Utuado
5. Francisco L. Anselmi Rodríguez	Coamo

Delegates	Residences
6. Francisco Arrillaga Gaztambide	Hato Rey
7. Carmelo Àvila Medina	Naguabo
8. José B. Barceló Oliver	Adjuntas
9. Ramón Barreto Pérez	Hato Rey
10. Ramón Barrios Sánchez	Bayamón
11. Jaime Benítez Rexach	Río Piedras
12. Francisco Berio Suárez	Comerío
13. Virgilio Brunet Maldonado	Hato Rey
14. Agustín Burgos Rivera	Villalba
15. Mario Canales Torresola	Jayuya
16. Angel M. Candelario Arce	Peñuelas
17. Ernesto Carrasquillo Quiñones	Yubucoa
18. Dionisio Casillas Casillas	Humacao
19. José A. Cintrón Rivera	Santurce
20. Luis Alfredo Colón Velázquez	Moca
21. Ramiro Colón Castaño	Ponce
22. Juan Dávila Díaz	Manatí
23. José M. Dávila Monsanto	Guayama
24. Lionel Fernández Méndez	Cayey
25. Antonio Fernos Isern	Santurce
26. Luis A. Ferré Aguayo	Ponce
27. Alcides Figueroa Oliva	Añasco
28. Leopoldo Figueroa Carreras	Cataño
29. Ernesto Juan Fonfrías Rivera	Carretera 2, K-19
30. Jorge Font Saldaña	Santurce
31. Juan R. García Delgado	Hatillo
32. Miguel A. García Méndez	Mayagüez
33. Jenaro Gautier Dapena	Caguas-La Muda
34. Rubén Gaztambide Arrillaga	Río Piedras
35. Fernando J. Geigel Sabat	Santurce
36. José R. Gelpi Bosch	Mayagüez
37. Darío Goitía Montalvo	Arecibo
38. María Libertad Gómez Garriga	Utuado
39. Héctor González Blanés	Santurce
40. Andrés Grillasca Salas	Ponce
41. Víctor Gutiérrez Franqui	Santurce
42. Celestino Iriarte Miró	Carretera Cataño
43. Jesús Izcoa Mouré	Naranjito
44. Lorenzo Lagarde Garcés	Ponce
45. Ramón Llobet Díaz	Guaynabo
46. Ramiro Martínez Sandín	Vega Baja
47. Juan Meléndez Baez	San Juan
48. Ramón Mellado Parsons	Río Piedras
49. Bernardo Méndez Jiménez	San Sebastián
50. Armando Mignucci Calder	Yauco
51. José Mimoso Raspaldo	Caguas

Delegates	*Residences*
52. Pablo Morales Otero	Santurce
53. Luis Muñoz Marín	San Juan
54. Luis Muñoz Rivera	Hato Rey
55. Eduardo Negrón Benítez	San Sebastián
56. Luis A. Negrón López	Sabana Grande
57. Abraham Nieves Negrón	Guayama
58. Mario Orsini Martínez	Juncos
59. Benjamín Ortiz Ortiz	Guaynabo
60. Cruz Ortiz Stella	Humacao
61. Lino Padrón Rivera	Vega Baja
62. Santiago R. Palmer Díaz	San Germán
63. Norman E. Parkhurst	Bayamón
64. Francisco Paz Granela	Santurce
65. Santiago Polanco Abreu	Isabela
66. Samuel R. Quiñones Quiñones	Carr. Isla Verde
67. Ubaldino Ramírez de Arellano Quiñones	San Germán
68. Ernesto Ramos Antonini	Hato Rey
69. Ramón María Ramos de Jesús	Aibonito
70. Antonio Reyes Delgado	Arecibo
71. Dolores Rivera Candelaria	Utuado
72. Heraclio H. Rivera Colón	Toa Alta
73. Alejo Rivera Morales	Ceiba
74. Alvaro Rivera Reyes	Río Grande
75. Carmelo Rodríguez García	Arecibo
76. Carlos Román Benítez	Santurce
77. Alfonso Román García	Fajardo
78. Joaquín Rosa Gómez	Manatí
79. Alberto E. Sánchez Nazario	Santurce
80. Angel Sandín Martínez	Vega Baja
81. Luis Santaliz Capestany	Las Marías
82. Yldefonso Solá Morales	Caguas
83. Juan B. Soto González	Gurabo
84. Rafael Torrech Genovés	Bayamón
85. Lucas Torres Santos	Orocovis
86. Pedro Torres Díaz	Gurabo
87. José Trías Monge	Guaynabo
88. Augusto Valentín Vizcarrondo	Mayagüez
89. Baudilio Vega Berríos	Mayagüez
90. Sigfredo Vélez González	Arecibo
91. José Veray Hernández	Aguadilla
92. José Villares Rodríguez	Caguas

Officials of the Convention
José Berríos Berdecía
Secretary
Cruz Pacheco Ruiz
Sergeant at Arms
Herminio A. Concepción De Garcia
Assistant Secretary

Nestor Rigual Camacho
Assistant Secretary
Julio Morales Rodríguez
Assistant Secretary
Felipe Jiménez Rivera
Assistant Secretary
Viriato San Antonio Hernández
Paymaster
Higinia Pastoriza
Property Clerk

Committees of the Constitutional Convention
Rules: Cruz Ortiz Stella, President; José Mimoso Raspaldo, Vice President; Luis Alfredo Colón, Secretary; Luis Santaliz Capestany, Lionel Fernández Méndez, Eduardo Negrón Benítez, Joaquín Rosa, Baudilio Vega, Juan R. García Delgado, José Rosario Gelpi, Ramón Barríos.

Publications and Disbursements: Santiago R. Palmer, President; Alfonso Román García, Vice President; Juan Dávila Díaz, Secretary; Agustín Burgos, Dionisio Casillas, Francisco Arrillaga, Abraham Nieves, Luis Muñoz Rivera, Norman E. Parkhurst, Juan R. García Delado, Enrique Àlvarez Vicente.

Judicial Branch: Ernesto Ramos Antonini, President; José Villares Rodríguez, Vice President; José M. Dávila Monsanto, Secretary; Lorenzo Lagarde Garcés, Santiago Polanco Abreu, Ernesto Juan Fonfrías, José Trías Monge, Angel M. Candelario Arce, Víctor Gutiérrez Franqui, Arcilio Alvarado, Miguel A. García Méndez, Juan B. Soto, Mario Orsini, Celestino Iriarte, Lino Padrón Rivera.

Legislative Branch: Luis Negrón López, President; Rubén Gaztambide Arrillaga, Vice President; Francisco Anselmi, Secretary; Heraclio Rivera Colón, Ramón Barreto Pérez, Augusto Valentín Vizcarrondo, Mario Canales, Ubaldino Ramírez de Arellano, Fernando Geigel, Celestino Iriarte, Lino Padrón Rivera.

Bill of Rights: Jaime Benítez, President; Ernesto Carrasquillo, Vice President; Bernardo Méndez, Secretary; Virgilio Brunet, Cruz Ortiz Stella, Alvaro Rivera Reyes, Francisco Paz Granela, José A. Cintrón Rivera, Alberto Sánchez, Juan Meléndez Baez, Arcilio Alvarado, Rubén Gaztambide Arrillaga, Héctor González Blanés, Leopoldo Figueroa Carreras, Juan B. Soto, Lino Padrón Rivera, Antonio Reyes Delgado.

Drafting, Style and Enrollment: Víctor Gutiérrez Franqui, President; María Libertad Gómez, Vice President; Jorge Font Saldaña, Secretary; Samuel R. Quiñones, Jaime Benítez, Benjamín Ortiz, Lionel Fernández Méndez, Jesús Izcoa Mouré, Juan Alemany Silva, Celestino Iriarte, Mario Orsini.

Preamble, Ordinances and Amendment Procedure:

Luis Muñoz Marín, President; José Trías Monge, Vice President; Jorge Font Saldaña, Secretary; Ernesto Ramos Antonini, Ernesto Juan Fonfrías, Ramón Mellado, Virgilio Brunet, Jenaro Gautier, Carlos Román Benítez, Luis Alfredo Colón, Luis A. Ferré, Ramiro Colón, Antonio Reyes Delgado, Héctor González Blanés, Ramiro Martínez Sandín.

Agenda: Benjamín Ortiz, President; Heraclio Rivera Colón, Vice President; Sigfredo Vélez González, Secretary; Carlos Román Benítez, Francisco Berio Suárez, Armando Mignucci, Pedro Torres Díaz, Lucas Torres, Leopoldo Figueroa Carreras, Miguel A. García Méndez, Ramón Barríos.

Transitory Provisions and General Matters: Yldefonso Solá Morales, President; Santiago Polanco Abreu, Vice President; Angel Sandín, Secretary; Francisco Anselmi, Carmelo Àvila Medina, Andrés Grillasca, José B. Barceló, Manuel Acevedo Rosario, Alcides Figueroa, Dolores Rivera Candelaria, Luis A. Ferré, Ramón Llobet, José Veray, Jr., Alejo Rivera Morales, Ramiro Martínez Sandín.

Executive Branch: Samuel R. Quiñones, President; Àlvaro Rivera Reyes, Vice President; Luis Negrón López, Secretary; Darío Goitía, Carmelo Rodríguez García, Pablo Morales Otero, Yldefonso Solá Morales, Rafael Torrech Genóves, Jose R. Gelpi, José Veray, Jr., Antonio Reyes Delgado.

We, the people of Puerto Rico, in order to organize ourselves politically on a fully democratic basis, to promote the general welfare, and to secure for ourselves and our posterity the complete enjoyment of human rights, placing our trust in Almighty God, do ordain and establish this Constitution for the commonwealth which, in the exercise of our natural rights, we now create within our union with the United States of America.

In so doing, we declare:

The democratic system is fundamental to the life of the Puerto Rican community;

We understand that the democratic system of government is one in which the will of the people is the source of public power, the political order is subordinate to the rights of man, and the free participation of the citizen in collective decisions is assured;

We consider as determining factors in our life our citizenship of the United States of America and our aspiration continually to enrich our democratic heritage in the individual and collective enjoyment of its rights and privileges; our loyalty to the principles of the Federal Constitution; the coexistence in Puerto Rico of the two great cultures of the American Hemisphere; our fervor for education; our faith in justice; our devotion to the courageous, industrious, and peaceful way of life; our fidelity to individual human

values above and beyond social position, racial differences, and economic interests; and our hope for a better world based on these principles.

Article I

The Commonwealth

Section 1.—The Commonwealth of Puerto Rico is hereby constituted. Its political power emanates from the people and shall be exercised in accordance with their will, within the terms of the compact agreed upon between the people of Puerto Rico and the United States of America.

Section 2.—The government of the Commonwealth of Puerto Rico shall be republican in form and its legislative, judicial and executive branches as established by this Constitution shall be equally subordinate to the sovereignty of the people of Puerto Rico.

Section 3.—The political authority of the Commonwealth of Puerto Rico shall extend to the Island of Puerto Rico and to the adjacent islands within its jurisdiction.

Section 4.—The seat of the government shall be the city of San Juan.

Article II

Bill of Rights

Section 1.— The dignity of the human being is inviolable. All men are equal before the law. No discrimination shall be made on account of race, color, sex, birth, social origin or condition, or political or religious ideas. Both the laws and the system of public education shall embody these principles of essential human equality.

Section 2.—The laws shall guarantee the expression of the will of the people by means of equal, direct and secret universal suffrage and shal l protect the citizen against any coercion in the exercise of the electoral franchise.

Section 3.—No law shall be made respecting an establishment of religion or prohibiting the free exercise thereof. There shall be complete separation of church and state.

Section 4.—No law shall be made abridging the freedom of speech or of the press, or the right of the people peaceably to assemble and to petition the government for a redress of grievances.

Section 5.—Every person has the right to an education which shall be directed to the full development of the human personality and to the strengthening of respect for human rights and fundamental freedoms. There shall be a system of free and wholly non-sectarian public education. Instruction in the elementary and secondary schools shall be free and shall be compulsory in the elementary schools to the extent permitted by the facilities of the state. No public property or public funds shall be used for the support of schools or educational institutions other than those of the state. Nothing contained in this provision shall prevent the state from furnishing to any child non-educational services established by law for the protection or welfare of children.

Section 6.—Persons may join with each other and organize freely for any lawful purpose, except in military or quasi-military organizations.

Section 7.—The right to life, liberty and the enjoyment of property is recognized as a fundamental right of man. The death penalty shall not exist. No person shall be deprived of his liberty or property without due process of law. No person in Puerto Rico shall be denied the equal protection of the laws. No laws impairing the obligation of contracts shall be enacted. A minimum amount of property and possessions shall be exempt from attachment as provided by law.

Section 8.—Every person has the right to the protection of law against abusive attacks on his honor, reputation and private or family life.

Section 9.—Private property shall not be taken or damaged for public use except upon payment of just compensation and in the manner provided by law. No law shall be enacted authorizing condemnation of printing presses, machinery or material devoted to publications of any kind. The buildings in which these objects are located may be condemned only after a judicial finding of public convenience and necessity pursuant to procedure that shall be provided by law, and may be taken before such a judicial finding only when there is placed at the disposition of the publication an adequate site in which it can be installed and continue to operate for a reasonable time.

Section 10.—The right of the people to be secure in their persons, houses, papers and effects against unreasonable searches and seizures shall not be violated.

Wire-tapping is prohibited.

No warrant for arrest or search and seizure shall issue except by judicial authority and only upon probable cause supported by oath or affirmation, and particularly describing the place to be searched and the persons to be arrested or the things to be seized.

Evidence obtained in violation of this section shall be inadmissible in the courts.

Section 11.—In all criminal prosecutions, the accused shall enjoy the right to have a speedy and public trial, to be informed of the nature and cause of the accusation and to have a copy thereof, to be confronted with the witnesses against him, to have compulsory process for obtaining witnesses in his favor, to have assistance of counsel, and to be presumed innocent.

In all prosecutions for a felony the accused shall have the right of trial by an impartial jury composed of twelve residents of the district, who may render their verdict by a majority vote which in no case may be less than nine.

No person shall be compelled in any criminal case to be a witness against himself and the failure of the accused to testify may be neither taken into consideration nor commented upon against him.

No person shall be twice put in jeopardy of punishment for the same offense.

Before conviction every accused shall be entitled to be admitted to bail.

Incarceration prior to trial shall not exceed six months nor shall bail or fines be excessive. No person shall be imprisoned for debt.

Section 12.—Neither slavery nor involuntary servitude shall exist except in the latter case as a punishment for crime after the accused has been duly convicted. Cruel and unusual punishments shall not be inflicted. Suspension of civil rights including the right to vote shall cease upon service of the term of imprisonment imposed.

No ex post facto law or bill of attainder shall be passed.

Section 13.—-The writ of habeas corpus shall be granted without delay and free of costs. The privilege of the writ of habeas corpus shall not be suspended, unless the public safety requires it in case of rebellion, insurrection or invasion. Only the Legislative Assembly shall have the power to suspend the privilege of the writ of habeas corpus and the laws regulating its issuance.

The military authority shall always be subordinate to civil authority.

Section 14.—No titles of nobility or other hereditary honors shall be granted. No officer or employee of the Commonwealth shall accept gifts, donations, decorations or offices from any foreign country or officer without prior authorization by the Legislative Assembly.

Section 15.—The employment of children less than fourteen years of age in any occupation which is prejudicial to their health or morals or which places them in jeopardy of life or limb is prohibited.

No child less than sixteen years of age shall be kept in custody in a jail or penitentiary.

Section 16.—The right of every employee to choose his occupation freely and to resign therefrom is recognized, as is his right to equal pay for equal work, to a reasonable minimum salary, to protection against risks to his health or person in his work or employment, and to an ordinary workday which shall not exceed eight hours. An employee may work in excess of this daily limit only if he is paid extra compensation as provided by law, at a rate never less than one and one-half times the regular rate at which he is employed.

Section 17.—Persons employed by private businesses, enterprises and individual employers and by agencies or instrumentalities of the government operating as private businesses or enterprises, shall have the right to organize and to bargain collectively with their employers through representatives of their own free choosing in order to promote their welfare.

Section 18.—In order to assure their right to organize and to bargain collectively, persons employed by private businesses, enterprises and individual employers and by agencies or instrumentalities of the government operating as private businesses or enterprises, in their direct relations with their own employers shall have the right to strike, to picket and to engage in other legal concerted activities.

Nothing herein contained shall impair the authority of the Legislative Assembly to enact laws to deal with grave emergencies that clearly imperil the public health or safety or essential public services.

Section 19.—The foregoing enumeration of rights shall not be construed restrictively nor does it contemplate the exclusion of other rights not specifically mentioned which belong to the people in a democracy. The power of the Legislative Assembly to enact laws for the protection of the life, health and general welfare of the people shall likewise not be construed restrictively.

Section 20.—The Commonwealth also recognizes the existence of the following human rights:

The right of every person to receive free elementary and secondary education.

The right of every person to obtain work.

The right of every person to a standard of living adequate for the health and well-being of himself and of his family, and especially to food, clothing, housing and medical care and necessary social services.

The right of every person to social protection in the event of unemployment, sickness, old age or disability.

The right of motherhood and childhood to special care and assistance.

The rights set forth in this section are closely connected with the progressive development of the economy of the Commonwealth and require, for their full effectiveness, sufficient resources and an agricultural and industrial development not yet attained by the Puerto Rican community.

In the light of their duty to achieve the full liberty of the citizen, the people and the government of Puerto Rico shall do everything in their power to promote the greatest possible expansion of the system of production, to assure the fairest distribution of economic output, and to obtain the maximum understanding between individual initiative and collective cooperation. The executive and judicial branches shall bear in mind this duty and shall construe the laws that tend to fulfill it in the most favorable manner possible.

Article III

The Legislature

Section 1.—The legislative power shall be vested in a Legislative Assembly, which shall consist of two houses, the Senate and the House of Representatives whose members shall be elected by direct vote at each general election.

Section 2.—The Senate shall be composed of twenty-seven Senators and the House of Representatives of fifty-one Representatives, except as these numbers may be increased in accordance with the provisions of Section 7 of this Article.

Section 3.—For the purpose of election of members of the Legislative Assembly, Puerto Rico shall be divided into eight senatorial districts and forty representative districts. Each senatorial district shall elect two Senators and each representative district one Representative.

There shall also be eleven Senators and eleven Representatives elected at large. No elector may vote for more than one candidate for Senator at Large or for more than one candidate for Representative at Large.

Section 4.—In the first and subsequent elections under this Constitution the division of senatorial and representative districts as provided in Article VIII shall be in effect. After each decennial census beginning with the year 1960, said division shall be revised by a Board composed of the Chief Justice of the Supreme Court as Chairman and of two additional members ap- pointed by the Governor with the advice and consent of the Senate. The two additional members shall not belong to the same political party. Any revision shall maintain the number of senatorial and representative districts here created, which shall be composed of contiguous and compact territory and shall be organized, insofar as practicable, upon the basis of population and means of communication. Each senatorial district shall always include five representative districts.

The decisions of the Board shall be made by majority vote and shall take effect in the general elections next following each revision. The Board shall cease to exist after the completion of each revision.

Section 5.—No person shall be a member of the Legislative Assembly unless he is able to read and write the Spanish or English language and unless he is a citizen of the United States and of Puerto Rico and has resided in Puerto Rico at least two years immediately prior to the date of his election or appointment. No person shall be a member of the Senate who is not over thirty years of age, and no person shall be a member of the House of Representatives who is not over twenty-five years of age.

Section 6.—No person shall be eligible to election or appointment as Senator or Representative for a district unless he has resided therein at least one year immediately prior to his election or appointment. When there is more than one representative district in a municipality, residence in the municipality shall satisfy this requirement.

Section 7.—If in a general election more than two-thirds of the members of either house are elected from one political party or from a single ticket, as both are defined by law, the number of members shall be increased in the following cases:

(a) If the party or ticket which elected more than two-thirds of the members of either or both houses shall have obtained less than two-thirds of the total number of votes cast for the office of Governor, the number of members of the Senate or of the House of Representatives or of both bodies, whichever may be the case, shall be increased by declaring elected a sufficient number of candidates of the minority party or parties to bring the total number of members of the minority party or parties to nine in the Senate and to seventeen in the House of Representatives. When there is more than one minority party, said additional members shall be declared elected from among the candidates of each minority party in the proportion that the number of votes cast for the candidate of each of said parties for the office of Governor bears to the total number of votes cast for the candidates of all the minority parties for the office of Governor.

When one or more minority parties shall have obtained representation in a proportion equal to or greater than the proportion of votes received by their respective candidates for Governor, such party or parties shall not be entitled to additional members until the representation established for each of the other minority parties under these provisions shall have been completed.

(b) If the party or ticket which elected more than two-thirds of the members of either or both houses shall have obtained more than two-thirds of the total number of votes cast for the office of Governor, and one or more minority parties shall not have elected the number of members in the Senate or in the House of Representatives or in both houses, whichever may

be the case, which corresponds to the proportion of votes cast by each of them for the office of Governor, such additional number of their candidates shall be declared elected as is necessary in order to complete said proportion as nearly as possible, but the number of Senators of all the minority parties shall never, under this provision, be more than nine or that of Representatives more than seventeen.

In order to select additional members of the Legislative Assembly from a minority party in accordance with these provisions, its candidates at large who have not been elected shall be the first to be declared elected in the order of the votes that they have obtained, and thereafter its district candidates who, not having been elected, have obtained in their respective districts the highest proportion of the total number of votes cast as compared to the proportion of votes cast in favor of other candidates of the same party not elected to an equal office in the other districts.

The additional Senators and Representatives whose election is declared under this section shall be considered for all purposes as Senators at Large or Representatives at Large.

The measures necessary to implement these guarantees, the method of adjudicating fractions that may result from the application of the rules contained in this section, and the minimum number of votes that a minority party must cast in favor of its candidate for Governor in order to have the right to the representation provided herein shall be determined by the Legislative Assembly.

Section 8.—The term of office of Senators and Representatives shall begin on the second day of January immediately following the date of the general election in which they shall have been elected. If, prior to the fifteen months immediately preceding the date of the next general election, a vacancy occurs in the office of Senator or Representative for a district, the Governor shall call a special election in said district within thirty days following the date on which the vacancy occurs. This election shall be held not later than ninety days after the call, and the person elected shall hold office for the rest of the unexpired term of his predecessor. When said vacancy occurs during a legislative session, or when the Legislative Assembly or the Senate has been called for a date prior to the certification of the results of the special election, the presiding officer of the appropriate house shall fill said vacancy by appointing the person recommended by the central committee of the political party of which his predecessor in office was a member. Such person shall hold the office until certification of the election of the candidate who was elected. When the vacancy occurs within fifteen months prior to a general election, or when it occurs in the office of a Senator at Large or a Representative at Large, the presiding officer of the appropriate house shall fill it, upon the recommendation of the political party of which the previous holder of the office was a member, by appointing a person selected in the same manner as that in which his predecessor was selected. A vacancy in the office of a Senator at Large or a Representative at Large elected as an independent candidate shall be filled by an election in all districts.

Section 9.—Each house shall be the sole judge of the election, returns and qualifications of its members; shall choose its own officers; shall adopt rules for its own proceedings appropriate to legislative bodies; and, with the concurrence of three-fourths of the total number of members of which it is composed, may expel any member for the causes established in Section 21 of this Article, authorizing impeachments. The Senate shall elect a President and the House of Representatives a Speaker from among their respective members.

Section 10.—The Legislative Assembly shall be deemed a continuous body during the term for which its members are elected and shall meet in regular session each year commencing on the second Monday in January. The duration of regular sessions and the periods of time for introduction and consideration of bills shall be prescribed by law. When the Governor calls the Legislative Assembly into special session it may consider only those matters specified in the call or in any special message sent to it by him during the session. No special session shall continue longer than twenty calendar days.

Section 11.—The sessions of each house shall be open.

Section 12.—A majority of the total number of members of which each house is composed shall constitute a quorum, but a smaller number may adjourn from day to day and shall have authority to compel the attendance of absent members.

Section 13.—The two houses shall meet in the Capitol of Puerto Rico and neither of them may adjourn for more than three consecutive days without the consent of the other.

Section 14.—No member of the Legislative Assembly shall be arrested while the house of which he is a member is in session, or during the fifteen days before or after such session, except for treason, felony or breach of the peace. The members of the Legislative Assembly shall not be questioned in any other place for any speech, debate or vote in either house or in any committee.

Section 15.—No Senator or Representative may, during the term for which he was elected or chosen, be appointed to any civil office in the Government of Puerto Rico, its municipalities or instrumentalities, which shall have been created or the salary of which shall have been increased during said term. No person may hold office in the Government of Puerto Rico, its municipalities or instrumentalities and be a Senator or Representative at the same time. These provisions shall not prevent a member of the Legislative Assembly from being designated to perform functions *ad honorem.*

Section 16.-The Legislative Assembly shall have the power to create, consolidate or reorganize executive departments and to define their functions.

Section 17.-No bill shall become a law unless it has been printed, read, referred to a committee and returned therefrom with a written report, but either house may discharge a committee from the study and report of any bill and proceed to the consideration thereof. Each house shall keep a journal of its proceedings and of the votes cast for and against bills. The legislative proceedings shall be published in a daily record in the form determined by law. Every bill, except general appropriation bills, shall be confined to one subject, which shall be clearly expressed in its title, and any part of an act whose subject has not been expressed in the title shall be void. The general appropriation act shall contain only appropriations and rules for their disbursement. No bill shall be amended in a manner that changes its original purpose or incorporates matters extraneous to it. In amending any article or section of a law, said article or section shall be promulgated in its entirety as amended. All bills for raising revenue shall originate in the House of Representatives, but the Senate may propose or concur with amendments as on other bills.

Section 18.-The subjects which may be dealt with by means of joint resolution shall be determined by law, but every joint resolution shall follow the same legislative process as that of a bill.

Section 19.-Every bill which is approved by a majority of the total number of members of which each house is composed shall be submitted to the Governor and shall become law if he signs it or if he does not return it, with his objections, to the house in which it originated within ten days (Sundays excepted) counting from the date on which he shall have received it.

When the Governor returns a bill, the house that receives it shall enter his objections on its journal and both houses may reconsider it. If approved by two-thirds of the total number of members of which each house is composed, said bill shall become law.

If the Legislative Assembly adjourns *sine die* before the Governor has acted on a bill that has been presented to him less than ten days before, he is relieved of the obligation of returning it with his objections and the bill shall become law only if the Governor signs it within thirty days after receiving it.

Every final passage or reconsideration of a bill shall be by a roll-call vote.

Section 20.-In approving any appropriation bill that contains more than one item, the Governor may eliminate one or more of such items or reduce their amounts, at the same time reducing the total amounts involved.

Section 21.-The House of Representatives shall have exclusive power to initiate impeachment proceedings and, with the concurrence of two-thirds of the total number of members of which it is composed, to bring an indictment. The Senate shall have exclusive power to try and to decide impeachment cases, and in meeting for such purposes the Senators shall act in the name of the people and under oath or affirmation. No judgment of conviction in an impeachment trial shall be pronounced without the concurrence of three-fourths of the total number of members of which the Senate is composed, and the judgment shall be limited to removal from office. The person impeached, however, may be liable and subject to indictment, trial, judgment and punishment according to law. The causes of impeachment shall be treason, bribery, other felonies, and misdemeanors involving moral turpitude. The Chief Justice of the Supreme Court shall preside at the impeachment trial of the Governor.

The two houses may conduct impeachment proceedings in their regular or special sessions. The presiding officers of the two houses, upon written request of two-thirds of the total number of members of which the House of Representatives is composed, must convene them to deal with such proceedings.

Section 22.—The Governor shall appoint a Controller with the advice and consent of a majority of the total number of members of which each house is composed. The Controller shall meet the requirements prescribed by law and shall hold office for a term of ten years and until his successor has been appointed and qualifies. The Controller shall audit all the revenues, accounts and expenditures of the Commonwealth, of its agencies and instrumentalities and of its municipalities, in order to determine whether they have been made in accordance with law. He shall render annual reports and any special reports that may be required of him by the Legislative Assembly or by the Governor.

In the performance of his duties the Controller shall be authorized to administer oaths, take evidence and compel, under pain of contempt, the attendance of witnesses and the production of books, letters, documents, papers, records and all other articles deemed essential to a full understanding of the matter under investigation.

The Controller may be removed for the causes and pursuant to the procedure established in the preceding section.

Article IV

The Executive

Section 1.-The executive power shall be vested in a Governor, who shall be elected by direct vote in each general election.

Section 2.-The Governor shall hold office for the term of four years from the second day of January of the year following his election and until his successor has been elected and qualifies. He shall reside in Puerto Rico and maintain his office in its capital city.

Section 3.-No person shall be Governor unless, on the date of the election, he is at least thirty-five years of age, and is and has been during the preceding five years a citizen of the United States and a citizen and *bona fide* resident of Puerto Rico.

Section 4.-The Governor shall execute the laws and cause them to be executed.

He shall call the Legislative Assembly or the Senate into special session when in his judgment the public interest so requires.

He shall appoint, in the manner prescribed by this Constitution or by law, all officers whose appointment he is authorized to make. He shall have the power to make appointments while the Legislative Assembly is not in session. Any such appointments that require the advice and consent of the Senate or of both houses shall expire at the end of the next regular session.

He shall be the commander-in-chief of the militia.

He shall have the power to call out the militia and summon the posse comitatus in order to prevent or suppress rebellion, invasion or any serious disturbance of the public peace.

He shall have the power to proclaim martial law when the public safety requires it in case of rebellion or invasion or imminent danger thereof. The Legislative Assembly shall meet forthwith on their own initiative to ratify or revoke the proclamation.

He shall have the power to suspend the execution of sentences in criminal cases and to grant pardons, commutations of punishment, and total or partial remissions of fines and forfeitures for crimes committed in violation of the laws of Puerto Rico. This power shall not extend to cases of impeachment.

He shall approve or disapprove in accordance with this Constitution the joint resolutions and bills passed by the Legislative Assembly.

He shall present to the Legislative Assembly, at

the beginning of each regular session, a message concerning the affairs of the Commonwealth and a report concerning the state of the Treasury of Puerto Rico and the proposed expenditures for the ensuing fiscal year. Said report shall contain the information necessary for the formulation of a program of legislation.

He shall exercise the other powers and functions and discharge the other duties assigned to him by this Constitution or by law.

Section 5.-For the purpose of exercising executive power, the Governor shall be assisted by Secretaries whom he shall appoint with the advice and consent of the Senate. The appointment of the Secretary of State shall in addition require the advice and consent of the House of Representatives, and the person appointed shall fulfill the requirements established in Section 3 of this Article. The Secretaries shall collectively constitute the Governor's advisory council, which shall be designated as the Council of Secretaries.

Section 6.-Without prejudice to the power of the Legislative Assembly to create, reorganize and consolidate executive departments and to define their functions, the following departments are hereby established: State, Justice, Education Health, Treasury, Labor, Agriculture and Commerce, and Public Works. Each of these executive departments shall be headed by a Secretary.

Section 7.-When a vacancy occurs in the office of Governor, caused by death, resignation, removal, total and permanent in- capacity, or any other absolute disability, said office shall devolve upon the Secretary of State, who shall hold it for the rest of the term and until a new Governor has been elected and qualifies. In the event that vacancies exist at the same time in both the office of Governor and that of Secretary of State, the law shall provide which of the Secretaries shall serve as Governor.

Section 8.-When for any reason the Governor is temporarily unable to perform his functions, the Secretary of State shall substitute for him during the period he is unable to serve. If for any reason the Secretary of State is not available, the Secretary determined by law shall temporarily hold the office of Governor.

Section 9.-If the Governor-elect shall not have qualified, or if he has qualified and a permanent vacancy occurs in the office of Governor before he shall have appointed a Secretary of State, or before said Secretary, having been appointed, shall have qualified, the Legislative Assembly just elected, upon convening for its first regular session, shall elect, by a majority of the total number of members of which each house is composed, a Governor who shall hold office until his successor is elected in the next general election and qualifies.

Section 10.-The Governor may be removed for the causes and pursuant to the procedure established in Section 21 of Article III of this Constitution.

Article V

The Judiciary

Section 1.-The judicial power of Puerto Rico shall be vested in a Supreme Court, and in such other courts as may be established by law.

Section 2.-The courts of Puerto Rico shall constitute a unified judicial system for purposes of jurisdiction, operation and administration. The Legislative Assembly may create and abolish courts, except for the Supreme Court, in a manner not inconsistent with this Constitution, and shall determine the venue and organization of the courts.

Section 3.-The Supreme Court shall be the court of last resort in Puerto Rico and shall be composed of a Chief Justice and four Associate Justices. The number of Justices may be changed only by law upon request of the Supreme Court.

Section 4.-The Supreme Court shall sit, in accordance with rules adopted by it, as a full court or in divisions. All the decisions of the Supreme Court shall be concurred in by a majority of its members. No law shall be held unconstitutional except by a majority of the total number of Justices of which the Court is composed in accordance with this Constitution or with law.

Section 5.-The Supreme Court, any of its divisions or any of its Justices may hear in the first instance petitions for habeas corpus and any other causes and proceedings as determined by law.

Section 6.-The Supreme Court shall adopt for the courts rules of evidence and of civil and criminal procedure which shall not abridge, enlarge or modify the substantive rights of the parties. The rules thus adopted shall be submitted to the Legislative Assembly at the beginning of its next regular session and shall not go into effect until sixty days after the close of said session, unless disapproved by the Legislative Assembly, which shall have the power both at said session and subsequently to amend, repeal or supplement any of said rules by a specific law to that effect.

Section 7.-The Supreme Court shall adopt rules for the administration of the courts. These rules shall be subject to the laws concerning procurement, personnel, audit and appropriation of funds, and other laws which apply generally to all branches of the government. The Chief Justice shall direct the administration of the courts and shall appoint an administrative director who shall hold office at the will of the Chief Justice.

Section 8.-Judges shall be appointed by the Governor with the advice and consent of the Senate. Justices of the Supreme Court shall not assume office until after confirmation by the Senate and shall hold their offices during good behavior. The terms of office of the other judges shall be fixed by law and shall not be less than that fixed for the term of office of a judge of the same or equivalent category existing when this Constitution takes effect. The other officials and employees of the courts shall be appointed in the manner provided by law.

Section 9.-No person shall be appointed a Justice of the Supreme Court unless he is a citizen of the United States and of Puerto Rico, shall have been admitted to the practice of law in Puerto Rico at least ten years prior to his appointment, and shall have resided in Puerto Rico at least five years immediately prior thereto.

Section 10.-The Legislative Assembly shall establish a retirement system for judges. Retirement shall be compulsory at age of seventy years.

Section 11.-Justices of the Supreme Court may be removed for the causes and pursuant to the procedure established in Section 21 of Article III of this Constitution. Judges of the other courts may be removed by the Supreme Court for the causes and pursuant to the procedure provided by law.

Section 12.-No judge shall make a direct or indirect financial contribution to any political organization or party, or hold any executive office therein, or participate in a political campaign of any kind, or be a candidate for an elective public office unless he has resigned his judicial office at least six months prior to his nomination.

Section 13.-In the event that a court or any of its divisions or sections is changed or abolished by law, the person holding a post of judge therein shall continue to hold it during the rest of the term for which he was appointed and shall perform the judicial functions assigned to him by the Chief Justice of the Supreme Court.

Article VI

General Provisions

Section 1.-The Legislative Assembly shall have the power to create, abolish, consolidate and reorganize municipalities; to change their territorial limits; to determine their organization and functions; and to authorize them to develop programs for the general welfare and to create any agencies necessary for that purpose.

No law abolishing or consolidating municipalities shall take effect until ratified in a referendum by a majority of the electors voting in said referendum in each of the municipalities to be abolished or consolidated. The referendum shall be in the manner determined by law, which shall include the applicable procedures of the election laws in effect when the referendum law is approved.

Section 2.-The power of the Commonwealth of Puerto Rico to impose and collect taxes and to authorize their imposition and collection by municipalities shall be exercised as determined by the Legislative Assembly and shall never be surrendered or suspended. The power of the Commonwealth of Puerto Rico to contract and to authorize the contracting of debts shall be exercised as determined by the Legislative Assembly.

Section 3.-The rule of taxation in Puerto Rico shall be uniform.

Section 4.-General elections shall be held every four years on the day of November determined by the Legislative Assembly.

In said elections there shall be elected a Governor, the members of the Legislative Assembly, and the other officials whose election on that date is provided for by law.

Every person over twenty-one years of age shall be entitled to vote if he fulfills the other conditions determined by law. No person shall be deprived of the right to vote because he does not know how to read or write or does not own property.

All matters concerning the electoral process, registration of voters, political parties and candidates shall be determined by law.

Every popularly elected official shall be elected by direct vote and any candidate who receives more votes than any other candidate for the same office shall be declared elected.

Section 5.-The laws shall be promulgated in accordance with the procedure prescribed by law and shall specify the terms under which they shall take effect.

Section 6.-If at the end of any fiscal year the appropriations necessary for the ordinary operating expenses of the government and for the payment of interest on and amortization of the public debt for the ensuing fiscal year shall not have been made, the several sums appropriated in the last appropriation acts for the objects and purposes therein specified, so far as the same may be applicable, shall continue in effect item by item, and the Governor shall authorize the payments necessary for such purposes until corresponding appropriations are made.

Section 7.-The appropriations made for any fiscal year shall not exceed the total revenues, including available surplus, estimated for said fiscal year unless the imposition of taxes sufficient to cover said appropriations is provided by law.

Section 8.-In case the available revenues including surplus for any fiscal year are insufficient to meet the appropriations made for that year, interest on the public debt and amortization thereof shall first be paid, and other disbursements shall thereafter be made in accordance with the order of priorities established by law.

Section 9.-Public property and funds shall only be disposed of for public purposes, for the support and operation of state institutions, and pursuant to law.

Section 10.-No law shall give extra compensation to any public officer, employee, agent or contractor after services shall have been rendered or contract made. No law shall extend the term of any public officer or diminish his salary or emoluments after his election or appointment. No person shall draw a salary for more than one office or position in the government of Puerto Rico.

Section 11.-The salaries of the Governor, the Secretaries, the members of the Legislative Assembly, the Controller and Judges shall be fixed by a special law and, except for the salaries of the members of the Legislative Assembly, shall not be decreased during the terms for which they are elected or appointed. The salaries of the Governor and the Controller shall not be increased during said terms. No increase in the salaries of the members of the Legislative Assembly shall take effect until after the expiration of the term of the Legislative Assembly during which it is enacted. Any reduction of the salaries of the members of the Legislative Assembly shall be elective only during the term of the Legislative Assembly which approves it.

Section 12.-The Governor shall occupy and use, free of rent, the buildings and properties belonging to the Commonwealth which have been or shall hereafter be used and occupied by him as chief executive.

Section 13.-The procedure for granting franchises, rights, privileges and concessions of a public or quasi-public nature shall be determined by law, but every concession of this kind to a person or private entity must be approved by the Governor or by the executive official whom he designates. Every franchise, right, privilege or concession of a public or quasi-public nature shall be subject to amendment, alteration or repeal as determined by law.

Section 14.-No corporation shall be authorized to conduct the business of buying and selling real estate or be permitted to hold or own real estate except such as may be reasonably necessary to enable it to carry out the purposes for which it was created, and every corporation authorized to engage in agriculture shall by its charter be restricted to the ownership and control of not to exceed five hundred acres of land; and this provision shall be held to prevent any member of a corporation engaged in agriculture from being in any wise interested in any other corporation engaged in agriculture.

Corporations, however, may loan funds upon real estate security, and purchase real estate when necessary for the collection of loans, but they shall dispose of real estate so obtained within five years after receiving the title.

Corporations not organized in Puerto Rico, but doing business in Puerto Rico, shall be bound by the provisions of this section so far as they are applicable.

These provisions shall not prevent the ownership, possession or management of lands in excess of five hundred acres by the Commonwealth, its agencies or instrumentalities.

Section 15.-The Legislative Assembly shall determine all matters concerning the flag, the seal and the anthem of the Commonwealth. Once determined, no law changing them shall take effect until one year after the general election next following the date of enactment of said law.

Section 16.-All public officials and employees of the Commonwealth, its agencies, instrumentalities and political subdivisions, before entering upon their respective duties, shall take an oath to support the Constitution of the United States and the Constitution and laws of the Commonwealth of Puerto Rico.

Section 17.-In case of invasion, rebellion, epidemic or any other event giving rise to a state of emergency, the Governor may call the Legislative Assembly to meet in a place other than the Capitol of Puerto Rico, subject to the approval or disapproval of the Legislative Assembly. Under the same conditions, the Governor may, during the period of emergency, order the government, its agencies and instrumentalities to be moved temporarily to a place other than the seat of the government.

Section 18.-All criminal actions in the courts of the Commonwealth shall be conducted in the name and by the authority of "The People of Puerto Rico" until otherwise provided by law.

Section 19.-It shall be the public policy of the Commonwealth to conserve, develop and use its natural resources in the most effective manner possible for the general welfare of the community; to conserve and maintain buildings and places declared by the Legislative Assembly to be of historic or artistic value; to regulate its penal institutions in a manner that effectively achieves their purposes and to provide, within the limits of available resources, for adequate treatment of delinquents in order to make possible their moral and social rehabilitation.

Article VII

Amendments to the Constitution

Section 1.-The Legislative Assembly may propose amendments to this Constitution by a concurrent resolution approved by not less than two-thirds of the total number of members of which each house is composed. All proposed amendments shall be submitted to the qualified electors in a special referendum, but if the concurrent resolution is approved by not less than three fourths of the total number of members of which each house is composed, the Legislative Assembly may provide that the referendum shall be held at the same time as the next general election. Each proposed amendment shall be voted on separately and not more than three proposed amendments may be submitted at the same referendum. Every proposed amendment shall specify the terms under which it shall take effect, and it shall become a part of this Constitution if it is ratified by a majority of the electors voting thereon. Once approved, a proposed amendment must be published at least three months prior to the date of the referendum.

Section 2.-The Legislative Assembly, by a concurrent resolution approved by two-thirds of the total number of members of which each house is composed, may submit to the qualified electors at a referendum, held at the same time as a general election, the question of whether a constitutional convention shall be called to revise this Constitution. If a majority of the electors voting on this question vote in favor of the revision, it shall be made by a Constitutional Convention elected in the manner provided by law. Every revision of this Constitution shall be submitted to the qualified electors at a special referendum for ratification or rejection by a majority of the votes cast at the referendum.

Section 3.-No amendment to this Constitution shall alter the republican form of government established by it or abolish its bill of rights.

Article VIII

Senatorial and Representative Districts

Section 1.-The senatorial and representative districts shall be the following:

I.-SENATORIAL DISTRICT OF SAN JUAN, which shall be composed of the following Representative Districts: The Capital of Puerto Rico, excluding the present electoral precincts of Santurce and Rio Piedras; 2.-Electoral zones numbers 1 and 2 of the present precinct of Santurce; 3.-Electoral zone number 3 of the present precinct of Santurce; 4.-Electoral zone number 4 of the present precinct of Santurce; and 6.-Wards Hato Rey, Puerto Nuevo and Caparra Heights of the Capital of Puerto Rico.

II.-SENATORIAL DISTRICT OF BAYAMON, which shall be composed of the following Representative Districts: 7.-The municipality of Bayamon; 8.-The municipalities of Carolina and Trujillo Alto; 9.-The present electoral precinct of Rio Piedras, excluding wards Hato Rey, Puerto Nuevo and Caparra Heights of the Capital of Puerto Rico; 10.-The municipalities of Catano, Guaynabo and Toa Baja; and 11.-The municipalities of Toa Alta, Corozal and Naranjito.

III.-SENATORIAL DISTRICT OF ARECIBO, which shall be composed of the following Representative Districts: The municipalities of Vega Baja, Vega Alta and Dorado; 12.-The municipalities of Manati and Barceloneta; 13.-The municipalities of Ciales and Morovis; 14.-The municipality of Arecibo; and 15.-The municipality of Utuado.

IV.-SENATORIAL DISTRICT OF AGUADILLA, which shall be composed of the following Representative Districts: 16.-The municipalities of Camuy, Hatillo and Quebradillas; 17.-The municipalities of Aguadilla and Isabela; 18.-The municipalities of San Sebastian and Moca; 19.-The municipalities of Lares, Las Marias and Maricao; and 20.-The municipalities of Anasco, Aguada and Rincon.

V.-SENATORIAL DISTRICT OF MAYAGUEZ, which shall be composed of the following Representative Districts: 21.-The municipality of Mayaguez; 22.-The municipalities of Cabo Rojo, Hormigueros and Lajas; 23.-The municipalities of San German and Sabana Grande; 24.-The municipalities of Yauco and Guanica; and 25.-The municipalities of Guayanilla and Penuelas.

VI.-SENATORIAL DISTRICT OF PONCE, which shall be composed of the following Representative Districts: 26.-The first, second, third, fourth, fifth and sixth wards and the City Beach of the municipality of Ponce; 27.-The municipality of Ponce, except for the first, second, third, fourth, fifth and sixth wards and the City Beach; 28.-The municipalities of Adjuntas and Jayuya; 29.-The municipalities of Juana Diaz, Santa Isabel and Villalba; and 30.-The municipalities of Coamo and Orocovis.

VII.-SENATORIAL DISTRICT OF GUAYAMA, which shall be composed of the following Representative Districts: 31.-The municipalities of Aibonito, Barranquitas and Comerio; 32.-The municipalities of Cayey and Cidra; 33.-The municipalities of Caguas and Aguas Buenas; 34.-The municipalities of Guayama and Salinas; and 35.-The municipalities of Patillas, Maunabo and Arroyo.

VIII.-SENATORIAL DISTRICT OF HUMACAO, which shall be composed of the following Representative Districts: 36.-The municipalities of Humacao and Yabucoa; 37.-The municipalities of Juncos, Gurabo and San Lorenzo; 38.-The municipalities of Naguabo,

Ceiba and Las Piedras; 39.-The municipalities of Fajardo and Vieques and the Island of Culebra; and 40.-The municipalities of Rio Grande, Loiza and Luquillo.

Section 2.-Electoral zones numbers 1, 2, 3 and 4 included in three representative districts within the senatorial district of San Juan are those presently existing for purposes of electoral organization in the second precinct of San Juan.

Article IX

Transitory Provisions

Section 1.-When this Constitution goes into effect all laws not inconsistent therewith shall continue in full force until amended or repealed, or until they expire by their own terms.

Unless otherwise provided by this Constitution, civil and criminal liabilities, rights, franchises, concessions, privileges, claims, actions, causes of action, contracts, and civil, criminal and administrative proceedings shall continue unaffected, notwithstanding the taking effect of this Constitution.

Section 2.-All officers who are in office by election or appointment on the date this Constitution takes effect shall continue to hold their offices and to perform the functions thereof in a manner not inconsistent with this Constitution, unless the functions of their offices are abolished or until their successors are selected and qualify in accordance with this Constitution and laws enacted pursuant thereto.

Section 3.-Notwithstanding the age limit fixed by this Constitution for compulsory retirement, all the judges of the courts of Puerto Rico who are holding office on the date this Constitution takes effect shall continue to hold their judicial offices until the expiration of the terms for which they were appointed, and in the case of Justices of the Supreme Court during good behavior.

Section 4.-The Commonwealth of Puerto Rico shall be the successor of the People of Puerto Rico for all purposes, including without limitation the collection and payment of debts and liabilities in accordance with their terms.

Section 5.-When this Constitution goes into effect, the term "citizen of the Commonwealth of Puerto Rico" shall replace the term "citizen of Puerto Rico" as previously used.

Section 6.-Political parties shall continue to enjoy all rights recognized by the election law, provided that on the effective date of this Constitution they fulfill the minimum requirements for the registration of new parties contained in said law. Five years after this Constitution shall have taken effect the Legisla-

tive Assembly may change these requirements, but any law increasing them shall not go into effect until after the general election next following its enactment.

Section 7.-The Legislative Assembly may enact the laws necessary to supplement and make elective these transitory provisions in order to assure the functioning of the government until the officers provided for by this Constitution are elected or appointed and qualify, and until this Constitution takes effect in all respects.

Section 8.-If the Legislative Assembly creates a Department of Commerce, the Department of Agriculture and Commerce shall thereafter be called the Department of Agriculture.

Section 9.-The first election under the provisions of this Constitution shall be held on the date provided by law, but not later than six months after the effective date of this Constitution. The second general election under this Constitution shall be held in the month of November 1956 on a day provided by law.

Section 10.—Constitution shall take effect when the Governor so proclaims, but not later than sixty days after its ratification by the Congress of the United States.

Done in Convention, at San Juan, Puerto Rico, on the sixth day of February, in the year of Our Lord one thousand nine hundred and fifty-two.

✳RESOLUTIONS APPROVED BY THE CONSTITUTIONAL CONVENTION RELATING TO THE CONSTITUTION OF THE COMMONWEALTH OF PUERTO RICO

Resolution No. 22

Approved by the Constitutional Convention of Puerto Rico in the Plenary Session Held February 4, 1952

To determine in Spanish and in English the name of the body politic created by the Constitution of the people of Puerto Rico.

WHEREAS, this Constitutional Convention, in accordance with the mandate of the people, is about to adopt the Constitution by virtue of which the Puerto Rican community will be politically organized;

WHEREAS, it is necessary to give an appropriate name in both English and Spanish to the body politic thus created;

WHEREAS, the word "commonwealth" in contemporary English usage means a politically organized community, that is to say, a state (using the word in the generic sense) in which political power resides ultimately in the people, hence a free state, but one which is at the same time linked to a broader political system in a federal or other type of association and therefore does not have an independent and separate existence;

WHEREAS, the single word "commonwealth", as currently used, clearly defines the status of the body politic created under the terms of the compact existing between the people of Puerto Rico and the United States, i.e., that of a state which is free of superior authority in the management of its own local affairs but which is linked to the United States of America and hence is a part of its political system in a manner compatible with its federal structure;

WHEREAS, there is no single word in the Spanish language exactly equivalent to the English word "commonwealth" and translation of "commonwealth" into Spanish requires a combination of words to express the concepts of state and liberty and association;

WHEREAS, in the case of Puerto Rico the most appropriate translation of "commonwealth" into Spanish is the expression "estado libre asociado", which however should not be rendered "associated free state" in English inasmuch as the word "state" in ordinary speech in the United States means one of the States of the Union;

THEREFORE, Be it resolved by the Constituent Assembly of Puerto Rico:

First: That in Spanish the name of the body politic created by the Constitution which this Convention is adopting for submission to the people of Puerto Rico shall be "Estado Libre Asociado", it being understood that in our case this term is equivalent to and an appropriate translation of the English word "commonwealth".

Second: That, as a consequence, the body politic created by our Constitution shall be designated "The Commonwealth of Puerto Rico" in English and "El Estado Libre Asociado de Puerto Rico" in Spanish.

Third: That the Committee on Style of this Convention is instructed to use these designations in the respective English and Spanish texts of the Constitution when submitting the documents for third reading.

Fourth: That this resolution shall be published in Spanish and in English as an explanatory and authoritative statement of the meaning of the terms "Commonwealth" and "Estado Libre Asociado" as used in the Constitution; and that it shall be widely distributed, together with the Constitution, for the information of the people of Puerto Rico and the Congress of the United States.

Resolution No. 23

Approved by the Constitutional Convention of Puerto Rico in the Plenary Session Held February 4, 1952

Final declarations of the Constitutional Convention of Puerto Rico.

WHEREAS, the Constitutional Convention of Puerto Rico, in fulfilling the important mission assigned it by the people, has approved a Constitution for the Commonwealth of Puerto Rico within the terms of the compact entered into with the United States of America;

WHEREAS, in accordance with the terms of the compact, said Constitution is to be submitted to the people of Puerto Rico for their approval;

THEREFORE, Be it resolved by this Constitutional Convention:

First: That, pursuant to the relevant regulations, a certified copy of the Constitution as approved be sent to the Governor of Puerto Rico so that he may submit it to the people of Puerto Rico in a referendum as provided by law.

Second: That copies of the Constitution be printed in Spanish and English, respectively, in numbers sufficient for general distribution to the end that it will become widely known.

Third: That the following final declarations of this Convention be entered on its journal and also published:

(a) This Convention deems that the Constitution as approved fulfills the mission assigned it by the people of Puerto Rico.

(b) When this Constitution takes effect, the people of Puerto Rico shall thereupon be organized in a commonwealth established within the terms of the compact entered into by mutual consent, which is the basis of our union with the United States of America.

(c) The political authority of the Commonwealth of Puerto Rico shall be exercised in accordance with its Constitution and within the terms of said compact.

(d) Thus we attain the goal of complete self-government, the last vestiges of colonialism having disappeared in the principle of Compact, and we enter into an era of new developments in democratic civilization. Nothing can surpass in political dignity the principle of mutual consent and of compacts freely agreed upon. The spirit of the people of Puerto Rico is free for great undertakings now and in the future. Having full political dignity the commonwealth of Puerto Rico may develop in other ways by modifications of the Compact through mutual consent.

(e) The people of Puerto Rico reserve the right to propose and to accept modifications in the terms of its relations with the United States of America, in order that these relations may at all times be the expression of an agreement freely entered into between the people of Puerto Rico and the United States of America.

Fourth: That a copy of this resolution be sent to the President of the United States and to the President of the Senate and the Speaker of the House of Representatives of the Congress of the United States.

4

Historic Landmarks

✹ Alabama ✹ Arizona ✹ California ✹ Florida ✹ Georgia ✹ Louisiana ✹ New Mexico
✹ Panama Canal Zone ✹ Puerto Rico ✹ Texas ✹ Virgin Islands

✹ALABAMA

Apalachicola Fort

One and a half miles east of Holy Trinity on the Chattahoochee River, Russell County. Established in 1690, it was the northernmost Spanish outpost on the Chattahoochee River built to prevent English inroads among the lower Creek Indians.

De Soto Caverns

Childersburg, 5 miles east on S.R. 76, southwest of Talladega. These spectacular caverns, containing 2000-year-old Indian burials and long stalagtites, were visited by Spanish explorer Hernando de Soto.

De Soto Falls

North of Gadsden, DeKalb County. One-hundred foot falls that were visited by Spanish explorer De Soto and named after him, as were the caverns (*see* above).

✹ARIZONA

Ajo

The site of the first commercial copper mine in Arizona, founded by Henry Lesinsky in 1855 when he hired Sonoran miners to build the mine and smelter and operate them. The open pit can be viewed from a lookout on S.R. 85, just past the town of Ajo.

Clifton and Morenci

The sites of copper diggings by Mexican placer miners since the 1860s. Laborers in the copper mines were predominantly Hispanic and were initially subjected to lower wages than those paid to Anglo miners. In 1915, Juan García, R. Rodrigues, Rifino García and Adolfo Palacio organized an historic

strike against the practice; the result was an end to wage discrimination.

Córdova House

173-177 N. Meyer, Tucson. This adobe house dates from c. 1750 and is the oldest continuously occupied house in Tucson.

Coronado National Memorial

Hereford, 22 miles south of Sierra Vista, 5 miles from S.R. 92 on R.R. 2. This is believed to mark the spot where, in 1540, Spanish explorer Francisco Vásquez de Coronado entered what is today the territory of the United States on his northward search, on behalf of the viceroy of Mexico, for the mythical gold of the Seven Cities of Cíbola. The memorial is on 5,000 acres of land, which provide habitat for many plants and animals. Open daily except major holidays.

Guevavi Mission

Ruins near Tumacacori. This was a small mission founded by Father Eusebio Kino in 1692 and abandoned in 1775. The building (probably erected in 1751), is considered the first church erected by Europeans in southern Arizona.

Morenci

See: Clifton and Morenci.

Quiburi

Near Fairbank. Site of the Presidio de Santa Cruz de Terrenato established to guard against Apache depredations. It operated from 1775 to 1780. It is also the site of a mission founded by Father Eusebio Kino before 1700.

135

San Bernardino de Awatobi

In the Painted Desert, east of the Grand Canyon. Visited by Spaniards in 1540 and 1583, the Franciscans founded a Hoi mission here and at four other sites in 1629. All were destroyed in the Rebellion of 1680, although San Bernardino may have functioned until 1700.

San Bernardino Ranch

Seventeen miles east of Douglas on the international boundary, Cochise County. Established in 1822 by Ignacio Pérez on the site of a watering hole on the old Spanish military trail, the ranch illustrates the continuity of Spanish and American cattle ranching in the Southwest. Abundant springs made the ranch a stopping place in the era of westward expansion.

San José de Tumacacori Mission

Tumacacori National Monument. These are the ruins of the northernmost of the mission chain. It was founded by the Franciscan Father Eusebio Kino in 1696. In 1844, Mexico sold the mission lands to a private citizen and the Tumacacori adobe church subsequently fell into ruins. The national monument, totaling ten acres, was established in 1908.

San Xavier del Bac

San Xavier Rd., 9 miles southwest of Tucson via Mission Rd., Pima County (in the Papago Indian reservation). Founded in 1700 by Father Eusebio Kino, it is one of the finest Spanish colonial churches in the United States, having a richly ornamented baroque interior. A good example of Spanish mission architecture, it was completed and consecrated by the Franciscans in 1797. Since 1911, it has been maintained as the primary school and church for the Papagos.

Tubac

Tubac Presidio State Park. The presidio of Tubac was established in 1752 and the Church of Santa Gertrudes in 1754. When Tucson was founded in 1772, the presidio was ordered to move to a new site to protect Tucson and Tubac was virtually deserted and

City of Tucson

Founded by Father Garcés in 1776 as the Mission of San José de Tucson, the town was originally surrounded by a high adobe wall to guard against Apache depredations. San José mission stood at the foot of "A" Mountain on the west side of the Santa Cruz River and the presidio was on the east side.

the mission was nearly closed. It survived only to the early 1830s. Museum on-site.

Velasco House

471-477 S. Stone, Tucson. This was the home of Carlos Ygnacio Velasco, publisher of the Spanish-language newspaper *La Fronteriza* (*The Border Newspaper*) from 1878 to 1914. The house was built in 1878.

❋CALIFORNIA

Carmel Mission

(Mission San Carlos Borromeo del Río Carmelo) 3080 Río Rd., Monterey County. Established by Father Junípero Serra in 1771, he used it as his residence and headquarters until 1784. It was the most important of the California missions.

José Castro House

On the south side of the plaza, San Juan Bautista State Historic Park, San Benito County. Built in 1840-41, the adobe structure was owned by the commandant general of the Mexican forces in northern California. On nearby Gabilon Peak, Castro routed the expedition of John Charles Fremont on March 9, 1846.

Custom House

Maine and Decatur Sts., Monterey, Monterey County. Built in 1814, it is the oldest government building in California. It was converted into a lodge in 1848 and opened as a museum in 1930. The custom House Plaza preserves Monterey's heritage as the capital of "Alta California" under Spanish rule.

Elysian Park

Los Angeles, Los Angeles County. This city park is the site of the camp of Don Gaspar de Pórtola and Padre Juan Crespi, who reached the area on August 2, 1769.

Estudillo House

4001 Mason St., San Diego, San Diego County. This twelve-room adobe house was built in 1827-1829 by Don José Antonio Estudillo, who eventually became mayor and justice of the peace of San Diego.

Feliciano Canyon

Near Los Angeles. On March 19, 1842, Francisco López discovered gold in profitable quantities here. For the next several years, he worked numerous claims in the area. But his discoveries did not set off the great gold rush.

Flores House

South Pasadena, Los Angeles County. Built c. 1840, it was the site of the withdrawal of the Mexican Army under José Flores after the battle of La Mira in December, 1846.

Fort Point National Historic Site

Golden Gate National Recreation Area, San Francisco, San Francisco County. This was the site where Juan Bautista de Anza raised the spanish flag in 1776.

Los Alamos Ranch House

Three miles west of Los Alamos on Old U.S. 101, Santa Barbara County. Founded c. 1840, it is a good example of a Spanish-Mexican hacienda.

Los Angeles

Los Angeles County. Its formal appellation was "El Pueblo de Nuestra Señora la Reina de los Angeles de Porciúncula" (The Town of Our Lady the Queen of the Angels of Porciúncula). It was founded in 1781, although friars had visited the area and built a chapel there twelve years earlier. Its remaining historic sites in the central area include the Plaza Church (1818) and the Avila House (1818), a typical Hispanic residence of the time, which was the home of the mayor Francisco Avila. It was later used as occupation headquarters by Commander Robert Stockton, and was last surrender to the United States in the Mexican War in 1847.

Monterey Old Town Historic District

Monterey, Monterey County. Monterey served as the Spanish and Mexican capital of California from 1776 to 1849 and was a center of political, economic and social activity. Forty-three nineteenth-century adobe structures are located in the district, including El Castillo, the fortress built to guard the anchorage in 1794; the Customs House (1828-1845); the Presidio Chapel (1790s); and the Casa Alvarado (1836), home of the poet, revolutionary and governor of California (1836-1842), Juan Bautista Alvarado.

Moraga House

Orinda, Contra Costa County. It was built c. 1841 for José Moraga, a descendant of the founder of San Francisco.

New Almadén

Fourteen miles south of San Jose on County Route G8, Santa Clara County. It was the site of the first mercury deposit discovered in north America, in 1824. Mercury from New Almaden's mines was essential to the mining process during the gold rush. The mine town of New Almadén was an early Hispanic population and cultural center.

Peña House

Vacaville, Solano County. Built in 1842, it was the home of Juan Peña, rancher and partner of Juan Manuel Vaca, holder of the 44,000-acre Vaca land grant in this area.

Peralta (Adobe) House

184 W. Saint John St., San José, Santa Clara County. It is the last remaining structure of the San José de Guadalupe Pueblo, the oldest civil settlement and first municipal government in Alta California (established 1777).

Petaluma Adobe State Historic Park

Adobe Rd., Petaluma, Sonoma County. It was built from c. 1836 to 1846 for General Guadalupe Mariano Vallejo, commandant of the Sonoma Pueblo. The large adobe house served as his home and the hacienda headquarters.

Pico Hotel

430 N. Main St., Los Angeles, Los Angeles County. Constructed in 1859, it was owned and operated by Don Pío Pico, the former governor of Alta California.

Pico House

1515 San Fernando Mission Blvd., Mission Hills, Los Angeles County. A two-story adobe house, once part of the San Fernando Rey de España Mission, it was sold by the Mexican government in the 1840s to pay for the defense of Alta California against Anglo invaders.

Pico House

Whittier, Los Angeles County. Home of Pío Pico, the last governor of Mexican California, a rancher and a businessman.

The Presidio

On the northern tip of the San Francisco Peninsula on U.S. 101 and Int. 480, San Francisco, San Francisco County. The fort was established by the Spanish in 1776 to guard the entrance to San Francisco harbor. In 1849, it became the headquarters of the U.S. Army on the Pacific Coast.

La Purísima Concepción Mission State Historic Park

Four miles east of Lompoc, near the intersection of California 1 and 150, Santa Barbara County. Originally founded in 1787, it was destroyed by an earthquake in 1812. The present buildings are a reconstruction of a second, Franciscan, mission which fell into disrepair after secularization in 1834.

Rancho el Encino

Los Encinos State Historic Park, 16756 Moorpark St., Encino, Los Angeles County. A 4500-acre ranch complex founded in the 1840s by Don Vicente de la Osa.

Rancho Santa Margarita

Camp Pendelton, Oceanside, San Diego County. This was a home owned by Pío Pico, the last Mexican governor of California. Several buildings and fragments remain.

Royal Presidio Chapel

550 Church St., Monterey, Monterey County. Built in 1789, royal Spanish governors worshiped here and state ceremonies were held here. It is the only remaining presidio chapel in California and the sole existing structure of the original Monterey Presidio, now the U.S. Army Language School.

San Carlos Borromeo (del Río Carvelo) Mission

3080 Río Rd., Carmel, Monterey County. Founded in 1771 by Father Junípero Serra, it became his place of burial in 1784. The current church dates from 1793-1794.

San Diego de Alcalá Mission Church

10818 San Diego Mission Rd., Mission Valley, San Diego, San Diego County. Founded in 1769 by Father Junípero Serra and built between 1808 and 1813, it was the first of the twenty-one California missions.

San Diego Presidio

In Presidio Park, San Diego, San Diego County. It is the site of the first permanent European and mestizo settlement on the coast of California. Founded in 1769, it was used as a base for exploratory expeditions into the interior and as the military headquarters for southern California.

Royal Presidio Chapel, Monterey. (Courtesy of the U.S. Department of the Interior and the National Park Service.)

San Francisco Bay Discovery Site

4 miles west of San Bruno via Skyline Drive and Sneath Lane, San Mateo County. In 1769, Spanish explorer Gaspar de Pórtola discovered the great inland bay which he named after Saint Francis. The discovery led to the founding of the mission and presidio of San Francisco in 1776.

San Francisco de Asís Mission (Mission Dolores)

16th and Dolores Sts., San Francisco, San Francisco County. Founded by Father Junípero Serra in 1776, construction began in 1782. Many of the mission's decorations came from Mexico and Spain.

San Francisco de Solano Mission

Sonoma State Historic Park, Sonoma, Sonoma County. It was the last and most northerly of the San Francisco missions to be built (1824), under the direction of Father José Altamira acting in contradiction to government authorities.

San Gabriel Arcángel Mission

Mission and Junípero Serra Drs., San Gabriel, Los Angeles County. Founded in 1771, it was operated until 1828 and thereafter served as a parish church until 1940.

San José Mission

43300 Mission Blvd., Fremont, Alameda County. Established in 1797, the last remaining building is dated c. 1810.

San Juan Bautista Mission

San Juan Bautista, San Benito County. Founded in 1797, finished in 1812, it is the largest of the California missions. It is still an active church.

San Francisco de Asís Mission (Mission Dolores). (Oriana Day Painting. Courtesy of the De Young Museum, San Francisco.)

San Juan Bautista Plaza Historic District

In San Juan Bautista, San Benito County. It is composed of five buildings, all completed between 1813 and 1874: Plaza Hall, Plaza Stable, Castro House, Plaza Hotel, mission, church.

San Juan Capistrano Mission

Olive St., San Juan Capistrano, Orange County. Founded on November 1, 1776, by Father Junípero Serra, it was constructed between 1797 and 1806.

San Luis Rey de Francia Mission Church

4 miles east of Oceanside on California 76, 4050 Mission Ave., San Diego County. Founded in 1798 and built between 1811 and 1815, the present building was one of two cruciform mission churches erected in California by the Spanish. Originally named for Louis IX, King of France, it was rededicated in 1893 as a Franciscan college.

San Miguel Arcángel Mission

801 Mission St., San Miguel, San Luis Obispo County. Constructed from 1816 to 1818, this is the third church on the original mission site. Its interior murals were painted by Esteban Munras, aided by Indian assistants.

San Pasqual

Battlefield State Historic Park, S.R. 78, San Pasqual. Site of the General Andrés Pico's defeat of General Stephen Watts Kearny on December 6, 1846. A significant battle in the U.S. conquest of California.

Santa Barbara Mission

2201 Laguna St., Santa Barbara County. Founded in 1786, it became the Franciscan capital and the see of the first Spanish bishop. The present church, the fourth on the site, was completed in 1820. This was the only California mission secularized in 1833.

Santa Barbara Presidio

El Presidio de Santa Barbara, State Historic Park, 122-129 E. Cañon Perdido, Santa Barbara, Santa Barbara County. Established on April 21, 1782, it was the last presidio built by the Spanish in Alta California.

San Luis Rey de Francia Mission, Oceanside. (Photo by Henry F. Whitey, 1936. W.P.A.)

Vallejo Adobe

Niles Blvd. at Nursery Ave., Fremont, Alameda County. This was the overseer's home, dated 1855, on the estate of José de Jesús Vallejo, the military commander of the Pueblo de San José (1841-1842) and prominent California rancher.

Santa Barbara Mission. (Photo by Henry F. Whitey, 1936. W.P.A.)

(General) Vallejo House

Third St. W., Sonoma, Sonoma County. Built 1851-53, it was the house of General Mariano Vallejo, founder of Sonoma.

☀FLORIDA

Cathedral of St. Augustine

Cathedral St., Saint Augustine, St. Johns County. St. Augustine Parish, established in 1594, is the oldest Catholic Parish in the United States. The cathedral, first constructed in 1797, is largely a restoration of a church constructed from 1887 and 1888.

Fort San Carlos de Barrancas

Pensacola U.S. Naval Air Station, Pensacola. Built of earthwork on the beach in 1559 by the Spanish, it was rebuilt of stone in 1696 at its present site. Following the turns of history, it passed from the Spanish to the French to the Spanish to the British and finally it was ceded to the United States in 1821.

General Vallejo House. (Photo by Roger Sturtevant, 1934.)

Fort San Marcos de Apalache

Eighteen miles south of Tallahassee on U.S. 319 and Florida 363, St. Marks, Wakulla County. Founded in 1660 by the Spanish, it was captured in 1818 by Andrew Jackson, which facilitated the American acquisition of Florida in 1819.

González-Alvarez House (the Oldest House in the United States)

14 St. Francis Street, St. Augustine, St. Johns County. Built c. 1723, it is a townhouse adapted to Florida's unique climatic conditions. The original one-story had *coquina* (broken coral and shell) walls and floors of tabby (oyster shells mixed with lime).

Plaza Ferdinand VII

S. Palafox St., Pensacola, Escambia County. It is the site of the formal transfer of Florida from Spain to the United States in 1821. Andrew Jackson, the governor of the territory, officially proclaimed the establishment of the Florida Territory.

Castillo de San Marcos, St. Augustine.

St. Augustine Town Plan Historic District

Founded as a Spanish military base in 1565, St. Augustine is the oldest continuously occupied European settlement in the continental United States. Laid out around a central plaza, Plaza de la Constitución, the present streets are all in the original town plan. Additionally, many of the colonial homes and walled gardens have been restored.

San Luis de Apalache

Mission Rd., 2 miles west of Tallahassee on U.S. 90, Leon County. Founded in 1633 as the administrative center for the Spanish Province of Apalache, it was abandoned in 1702 when Great Britain began the destruction of the Spanish missions in Florida.

✷GEORGIA

St. Catherines Island

Part of the Sea Islands (the "Golden Isles of Guale"), 10 miles off the Georgia coast, Liberty County. The island was an important Spanish mission center from 1566 to 1684.

✷LOUISIANA

The Cabildo

Jackson Square, New Orleans, Orleans Parish. Built in 1795, the building originally housed the administrative and legislative council that ruled Spanish Louisiana. The transfer of Louisiana from Spain to France, and the subsequent transfer from France to the United States, both took place in the statehouse in 1803. Now part of the Louisiana State Museum, the structure exhibits the strong influence of Spanish architecture in the territory.

Jackson Square (Place d'Armes)

New Orleans, Orleans Parish. Center of the city since the first plan was drawn up by the Spanish in 1720. Here, in 1803, the American flag was raised for the first time over the newly purchased Louisiana Territory.

Vieux Carré Historic District

New Orleans, New Orleans Parish. Known as the "French Quarter," this eighty-five block district almost coincides with the original city plan laid out by the Spanish in 1721. In spite of the name, the architecture is predominately Spanish.

✷NEW MEXICO

Albuquerque

Bernalillo County. The town was founded in 1706 by Don Francisco Cuervo y Valdés. Old Town is the Spanish center of the city and is a historic zone, telling much about the history of the city through its varied arcitecture. *See* San Felipe de Neri church.

Barrio de Analco Historic District

518 Alto Street, Santa Fe, Santa Fe County. This district is unique because it represents a still active, working-class neighborhood of Spanish Colonial heritage that goes back to 1620. The district contains numerous examples of Spanish Pueblo architecture, characterized by the adobe construction indigenous to the Southwest.

Donciano Vigil House

518 Alto St., Santa Fe, Santa Fe County. From 1800 to 1832 this house served as the home of the important political leader Donciano Vigil.

Hawikuh

Valencia County. A Zuni city, it was the largest of the "Cities of Cíbola"; it was conquered by Coronado in 1540 and abandoned in 1680.

Las Trampas Historic District

Founded in 1751, the village of Las Trampas, a Spanish-American agricultural community, preserves its eighteenth-century heritage in appearance and culture.

The Cabildo in New Orleans. (Courtesy of the U.S. Department of the Interior and the National Park Service.)

Las Vegas Old Town Plaza

Las Vegas, San Miguel County. The plaza dates from 1835. In 1846, General Stephen Watts Kearny proclaimed New Mexico a U.S. territory here. Once a center of commerce on the Santa Fe Trail, Las Vegas, NM, is a modern center of activity.

Laureano Córdova Mill

Vadito, Taos County. This is a gristmill built c. 1870 in the traditional Mexican fashion, with a horizontal waterwheel; it is the only one of this type still commercially operated in New Mexico.

Mesilla Plaza

Two miles south of Las Cruces on New Mexico 28, Doña Ana County. On July 4, 1854, the American flag was raised over the plaza, confirming the Gadsden Purchase Treaty. The town retains the flavor of a Mexican village. The town was founded by the Spanish in 1598.

"El Morro" National Monument

Forty-five miles southwest of Grants, Valencia County. Site of Inscription Rock, bearing the 1605 graffitto of Juan de Oñate, New Mexico's governor and colonizer. The sandstone mesa was called "El Morro" (or "The Bluff") by the Spanish. Other settlers also carved their inscriptions in the soft rock.

Palace of the Governors

Lincoln and Palace Aves., the Plaza, Santa Fe, Santa Fe County. Originally constructed in 1610-1612, it is the oldest public building in the continental United States. It was used as the territorial capitol and Governor's residence during the Spanish, Mexican and American territorial rules.

San Estevan del Rey Mission church

On New Mexico S.R. 23, Acoma, Valencia county. Constructed from 1629 to 1642, and repaired from 1799 to 1800, San Estevan is an example of Spanish colonial architecture blending a European plan and form with American Indian construction and decorative detail. The mission served the Acoma pueblo.

San Felipe de Neri Church

On Old Town Plaza, Albuquerque, Bernalillo County. Founded in 1706, the present building was built in 1793 on the site of the earlier church.

San Francisco de Asís Mission Church

The Plaza, Ranchos de Taos, Taos County. Constructed c. 1772, it is an example of a New Mexican Spanish colonial church, covered with stuccoed adobe. It was built with exceptionally massive walls.

San Gabriel del Yungue-Ouige

Four miles north of Española via U.S. 64 and secondary roads, Río Arriba County. The ruins of this Tewa Indian pueblo mark the site of the first Spanish-built capital of New Mexico (1598-1610), established by Juan de Oñate. The capital was removed to Santa Fe in 1610.

San José de Gracia Church

The plaza, Las Trampas, Taos County. Built from 1760 to 1776, it is one of the best-preserved Spanish Colonial pueblo churches in the state. Its interior features old paintings on the reredos and designs painted under the balcony.

San José de los Jémez Mission

Jémez State Monument, Jémez Springs, San Miguel County. The mission was founded here in 1617 to serve the Pueblo of Giusewa. It was abandoned in 1622 due to Apache depredations.

San Miguel Church

Old Santa Fe Trail and E. De Vargas St., San Miguel of Santa Fe Mission, Santa Fe, Santa Fe County. Built c. 1636 for the use of Indian slaves and servants, it was almost completely destroyed during the Pueblo Revolt of 1680.

San Miguel del Vado Historic District.

San José, San Miguel County. Founded in the 1790s as a northern frontier outpost, this is an example of an early Hispanic village.

Santa Fe

Santa Fe County. It was founded by Don Pedro de Peralta in 1610 as a new capital for New Mexico. It was abandoned in 1680 due to the revolt of the Pueblos and re-occupied in 1692. The Fiesta de Santa Fe, held in September, celebrates this reconquest.

Santa Fe Plaza

Santa Fe, Santa Fe County. Founded c. 1610, it was historically the city's commercial and social center and the terminus of the Santa Fe Trail. The Palace of the Governors on the Plaza, was the site of the flag raising in 1846, establishing American rule.

Santuario de Chimayó

South of Truchas in Chimayó, Santa Fe County. The Sanctuary is a well-preserved, unrestored, small adobe church built in 1816 as an offering of thanks by Don Bernardo Abeyta. Its original wall paintings remain in good condition.

✳PANAMA CANAL ZONE

Fort San Lorenzo

Near the mouth of the Chagres River on the Atlantic side of the Isthmus of Panama, Panama Canal Zone. The fort was built by Spain between 1597 to 1601 to guard one terminal of the overland route used to avoid the dangerous voyage around Cape Horn.

✳PUERTO RICO

The Convent of Porta Coeli

San Germán. Built in 1530, it is one of the oldest religious structures built by Europeans in all of the Americas. It is the birth place of Santa Rosa de Lima.

La Fortaleza

San Juan Island, San Juan. The fort was built by the Spanish between 1533 and 1540, and remodeled and enlarged between 1845 and 1846 as a defense against raids by French and English pirates. It also became the residence of the island's governors.

✳TEXAS

The Alamo

Alamo Plaza (downtown), San Antonio, Bexar County. Founded by the Spanish in 1718 and built by Franciscans in 1744 as the San Antonio de Valero mission church, it was the site of the 1836 battle between Mexican troops and Texan rebel separatists. The defeat of the Texas rebels here spurred the Texas independence movement. There are two on-site museums.

Camino Real

El Paso, El Paso County. Because the road was once used by Spanish conquistadors, the "Camino Real" (King's Highway) and "the Old San Antonio Road" were the names given the route connecting settlements on the Rio Grande and the east Texas missions, including Corpus Christi de la Ysleta. (See below).

Chamizal National Monument

700 E. Marcial, El Paso, El Paso County, on the border with Mexico. Locale of the ninety-nine-year border dispute between Mexico and the United States. The dispute was settled in 1963.

The Convent of Porta Coeli in San Germán.

Concepción Mission

807 Mission Road, San Antonio, Bexar County. Built from 1731 to 1755 by the Spanish under the leadership of Franciscan friars, it is the best preserved of the Texas missions. The massive church building is designed in Mexican Baroque style, with twin bell towers.

The Alamo, San Antonio. (Courtesy of the Department of the Interior and the National Park Service.)

Corpus Christi de la Ysleta Mission

Ysleta, El Paso County. Established in 1682, the current structure dates from 1744. It has served the Tigua Indians since its founding and adjoins the Tigua Indian Reservation.

Dolores Viejo

On the north bank of the Rio Grande, near Laredo, in Zapata County. Here are the remains of the oldest Spanish settlement in Texas. It was founded in 1750 by José Vásquez Borrego, lieutenant to José de Escandón.

Espada Aqueduct

San Francisco de la Espada Mission, San Antonio Missions National Historical Park, San Antonio Bexar County. Built from 1731 to 1745 by the Spanish, it was once a part of an irrigation system serving five area missions. It is the only remaining spanish structure of its type in the United States.

José Antonio Navarro House

228 S. Laredo St., San Antonio. Built c. 1850, it was home to one of two native Texans to sign their names to the 1836 Texas declaration of independence. The house and grounds are now a state historic site.

Laredo (Villa de San Agustín de Laredo)

Laredo, Webb County. Founded in 1755 by Tomás Sánchez, an officer of the Royal Army of Spain, the buildings around the old plaza reflect the distinct Spanish/Mexican architectural and cultural heritage. Laredo was also the home to the small stone-and-adobe capitol of the short-lived (1839-1840) Republic of the Rio Grande, which included south Texas and what became three northern states of Mexico.

Los Nogales

Seguin, Guadalupe County. A house built prior to 1765 on the Old Spanish Trail. In 1825, it served as a post office operated by Juan Seguín, the Texan freedom-fighter.

Nuestra Señora de la Luz Mission

Wallisville, Chambers County. The mission and presidio were established in 1756.

Nuestra Señora del Rosario Mission

Goliad County. Established in the 1750s, it was built to minister to the Karankawan tribes.

San Francisco de la Espada Mission, San Antonio.

Nuestra Señora del Socorro Mission

Moon Rd. and Farm Rd. 258, Socorro, El Paso County. Founded in 1680, the present structure dates from 1840-1848.

Palo Alto Battlefield

Six and a half miles north of Brownsville, Farm Rd. 511, Cameron County. It is the site of the first of two

Espíritu Santo de la Bahía Mission, Goliad County.

Monument honoring the fallen at the Alamo, San Antonio.

important Mexican War battles fought in Texas. General Zachary Taylor's victory here in 1846 made invasion of Mexico possible.

Presidio Nuestra Señora de Loreto de la Bahía

One mile south of Goliad State Park on U.S. 183, Goliad County. It was constructed in 1749 to protect the Espíritu Santo de la Bahía Mission. After the 1810 Mexican revolution for independence, its name was changed to Goliad, supposedly an anagram for the patriot of the revolution, (H)idalgo. During the Texas War of Independence, it served as a prison. Execution of the prisoners held there was a rallying point for Texas partisans.

Presidio Saint Louis

Inez, Victoria County. The fort was established in 1685 by Sieur La Salle's French forces; it was refounded by Spanish forces from 1722 to 1726 to prevent further French incursions.

Rancho de las Cabras

Floresville, Wilson County. A former stock ranch for the San Francisco de la Espada Mission (established in 1731), which was thirty miles north.

Resaca de la Palma Battlefield

On the north edge of Brownsville on Parades Line Road, Cameron County. It is the site of the second battle of the Mexican War. On May 9, 1846, the battle involving forces of General Zachary Taylor and the Mexican Army, begun at Palo Alto, continued here. The defeated Mexican force retreated across the Río Grande.

San Antonio

Bexar County. San Antonio, named for the Franciscan mission, San Antonio de Valero, was first settled in 1718 as a way station between the Río Grande and Los Adaes, which was the first capital of Texas. San Antonio developed into an important commercial center and, in 1773, became the capital of Texas. After Mexican independence, it became the headquarters of the lieutenant governor of the state of Coahuila y Tejas. After the war of Texas independence, San Antonio was no longer a political capital, but continued to develop as a commercial center, becoming the most populous city in Texas by the turn of the century. Today, Houston holds that honor.

San Diego

Duval County. A program was created here for an uprising February 20, 1915, by Mexican-Americans along the Mexican border and the creation of a republic, with a possible eventual union with Mexico. The uprising was to be led by the Supreme Revolutionary congress, which called for the killing of all Anglos over the age of sixteen, except for the elderly. There was considerable unrest after the plan had been revealed and it led to some Anglo vigilantism against Mexicans. By Autumn of 1915, order was restored.

A reconstruction of the San Francisco Mission in East Texas, the first mission in Texas. (Courtesy of the *Texas Catholic Herald*.)

San Fernando Cathedral

Main Plaza, San Antonio, Bexar County. It was founded in 1734 by colonists from the Canary Islands, who were sent by King Philip of Spain. The present-day stone church was reconstructed in 1873, after a fire. Alamo heroes are buried here.

San Francisco de la Espada Mission

Espada Rd., San Antonio Missions National Historical Park, San Antonio, Bexar County. Built in the mid-eighteenth century, it was used in 1835 as a fortification against Mexican forces. *See also*: Espada Aqueduct; San Francisco de los Tejas Mission.

San Francisco de los Tejas Mission

Near Weches, Houston County. Established in March 1690 by Father Massanet to minister to the Caddo Indians and to establish a Spanish presence and ward off French incursions into Texas. It was the first Spanish mission in Texas. It was abandoned in 1693 after the Indians became hostile. It was re-established in 1716 and in 1721 the Marquis de Aguayo reopened the mission as San Francisco de los Neches a few miles from the original site. Finally, in 1731, the mission was moved to San Antonio and became San Francisco de la Espada. Today, a replica stands on the original site of the San Francisco de los Tejas Mission.

San Jacinto Battleground

Twenty-two miles east of Houston, on Texas S.R. 134, Harris County. In 1836, General Sam Houston's forces won the decisive engagement of the Texas Revolution here gaining Texas' independence from Mexico. A heavily monumented Shrine of the Texas Republic now stands on the site.

San José de Palafox

Thirty miles north of Laredo, Webb County. The remains of the Palafox Villa, founded in 1810 by Don Antonio Cordero y Bustamante, Governor of Coahuila, Mexico.

San José y San Miguel de Aguayo Mission

6539 San Jose Dr., San Antonio Missions National Historical Park, San Antonio, Bexar County.

Founded in 1720, it was one of the most successful and prosperous missions of New Spain. By the time of secularization (1794), it boasted a church, a chapel, Indian quarters, barracks, mill, granary, workshop and storerooms.

San Juan Capistrano Mission

Berg's Mill-Graf Rd., San Antonio Missions National Historical Park, San Antonio, Bexar County. It was built in 1731, secularized in 1824. Ruins of the church and granary are on the site; the chapel was restored in 1909.

San Luis de las Amarillas Presidio

Near Menard, Menard County. The fort was established in 1758 as a base for Spanish mineral explorations. It was abandoned in 1768.

San Xavier Mission complex

Rochdale, Milam County. The site of three missions that were later abandoned due to friction between the presidio troops and the missionaries: San Francisco Xavier (1747), San Ildefonso (1749) and Nuestra Señora de la Candelaria (1749).

San José y San Miguel Aguayo Mission. (Photo by Arthur W. Stewart, 1936. W.P.A.)

Socorro Mission

Socorro, El Paso County. Established c. 1840, La Purísima Socorro Mission replaced a much earlier mission on this site which had served the Piro, Tano, and Jémez Indians displaced from New Mexico.

Spanish Governor's Palace

105 Military Plaza, San Antonio, Bexar County. It is the only remaining example in Texas of an aristocratic eighteenth-century Spanish residence. It served as the headquarters for the captain of the presidio.

"La Villita"

Villita St., San Antonio, Bexar County. Heart of the original Mexican community, it is made up of a little village of restored houses which now are tourist curio shops.

San Miguel Mission, Santa Fe, New Mexico.

✳VIRGIN ISLANDS

Columbus Landing Site

Salt River Bay, St. Croix Island. This is the earliest site now under the United States flag which is associated with Christopher Columbus. The skirmish here with the Carin Indians in 1493 was the first recorded conflict between European explorers and American aborigines.

References

Balseiro, José. *The Hispanic Presence in Florida*. Miami: Seemann Publishers, 1976.

Federal Writers Project. *New Mexico: A Guide to the Colorful State*. New York: Hastings House, 1953.

Forrest, Earle R. *Missions and Pueblas of the Old Southwest*. Cleveland, Oh.: Arthur H. Clark, 1929.

Johnson, Paul. *Pictorial History of California*. New York: Doubleday, 1970.

National Park Service. *Catalog of National Historic Landmarks*. Washington, D.C.: U.S. Department of the Interior, 1985.

Robinson, W. W. *Los Angeles: A Brief History and Guide*. San Francisco: California Historical Society, 1981.

Welch, June Rayfield. *Historic Sites of Texas*. Dallas, Texas: G.L.A. Press, 1972.

Nicolás Kanellos

5

The Family

The United States harbors one of the most diverse Hispanic populations in the world. Large urban populations are present on both the Pacific and Atlantic coasts, rural pockets dot every state of the union, and large expanses of Hispanics are found in the major states from California to New York. The first impression a person gets of this population is the basic similarity that is expressed in social and cultural behavior regardless of urban or rural setting. The entire population is Spanish-language oriented, and indeed many newcomers and settlers speak nothing but Spanish.

Cultural manifestations expressed in dance, music, fiestas, and so forth, help paint a picture of similarity. The broad similarities in culture and language, however, mask a diverse people that represent every Hispanic-Latino country and group of people in the world. This diversity is a product of widespread Hispanic immigration and the different ways Hispanics have adapted to the United States. These are complex processes in which Hispanics, like other immigrant and settler groups, have relied on both traditional and hybrid cultural institutions in relating, adapting, and surviving in the new cultural milieu that is the United States.

Fundamental to this adaptation process, and indeed to Hispanic culture in general, is the institution of the family. The family is considered the single most important institution in the social organization of Hispanics. It is through the family and its activities that all people relate to significant others in their lives and it is through the family that people communicate with the larger society.

Although these primary functions of the family are evident among all peoples, the family among Hispanics has been a central thread that connects a multitude of strands that make up their social world. The central importance in social-cultural functions and the values of cultural life expressed through the family are emphasized in all studies focusing on Hispanics both in the United States and throughout the Hispanic world. There is no argument that when compared to the U.S. population in general, Hispanics place special emphasis, sentiment, and value on the family.

The Hispanic family is organized around a group of primary institutions that are common to all Hispanic groups in the United States, but the family is expressed in different ways. The literature refers to a Hispanic family structure that is composed of elements (institutions) that provide important social and cultural meaning and to one degree or another are identifiable in all groups. But this hides the specific and rich cultural diversity and the complex cultural adaptations of Mexicans, Puerto Ricans, Cubans, Dominicans, and Central and South Americans to the United States. Each of these cultural groups exhibits a broadly identifiable "Hispanic family" that is organized around a number of supportive institutions. The variations, however, of the Hispanic family are seen both within and across all groups.

Understanding the diversity of the family among Hispanics requires a fundamental understanding of the different Hispanic groups in the United States. Each group has a particular history within the United States that has affected the manner in which the family and its supportive institutions have been expressed. Only one group, Mexican Americans/Chicanos originates in the area that is the continental United States, but the bulk of the Hispanic population, like Puerto Ricans, Cubans, Dominicans, and Central and South Americans, immigrated to this country. Puerto Ricans on the other hand are the only "colonized" group that has migrated and settled in the United States in mass. Significantly, Puerto

The Lugo Family at Bell Gardens, California, circa 1888. (Courtesy of Los Angeles County Museum of Natural History.)

Ricans are U.S. citizens and move freely between the island of Puerto Rico and the mainland. The adaptation of the Hispanic population in both urban and rural settings stems from the socioeconomic and historical relations of home countries with the United States, a continuing migration based primarily on labor needs, and, to varying degrees, a continued relationship with home regions. Hispanics have used and generated new social processes based on the traditional family patterns in the migration process and in adapting to life in the United States.

Understanding the family as it has evolved among Hispanics in the United States requires a consideration of the societal contexts that influence and condition Hispanic socialization in the United States. The settlement of Puerto Ricans in New York and the creation of urban barrios in Spanish Harlem, Brooklyn, and Manhattan have been conditioned by continuous high unemployment, lack of housing, and poverty, which are exacerbated by the dense population in the city. This is very different from the Cuban settlement in Miami, where strong economic enclaves of primarily middle-class entrepreneurs are thriving in what is now known as Little Havana.

Additional social factors differentiating the His-

panic family include race and class. Although Hispanics stem from a similar origin, their ethnic/racial makeup differs because of the historical patterns in their countries of origin. Among those groups from the Caribbean (Dominicans, Puerto Ricans, Cubans), for example, a rich African element exists in the population that stems from the importation of slaves in early colonial periods. Mexicans, on the other hand, are primarily mestizo, rich in Indian (native American) background mixed with descendants from Spain. And Hispanics come from every socioeconomic class that is represented in the United States. The majority of Hispanics, however, are to be found in the lower economic strata of society, and a great percentage continue to remain below the poverty line. Racial attitudes toward people of color in the United States have had a great influence on their adaptation. Discrimination toward blacks and Hispanics and others has restricted access to employment, education, and housing, and in turn has influenced patterns of family and household development.

Although Hispanics are among the newest groups of immigrants to the United States, they are also some of the first settlers. Indeed, the ancestors of the populations in the southwestern United States (Califor-

A child's birthday party in New York City. (Justo A. Martí Collection, Center for Puerto Rican Studies Library, Hunter College, CUNY.)

nia, Arizona, New Mexico, Colorado, and Texas) settled in these states long before the U.S. colonies severed their ties from England. There have also been successive waves of immigrants for many generations. The Puerto Rican migration began at the turn of this century, after the United States took that island from Spain, and Mexican immigration began in great earnest early in the century and escalated after the Mexican Revolution of 1911. The long-time residence and established settlements mean that many generations of Hispanics can be counted in the United States. The family must be viewed across these generations as well as within the generations to fully appreciate its role. For example, early settlers and migrants created and utilized social networks based on family relations, while later generations illustrate a more nuclear family preference and maintain family values and kin extensions in different ways.

The focus here is not just the different elements but the primary processes that together make up the family. The idea of a static and unchanging family, although once a major depiction in the scholarly literature, is not accepted by current scholars and practitioners. (This is partly because of the emergence of critical research that has reanalyzed and often interpreted social science from a Hispanic perspective, by Chicano, Puerto Rican, Cuban, and other Hispanic scholars who are focusing on their own communities and people). In the past, the family has been viewed as an archaic vestige of former societies to which men, women, and children were tied. The sense of a "traditional family" among Hispanics emphasized a nonchanging and out-of-date institution that kept Hispanics from becoming productive and contributing to the larger U.S. society. The contrary, however, is in fact the rule. The Hispanic family is an institution that provided the social mechanisms which helped people, at least initially, in the processes of migration and settlement. It is the one institution, in varying forms, that provided the initial contacts and ties to employment, friends, kin, and new settlements in the United States. There are, to be sure, elements that have not fit certain aspects of the larger U.S. Hispanic society, but these elements appear generally after initial settlement, in later generations. A high rate of divorce, for example, is found

Community action through family and parent power: United Bronx Parents, Inc. (Records of the United Bronx Parents, Inc. Courtesy of the Center for Puerto Rican Studies Library, Hunter College, CUNY.)

among the second-generation population compared to first pioneers.

✸THE INSTITUTIONS OF THE HISPANIC FAMILY

What then, are the primary elements that make up the social-cultural "machinery" of the Hispanic family in the United States? The concept of "family" among all Hispanics refers to more than just the nuclear family that consists of a household of man and wife with their children. The family incorporates the idea of *la familia* (the greater family), which includes in addition to the immediate nuclear household, relatives that are traced on both the female and male sides. There include parents, grandparents, brothers and sisters, cousins, and to a certain extent any blood relatives that can be identified through the hierarchy of family surnames. This broad-ranging concept has important consequences for actual social and cultural behavior. It places individuals as well as nuclear families into a recognizable network of social relations within which mutual support and reciprocity occur.

A Puerto Rican mine worker, at home with his family after work in Bingham Canyon, Utah. (Historical Archive, Departamento de Asuntos de la Comunidad Puertorriqueña. Courtesy of the Center for Puerto Rican Studies Library, Hunter College, CUNY.)

Before describing the particular aspects of each of the major groups of Hispanics in the United States, the distinction between household and family needs to be made. "Household" has been a focus of anthropological inquiry because households are the entities in which people actually live. According to Baca-Zinn (1983), families are groups of persons bound together by ties of kinship both real and fictive, as we have seen, and households are groups of persons bound to place. Households are the units within which people pool resources and perform specific tasks. They are units of production, reproduction, and consumption. They are residential units where persons and resources are connected and distributed.

Important supportive institutions of la familia include the extended family, *parentesco*, (the concept of familism) *compadrazgo* (godparenthood), *confianza* (trust), and family ideology. Family ideology is more than just the way people think about family. Family ideology among Hispanics sets the ideal and standards to which individuals aim; it is the guiding light to which all look and attempt to shape their behavior for themselves as well as for the perception others have of them. Family ideology consists of the conceptual rules that people try to maintain, the values that are expressed about what the family should be and how it is maintained. For Hispanics, the ideal of family is that it is the central and most important institution in life. It holds all individuals together and all individuals should put family before their own concerns. It is the means of social and cultural existence. Ideology also defines the ideal roles and behaviors of family members. Although there is truth to family ideology in that it influences actual behavior, this ideology is never totally realized among Hispanics. Like all ideology, the ideology of la familia is a guide for behavior, a basis from which to act.

Family ideology also defines the ideal roles and behaviors of family members. The ideal family is a patriarchy that revolves around a strong male figure who is ultimately responsible for the well-being of all individuals "under his roof." The concept of "machismo" is embedded in this ideal, in which men are viewed as virile, aggressive, and answerable only to themselves. In real life, however, this is rarely realized. There are degrees of male authoritarianism that vary both within and across groups, but for the most part women are strong contributors to decision making and are often the internal authority figures in the family. In both subtle and direct ways, women not only contribute to decision making but often have the authority in the family. This is contrary to the stereotype in which the woman is viewed as subservient and deferent to "her man" and that child rearing and household chores should be her main concern. In fact, one of the greatest of changes in the Hispanic family in the United states is in the woman's role. There is a very high percentage of woman-headed households,

especially among Puerto Ricans in New York. A high percentage of women in all Hispanic groups are employed and are the primary household wage earners. This, as might be expected, has caused tremendous changes in family structure and role behavior. However, family ideology continues to be verbally expressed as a value and cultural norm, often in contradiction to actual family behavior.

The role of children in the family ideology is one in which they, as stated in the age-old dictum, "are to be seen but not heard." Children should be subservient and show respect to all elders, *respeto* (respect) being a concept held by all individuals. In a variety of studies in education, Hispanic children, especially those of new migrants, do behave in a "culturally prescribed manner" that is congruent with family ideology. However, as in all other aspects of family ideology among Hispanics, children's roles have experienced drastic changes. Education in the American system and exposure to people outside the immediate family and network of relatives has affected children in many ways. Children often become the social brokers between their parents and the outside

Mexican Mother of the Year, 1969: Mrs. Dolores Venegas and her husband, Miguel, Houston, Texas. (Courtesy of the *Texas Catholic Herald*.)

world. They are the best speakers of English and
know the outside more thoroughly than parents.

Among all Hispanics some form of the extended
family is present. The extended family is an important
part of the la familia concept, because it includes
more than one generation of individuals that are
related, and who express immediate support to one
another as a primary value. The ideal extended family
includes a husband and wife, their children, grandparents (mothers and fathers of husband and wife),
and siblings of the husband and wife. Many members
of this extended family live together under one roof
and share economic and social activities. Although a
number of variants to the ideal type do exist, Hispanic groups in the United States do not generally
live in an extended family household. The reality is
that Hispanics tend to favor the nuclear family and a
separate household. This is especially true of later
settlers and individuals born in the United States.
The extended family living in single households is
generally a transitory stage in family and household
development. It is seen primarily during the migrant
stages of first arrival when newcomers need support
and help in adjusting and finding their way in a new
environment. The reality of the extended Hispanic
family is that it transcends geographical barriers and
has functioning units in both the country of origin as
well as in the United States. It is in this sense that the
institution of the family has taken on a hybrid form
through the strategic expression of migrants adapting to a new environment.

Hispanics have used the extended family in conjunction with other kinship institutions that form
part of the greater familia and family ideology. As in
the family in general, the Catholic religion has had a
very strong influence in familia institutions. Religious rites of baptism and marriage take on special
meaning that have evolved into sociocultural expressions important among Hispanics in the United
States. *Compadrazgo* (godparenthood), marriage,
and *parentesco* (kinship sentiment) are primary institutions that need to be understood in relation to the
family. These are multidimensional elements that together help maintain la familia. Compadrazgo is
formed usually through the baptism of a child, with
parents choosing *padrinos* (godparents) from close
friends or relatives. Compadrazgo is the extension of
kinship to nonrelatives and the strengthening of responsibilities between kin. Padrinos also sponsor the
child in baptism and confirmation ceremonies. They
are also chosen to be best man and bridesmaid at
weddings. *Compadres* (co-parents) ideally have special responsibilities toward the godchild and in the
past have been expected to take the parental role if
parents were to pass away, except in the case of

marriage sponsorship. This special parental relationship is maintained throughout life. In addition, although not recognized in much of the literature, the
ahijado/a (godchild) has a special responsibility
towards the padrino. This is manifested in varying
degrees, but can be seen when the padrino is elderly;
ahijados may pay special attention almost as if the
padrino/a were a grandparent. However, the strongest relationship in compadrazgo is that between the
child's parents and godparents, who call each other
compadres (literally co-parents). Godparents often
address each other as *comadre* (co-mother) or
compadre (co-father), illustrating the special relationship they have toward one another. Compadrazgo forms an intimate relationship in which those
sharing the role have specific expectations of each
other. Much of the literature focuses on the reciprocal nature of the relationship between compadres,
especially in the early period of adaptation to the
United States. Compadres are expected to provide
each other with mutual help, to care for one another
in time of need, and to be readily available in times of
crisis. Compadrazgo has been, as might be expected, a
key institution embraced by migrants from all the
Hispanic countries. Compadres, as kin, have provided shelter for newcomers, access to jobs, and a
base from which people can become acclimatized to
the new environment. Compadrazgo is a means to
further "extend" the family by adding new members
and ensuring support in times of need.

In addition to the compadrazgo, which extends
reciprocity to nonrelatives, *parentesco* (kinship sentiment) has been an important institution that has
taken on new meaning in the early periods of migration and settlement. Parentesco has been especially
utilized by Mexican immigrants. As used in the border area, it became a broader concept than that
understood in the home region, where parentesco was
reserved for kin. In the United States it was expressed
on the basis of regional affiliation, the migration
experience, or the mutual settlement in a foreign
environment. Families did not just extend parentesco
to other migrants; they were extending parentesco to
families and individuals who shared a specific history
in the country of origin. Parentesco is not familism,
which is the recognition of the importance of family,
family ties, family honor, and the ideal of respect.
Familism incorporates the altruistic value that the
family is more important than any of its members.
This recognition carries a responsibility to kin in
general. Parentesco is a kinship sentiment used by
Hispanics to incorporate kin as well as nonkin into
family networks. It is the extension of family sentiment to kin and nonkin.

Parientes (blood relatives), because of their natu-

A Hispanic family attends mass, Houston, Texas. (Photo by Curtis Dowell. Courtesy of the *Texas Catholic Herald*.)

ral relation as bloodkin, are automatically part of a family network. Similarly, compadres, if not already kin, are brought into the network as well. However, among Hispanics in the United States, the sentiment of parentesco is extended to individuals who share regional or specific geographic origins, especially a town or township in the country of origin. This was especially evident among early migrants to the United States who came from primarily rural backgrounds; often similar origins in towns did indicate kinship even if distant. The new environment in the

United States utilized the sentiment toward kin and friends from home regions to build the support and reciprocity networks needed in the new settlements. Kin terms are used to express this relationship— *primo/a* (cousin), *tío/a* (uncle/aunt), for example.

Confianza (trust) is of particular importance to both the institutions of compadrazgo and parentesco among Hispanics in the United States, and is the basis of the relationships between individuals in many spheres of social activity. It is evident in business relations among entrepreneurs who work on the

The rehearsal of a *posada* sponsored during the Christmas season for families by the Club Sembradores de la Amistad in Houston, Texas, 1988. (Photo by Curtis Dowell. Courtesy of the *Texas Catholic Herald*.)

basis of trust and among friendships in which trust is fundamental. But confianza goes beyond relationships between individuals and forms the underlying base of reciprocity of all types. Confianza is the underlying factor that builds relationships and forms the basis for trust in the institutions of parentesco and compadrazgo. In a sense, the combined expression and practice of compadrazgo and parentesco produce the continued trust that is expressed as confianza. To have confianza with an individual is not just to regard that person with trust, but it signifies a relationship of special sentiment and importance involving respect and intimacy. Confianza developed in friendship can, for example, lead to a relationship of compadrazgo and to expressing parentesco to individuals who are not kin, as for example an individual who is from a home region and is a friend or compadre of kin.

A unique characteristic of the extended family among Hispanics in the United States is regionalism.

Because of the migration over time of different generations from specific home regions, the family has been extended to include both U.S. and home country components. The family has become in many instances a binational or transnational institution even after several generations of time. Among Dominicans and Mexicans this is especially evident, but it is true to varying degrees among all Hispanics in the United States. Extensions of the family in the United States form part of a social network that includes not just regions but actual ties to specific hometowns. Among early pioneers and first migrants, kinship forms the basis for help in settling and finding jobs in the United States; later as settlements became more established, these early migrants host and assist both relatives and friends from their home areas. And migrants themselves return to home countries and regions, setting up a back-and-forth flow that depends on the support of family members in both areas. This actually extends the family across geographic space, creating the reciprocity, mutual help, and parentesco in the country of origin as well as in the United States. Hence the extended regional family becomes a basis of reciprocity between families in the home and the country of origin, as well as a potential basis for continuing migration to and from the United States.

The institution of marriage varies tremendously among Hispanics in the United States, and like the family in general has been adapted to a number of different socioeconomic conditions. The value of a religious wedding is not, nor has it ever been, the sole means for recognizing unions between men and women. Among Dominicans, for example, marital unions consist of *matrimonio por la iglesia* (church wedding), *matrimonio por ley* (civil marriage), and *union libre* (free union). Church weddings carry higher prestige and are more prevalent among persons of higher socioeconomic status, but free unions allow for early cohabitation in the migrant settlement. Marriage, however, has been an institution that strengthens extended family ties and incorporates individuals and their kin into network alliances under parentesco. Marriage, in addition to its important function of uniting conjugal pairs in critical household formation and procreation of children, is an institution used in the primary adaptive processes to the United States. Marriage among Hispanics continues to be within their own group (endogamous), that is, Mexicans marrying Mexicans, Puerto Ricans marrying Puerto Ricans, and so on. There is some intermarriage between groups, but this is infrequent, and there is a growing rate of intermarriage with Anglo-Americans, especially among second-generation Hispanics. This is especially true of Mexican Americans.

La familia, then, incorporates the institutions of ideology, parentesco, compadrazgo, marriage, and confianza that together have formed the basis of migration and settlement in the United States. Through the variant forms of the extended family, Hispanics have adjusted and adapted to a new environment. The family, however, continues changing as seen in the shift from extended to nuclear family preference in later generations and among U.S.-born persons. This, however, is not an indication of abandoning extended family ties, but a change in the manner in which extended ties and relations are expressed that are congruent with life in the United States. Although these institutions can be viewed as separate strands of a single thread, they are strands that together form the social fabric in unique products of expression. Social networks composed of extended families are the basis of communities in urban and rural barrios of Chicanos, Mexicans, Puerto Ricans, Cubans, and the other Latinos in the United States.

Because families live in households, they are often taken as one and the same thing. Hispanics make the differentiation clearly, as they refer to the nuclear family living under one roof as *la casa*, as opposed to the broader institution la familia. Households, however, are a good indication of the changing nature of adaptation and settlement of Hispanics in the United States. Households include the extended family as people first migrate and begin to settle in the United States. It is the first step in becoming permanent settlers.

✷ PUERTO RICANS: BORN IN THE U.S.A.

Puerto Ricans are the second-largest Hispanic group in the United States and have been migrating to the mainland United States since the turn of the century. In 1917, the Jones Act granted all Puerto Ricans born on the island U.S. citizenship. This is a striking difference to all other Hispanic immigrants to the country, as Puerto Ricans can move freely between their country of origin without legal restrictions and entanglements of U.S. immigration law.

Migration to the continental United States became a viable alternative to the deteriorating economic and social situation on the island. Economic changes on the island brought about by foreign control of land for sugar and coffee plantations and tobacco created high unemployment and a steady stream of migrants to the United States that has continued to the present. One of the first casualties of this economic change was the incremental decline of family patterns that were based on subsistence. High unemployment coupled with a gradual industrialization caused both increased unemployment and dependence on outside commodities. This imbalance created surplus labor at a time when jobs in New York City and elsewhere on the mainland needed to be filled. Puerto Ricans began migrating to the United States and, in particular, to New York City. Initially, as is the case with the majority of Hispanics in the United States, the early migration was intended to be only temporary. Puerto Ricans did not want to leave the island, but the high unemployment and the draw of jobs in New York created the flow of people between the mainland and the island.

In the late 1890s, during the Spanish-American War, a small group of Puerto Ricans fled the island and sought refuge in New York City while they worked for independence. Most of these people returned after the United States obtained the island from Spain. They felt betrayed when the United States maintained jurisdiction over the island and did not support the liberation movement. However, the early colony helped establish New York as a receiving area, and it grew geometrically in the following years. In the early part of the century, migration to the United States continued and New York became the preferred area for the majority of migrant Puerto Ricans, establishing one of the largest concentrations of Hispanics in the United States. The early migration was composed of people moving from rural to urban areas in Puerto Rico as well as people who immigrated to New York directly from rural areas of the island. Of importance here is that these people maintained what might be called the traditional family as it was known in Puerto Rico. Some of these people joined the migrant labor circuits on the mainland doing agricultural work, but the majority went to the city of New York. The early conditions of this migration created a relationship that was to have enduring consequences for settlement and adaptation of Puerto Ricans and their families as well as for the subsequent forms the family would take in the United States.

In the 1940s, airline flights between the island and New York became regular, were relatively inexpensive, and travel time was short. Air travel became the common means of leaving and returning to the island and paved the way for what was to become the "Great Migration" from the mid 1940s to the 1970s. The decades before 1945 are considered the period of pioneer migration. Many of the people emigrating from Puerto Rico were contract laborers who came to work in industry and agriculture. These individuals were the basis for many of the Puerto Rican communities that currently exist outside New York City. However,

the majority of migrants continued to pour into New York City. By 1940, there was a total of almost 70,000 Puerto Ricans in the United States; more than 87 percent, or almost 61,000, were living in New York City.

During the war years, there were not many migrants who crossed from the island because of the danger in the Atlantic. But when the war ended, there was a sizable unemployed population looking to leave for jobs in the United States. It was at this time that the Great Migration began. The economic situation in Puerto Rico had worsened before this period and the island fell further under the domination of a market economy controlled by U.S. interests. By 1960, a total of 887,662 Puerto Ricans had migrated to the United States; 69 percent of these people, or about 612,000, resided in New York City. By the end of the next decade, a total of 1,391,463 people had left the island and had become residents of the United States, with 817,712 of them residing in the city of New York.

Similarly to other Hispanic immigrants, Puerto Ricans did not travel together in family groups at the beginning of the migration. Usually, young men immigrated to find work, then began sending for spouses and families. But the social conditions in the United States, especially in New York, where new communities were established, set parameters that changed family patterns and conditioned the adaptation of Puerto Ricans to the city.

In Puerto Rico, unemployment in these later years continued to worsen, and the educational system was not meeting the needs of the population. The majority of people worked *la zafra* (the sugar harvest), but this work lasted only five months of the year. Workers were idle for the remaining seven months. During the years after the 1940s, unemployment was heightened by a growing working-age population. A rising population coupled with a drop in the death rate created a large, young, unemployed working class.

Poverty became a significant factor in the lives of families in both Puerto Rico and the United States. It is impossible to discuss the Puerto Rican family in the United States without discussing the extreme conditions that have pervaded the Puerto Rican community here. From a historical perspective, Puerto Ricans have never recovered from the early colonial period when U.S. capital interests took over the ownership of the majority of land on the island and created a labor force that was dependent on cash crops. Puerto Rico had one of the highest infant mortality rates in the world and one of the lowest rates of average income per worker during the early years of U.S. jurisdiction over the island. Consider for example that in 1899 Puerto Ricans maintained ownership of 93 percent of all farms, but by 1930 foreign (U.S.) interests controlled 60 percent of sugar cultivation, 80 percent of tobacco lands, 60 percent of all banks, and 100 percent of maritime lines that controlled commodities entering and leaving the island. Prior to the capitalist sugar economy, the family was very important in the subsistence economy. The diminished importance of the family in agriculture, continued unemployment and poor education in Puerto Rico resulted in poverty on the island. Similar factors account for its existence in the United States. People arrived in the States with low skills because of both a rural background and little or no schooling. The jobs they worked at were poor-paying. Of all Hispanic groups in the United States, Puerto Ricans continue to be the most socioeconomically disadvantaged group in the country, especially in New York City. In 1980, the median family annual income for Puerto Ricans was $9,900, compared to $15,000 for all Hispanics and $19,500 for all U.S. families. Forty-five percent of Puerto Ricans in New York City live below the poverty level. Much of this poverty is found among female-headed households, a family configuration that is increasing among Puerto Ricans, Dominicans, and other Hispanics in the United States. Poverty, then, is a consistent factor and an underlying force among the Puerto Rican families in the United States. It has conditioned change and the adaptation of families to the social and cultural environment of the United States.

At the end of the 1960s and into the early 1970s, what has become known as "revolving door" migration began. This is a back-and-forth stream of people moving between the United States and the island. It is no longer focused in New York, although a majority of Puerto Ricans continue to migrate and settle in the Northeast.

This back-and-forth movement has encouraged the unification and extension of families on the mainland with those in Puerto Rico. Travel of family members to and from households on the island and on the mainland is now a natural part of the migration cycle. Even "Nuyoricans," Puerto Ricans born in New York, have migrated to the island and have begun to adapt to life there.

A significant problem in New York and in other urban areas that has greatly influenced Puerto Rican families and individuals is access to housing. Housing in New York has always been a problem, but among Puerto Ricans who earn low wages and are often unemployed in the city, housing is poor, crowded, and a major adaptational factor, especially for those Puerto Ricans who are on the lowest rung of the socioeconomic ladder. An example of the seriousness of the housing conditions for inner-city Puerto Rican families is Hartford, Connecticut. According to Pelto, Roman, and Liviano (1982), housing conditions have become desperate as apartments are converted to more expensive condominiums and residential space is taken over by offices and businesses. Housing problems are contributing to household fragmentation and unemployment is contributing to serious problems in family life. Two of every three households were reported to lack employment, even part-time. This has contributed to a number of household types: dual-parent households where at least one of the two parents is employed; households with two parents but with neither employed; and single-parent households where the parent is not employed. These variations, however, illustrate the workings of the extended family in that the households with two unemployed parents are often helped by other relatives living in the Hartford area. Similarly, among single-parent households, there are relatives in the city who appear to be providing help and support. Here again the range of assistance received from others outside the household demonstrates the general patterns of exchange and reciprocity. It is clear, then, that the urban milieu in the United States has influenced Puerto Rican family patterns and households.

Although poverty among Puerto Ricans is a significant factor, not all Puerto Ricans are suffering from unemployment and poverty. Although the majority of early migrants were unskilled, Puerto Ricans have slowly penetrated the white-collar world associated with the middle class in the United States. Even with great poverty, the children of migrants, the second generation, are improving their socioeconomic position. Less unemployment, higher educational achievement, and higher incomes are not the rule but are evident in the population as a whole.

The ideal of the family as a cultural expression is still adhered to and the institutions of *parentesco*, *compadrazgo*, *confianza*, and varying degrees of patriarchy are maintained among Puerto Ricans in the United States. One significant change among the general population is the increasing influence of the role of women. This has been a direct result of women working, often when the male in the house is unemployed. Women in many cases have become the breadwinners of the household. This has led to an increasing trend toward stronger egalitarian relations among spouses, but this generally means that the wife has taken on traditional male tasks, not that men have taken on the wives' roles and tasks in the household. Marriage preference continues to be a religious ceremony in the Catholic church, and there is a low rate of Puerto Ricans marrying outside the community, although this has increased among second-generation U.S.-born persons.

Puerto Ricans continue to identify strongly with their cultural and ethnic past. A study by Rogler and Cooney (1984) of one hundred parents and their married children (a total of two hundred married couples) in New York reported that not one member of the children's generation, almost all born in the United States, reported feeling closer to Anglo-Americans than to Puerto Ricans, nor did anyone in their generation consider Anglo-Americans to be his or her real people.

What we see in the family among Puerto Ricans in the United States is a great variation in form, but it is still based in part on the ideal type of Hispanic family. Major institutions appear to be alive and well, but the dearth of research in this area of family life does not allow any assured conclusions. As illustrated above, the research and documentation of the Puerto Rican family centers around the revolving-door migration between the island and the mainland United States and focuses on New York City. However, the extreme socioeconomic conditions in which Puerto Ricans have lived are significant factors in the formation of variant types of households. The extended family is an important institution that has been utilized in situations of mutual help and reciprocity, but the preferred family living pattern is the nuclear family with a woman, man, and children living in one household. The variety of family types include intergenerational forms where the nuclear family enjoys considerable autonomy from kin, but where frequent visits and exchanges of gifts and help, especially on ceremonial occasions, keep the extended nature of the family alive. Also, there are families in which married children are completely dependent on their parents and where the younger generation is almost totally absorbed and nurtured by the parents. The range of behavior includes situations where strong mothers have created matriarchal patterns of organization in which they control and bind the family together. Although there is variation among households and families in general, there are strong underlying bonds that maintain the norms that bind the family together, allowing a flexibility that has provided for successful adaptation in numerous areas of the United States.

❋ DOMINICANS

The Dominican population in the United States, like Puerto Ricans and Mexicans, began arriving at the turn of the twentieth century, but the political and economic conditions in the Dominican Republic fostered a pattern of migration and settlement in the United States that affected the formation and structure of families differently from the way it did other groups. The Dominican Republic has had a history of strong economic and political dependency on the United States that, as in other Caribbean nations, began around 1900. However, unlike Puerto Rico, the Dominican Republic experienced an internal domination during the "Trujillato," the reign of dictator Molina Trujillo from 1930 to 1960, that created a constriction of the migrant flow from the Republic. After the death of Trujillo in 1960, a surge of Dominicans began leaving for the United States. Throughout this period and into the present, the family and its constituent institutions have been a major factor for Dominicans in both initiating migration to the United States and in the initial settlement and adaptation to the United States. Through the institution of the family, Dominicans have maintained a continuous chain of movement between the Republic and the mainland United States. Understanding the basic causes of the migration helps comprehend the development of the Dominican family as an institution responding to socioeconomic circumstances in both the United States and the Republic.

According to Georges (1990), Dominicans are the fourth-largest Hispanic group in the United States, but, like Puerto Ricans, in New York City and the northeastern United States they are the second-largest group. Estimates of their numbers range for 300,000 to over 500,000, but the actual figure is probably closer to 300,000. In 1981, Dominicans in the United States represented 5 to 8 percent of the total Dominican Republic's work force. Dominicans are primarily working-class. Of all the major immigrant groups (Hispanics and others) who entered the United States between 1970 and 1980, Dominicans had the lowest family income ($9,569). Like the majority of Hispanics, they are a young population.

The presence of the United States was felt in the Dominican Republic early in the century and continues to the present. This influence helped set the economic structure that was to change the basic pattern of subsistence in the island, convert land to foreign interests, and create a labor force that was initially confined to work in the Dominican Republic. However, after the death of Trujillo, that labor force poured into the United States.

At the turn of the century, there was little migration to the United States from the Dominican Republic. By the second quarter of the century, sugar, as in the other Caribbean islands, became an important crop that attracted investors to the island. North Americans, Europeans, Cubans, and others looking for expanded or new areas in which to invest went to the island. In addition, investment in coffee, cacao, and cattle ranching became popular. These investments created a demand for land and, as in Puerto

Rico, people were forced out of subsistence agriculture and into a labor force that was dependent primarily on sugar cultivation.

The early part of the century was marked by economic distress and political instability, opening the way for U.S. intervention. The intervention took the form of an eight-year occupation that became the basis for major changes in Dominican health services, education, and public works. Under U.S. guidance, schools and hospitals were built where they had never existed; new roads and bridges connected once remote areas. One of the lasting results of the public works program was political centralization. Unification of the country neutralized the power of local political leaders. These processes helped form a new relationship with the United States and created a mass of people who came to rely on wage labor, first in the Republic itself and then, as unemployment became a serious problem, in the urban Northeast of the United States.

By the end of the U.S. occupation in 1924, sugar companies controlled almost a quarter of all agricultural land; 80 percent of this control was by U.S. companies. During this period, the Dominican National Guard was created, which came to have lasting effects on the Republic. The guard was trained by the United States, and it produced a military establishment that was strongly favorable to the United States. A result of this establishment was the rise of Trujillo, who worked his way from a guardsman into the presidency of the Republic.

President Trujillo instilled a strongly pronational industry that relied on a large and stable work force. During his reign from 1930 to 1960, migration to the United States was a mere trickle; the population was restricted to the Dominican Republic. Trujillo also encouraged population growth to both counter a long-standing territorial conflict with Haiti and to boost the national labor force. During the period form 1930 to 1961, the population of the Dominican Republic doubled from 1.5 to 3 million people. Some of this growth was, to be sure, the result of improved health. The result, however, at the time of Trujillo's death, was a sizable population that was dependent on wage labor.

In the early 1960s, constraints in the agricultural sector created a massive rural-urban migration. In 1970, over one-half of the population of the capital city, Santo Domingo, was composed of migrants from the countryside. By the end of the following presidential period (of Joaquín Balaguer), a 1980 study reported that in the five poorest neighborhoods around Santo Domingo, 91 percent of household heads were migrants, most from rural areas (Georges 1990). This migration became international as household heads and families left the Republic for Puerto Rico and the United States.

In the final years of Trujillo's dictatorship between 1950 and 1960, 9,800 people immigrated to the United States. In the next two-year period, from 1960 to 1962, this number increased sixfold, and in almost every year after 1962, a number equal to or greater than the total for the previous decade migrated to the United States. Between 1966 and 1980, the number of legal immigrants admitted to the United States averaged about 14,000 per year. It is obvious that both legal and undocumented migration became a partial solution to a growing unemployment problem in the Republic.

A significant aspect of the Dominican migration that affects the settlement of families in the United States is the influx of undocumented migrants, or migrants that enter on tourist or other types of temporary visas and remain in the United States illegally. By the mid-1960s, more than 150,000 nonimmigrants were being admitted annually, and between 1961 and 1978 approximately 1,800,000 entered the United States on nonimmigrant visas. Although most of these people did not choose to stay in the United States, some did indeed regularize their status through marriages and other means. Estimates of the undocumented migrants are between 14 to 17 percent of the total Dominican U.S. population (Georges, 1990).

The closeness of the Republic to Puerto Rico and the mainland has made travel back and forth to the island relatively easy. Most immigrants travel directly to the United States, others go first to Puerto Rico. Recently, undocumented Dominicans have begun to enter the United States through Mexico, crossing into the United States as do many Mexicans and Central Americans at the U.S.-Mexican border. The migrant stream between the Dominican Republic and the United States has become one social field in which family connections at both ends of the stream are important. Indeed, it is the family in its extended form that helps initiate the migration to the United States and helps in initial adaptation and settlement. Once settlement is accomplished, the connection to the Republic is maintained.

In many ways, the Dominican migration illustrates in dramatic fashion how Hispanics strategically use *familia* institutions in new ways. Although all Hispanic groups utilize *parentesco*, *compadrazgo*, extended kin, and *confianza*, the massive and direct migration of Dominicans from the Republic in a relatively short time period to dense urban areas in the United States shows an intense use of these institutions.

Because of the direct contact with the home country, modern transportation, and the proximity of the

Republic to the United States, Dominicans have maintained a very strong ethnic identity in the United States. In addition, the recent immigration of numerous first-generation Dominicans has helped transfer social patterns from the Republic to the United States. The large, existing Hispanic population in the northeastern United States has been a further incentive both to keep cultural ties alive and to settle in Hispanic neighborhoods where identity and adaptation appear to be easier than in purely Anglo areas.

The household based on the ideal of the nuclear family with two spouses and children is the elementary unit of social and economic relationships in the Dominican Republic. This ideal has been carried over to the United States, but it is not realized. What has occurred is a hybrid form of the family that is begun in the Dominican Republic. The basis of this new form is reciprocal exchange and mutual help. As with other Hispanic groups, individuals in the household are connected through the extended family and network of friends traced through both spouses. Compadrazgo, confianza, parentesco, and marriages unite and extend reciprocal relations and sentiment between individuals and groups of individuals. The principal relationships of the extended family play an important role in connecting individuals not only at local and regional levels, but also beyond national boundaries.

When migration to the United States began in earnest, individuals relied on the extended family for support in initiating the move. Branches of the (kindred) extended family were sent first to the cities of the Republic or to the United States to secure contacts there. Once in the United States, family members and kindred branches utilized the institutions of confianza and parentesco with other Dominicans, forming large networks of mutual support that led to the extension of kinship ties through marriage and other familial institutions. In 1974, Hendricks reported that in the village he studied in the Republic, 65 percent of families had immediate family members living in the United States and 87 percent of these families were receiving money from kin in the United States. The extended family has become so important that seldom do immigrants leave home without some assurance of help from contacts in the United States.

Because individuals have traveled to the United States often without spouses, household and marriage relations have been adapted to the new environment. In the Dominican Republic and in the United States, the authority of the male is an ideal standard in which (as stated earlier) the man of the house is the final authority and decision maker. There are few households, however, in which this form is evident.

Circumstances in the United States and in the Republic are encouraging change in sex roles, especially among women.

Because of migration and settlement in the United States, the role of women is the most affected and changed in family relationships. In the Dominican Republic, as men leave, women are left as the main authority figures in the households. Although many women were always in the position of head of household, this seems to have increased because of migration. The greatest change, however, is seen in the United States. Here women have the opportunity to work, changing the traditional roles they occupy, but also influencing the role of the male as provider and principal head of the household. Women are becoming heads of household primarily because of their financial contributions to the home, which, in the absence of a male head, is often essential in maintaining family needs, goals, and even survival. Women are being exposed to the outside environment, and new social situations are providing them with important social skills that many men do not have.

Not all women, however, are becoming more independent. Those women who do not work are confined to the household to care for children. This encourages the strengthening of the male's authority and the isolation of women, who, unlike those in the Dominican Republic, have less freedom in general. They are confined to the household, seldom have outside contacts, and are the caretakers of children.

In addition to the change in women's roles, a significant change in the Dominican family in the United States is the number of children in families. In the United States, Dominicans have fewer children than in the Republic, primarily due to financial constraints. Economic restrictions in housing, food, clothing, and child care limit the ability of women to work. Parents are often brought from the Dominican Republic to help with children, and other kin in the United States are often caretakers of children while parents work, thus making the extended family a further support. Interestingly, migration has increased the likelihood that children will live with or be cared for by a variety of individuals.

Heads of household are often those individuals who are the financial providers, are proficient in English, and are the ones to whom the family is obligated because of financial support. Hendricks (1974) has shown that this is often not the man in the household, especially if he has come to the United States as a mature adult. For many U.S. households, the father or elderly male is often the least able to perform this role.

The Dominican acceptance and acknowledgment of different conjugal unions has been a factor in U.S.

settlement and continued ties to the Republic. Three types of marriage are acknowledged by Dominicans: *matrimonio por iglesia* (church marriages), *matrimonio por ley* (civil marriages) and *unión libre* (free union). According to Hendricks (1974), all three are legitimate types of conjugal unions that cut across all classes, legitimizing the children of the unions. In addition to accommodating U.S. legal requirements for securing visas, these three types of marital unions help Dominicans to adapt socioeconomically to the United States. Religious marriages are often forgone because they are more expensive than civil unions. Civil unions are legal in the United States and help unite conjugal pairs. Free unions have played a significant role in maintaining family connections in the Republic because they allow individuals to cohabit and share households and expenses in the United States while maintaining legal spouses and households in the Republic. In the Dominican Republic, polygamous marriage, that is, men having more than one "wife," and men supporting and having a union with more than one woman, was socially and legally approved. Although not approved legally in the United States, the acceptability of these norms allows men and women to engage in relations in the United States while families are maintained in the home country.

❋ CUBANS

The experience of Cubans in the United States has been markedly different, although there are similarities they share with other Hispanics. The Cuban immigration and settlement in the United States was primarily a politically instigated migration caused by the Cuban Revolution of 1959 headed by Fidel Castro. Prior to the revolution there had been some migration into Florida and New York. At the turn of the century tobacco workers were relocated to work in Tampa in companies that had been moved from Cuba. According to Moore and Pachón (1985), there were some 18,000 to 19,000 Cubans living in the United States in 1930. And there was a slow trickle of Cubans who entered the United States prior to the 1950s. But of the total, now nearing 1,000,000 Cubans in the United States, more than half have arrived since 1959.

The United States played a significant role in the early history of the Republic of Cuba and established strong economic ties there early in the century. This history, like that of other Hispanics, is important in understanding the Cuban immigration to the United States and the sentiment that Cubans hold for their home country. As in Puerto Rico and the Dominican Republic, the United States played a significant role in bringing Cuba into the new industrial epoch of the twentieth century and a world economy (dominated by capital interests primarily from the United States).

Just before the turn of the century, Cuba had begun to resist the Spanish government and rebelled. In 1898, the United States intervened, supported the Cuban revolutionaries who were fighting Spain for independence, and began the Spanish-American War. (The U.S. entrance into the war was justified by blaming Spain for sinking the battleship *Maine* in Havana Harbor in February 1898.) In December 1898, the conflict ended and a treaty was signed in which Spain relinquished sovereignty over Cuba. The United States ruled until 1902, when the Cuban Republic was formally instituted. However, political unrest continued and the United States, with the right of intervention secured in the original Cuban constitution, intervened from 1906 to 1909 and again in 1912. During this period and after World War I, U.S. interests dominated Cuba's economy through the control of land dedicated to the production of sugar. Through the next thirty years and into the decade of the 1950s, Cuba experienced continued economic instability and unrest.

During the Second World War, Cubans experienced continued food shortages and political instability owing to fluctuations in world sugar prices, the primary export crop of the Cuban nation. High costs of living and continued inflation led to unrest and political violence in the late 1940s. In 1952, Fulgencio Batista, the head of the Cuban Army, seized power, suspended the constitution, dissolved the Cuban Congress, and set up a provisional government. Batista, running unopposed, held elections in 1954 and was inaugurated in February 1955. The entire first half of the twentieth century had been marked by unrest, economic instability, and a strong foreign interest that controlled sugar production and export. Batista's strong hand, in conjunction with the stabilization of world sugar prices, brought initial suppression of the political unrest and economic stability through an economic development program supported by the United States.

During the later years of Batista's dictatorship, 10,000 to 15,000 Cubans entered the United States annually. This early migration was composed of ruling elite and the politically and socially alienated, as well as individuals who were unemployed. But it was overrepresented by the upper classes. This migration was to continue in earnest after the next Cuban revolution that brought Fidel Castro into power in 1959.

That early period of Cuban history set up a stratified society favoring the ruling class and foreign interests in sugar, primarily from the United States. Although initially stymied by Batista, unrest grew and erupted in the Cuban Revolution of 1959, led by Fidel Castro. It was this revolution that initiated the first major wave of exiles into the United States. The revolution was supported by all classes and all generations in Cuba. In "Dilemmas of a Golden Exile," Alejandro Portes (1969), a well-noted Cuban sociologist, states that "seldom has history seen a more complete example of social consensus." However, Castro's plan was to return Cuba to the ordinary people, and he began a program of socialization in which the powerless working class took control. Castro initiated agrarian reform affecting plantations controlled by U.S. companies. The operation of plantations by non-Cuban stockholders was prohibited and Castro eventually deemphasized sugar for food crops. Upper-class Cubans, the wealthy, the educated, and the powerful saw their status challenged and their influence radically curtailed. The lower strata of Cuban society was now in control and in power.

This restructuring of Cuban society resulted in the first massive immigration of Cubans to the United States in 1960. Between 1959 and 1962, more than 155,000 people left the island. This migration was slowed because of a three-year suspension of airline flights from Cuba to the United States. But in 1965, when the airlift was reestablished, daily flights brought some 257,000 Cubans to the United States between December 1965 and December 1972. These individuals were fleeing the Castro government and felt betrayed by the revolution. They brought a fierce hostility toward the Castro regime, but also an attachment and pride to their values and style of life, a clearly defined identity as Cubans, and a strong desire to return to Cuba.

The majority of this first wave of Cubans went to Miami, Florida. In Miami, they were close to Cuba and were in a climate that was very much like home. In addition, the previous tobacco-worker immigration to Florida had established communities there. This first wave of refugees was followed by a subsequent group of people who left Cuba in the 1980s. In April 1980, 10,000 people took refuge in the Peruvian embassy in Havana, hoping to leave Cuba. The Castro regime allowed these people and an additional 118,000 others to leave. The majority of them left from the port of Mariel and are known as the Marielitos. Hence, the prerevolution, the immediate postrevolution, and the Mariel migrations constitute the three waves of migrations for Cubans entering the United States.

Most Cuban immigrants settled in Miami, although there are smaller communities in Los Angeles, New York City, and Union City, New Jersey. In addition to having a history of settlement in Miami, the first wave of refugees who had come from the professional and entrepreneurial classes came equipped to begin new businesses and prosper from the economy. Unlike many other Hispanic groups, most of the Cubans arrived with resources in the form of capital, education, and both professional and semi-professional skills, allowing them to take advantage of their new situation in the United States. In addition, there were many political groups in the United States who provided help and resources because of their anti-Communist sentiments. The result was a strong economic foothold in Miami. The success of the early immigrants provided fertile ground for the successive immigrant waves in the form of jobs and opportunities that were not available other groups. This has been described as an ethnic economic enclave in which Cubans have provided viable alternatives to the U.S. labor market. The enclave is characterized by ethnic (Cuban) businesses that employ and do business within the ethnic community and provide upward mobility for labor. Hence, the early immigrants were able to get a strong foothold, with succeeding waves providing continued input into the enclave in the form of resources and labor. The result in Miami is a strong Cuban community that has influenced not only the economy but also politics. Spanish, for example, is the primary language spoken, making it possible even for monolingual Spanish-speakers to succeed. This environment has had strong binding effects on the families of Cubans in the United States.

Portes (1969) has shown the adaptive nature of Cuban immigrants in Milwaukee. He noted that educational attainment, occupational skills that were in demand in the United States, and a middle-class ethic and style of life combined to produce a fast process of adaptation. Significantly, the adaptation of Cuban families in Milwaukee was generally not a problem. They had come with strong values in individualism, self-concept, personal rights, and belief in the improvement of one's position in the stratification system. The satisfaction and attraction to life in the United States was almost an exclusive result of the level of socioeconomic rewards these people received. These socioeconomic rewards were the only factors that overcame old attachments among the families studied, which, according to Portes, is in "perfect agreement with the beliefs they supported and the role they played during the revolutionary process."

The individuals who are now in the United States are primarily exiles, but there is a significant difference in the people who arrived in the United States at different times. During the first waves just before and during the revolution in 1959, Cubans coming to the United States were primarily the more privileged classes consisting of managers, entrepreneurs, and landowners. Later, after a decade of socialism, immigrants of lower-middle and working-class backgrounds predominated. This resulted in a U.S. population that was a truly historically representative strata of Cuban society, a factor that is not seen in the other Hispanic groups who have come to the United States.

Cubans in the United States are also different in other ways from Mexicans, Puerto Ricans, Dominicans, and other Hispanic immigrants and settlers. Although the exiled population represents all sectors of the prerevolutionary society, it is overrepresented by professionals and semiprofessionals. In general, the upper occupational strata of the Cuban population are overrepresented. Because the Caucasian population in Cuba was in the upper strata, Cuban Caucasians are also overrepresented in the United States. A 1953 Cuban census indicated that 72 percent of the population was Caucasian; in the 1970 U.S. census, the Cuban Caucasian population was 95 percent. In addition, the Cuban population is disproportionately elderly. Currently, 10 percent of Cubans in the United States are over 65, a proportion three times larger than for other Hispanic groups. When viewed as a whole, Cuban Americans are also a highly educated group. Of the pre-1953 population, only 4 percent had completed the twelfth grade or more, but the later post-Castro group reported that 36 percent of the immigrant group had completed twelve or more years of schooling. These factors along with settlement patterns illustrate a highly adapted and successful population. As with Puerto Ricans, Dominicans, and Mexicans, however, the family played an initially important role in adjustment.

As in pre-Castro Cuba, the family and its structure varies according to class. Since the 1930s, according to Queralt (1984), Caucasian Cubans have been oriented toward the nuclear family, with both spouses and children living together as the norm. The immigration and consequent adaptation to the United States has encouraged this trend even more. The middle and lower classes have relied more on the extended family because of its supportive nature in initial settlement and employment. But the trend is toward a nuclear family household for all Cubans in the United States.

There is no doubt that family ideology is of central importance among Cubans in the United States. The concept of a good family, in particular in the value placed on conserving and exhibiting a strong and good family name, has helped keep the traditional family ideology among Cubans. One example of this has been the reestablishment of strict chaperoning of daughters. Although changes in family relationships and roles are taking place, Cubans continue to uphold the ideals of male authority and paternally centered families. The traditional view of the role of children and adolescents, however, has begun to cause conflict between the generations. A study in west New York and Union City, New Jersey, indicated that 86 percent of parents interviewed reported having great difficulty accepting similar freedom and independence enjoyed by other U.S. teenagers for their own children (Casal, 1980). It appears that the trend and focus on the nuclear family has had influences on more traditional institutions of Hispanic family structure among Cubans. According to Queralt (1984), compadrazgo, for instance, does not appear as strong or pervasive an institution as for other Hispanic groups. Marriages appear to have remained primarily within the Cuban community, but this appears to be changing. Parental pressure, intergenerational language barriers, and the tightness and completeness of the Cuban community help keep marriages within the group. The immigration of more women in recent years as compared to men of marriageable age has not yet had an impact on marriage patterns. The Cuban law prohibiting the emigration of males of military service age has resulted in an uneven distribution of the sexes among U.S. Cubans of marital age. In 1970, in the age category of 20-29, there were seventy-six males for each one hundred females in the United States. Although marriages continue to be within the group (called endogamy), the rate of divorce among Cubans is higher than for other Hispanic groups and in fact is higher than for the U.S. population in general. According to the *Harvard Encyclopedia of Ethnic Groups* (1980), between 1960 and 1970, there were 6.2 divorces per 100 marriages among Cubans, 5.3 for the general population, and only 2.9 for other foreign-born immigrants.

The generational differences produced by the different waves of immigrants from both prerevolutionary Cubans who adhere to traditional values and those who have been exposed to the socialist change are significant to family and sex roles in the United States. Generally speaking, Cubans in the United States continue to hold a stronger traditional value about the family when compared to Anglo-Americans. For example, emphasis on the male authority is still present. However, the Castro regime placed considerable emphasis on incorporating more women into the labor force and has questioned the norms about sex roles. Individuals who have entered the United States more recently have been exposed to these and other more liberal ideas. A consequence has been a more open attitude toward women in the work force and change in the family. Cuban women have the highest rate of participation, 54 percent, in the labor force among Spanish-speaking women. Cuban women actually have a higher rate of participation than do Caucasian women as a percentage of the total U.S. population.

Although working women appear to have more freedom and access to social relations outside the family, work for Cuban women also has negative consequences. Work can be an increased burden, as men have yet to take on any of the domestic responsibilities of women in the household. In addition, for Cuban women the lack of domestic help increases their responsibility in the home. However, there continues to be an increase in the percentage of working wives. As with many other Latino groups in the United States, those in the grandparental generation serve as baby-sitters and instillers of traditional values.

In general, it appears that when compared to other Hispanic groups in the United States Cubans are adapting successfully to American life. They have not exhibited the severe poverty nor severe socioeconomic constraints suffered by Puerto Ricans, Mexicans, and Dominicans. Their adaptive success is the result of a strong and viable economic structure that is based within the community itself and a set of values based on individualism that parallel those of the United States generally.

The tendency toward a nuclear family, however, does not discount the importance of the use of the extended family and its institutions in adapting to the United States. In fact, when viewed from a sociological point of view, the extended family in the form of social networks is a prevailing institution that has had significant impact for Cubans. This may in fact be stronger for Cubans than for other Hispanic groups. Dense kinship networks provide the basis for a pattern of social relationships that revolve around the ethnic community. In fact, according to Portes and Bach's book *Latin Journey* (1985), Cuban refugees in 1976 reported that 87 percent had received help from relatives living in the United States. The social world of Cuban immigrants is one that is full of kin and ethnic ties. In 1973, on arrival to the United States, Cuban exiles reported having an average of 10 relatives and friends awaiting them. Three years later, they reported an average of 4 relatives living in the same city and 2.5 relatives living elsewhere in the United States. This was true for both men and women. Cuban wives had numerous relatives in cities where they lived. Similarly, Cubans reported an average of 8 close friends living in the same city, 7 of which were Cuban. Of these, 93 percent stated they had no American friends. These figures illustrate of the thick kinship and friendship networks to which Cuban immigrants belong and upon which they depend. Although the family has taken different forms, its role as an adaptive institution continues to be a significant factor in the U.S. Cuban community.

✴ MEXICAN AMERICANS

The Mexican-origin population is the largest Hispanic group in the United States, numbering over twelve million according to the 1990 U.S. census. Because of its size and geographic range both in the United States and in Mexico, this population is also the most diverse. Indeed, some of the Mexican regions from which immigrants have come are larger than any of the other Hispanic-origin countries. The U.S. East Coast is represented by Mexicanos from Tamaulipas, Saltillo, Torreón, and the southeastern seaboard of Mexico, including Vera Cruz and other Caribbean-like regions. The core sending area of Mexico, however, is the central states of Durango, Zacatecas, San Luis Potosí, Guanajuato, Jalisco, and Michoacán. The majority of these people from the core sending states have come to the southwestern United States, principally to California and Texas. But people from throughout Mexico are represented in all areas of the United States. People have also migrated from the northern Mexican border states of Sonora, Chihuahua, Coahuila, Nuevo León, and the states of the Pacific coast, Sinaloa and Nayarit. Even remote Mexican areas and regional cultures are represented in the United States. In fact, Mexican colonies in the United States are often dense settlements of people from specific Mexican regions and states. Neighborhoods in Los Angeles, for example, are made up of people from Sonora, others from Michoacán and Sinaloa. Each group expresses a regional pride and specific cultural practices. Neighborhoods exhibit commercial establishments that boast native restaurants and shops specializing in regional specialties. This variety, a product of recent immigration, is complicated by the fact that Hispanics were also original populations in much of the Southwest.

The historical conditions between the United States and Mexico set the tone for current relationships. Of extreme importance in these relationships are the southwestern borderlands, which were first Spanish outposts in the New World, then Mexican territory before the Mexican-American War of 1846. This is the area currently separated by a two-thousand-mile border. It consists of the U.S.-Mexican border states of Texas, New Mexico, Arizona, Colorado, and California. Although indigenous Americans first lived in this region and continue to do so, each state is historically Spanish-Mexican. Unlike the political-economic influence and domination of the United Staes in other countries of Hispanic origin, the United States conquered the Southwest and took it from Mexico. This conquest was the beginning of a U.S.-Mexican relationship that shaped present attitudes, economic dependencies, and immigration. The Southwest borderlands, currently the area of the highest density of the Mexican-origin population, stretches from the Pacific Ocean at San Diego, California, to the Gulf of Mexico at Texas. This two-thousand-mile zone has been a frontier since indigenous periods when trade routes between the civilizations in Mexico and the Pueblo Indians in the north were established before the arrival of the Spanish. It is an area of immense geographic variety and isolation. The history of settlement here reflects this diversity, a long-standing Mexican and Spanish heritage. The names of states, major settlements, and geographic sites bear witness to this heritage.

However prominent the Spanish-Mexican heritage of the Southwest, the population, both native and immigrant, has been subordinate to the dominant Anglo and has lived a history of segregation and racial conflict that only recently has begun to change in meaningful ways. Before the Anglo arrived, there were only outpost settlements in the region that had very small populations. According to Moore and Pachón (1985), Texas had some 5,000 Mexicans; New Mexico, the farthest outpost yet the largest, had some 60,000; California, around 7,500; and Arizona, perhaps 1,000 people. Each of these states has a specific history of Mexican and Anglo social interaction that conditioned the modern incorporation and adaptation of Mexicans, both U.S.-born and immigrants.

The adaptive response of the family during this early period was conditioned both by the frontier nature of the Mexican settlements and the ensuing conflict of conquest and entrance of the Anglo population. The long-standing Hispanic presence in the United States is exemplified by New Mexican settlements around Albuquerque and Santa Fe. New Mexicans to this day consider themselves Hispanos, direct descendants of the original Spanish settlers who arrived in the seventeenth century. Similarly, the towns along the Texas Rio Grande frontier had been settled early in the original Mexican settlement. And in California, the Spanish-Californio families became landowners and ranchers, establishing a specific culture that was a product of their lives there.

It was the early Spanish and Mexican settlements that were the basis for the Mexican-American and Hispanic Southwest. Mexico had lost nearly one-third of its territory in the Mexican-American War.

The Treaty of Guadalupe Hidalgo set both the boundaries for the international border separating the United States and Mexico and outlined the rights of the Mexican population that remained in the territory ceded to the United States. In each region and state, the new American presence capitalized on a variety of economic pursuits. Mexicans, once landowners and dominant entrepreneurs throughout the region, fell prey to the new economies and became wage laborers, although a few upper-class families survived. The overall result was the subjugation of the Hispanic population from a dominant economic and political entity to one of a prevailing wage labor in which Anglo economic interests controlled the regions. In Arizona, mining became a major resource for American capitalists that depended on Mexican labor, both native and immigrant. Agriculture became prominent in both California and Texas, establishing the migrant streams of Mexican workers.

In the late 1880s, the termination of the transcontinental railroad brought an onslaught of Americans from the eastern seaboard who made the Southwest their home. According to Moore and Pachón (1985), in 1887 the railroad brought in 120,000 Anglo settlers to southern California when the total population was only 12,000 for all Mexicans. The early families of these Mexican populations slowly lost power and social status. To Anglos they became socially indistinguishable from the Mexicans who began arriving in great numbers after the turn of the century.

The historic connection of the Southwest and Mexico continues to be prominent. Spanish is still spoken in much of the area, the geographic proximity makes travel back and forth to Mexico easy, and many of the border towns became truly a part of both cultures. The names for Calexico (California-Mexico) and Mexicali (Mexico-California), for example, were derivatives of the frontier and binational status along the California-Mexico border.

Small Mexican settlements developed throughout the Southwest and became the basis for the onslaught of Mexican immigration that was to begin in the early 1900s. The early settlements, however, had been closely tied to specific regions in Mexico. In California, for example, the regional ties between Baja California and Alta California during Spanish and Mexican periods provided traditional patterns of movement for families migrating into the United States. These regional ties helped people maintain affiliation to hometowns and kin in the south. By the 1900s, colonies of Mexicans from specific regions of Mexico had established themselves in southwestern towns and cities, providing links to hometowns and the country of origin. Many of these settlements were agricultural camps, others the result of mining, and many Mexicans began moving to the growing cities of the West.

Mexican immigration has been the result, as in other Hispanic immigration and settlement, of the ongoing economic and political relationship of the home country with the United States. The concurrent conditions in Mexico coupled with the demand for wage labor in the United States, and the history of the Spanish-Mexican Southwest, influenced the massive and continuous movement of people between the two countries. The development of Mexican railroads, financed and controlled by American capitalists in the early 1900s, provided access to raw resources and human labor. The railroads made labor accessible to every major economic center in the United States. Mexican labor was contracted for work in the Southwest and later in the industrial middle-eastern states.

The onslaught of the Mexican Revolution, a result of the tyrannical control of Porfirio Díaz, uprooted and literally opened the doors for mass migration from the previously landlocked peasantry. Díaz, who was dictator of Mexico from 1887 to 1911, ruled Mexico with an iron hand. He took millions of acres from the Mexican *campesino* and fostered a laissez-faire development program that favored foreign interests in the republic. Díaz gave up huge land grants to foreign capitalists under the rubric of development. Many of these schemes were in the mining industry. One of his most amazing land grants was to an American company that went by the name of the International Company of Mexico in Baja California; the company was given some eighteen million acres (twenty-eight thousand square miles). The confinement and destitution of the major Mexican population, together with continued land takeover, led to civil disorder and finally the Mexican Revolution of 1911. Many people fled Mexico at this time, many with hopes of returning.

At the end of the revolution, the migration to the United States did not abate, and through 1930 continued in a steady stream, with only brief stoppage during the First World War. In 1930, the Great Depression in the United States caused economic upheaval and the Mexicans became a threat to the nation's unemployed and were displaced by Anglo Dust Bowl migrants. Mexicans became the scapegoats for the economic crisis in America. Then, President Hoover initiated a repatriation program aimed at returning the Mexican-origin population to Mexico. The result was the deportation of almost one-half million Mexicans and Mexican Americans to Mexico. Much of this was voluntary, but social pressures and the country's mood influenced the return of many Mexican Americans, even some who had been born U.S. citizens. The 1940s reversed this pattern and the Second World War provided new opportunities for Mexican Americans in the United States. This period was characterized by a move out of agriculture, railroad work, and mining. Significantly, 300,000 to 500,000 Mexican American men served in the U.S. armed forces during the war. This was also a period in which the majority of Mexican people made a shift from a basic rural to an urban existence. In 1950, about 25 percent of Mexican Americans were rural; by 1970 only 15 percent were rural. In some areas, 90 percent of the Mexican population today is urban.

What has occurred is a slow movement into the middle class for many Mexican Americans. Even though immigrant Mexicans have continued to be primarily unskilled, there has been a steady incorporation of Mexican Americans into the primary labor market of the United States. Immigrants and undocumented Mexicans continue to be at the bottom strata of the labor market, filling nonskilled jobs primarily in the service sectors. However, Mexican Americans now represent three and four generations in the country; many are U.S.-born citizens. This residential longevity has provided for a basic adaptation and slow movement into the mainstream of American society.

The 1950s through the present has seen the continued movement of Mexicans into the United States. Much of the migration has been the result of voluntary immigration by Mexicans who come in search of better jobs that will help support their families and kin in home areas; others arrive with hopes of settlement. U.S. programs have also influenced the migration. For example, the Bracero Program, a labor contract program for agricultural workers in the United States, brought hundreds of thousands of Mexicans into the Southwest in the early 1960s. Many Mexicans returned to Mexico when the program was ended, but many "braceros" had made their home in the United States. This period (the 1960s) also saw the beginnings of real political involvement. Mexican Americans became involved in the Chicano movement and in politics in general. Ethnic identity became an important issue for Mexican Americans/Chicanos and brought visibility to the population as a national minority. It was no longer perceived as an isolated population of the Southwest but recognized as the fastest-growing minority in the United States.

This brief outline provides some idea of the complexity of the immigration and origin of the Mexican-American population in the United States. There are major differences in Mexican immigration from that of other Hispanic groups, and these discrepancies explain how these processes have influenced family patterns of socialization and change among Mexicans. In the first place, it is easy for Mexicans to get to the major cities of the United States. All are accessible by inexpensive travel (car, bus, and railroad) in addition to air travel. Mexicans and Mexican Americans often return to Mexico to visit relatives and to enjoy cultural and social events not available in the United States. These and other factors have had an impact on the development and change of the family and its institutions among Mexican Americans.

Mexican traditions, including the family, have survived more widely among Mexican Americans because of the historic isolation of the southwestern settlements and the geographic proximity to Mexico. The earliest of settlements as well as newcomer *colonias* (settlements) are rejuvenated by the continuing migration and the easy access to the border and the home regions of early pioneers. Furthermore, the residential segregation of Mexican communities and neighborhoods has fostered strong ethnic ties and boundaries to the greater society. These factors, along with racial conflict and discrimination toward Mexicans, have sustained a fierce pride and commitment to sociocultural institutions, which have in many ways become cultural symbols among Mexican Americans.

The family continues to be held as a particularly important institution among Mexican Americans. But family and familism is also a source of stress and conflict. Although the extended family is instrumental in socialization, especially in early settlement, it is also seen as creating inner barriers to adaptation to the outside world. The concept that family is all-important and that the individual should sacrifice for the good of the family has its costs, especially if individuals forgo immediate opportunities that may aid in long-term adaptation. Education is one example. Among migrant farm labor families, the economic necessity of having all family members participating and contributing to the family helped lead to one of the worst dropout rates for Hispanics in the country. Among second- and third-generation Mexican Americans, the traditional family values can be sources of stress in that they are not congruent with modern life-styles. However, the values of *la familia* are still adhered to by many, albeit only ideologically.

However, as with other groups of Hispanics, the family has played an instrumental role in the early adaptation and settlement of Mexicans to the United States. Among Mexican and Mexican Americans, the concept of the family is rooted in Mexico's agrarian past. This concept was emphasized first by the severance of the original native Mexican population from political and economic standing, then with the continuing entrance of rural immigrants from across the border. Once pioneer migrants settled in the United States, loved ones were brought north. This began a migration stream that included whole branches of families, representing the towns and regions to which they were connected. It is not uncommon for migrations between specific Mexican and U.S. regions to have three and four generations of continual back-and-forth flow, with established U.S. branches that receive and aid newcomers from Mexico.

Familism is perhaps the single most consistent aspect of Mexican-American culture. The strong sentiment toward family, family cohesiveness, and incorporation of the individual into family membership has provided a base for settlement in the form of community for people in the United States. Migrants faced with strange and often threatening social environments naturally sought each other out and extended the relationships used in home regions. These were the institutions of ideology, *confianza*, *compadrazgo*, *parentesco*, and marriage. In some U.S. areas, migrants maintained strong regional ties through these institutions, whereas people who had migrated out of the same home regions and remained in Mexico did not maintain the regional and familial ties. These latter individuals were absorbed into new Mexican regions as Mexicanos, but in the United States the socioeconomic environment incurred a boundary maintenance and cohesiveness. People count on their personal connections in the United States for housing, help in finding jobs, and in adapting.

Although the nuclear family and household is preferred to the extended family household, connections to kin and the relations of the extended family continue to play important roles in the lives of Mexicans and Mexican Americans in the United States. There is a great range here, however, especially when one considers the generational differences of family branches in the United States. Recent and early immigrants rely on kin and the extended family for the majority of their social relationships, while individuals born as U.S. citizens have less extended kin relations (especially after the second generation). Education in the United States, geographic and social mobility, and economic stability have all contributed to strengthen the nuclear family and household for Mexican Americans. The nuclear family is in fact the desired type of family for both Mexican Americans and Mexicans.

The relationships of the extended family often take different forms for these more acculturated individuals. Frequent visiting between immediate kin and special celebrations such as birthdays, baptisms, marriages, and funerals serve to bring kin together and rekindle family ties, whereas among newer immigrant Mexicanos the extended family is the center of social and kin relations. Marriage has continued to be primarily within the group, but a growing number of Mexican Americans have wed non-Mexican-origin individuals. This is greatest among Chicanos in California, but it is not uncommon among all the U.S.-born Latinos, especially after the first generation.

Mexicans, as with other ethnic groups, first live in segregated neighborhoods and are schooled with peers of the same ethnic background. However, as families get better jobs, the first priority is to move out of the ethnic neighborhoods, thus ensuring more exposure to American society for offspring. Schooling and the continued upward mobility of families has resulted in the economic severance from the reciprocity and mutual help among kin, so needed in early settlement and adaptation. The reciprocal duties of kinship obligations through compadrazgo, for example, continue to be ideological values that are not expressed or carried out as in previous periods. But it must be remembered that the migration from Mexico continues to emphasize these values and the actual expression of compadrazgo and other kin institutions in social behavior.

Compadrazgo has been a very strong institution among Mexican Americans. The *compadre/comadre* relationship often stands above even sibling relationships. The asking of individuals to be padrinos in baptisms or marriage is a high honor that brings with it kinlike obligations that are often considered of special importance. Compadres are expected to provide help and advice in time of crisis, and in the migration process the compadre/comadre is often the central individual who provides mutual help in the first stages of settlement. These are life long relationships in which compadres provide help such as needed information, access to jobs, and other essential social-economic benefits. As with all Latinos and other family institutions, compadrazgo varies within the generations. As with marriage and familism in general among second and later U.S.-born generations, compadrazgo has lost much of its reciprocal obligatory and mutual help functions, and when it is still practiced, this is sometimes only symbolic and expressive of ethnic pride and identity.

Although the actual role of the male in the family has changed, the ideals of the patriarchical family with father as decision maker and authoritarian is still expressed. Respect and deference to the male is expected ideal behavior. Children, especially, are expected to regard the father as the final voice and decision maker without exception. However, in actual behavior, fathers and mothers have taken on a more dualistic role in the management of the family, with the mother having increasingly more responsibility, especially regarding economics.

Children have been exposed to American education and have had much more exposure to the outside world than parents. The natural outcome of this exposure and education is the acceptance of mainstream values and goals for normalized American life-styles. This, as with other Hispanic groups, has been the root cause of conflict within the home and family. Mexican-American youths, like other youth, now spend most of their time being schooled in an educational system that stresses the norms and values of American society. These norms are often in conflict with the expected behavior of the family and its institutions.

Women's roles have changed the most dramatically among Mexican Americans. As with the other Latino groups, it is the female's entrance into the work force that has initiated the major changes in sex roles and division of labor. Mexican women have a long history of working in various industries in the United States. In southern California during the Second World War, Mexican-American women worked in the aviation industry on assembly lines and afterward in the canneries throughout the state. Their history as migrant laborers throughout the United States is also well noted. The garment industry and other industries employed Mexican women as well.

Working women have gained more access to society in general and more of an egalitarian role in the household. As with other Hispanic groups, however, Mexican-American families exhibit change in women's roles but not necessarily in those of men. Men generally continue not to participate in the sharing of household duties. It is the woman who has taken on some of the male responsibilities. Although these are generalizations about the changes taken place in sex roles, women, regardless of the value and ideal of the father-centered household, in the past have had a strong input into decisions and acted as the final authority within the family and household. In fact, women are often seen as central individuals who are primary catalysts and authoritarian figures in family relationships.

As with other groups, Mexican Americans must be viewed in the range of their historical experiences and relationships in the United States. A look at any single region, town, or neighborhood that is characterized as Mexican or Mexican-American/Chicano will illustrate many inter- and cross- generational differences. Families of well-adapted and acculturated individuals who hold strong Mexican familial patterns live side by side with families who have opted for more nuclear family patterns. In addition, bilingual families can be found in neighborhoods where monolingual Spanish- and monolingual English-speakers are also residents. Some values are held on to more stringently than others, as for example the respect held for the elderly. This continues to be a strong value among Mexicans and Mexican Americans, illustrated by the low rates of elderly in nursing or old-age homes. They continue to be cared for in the homes of kin and children.

When compared to other Hispanic groups and to the U.S. population in general, Mexican Americans have the largest family size, averaging almost five people per family. Puerto Ricans have almost four (3.67) people per family, and Cubans, 3.5. These averages illustrate a growing population and, when viewed in conjunction with the median age of Hispanics, indicate very high population projections for the future. It is estimated, for example, that by the turn of the next century, Hispanics will be the largest minority population in the United States. The Mexican-origin population is currently 60 percent of this total.

The fact that the Mexican-American and Hispanic population is growing and will have a greater impact on the United States in the future is obscured by the fact that Hispanics continue to be at the bottom rungs of the economic and social classes. Poverty among Mexican Americans, as with other Hispanic groups and particularly Puerto Ricans, is a continuous problem that affects family life-styles and well-being. A full quarter of Mexican Americans in the late 1970s were living in poverty. What is shocking is that it appears that instead of decreasing, poverty is increasing. The Mexican-American family will continue to be an important adaptive mechanism, utilizing the support institutions and evolving in ways that fit the sociocultural milieu of the United States.

References

Alvarez, Robert R., Jr. *Familia: Migration and Adaptation in Alta and Baja California 1850-1975.* Berkeley: University of California Press, 1987.

Baca-Zinn, Maxine. "Marital Roles and Ethicity: Conceptual Revisions and New Research Dimensions." In *Hispanic Report on Families and Youth.* The National Coalition of Hispanic Mental Health and Human Services Organizations. Washington, D.C.: Cosmho, 1978.

———. "Ongoing Questions in the Study of Chicano Families." In The State of Chicano Research in Family, Labor, and Migration Studies, edited by Armando Valdez, Albert Camarillo, and Tomas Almaguer. Palo Alto, Calif.: Stanford University, Center for Chicano Research, 1983.

Casal, Lourdes, and Andrés R. Hernández. "Cubans in the United States: A Survey of the Literature." In *The Cuban Experience,* edited by Carlos E. Cortez. New York: Arno Press, 1980.

Cross, Harry E., and James A. Sandos. *Across the Border: Rural Development in Mexico and Recent Migration to the United States.* Berkeley: University of California, Institute of Governmental Studies, 1981.

Fitzpatrick, Joseph P. *Puerto Rican Americans. The Meaning of Migration to the Mainland,.* 2d ed. Englewood Cliffs, N.J.: Prentice-Hall, 1987.

Gallagher, P. *The Cuban Exile.* New York: Academic Press, 1980.

Galarza, Ernesto. *Merchants of Labor: The Mexican Bracero Story.* San Jose, Calif.: Rosicrucian Press, 1965.

García, Mario T. *Mexican Americans.* New Haven: Yale University Press, 1989.

Georges, Eugenia. *The Making of a Transnational Community: Migration, Development and Cultural Change in the Dominican Republic.* New York: Columbia University Press, 1990.

Harvard University. *Harvard Encyclopedia of American Ethnic Groups.* Cambridge: Harvard University Press, 1980.

Hendricks, Glenn. *The Dominican Diaspora.* New York: Teachers College of Columbia University, 1974.

Moore, Joan, and Harry Pachón. *Hispanics in the United States.* Englewood Cliffs, N.J.: Prentice-Hall, 1985.

Morales, Julio. *Puerto Rican Poverty and Migration: We Just Had To Try Elsewhere.* New York: Praeger, 1986.

Pelto, Pertti J., Maria Roman, and Nelson Liriano. "Family Structures in an Urban Puerto Rican Community." *Urban Anthropology* 11 (Spring 1982): 39-58.

Portes, Alejandro. "Dilemmas of a Golden Exile: Integration of Cuban Refugee Families in Milwaukee." *ASR* 34 (1969): 505-18.

Portes, Alejandro, and Robert L. Bach. *Latin Journey: Cuban and Mexican Immigrants in the United States.* Berkeley: University of California Press, 1985.

Queralt, Magaly. "Understanding Cuban Immigrants: A Cultural Perspective." *Social Work,* (March-April 1984): 115-21.

Rodríguez, Clara. *Born in the U.S.A.* Boston: Unwin Hyman, 1989.

Rogler, Lloyd H., and Rosemary Santana Cooney. *Puerto Rican Families in New York City.* New York: Intergenerational Processes, 1984.

Zaragoza, Alex. "The Conceptualization of the History of the Chicano Family." In *The State of Chicano Research in Family, Labor and Migration Studies,* edited by Armando Valdez, Albert Camarillo, and Tomas Almaguer. Palo Alto, Calif.: Stanford University, Center for Chicano Research, 1983.

Robert R. Álvarez, Jr.

6

Relations with Spain and Spanish America

Because of their colonial experiences, relations between the United States and Latin America began inauspiciously. From the beginning, however, the United States became the dominant player, largely because it had clearly defined foreign policy objectives. As a result, the Latin Americans found themselves responding to U.S. initiatives. Since independence, three distinct time periods characterize inter-American relations. During the nineteenth century each sought its own place in world affairs, but, motivated by similar factors near the end of the century, the United States and Latin America came closer together. During the second time period, from 1903 to 1954, U.S. concern with securing the Panama Canal contributed to its intervention in the internal affairs of the Caribbean nations; its actions increased Latin America's distrust of its northern neighbor. In the final time period, from 1954 to the present, the political leaders in both hemispheres focused their attention on Communist subversion, but in so doing ignored the economic and social disparities that needed to be addressed. As the twenty-first century approaches, the nature of inter-American relations will need to be refocused.

✳POLICY FOUNDATIONS

From their founding in the sixteenth and seventeenth centuries until U.S. independence in 1783, the British and Spanish New World colonies had little contact with one another. By agreement in 1670, intercolonial trade required a special license that greatly restricted commerce and led to the development of clandestine trade, particularly between New England and the Caribbean basin region. Beyond this limited commerce there was little interchange and, without it, colonials both north and south knew little about each other.

After 1783, U.S. commercial interests expanded in the Caribbean Basin region. North American merchants took flour, spirits and wine, lumber, iron, shoes, hats, dry goods, and furniture and brought back principally sugar, molasses, brandy, rum, coffee, tobacco, cocoa, and indigo. In this trade, U.S. merchants were often at the mercy of Spanish naval ships sent to intervene on behalf of Madrid's regulations. Looking beyond the Caribbean before 1810, most North Americans anticipated that Latin America would be a marketplace for its eastern manufactures and western agricultural produce.

Also, during the generation following its independence the United States sought to remove the dangers posed by the presence of the British, French, and Spanish on its borders. The greatest threat came from the Spanish along the southern and western boundaries provided by the 1783 Treaty of Paris.

Like its European neighbors, Spain did not wish the United States to become a strong nation after 1783, nor did Spain want the North Americans to influence its New World colonies. These considerations prompted Spain to contest the generous southern boundary granted the United States at Paris, to stir Indian discontent against U.S. expansion in the old southwest, and to thwart U.S. shipping on the Mississippi River and in the Gulf of Mexico. Part of these difficulties were solved with the Pinckney

Treaty of 1795. But in a weakened position and suspecting that the United States had reached a secret accord with the British in 1794, Spain accepted a diplomatic solution. In the treaty, Spain recognized the 31st parallel as the southern boundary of the United States and granted it free navigation of the Mississippi River with the right of deposit at New Orleans.

Spain's concession did not reduce the U.S. fear that Louisiana and the Floridas might pass to a first-rate European power, specifically Britain or France, either of which could threaten U.S. security, expansion, and prosperity. The U.S. fear became a reality following the 1800 Treaty of San Ildefonso, which provided Napoléon Bonaparte an opportunity to reestablish a French empire in the New World, with an agricultural base in Louisiana and a naval station on Hispaniola in the Caribbean. Haiti's independence in 1802, however, laid waste to Napoléon's plans and made Louisiana expendable. The United States proved to be a willing customer. In 1803, President Thomas Jefferson persuaded a reluctant Congress to pay $15 million to purchase the Louisiana Territory from France in order to expand and secure the nation's western boundary and its use of the Mississippi River.

Still, the Spanish presence in the Floridas made the U.S. southern boundary unsafe. The U.S. efforts to secure the area were piecemeal. In 1804, President Jefferson induced Congress to pass the Mobile Act, which annexed into the Mississippi Territory all navigable waters, rivers, creeks, bays, and inlets that were located within the United States east of the Mississippi River and emptied into the Gulf of Mexico. In 1810, when Spanish authority in west Florida crumbled, President James Madison directed the seizure of the territory between the Mississippi and Perdido Rivers and unsuccessfully urged Spain to temporarily permit the occupation of the remainder of the Floridas in order to prevent its transfer to another power. Congress was more emphatic. In secret session on January 11, 1811, it approved a resolution declaring that the United States could not accept the passing of any part of the Floridas into the hands of a foreign power. It then passed enabling legislation that authorized the president to negotiate with local authorities an agreement that would permit the United States to take custody of east Florida should it be threatened by a foreign power. Known as the "no-transfer resolution," it became a cornerstone of U.S. hemispheric policy.

From 1812 until 1818, the Florida and western boundary questions became peripheral issues to Latin America's independence movements, at which time Great Britain failed to respond to the execution

of two of its citizens by General Andrew Jackson during his foray into Florida. The incident served as the final signal that Spain could not obtain European assistance with its New World difficulties and prompted Washington to step up its pressure on Madrid. The result was the 1819 Adams-Onís or Transcontinental Treaty, which granted the remainder of the Floridas to the United States and defined clearly the western boundary of the Louisiana Territory. In return, the United States agreed to pay up to $5 million in claims by U.S. citizens against Spain. With its boundaries secure, the United States increased its interest in Latin America.

By the time of the Adams-Onís Treaty in 1819, Latin America's independence movements had significantly progressed, but the United States had been reluctant to become involved, in part because of the Floridas and in part because of its ignorance about Latin America. The North Americans had little knowledge of Latin America's colonial life or of the independence movements' historical causes. Only a small body of readers were familiar with the few books in English available in the United States during the early nineteenth century. Newspapers and periodicals emphasized the intrigues and complications of the Spanish revolt that Napoléon had stirred in Europe. As a result, U.S. policy evolved only slowly.

On October 22, 1808, Jefferson's cabinet instructed its agents in Cuba and Mexico to express their nation's sympathy with the independence cause, but nothing more. In 1811, motivated by ideological sympathy and commercial prospects, President James Madison appointed consuls to Buenos Aires and Mexico. When the Napoleonic Wars ended in 1815, Madison steered a more neutral course, which did nothing to halt the private assistance that flowed to Latin America from Baltimore and New Orleans. Even the neutrality laws in 1817 and 1818 failed to stem the tide. U.S. public sentiment grew in favor of Latin American independence as émigrés found a sympathetic ear in the newspapers in the eastern U.S. cities. Soon, smaller periodicals throughout the country picked up on the patriotic call against European imperialism. At the same time, Representative Henry Clay of Kentucky began to champion the cause of Latin American independence, paralleling its cause to the lofty ideals of the American Revolution of 1776. Clay engineered a House resolution in 1819 that granted the president authority to send ministers to South American governments that had achieved independence from Spain. Another Clay-sponsored resolution approved by the House in 1820 called for support of Latin America's independence. The momentum toward recognition culminated on

An early rally in East Lower Harlem (El Barrio) in Manhattan in support of the independence of Puerto Rico. (The Jesús Colón Papers. Courtesy of the Center for Puerto Rican Studies, Hunter College, CUNY; Benigno Giboyeaux for the Estate of Jesús Colón and the Communist Party of the United States of America.)

March 8, 1822, when President James Monroe informed Congress that La Plata (Argentina), Chile, Peru, Colombia, and Mexico had sustained independence and were entitled to recognition in order to protect them from European intrigues.

The growing sentiment continued until December 1823, when President Monroe, in his annual address to Congress, announced that the Western Hemisphere was off limits to further European expansion and political ideology. Monroe's ideas were not new or novel except for the vague implication that the United States might go to war to defend the Spanish-American republics. The Monroe Doctrine expressed the United States' long-standing desire to secure itself from any European threat, but as so often happened in the nineteenth century, U.S. policy was influenced by events in Europe. With the restoration of Ferdinand VII to the Spanish throne in 1823, rumors abounded that a European force would help Spain regain its colonies in the Western Hemisphere. Great Britain, which had placed a heavy financial stake in Latin America's independence movement, wanted no part of any restoration movement and

sought a joint declaration to that effect from the United States. Monroe spurned the suggestion and acted alone. In response, the embarrassed British closed their West Indian islands to U.S. merchants for several years. The Latin American leadership gave little credence to Monroe's message because they understood that the British, not the North Americans, had supported their independence movement and possessed a navy second to none.

The United States was not alone regarding Spanish intentions in the New World. Simón Bolívar anticipated a Spanish effort to retake its former New World empire. To meet the challenge and to work together in other common areas of interests, Bolívar envisioned a Latin American League. Toward that end, in 1825 he issued a call for a congress at Panama. Only at the insistence of Colombia, Central America, and Mexico was an invitation extended to the United States. While all shared concern over Spain's intentions, Colombia and Central America appealed to the U.S. interests for the preservation of neutral rights on the high seas and its desire for republican governments. President John Quincy Adams immediately expressed interest, but Congress delayed the approval of delegates while it debated (1) concern that any linkage to Latin America would destroy the United States' freedom of action, (2) suspicion that Latin America had already reached a secret agreement with Europe, and (3) fear of Southern congressmen that slavery, already outlawed in Latin America, might be a topic of discussion. When delegates Richard C. Anderson and John Sergeant were finally appointed, their instructions reaffirmed U.S. opposition to the reestablishment of European colonies in the Western Hemisphere and the transfer of Cuba to a third party, continued commitment to neutral rights on the high seas, and insistence that any transisthmian canal be opened equally to world commerce and be maintained by tolls. While only four Latin American nations sent delegates to the congress, which ended in failure, the arrival of Anderson and Sergeant after the congress had ended only confirmed Latin American suspicion about U.S. indifference toward the Southern Hemisphere.

Throughout this early period, the United States did not have a monopoly on ignorance. Largely because of the limited contact with North America during the colonial period and the minimal contact after 1776, the Latin American colonials knew little about the United States. In fact, only a few individuals in all of Spanish America had any knowledge of the United States, most of which came to the New World from France in translation. Discussions in Spanish America about U.S. independence focused on Europe, not the revolting colonies. After 1776, a few books dealing with the United States began to filter southward, again mostly via Europe. There is evidence that most of the Spanish-American patriots read the Declaration of Independence, federal constitution, and some of Tom Paine's writings. Apparently, works by other U.S. revolutionaries were not read in Spanish America. In short, there was limited knowledge in all of Spanish America about the United States.

Several U.S. agents and consuls, such as Joel Poinsett in Argentina and Chile from 1810 to 1814 and William Shaler in Cuba and Henry M. Brackenridge in Argentina after 1817, often acted as informal cultural emissaries. They also sympathized with the Latin American independence cause. Little is known about the impact that North American mercenaries made when fighting in the armies of Francisco de Miranda, Xavier de Mina, or José Miguel Carrera, and even less is known about impact made by the sailors and merchants who engaged in clandestine trade.

In Latin America, perceptions of the United States varied. Those prone to the Spanish-American brand of liberalism looked more favorably upon the United States and its leaders. George Washington, for example, was revered by Ecuadoran Vicente Rocafuerte, Colombian Miguel de Prado, and Argentine Manuel Belgrano. The great liberator Simón Bolívar hoped to be placed in the same pantheon of heroes as Washington, Benjamin Franklin, John Hancock, and John and Sam Adams. Several Spanish-American writers, including Rocafuerte, and such travelers as Francisco Miranda, praised the extent of religious, civil, and political freedoms, social equality, literacy, and lack of pomp and ceremony in the United States.

In contrast to the liberals stood the conservatives, who were not convinced that the North American cultural, social, and political institutions were applicable to the Spanish Americans. Liberators Bolívar and José San Martin and Colombian statesman José Manuel Restrepo understood that the societies differed and suggested that the federal form of government might not apply to Latin America. In short, the Latin American conservatives feared that any changes in the existing institutions would destroy their orderly world.

When Latin America achieved its independence, it did not have a clearly defined foreign policy. Since the beginning of the nineteenth century it had focused attention on separation from Spain and the type of government that would replace the Spanish Crown. After independence, the Latin Americans cast about for new friends and found particular solace with the British, who had invested a considerable amount of energy and money in the independence movements, which was the primary factor that contributed to Latin America's disdain toward the Monroe Doctrine in 1823. Politically, the liberals and conservatives vied for power and the type of government to be established after independence. There were efforts at a form of federalism adapted to the local cultures, such as the United Provinces of Central America and the Gran Colombia experiment, but during the 1830s the conservatives held sway and the principles of centralized government with limited participation became the norm across the Southern Hemisphere. Thereafter, until the 1880s, with few exceptions, inter-American relations were unimportant. Europeans, led by the British and followed by the French, Germans, and Dutch, became the beneficiaries of commerce as U.S. consuls and agents across the continent struggled to keep apace.

As the hemispheres drifted apart in the generation following Latin America's independence, the former Spanish colonies struggled to establish stability and seek new trading partners. The United States engaged in its own struggle for national identity and experienced a surge in social reform, the most important being the slavery issue, and developed an urge for expansion westward. The latter again brought it into contact with Latin America, this time in the form of a Mexico plagued by political instability.

✳DEVELOPING A RELATIONSHIP: THE NINETEENTH CENTURY

When the U.S. Senate finally ratified the Adams-Onís treaty, which provided for the acquisition of the Floridas, in 1821, the United States also surrendered its stake in Texas by defining the western boundary of Louisiana. While some western spokesmen, such as Henry Clay, expressed disappointment at the time, the treaty might never have been completed had the United States not yielded on the Texas issue, because the Spanish minister had to show something in exchange for the loss of the Floridas. The loss of Texas did not mean loss of interest. In 1825 and again in 1827, President John Quincy Adams proposed to purchase a portion of the Texas territory. In 1829, President Andrew Jackson made a similar effort, but when his emissary Anthony Butler suggested that $500,000 be used to bribe Mexican officials, the proposal died. Butler's suggestion also infuriated the Mexican government beyond its normal admonishment of U.S. expansionist fever.

In 1821, the Spanish government at Mexico City sowed the seeds for the loss of Texas by granting a huge tract of land to an enterprising Missourian named Moses Austin, with the understanding that he would settle three hundred American families on it. Following Austin's death, the actual colonization was begun by his son Stephen. Instead of canceling the contract after its independence, Mexico legalized the pact. By 1835, fourteen years after the Austin grant, approximately thirty thousand Americans resided in the Texas territory. Friction quickly developed between the newcomers and the Mexicans. The Protestant Americans protested against the requirements to support the Catholic church, to take up Mexican citizenship, and to pay tariffs imposed on goods imported from the United States. Many Texans along the Gulf Coast worried about the precarious status of black slavery, which they deemed essential to their cotton plantations. Finally, the Mexican dictator Santa Ana imposed a centralized government, which the Americans in Texas regarded as a violation of their rights under the 1824 Mexican constitution.

In 1835, the Texans rose in revolt, but Santa Ana led the Mexican forces to brutal victories at the Alamo and Goliad. The massacre of Americans escalated nationalism in the United States, while it gave increased confidence to Santa Ana to drive all the Americans from Texas. Sam Houston's army pre-vented Santa Ana from achieving his goal. On April 21, 1836, at San Jacinto, Houston routed the Mexicans and forced Santa Ana to sign two vague treaties that ended the conflict and provided for an independent Texas as far as the Rio Grande. Houston's victory was made possible with men and materiel from the United States, a clear violation of the 1818 neutrality law, contributing to the Mexican government's disavowal of the treaties.

After independence, the Texans faced an uphill battle in their desire to be annexed to the United States. The slavery issue impeded the expansionist march. President Jackson understood the impassioned arguments between the pro- and antislavery forces. He also understood that the annexation of Texas might not only split his Democratic party, but also the nation. Thus, he delayed the recognition of Texas until the eve of Martin Van Buren's entry into the White House. The storm passed, and for the next several years the Texas question became a secondary issue as the United States concerned itself with a severe economic downturn.

Infuriated by Washington's failure to annex, the Texans struck an independent course. Plagued by the high cost of maintaining a military to defend the constant threat of Mexican invasion, in 1838 they sent agents to Europe to negotiate treaties of recognition and commerce and to borrow money to develop their economy and build a government. The British, ever anxious to thwart U.S. expansion and in order to safeguard its Caribbean possessions and provide a source of raw cotton for its textile industry, was most receptive. France, not to be outdone by the British, also extended recognition to the Lone Star Republic. The European presence immediately threatened U.S. security and blunted any future expansionist plans.

The issue rested there until the eve of the 1844 presidential contest when President John Tyler submitted an annexation proposal to the Senate. Although the proposal was defeated, Tyler's action threw the issue into the center of the presidential campaign between Henry Clay and James K. Polk. Clay attempted to straddle the issue, but Polk made it clear that he intended to annex Texas (and Oregon). Following Polk's electoral victory, the lame duck incumbent Tyler sought to annex Texas before leaving office. The clever Texans capitalized on the situation, playing British and American interests against each other. Under these conditions Tyler called for a joint resolution, never before used to annex a foreign territory. The House passed the annexation resolution in January 1845, and the Senate a month later. On March 1, 1845, with only three days left in office, Tyler signed the resolution. The annexation resolution so infuriated the Mexicans that its minister in Washington immediately withdrew his credentials and returned home. Several months later the U.S. emissary in Mexico City was obliged to leave. Diplomatic intercourse ceased between Mexico City and Washington.

While attention was focused on Texas, North American traders ventured into New Mexico and by the early 1840s became the leading merchants along the northern portion of the Sante Fe Trail, which connected Santa Fe and Albuquerque to Zacatacas and Mexico City. California, whose link to Mexico was tenuous at best, also lured the North Americans. As early as 1835, the Mexican government refused President Jackson's offer of $500,000 for San Francisco and some surrounding areas. Thereafter, hundreds of North Americans migrated to California and, like their Texas brethren in the 1840s, demonstrated contempt for Mexican authority and hinted at a secessionist movement. Other factors increased U.S. interest. A series of treaties in 1843 opened five Chinese ports to international commerce, prompting some New England merchants to call for a U.S. port on the Pacific coast of North America. When British agents appeared in California in the 1840s to promote the territory's annexation to Great Britain, President Polk responded by appointing Thomas O. Larkin as his confidential agent to California to counteract foreign influence. The president also aroused the public against the British by pointing to the Monroe Doctrine.

The expanded U.S. interests in New Mexico and California exacerbated Washington's tenuous relations with Mexico City. Polk sought a favorable diplomatic solution to the growing crisis and dispatched John L. Slidell to Mexico City in 1845 to discuss the claims of U.S. citizens against the Mexican government, the disposition of California, and the Texas boundary. Knowing that the Mexican government was penniless, Slidell carried instructions to settle the Texas boundary at the Rio Grande. In return, the U.S. government would assume its citizens' claims. At most, Slidell was to offer $25 million, if it included California and all intervening territory. The Mexicans refused Slidell when he arrived in their capital on December 6, 1845, and again on January 13, 1846, following the overthrow of the Herrera administration.

Slidell returned to Washington, where he found Polk promoting war against Mexico. But Polk was restrained by his cabinet, which argued that if hostilities were to start, the Mexicans would have to initiate them. Coincidentally, that is what happened. Polk determined to push the issue. He ordered General Zachary Taylor from Corpus Christi, Texas, to move to the Rio Grande, where he threatened the town of Matamoros. On April 25, 1846, Taylor reported that Mexican troops had crossed the Rio Grande, attacked his fort, and killed and wounded sixteen of his men. The subsequent public anguish and congressional outcry prompted Polk to submit a war message to Congress on May 11, 1845, that summarized twenty years of alleged Mexican offenses against the Americans in Texas. Two days later Congress declared war and appropriated $10 million to cover its costs.

Despite quick victories by Taylor in northern Mexico and General S. W. Kearney in California, the Mexicans refused to capitulate until General Winfield Scott took an expeditionary force from Veracruz to Mexico City, which he captured on September 14, 1847. Accompanying Scott to Mexico City was Minister Plenipotentiary Nicholas Trist, who was to negotiate a settlement, but he was recalled within a month after Scott's victory. The recall notice arrived after Trist had begun negotiations that dragged on to February 2, 1848, when he concluded a peace treaty at Guadalupe Hidalgo. The treaty met all U.S. objectives at a cost less than the $25 million originally offered. The treaty ceded New Mexico and California to the United States and confirmed the U.S. title to Texas as far south as the Rio Grande. In return, the United States agreed to pay $15 million and assume claims of its citizens up to $3.25 million. The North Americans might have fulfilled their Manifest Destiny, but the event embittered the Mexicans and resulted in charges of U.S. imperialism throughout the remainder of Latin America.

With victory in the Mexican War, many North Americans looked as far south as the Central American isthmus in anticipation of an interoceanic canal. Despite a decade-long string of warnings made by U.S. consuls on the isthmus, Washington policymakers expressed surprise in 1848 at the well-entrenched British in the region. British interests in Central America dated to their logging encampments in the 1620s along the ill-defined Mosquito Coast in present-day Belize. Those encampments were secured by a series of agreements with the Spanish Crown in the early 1800s, and the British claimed to inherit them after Central American independence in 1821. Guatemala thought otherwise and unsuccessfully sought U.S. assistance to dislodge the British in 1835. In the 1840s, the British expanded their interests as far south as the San Juan River on the Costa Rican-Nicaraguan border, long the favored site for a transisthmian canal.

Washington's first effort to counter the British came in 1846, when the U.S. chargé d'affaires in Bogotá, Benjamin Bidlack, completed a treaty with

New Granada that granted the United States government and its citizens the right to construct a canal across the isthmus at Panama, provided that the United States guarantee the territory's neutrality and New Granada's sovereignty over it. But Polk hesitated to commit the treaty to the Senate until after the Treaty of Guadalupe Hidalgo was completed. Because the Guadalupe Hidalgo did not contain a provision for canal rights at Tehauntepec, Polk submitted the Bidlack accord instead and the Senate ratified it in March 1848.

Sensing U.S. expansion, the British raised the Union Jack over the Mosquito Territory in June 1848 and claimed a protectorate over the territory under the administration of the governor at Jamaica. To check the British in Central America, Polk dispatched Elijah Hise to the isthmus in June 1848. A year later he returned with a Nicaraguan treaty that granted the United States canal rights along the San Juan River, provided it protect Nicaraguan sovereignty, an indirect reference to the British presence along the Mosquito Coast. Anxious to avoid a debate over an entangling alliance, Polk withheld the treaty from the Senate. But the United States did not alter its strategy with the new administration of Zachary Taylor. He dispatched Ephraim G. Squier to Central America to obtain canal rights for U.S. business interests. Squier quickly reached an agreement with Nicaragua that granted the U.S.-owned (Cornelius Vanderbilt) Atlantic and Pacific Ship and Canal Company exclusive rights along the San Juan River. Squier then moved on to Honduras, where he negotiated a treaty that ceded to the United States Tigre Island in the Gulf of Fonseca, considered to be the western terminus of the Nicaraguan canal. Squier's actions infuriated the British minister in Central America, Frederick Chatfield, who directed the HMS *Gorgon* to the gulf, where he personally led the British troops ashore at Tigre Island. Chatfield's actions were subsequently rebuked because cooler heads prevailed in Washington and London.

In Washington, Secretary of State John M. Clayton recognized that his country's recent diplomatic efforts did not prevent the British or any other power from constructing a canal across the isthmus. At the same time, the British confronted a crisis on the European continent that prompted them to seek an accommodation. Subsequently, Sir Henry Bulwer was dispatched to Washington to work out an agreement. The 1850 Clayton-Bulwer Treaty prevented either nation from constructing a transisthmian canal, but with language deliberately ambiguous that immediately satisfied Washington's desire to curtail British expansion in Central America, while protecting British honor and interests along the ill-defined Mosquito Coast. More significant was the precedent that the treaty set for Central America's tortuous history: during a crisis that involves a foreign power, it usually is settled without Central America's consultation.

In the decade following the Clayton-Bulwer Treaty, Central America remained the focal point of U.S.-Latin American relations. The British slowly extricated themselves from the region, save for the 1859 treaty with Guatemala by which it promised to construct a railroad from the Caribbean coast to Guatemala's interior in return for Guatemala's recognition of a British possession there (Belize). The railroad was never built, provoking a Guatemalan dispute with Belize that has lasted to the present. Meanwhile, the U.S. government did not openly disavow, or even discourage, the attempts of William Walker to establish himself as maximum leader in Nicaragua, from which he planned a Central American confederation under his leadership. Also, during the U.S. Civil War, President Abraham Lincoln proposed the relocation of freed blacks to Central America. Both ventures failed, but they demonstrated the North Americans' lack of sensitivity toward Central America and also served as a basis for the long-standing ill will that the isthmian republics have toward the United States.

In the years immediately after the American Civil War, there was an ebb in inter-American relations. The North American people were more caught up in westward expansion, rapid industrial growth, and Reconstruction in the South than in the possible purchase of the Dominican Republic in 1869 or Mexican border problems in the early 1870s. Even in the 1880s, Secretary of State James G. Blaine received little credit for attempting to serve as an honest broker in the Mexican-Guatemalan border dispute and as a mediator in the War of the Pacific. Both incidents, however, fueled the charges of U.S. interference in Latin America's internal affairs.

These events appeared minor in the context of larger inter-American relations, but not so the Venezuelan boundary dispute that erupted in 1893. The dispute along the Venezuelan border with British Guiana dated to the 1840s, when the British determined a line of demarcation that the Venezuelans refused to accept. The issue was complicated by the discovery of gold in the disputed area, which attracted some forty thousand British subjects that Downing Street felt obliged to protect. A new complication arose in 1895 when the British sent troops to the Bluefields, Nicaragua, to protect its citizens there against the arbitrary rule of José Santos Zelaya. Although the Cleveland administration sided with Zelaya to force out the British, the U.S. press turned the Nicaraguan issue into a question of defending the Monroe Doctrine and made comparisons to the British presence in the disputed Venezuelan territory.

Amidst the jingoism, Cleveland and Secretary of State Richard Olney seized the issue. On July 20, 1895, Olney sent a missive to London reasserting the noncolonial principles of the Monroe Doctrine and demanded that Britain adhere to U.S. arbitration of the dispute. Obviously unimpressed, Lord Salisbury responded with the charge that the Monroe Doctrine was not recognized by international law and that it did not apply to boundary disputes. Not to be outdone, Cleveland asserted that the United States would unilaterally determine the boundary line and would be prepared to defend it. Congress agreed when it approved $100,000 for a boundary commission. Throughout the United States a wave of jingoism followed. Again, Britain was in a vulnerable position, with the rising German power on the European continent and its search for colonies abroad. London backed off and submitted to U.S. arbitration in 1897. When handed down in 1899, the commission's decision favored Venezuela, but was not far out of line with the original British offer. Although the jingoism and public interest had passed, the incident gave recognition to the Monroe Doctrine.

While these issues festered, internal changes in Latin America and the United States brought the two hemispheres closer together by the century's end. In Latin America, liberals returned to the presidential palaces after 1870 and brought with them a desire to modernize their societies. Espousing "positivism," the liberals believed that economic growth and prosperity were essential before true political democracy could take hold. To achieve modernity, these new political leaders directed the construction of modern national capitals replete with theaters, libraries, and universities. As a result, Buenos Aires, Santiago, Guatemala City, and others resembled European cities, but provincial towns remained backwaters. The new political leadership remained obsessed with material development, faith in scientific and technical education, and imitation of U.S. and western European values, but they postponed political democracy. Economically, the liberals focused on the development of an export economy, diversification of agriculture, mining, transportation, communications, and manufacturing. In effect, they opened their doors to foreign investment, but it was the Europeans, primarily the British, not the North Americans, who capitalized on the situation. Argentine beef and wheat, Chilean copper and nitrates, Brazilian sugar and coffee became dependent on the vicissitudes of the world economy. North Americans continued their investments in Cuba and also expanded their interests in Mexico and Central America.

During the same period, the United States had its own proponents of a larger world policy, such as Albert C. Beveridge, Henry Cabot Lodge, Sr., Alfred T. Mahan, and Theodore Roosevelt. These men advocated that the United States compete with the Europeans in the global economy, construct a two-ocean navy, establish the requisite coaling stations, and build an interoceanic canal. In the diplomatic arena, the leading spokesman was James G. Blaine, who as secretary of state briefly in 1881 and again from 1889 to 1893 advocated an expansion of North American interests in Latin America.

Like Henry Clay, Blaine envisioned a Latin American market awaiting to be tapped. In 1881, he noted the $100 million adverse balance of trade that the United States had with Latin America because the Latin countries shipped large quantities of raw materials to the United States but bought the bulk of their manufactured goods from Europe. Blaine suggested an inter-American conference, but for internal political reasons, Washington did not issue invitations until late 1888. Not until early October 1889 did the delegates of seventeen Latin American nations assemble in Washington to hear Blaine extol the virtues of American industry. Blaine then took his guests on a special six-thousand-mile train tour through forty-one cities to view giant factories and other mechanical marvels, listen to speeches and brass bands, and witness displays, including the firing of a natural gas well.

The conference failed to achieve Blaine's primary objectives: the creation of an inter-American customs union and the establishment of arbitration machinery. The Latin American delegates were sympathetic to the concept of a customs union, but they thought it impractical and instead favored separate reciprocity treaties. Long-standing mistrust of the United States and mutual jealousies among the Latin American states contributed to defeat the measure to establish an arbitration mechanism. The first inter-American conference resulted in only one tangible achievement: the creation of the agency that came to be called the Pan American Union, which was designed as a clearinghouse for spreading information among the constituent American republics, as well as for encouraging cooperation among them. In 1907, U.S. industrialist Andrew Carnegie donated the money for construction of the building that still houses the Organization of American States (OAS). Despite few tangible results, the 1889 conference momentarily improved inter-American relations.

Blaine moved quickly to capitalize on the reciprocity agreements, asking Congress to give him a free hand in making the necessary arrangements. But the high-tariff Harrison administration was suspicious of attempts to lower trade barriers, and the McKinley Tariff Bill of 1890 was so unsatisfactory to Blaine that he appeared before the Senate committee to forcefully plead for reciprocity. Although he eventually was able to negotiate six such treaties, the Democrats, after returning to power in 1893, reversed the policy to the accompaniment of bitter outcries from the Latin American countries.

While the U.S. Congress continued to debate the nuances of a foreign economic policy after the economic downturn that began in 1893, Cuba came to the center stage of diplomatic interest. Cuba's importance rested with its location at the crossroads of the Caribbean, from which an unfriendly power could bottle up U.S. trade and militarily threaten the U.S. underbelly. U.S. interest in Cuba dated to Thomas Jefferson, who had expressed an interest in acquiring the island. During the wars of Latin American independence, the United States was preoccupied with acquiring the Floridas but was not unhappy that Cuba remained a Spanish colony. In 1823, Secretary of State John Quincy Adams informed the Spanish government that the annexation of Cuba to the United States would be indispensable to the Union's integrity. From then until the Mexican War, the United States remained passive about Cuba.

In 1848, the expansionist-minded President Polk dispatched a special minister to Spain with an offer to pay up to $100 million for the island. But Spain vehemently responded that the island was not for sale at any price. In the 1850s, Cuba again became a focal point of expansion. In anticipation of a congressional imbalance with westward expansion, the Southern slave states looked toward Cuba. Given the Democratic party's Southern proclivity at the time, President Franklin Pierce proposed the purchase of the island for a price of up to $130 million and, if that failed, indicated that the United States would move to detach Cuba from Spanish rule and make the island independent in order to pave the way for annexation. In October 1854, the three U.S. ministers to Europe met at Aix-la-Chapelle, where they affirmed Pierce's proposal. Their declaration, named the Ostend Manifesto, became the object of European vilification of U.S. imperialism and caused Spain to become more recalcitrant than ever in resisting Washington's advance. As the U.S. Civil War approached, Cuba faded into the background.

But events on the island signaled future complications. Many Americans migrated to Cuba and invested in the sugar and tobacco industries, while the Cuban elite developed close ties to the United States. The latter's increased clamor for self-govern-

ment, if not independence, erupted into a war in 1868 that lasted for ten years. During that decade, many North Americans were arrested and executed by Spanish authorities, while others had their properties destroyed for sympathizing with the Cubans. The uprising caused a widespread cry for interference, but Secretary of State Hamilton Fish persuaded Congress not to become involved. When the war ended, the North Americans continued their investment in Cuban agriculture, and the Cuban elite strengthened their informal links to the United States through the large Cuban colony in New York City.

On the island, the independence spirit did not die. Early in 1895, the Cubans again rose up in rebellion. This time, the insurgents were hardly less ruthless than the Spaniards, who practiced a "scorched earth" policy. The North Americans, who by this time had $50 million invested in Cuba and whose trade totaled some $100 million, were caught in the middle. The insurgents put the torch to U.S. properties in hopes of drawing the North Americans into the fracas, while Cubans in the United States disseminated vicious propaganda about the Spanish. Also, the United States became the center of the rebels' gunrunning enterprises.

Madrid decided on harsh measures to quell the insurrection. In 1896, it sent to Cuba General Valeriano Weyler, who rounded up thousands of Cuban men, women, and children in concentration camps. Such barbaric treatment prompted a U.S. congressional resolution calling for recognition of Cuban independence, but national attention was diverted by the 1896 presidential campaign. Following the election of William McKinley, the yellow journalism renewed the call. It portrayed the Spanish atrocities on the island in a most exaggerated fashion. A subsequent change in Spanish government resulted in the recall of Weyler, modification of the reconcentration methods, release of U.S. citizens that were imprisoned, and a grant of partial autonomy to the Cubans. The concessions failed to pacify the island. The Spanish loyalists in Havana rioted in protest of the concessions, while the Cuban nationalists demanded independence. Amidst the tension, the United States dispatched the battleship *Maine* to Havana harbor, hoping to impress both groups. While in port, the *Maine* was ripped by an explosion that took more than 250 lives. Despite cries for reason until an investigation could be completed, the yellow press played into the hands of the Americans already riled at the Spanish.

In the meantime, William Randolph Hearst's *New York Journal* printed a private letter from the Spanish minister in Washington, Dupuy DeLome, that described McKinley as a weak leader. Its publication further irked the public and Congress. Together these events prompted Congress to vote for a declaration of war on March 19, 1898, and appropriate $50 million for its preparations. Nine days later, the Naval Court of Inquiry reported that the *Maine* had been blown up by a submarine mine, leaving the impression that Spain was responsible. The Navy report increased the public clamor for some action.

Still, McKinley sought a diplomatic solution. He instructed the U.S. minister in Madrid to determine if Spain would end its reconcentration camps and offer amnesty to the insurgents and accept future U.S. mediation. On April 9, Spain accepted the need for peace but balked at the proposed amnesty. Rather than respond to the Spanish offer, McKinley, caught in the tide of public opinion and its demand for U.S. intervention to liberate Cuba, asked Congress for authority to send troops to the island to bring an end to the hostilities. Congress, also caught up in the war hysteria, passed a four-part resolution on April 19 effectively equivalent to a declaration of war. McKinley approved the resolution on April 29, but stated that war had existed since April 21.

It was not much of a conflict. The war lasted fewer than three months, ending on August 12, 1898. In the subsequent negotiations that led to the Peace of Paris on December 12, 1898, Spain relinquished her sovereignty over Cuba and opened the door to U.S. tutelage of the island.

In 1898, when President McKinley declared that the nation's objective was to construct a canal under its control, he only reaffirmed his predecessors' proclamations of thirty years. As early as 1869, President Ulysses S. Grant had asserted that a transisthmian canal would be built by the United States. Twelve years later, Rutherford B. Hayes repeated the charge. Both presidents, like many individuals before them, focused attention on the Nicaraguan route at the San Juan River. Only the attempt by Ferdinand de Lesseps, of Suez Canal fame, momentarily diverted attention to Panama. More important than the location was a round of jingoism it ignited that demanded a U.S.-controlled canal. Writing in *The Nation* in 1881, John A. Kasson warned that U.S. intransigence would permit Europe to turn the Caribbean into another Mediterranean. Although the jingoism subsided after De Lesseps failed in 1881, interest in a transisthmian canal did not.

Since the 1820s, most canal observers and promoters had expected the canal's construction to be a private undertaking. The last such effort was made between 1887 and 1893 by A. G. Menocal's Maritime Canal Company, which spent some $4 million in clearing jungle and doing other preliminary work before collapsing for lack of funding.

In the 1890s, there were increased calls for a U.S.-government canal project. Their position was strengthened by the ninety-eight-day trip of the USS *Oregon* from Puget Sound to Cuban waters during the Spanish-American War and the increased call by the business community for access to the Asian and west coast Latin American markets. In addition to the material factors, the expansionists offered an ideological explanation. They pointed to the moral obligation to take western culture to the so-called backward areas of the world. The experience in Cuba reinforced these thoughts, and President McKinley uttered the same to justify the annexation of the Philippines in 1898.

By the century's end, there developed a national demand for an isthmian canal, built, owned, and operated by the U.S. government. What began as a desire to prevent Europeans from building and operating a canal became a national obsession for security and markets and also became a moral crusade. Only the Clayton-Bulwer Treaty stood in the way. The British, suspicious of Germany and experiencing a bogged-down Boer War, were ready to capitulate. The result was the second Hay-Pauncefote Treaty in 1901, which permitted the United States to construct and fortify a transisthmian canal.

That same year the Walker Commission recommended that the United States pursue the Nicaraguan route at an estimated cost of $189 million, as opposed to the $149 million for a route across Panama. The figure did not include the $109 million that the New Panama Canal Company, successor to the De Lesseps company, wanted for its rights and property. In early 1902, the House of Representatives approved the Hepburn bill, putting it on record as favoring the Nicaraguan site. Given this favorable ambiance, Secretary of State John Hay, also an advocate of the Nicaraguan route, and William L. Merry, the minister assigned to both Costa Rica and Nicaragua, commenced negotiations in both Washington and Central America. Like many of their predecessors, Nicaraguan president Zelaya and Costa Rican president Rafael Igesias believed that a canal would bring economic prosperity to their countries. With their hopes raised, the Central Americans signed preliminary protocols that gave the United States the exclusive right to build a canal along their common border and then through Nicaragua.

While Hay and Merry busied themselves, forces favoring the Panama route crystallized, particularly after the New Panama Canal Company dropped its asking price to $40 million. In response, the Walker Commission issued a supplemental report favoring the Panama route, and the Senate Committee on Interoceanic Canals followed suit. At the same time

Hay received a promising proposal from Colombia for the Panama route. The stage was set for a great debate on Capitol Hill. It began in June 1902, and when it ended, the Spooner Amendment to the Hepburn Bill authorized the president to pursue the Panama route first and, only if unsuccessful, to turn to Nicaragua.

The newly elected president, Theodore Roosevelt, determined to bring the canal project to fruition. Subsequent negotiations resulted in the 1903 Hay-Herrán Treaty. It granted the United States the right to build a canal in a six-mile-wide zone across Panama in return for a $10 million cash payment and an annual subsidy of $250,000. The Colombian senate rejected the treaty but called for new negotiations in the hope of wringing greater financial concessions from the United States.

The displeased North Americans found a willing ally in Panama, where the local citizens resented Bogotá's political domination. The Panamanians also received encouragement from Philippe Bunau-Varilla, who feared losses for the New Panama Canal Company, which he represented. The upshot of this intrigue was a revolt in Panama on November 2, 1903, independence two days later, and U.S. recognition two days after that. Roosevelt did little to conceal his joy for the revolutionary plot, which he at least tacitly encouraged. Bunau-Varilla then negotiated a treaty with Hay in the Waldorf Astoria Hotel in New York City. When completed on November 18, 1903, without Panamanian representation, the Hay-Bunau-Varilla Treaty gave the United States the same privileges as the proposed Hay-Herrán Treaty, except for a ten-mile-wide canal zone.

While Democrats and European leaders criticized Roosevelt's cowboy diplomacy, there was no public outcry against his action. In fact, *Public Opinion* best summarized North American opinion when it wrote that the public "wanted a canal even though this course of action cannot be justified on moral grounds." Latin Americans who had grown impatient with Colombia's dalliance acquiesced to Roosevelt's precipitous diplomacy. While some chastised his questionable tactics, commercial interests generally condemned Colombia, congratulated the Panamanians, and condoned the United States. In Central America, the abrupt change of the canal venue revived latent anti-Americanism. While Costa Rica retreated to its traditional isolationism, the mercurial Nicaraguan president, Zelaya, reacted with a vengeance. He interfered with diplomatic mail, discriminated against North American businessmen, and resisted settling pecuniary claims. The United States did little more than protest until he attempted a Central American union under his leadership.

The selection of Panama also severed U.S.-Colombian friendship. When the Colombians proposed arbitration of their grievance against the United States, the North Americans, long-time advocates of arbitration, demurred. Roosevelt viewed such action as a confession of wrongdoing. Roosevelt's successor, William Howard Taft, made several unsuccessful attempts to placate Colombia, and President Woodrow Wilson sought forgiveness with a 1914 treaty that professed "sincere regret" for the Panama affair and offered $25 million in compensation. But Roosevelt encouraged his fellow Republicans in the Senate to reject the treaty. Finally, in 1921, the William Harding administration dusted off the Wilson treaty and eliminated the "sincere regret" phrase. Colombia accepted the indirect apology and the $25 million.

✳A PERIOD OF U.S. DOMINANCE: 1903-1954

The acquisition of the Panama Canal Zone marked a major turning point in U.S. relations with the Caribbean region. Under three presidents - Theodore Roosevelt, William Howard Taft, and Woodrow Wilson - the United States actively sought political and financial stability in the region for fear that any instability would threaten the Panama Canal. The navy played an important part in carrying out Washington's assertive Caribbean policies. New facilities were needed to protect regional sea-lanes and the canal. Naval squadrons were upgraded and stood ready to implement Washington's policy. Washington was also motivated by an altruistic crusade to improve the quality of life for the downtrodden and inferior peoples of the Caribbean. At the same time, U.S. businessmen and bankers took advantage of the situation to turn a profit, and in so doing linked themselves to local elites, establishing an informal alliance that sought preservation of the existing social and political system. Although presidential policies differed, the Caribbean region became an American lake by 1920. Because of this, the United States provoked the ire of not only the Caribbean peoples but also all of Latin America.

The character of U.S. policy in the Caribbean was shaped in a large part by the postwar experience in Cuba. Because the Teller Amendment denied the United States the right to annex Cuba after the Spanish-American War, President McKinley, as commander in chief, directed the American presence on the island through Generals John R. Brooke and Leonard Wood. Because Brooke and Wood viewed the Cubans as an inferior people who needed uplifting, they governed them with a paternalistic attitude. With the Panama Canal about to become a reality,

Washington determined to protect the island from any foreign intervention. The means came with an amendment to the Army Appropriation Act of 1901 sponsored by Senator Orville Platt of Connecticut. It proscribed postoccupation U.S.-Cuban relations by pledging the republic to a low public debt, preventing it from signing any treaty that impaired U.S. interests, granting the United States intervention rights to protect life, liberty, and property, according the United States the right to validate the acts of the military government, and granting the United States the right to construct naval facilities. Before withdrawing from Cuba, U.S. authorities ensured that the Platt Amendment was annexed to the 1901 Cuban constitution and formalized by treaty two years later. Over the next generation, U.S. troops supervised Cuban elections to ensure the peaceful transfer of power. Given the guarantee of security, American investment on the island climbed to $100 million, most of it in tobacco and sugar.

The principles of the Platt Amendment also found their way into the 1903 Hay-Bunau-Varilla Treaty with Panama, which prevented Panama from pursuing an independent foreign policy and incurring excessive foreign debt and granted the United States rights to construct sanitation facilities in the terminal cities and to intervene in Panama to maintain public order. As in Cuba, the marines marched into the Panamanian republic before the decade was out.

In 1904, Roosevelt anticipated new challenges from Europe. In the aftermath of a debt crisis that resulted in an Anglo-German blockade of the Venezuelan coast, The Hague's Court of Permanent Arbitration upheld the right of creditor nations to use force to collect debts from recalcitrant debtor states. In 1903, with the prospect of European creditors intervening in the politically corrupt and financially bankrupt Dominican Republic, Roosevelt had the choice of either accepting European intervention or assuming responsibility for foreign nationals. With the Panama Canal under construction and the assessment that after one hundred years of independence, these "incompetent" states would inevitably come under U.S. protection and regulation, Roosevelt chose the latter course. In December 1904, he added a corollary to the Monroe Doctrine, declaring that "chronic wrongdoing" in the Western Hemisphere would force the United States to act as an "international police power" (See chapter on Documents.) A month later, a protocol with the Dominican Republic provided for the establishment of a U.S.-administered customs receivership by which New York bankers paid off the Dominican debts to Europe and U.S. Marines occupied Dominican customs houses. Part

of the money they collected paid off the U.S. bankers, while the remainder was used to improve the island's infrastructure.

In Central America, Roosevelt noted that the inter- and intrastate rivalries and fiscal irresponsibilities that begged European intervention could no longer be tolerated because of their potential threat to the Panama Canal. To ward off the dangers, the Roosevelt administration determined to establish constitutional governments across the isthmus. The opportunity came in 1907 when the machinations of Nicaraguan leader José Santos Zelaya threatened the isthmus with war. In response, Roosevelt and Mexican President Porfirio Díaz called for a general peace conference in Washington. The resultant General Treaty provided for nonrecognition of governments that came to power by coup d'état, banned the Central American governments from interfering in each other's internal affairs, and established the Central American Court of Justice. Roosevelt was pleased with the imposition of constitutional order through a treaty system, but so too were the incumbent Central American leaders, because the treaty system seemed to ensure their terms in office.

Roosevelt's successor, William Howard Taft, entered on a course in Nicaragua that soon became a quagmire from which the United States did not extricate itself until 1933. By 1909, Zelaya had become a hindrance to the American policy of regional stability, and Taft asserted that the United States might support any nation that would force Zelaya's ouster from office. It was the Nicaraguan conservatives who took up the call and, with support from U.S. private interests in the country, ousted Zelaya. As war ensued, Taft sent Thomas C. Dawson to Nicaragua, who worked out a series of agreements that abolished Zelaya's monopolies, established a customs receivership, and created a political arrangement that made liberal Juan B. Estrada president and conservative Adolfo Díaz vice president. Subsequently, the Knox-Castrillo convention put Nicaragua's financial house in order by providing for the refinancing of the country's foreign and domestic debts with a loan from U.S. banking interests secured by a U.S. customs receivership. When the political peace broke down in July, 1912, U.S. Marines were landed to supervise the November election that confirmed Díaz in the presidency. The marines also supervised the 1916 and 1920 elections. To address Nicaragua's financial plight, private bankers advanced loans collateralized by the Nicaraguan national railroad and bank. Nicaragua's financial plight contributed to its acceptance of the Bryan-Chamorro Treaty in 1914. In return for $3 million to pay its creditors, the Nicaraguans granted the United States canal rights in the country, thus securing the route from another canal venture, or at least the sale of the rights to a foreign nation that could then use Nicaragua to threaten U.S. regional security interests. By 1920, Nicaragua had become an American client state.

Taft was not successful in extending "dollar diplomacy" in Honduras or Guatemala. Neither the U.S. Congress nor the Honduran legislature was willing to commit itself to another customs receivership. In Guatemala, President Manuel Estrada Cabrera resisted U.S. pressure for restructuring his nation's foreign debt until 1913, when the British threatened naval intervention. Because the British actions served U.S. interests, the State Department turned its head to this violation of the Monroe Doctrine.

In the first generation of the twentieth century, the most extensive and systematic U.S. intrusion into the internal processes of Caribbean countries came in Haiti and the Dominican Republic. The origins of the Haitian intervention lay in American racial fantasies, economic interests, and strategic requirements. Haiti's independence dated to 1803, but owing to its racial makeup, the United States did not extend recognition until the Civil War. From 1876 to 1910, U.S. Marines landed on eight occasions to protect life and property. An effort also was made to purchase Molé Saint-Nicolas on the island's isolated north coast for a naval coaling station. Despite U.S. disdain for the Haitian blacks, the island's elite lived in a European style, and, in fact, in the first part of the twentieth century the Germans had made significant inroads there. Still, on the eve of intervention, the United States controlled about 60 percent of the republic's import market. For President Woodrow Wilson, the immediate Haitian problems rested with its political turmoil. Haitian presidents were regularly removed forcibly from office and oftentimes assassinated in the process.

By the summer of 1915, the State Department rationalized that some form of intervention was necessary to maintain order and to protect lives and property. The brutal killing of President Guillame Sam and the subsequent threat of revolution became the catalyst to U.S intervention. Admiral William B. Caperton landed bluejackets. Subsequently, the State Department fashioned a treaty that authorized U.S. control of the customs houses, construction of roads and schools, and organization of a constabulary. Under duress, the Haitians accepted the treaty that the North American military implemented, but not without sporadic violence in opposition to its presence. In addition to running the government, the U.S. military administrators demonstrated racism, holding the Haitians to be inferior people.

The origins of the 1916 Dominican occupation lay in the customs receivership established by Theodore Roosevelt in 1905. Financial and political prospects in the republic improved until 1911, when President Ramón Cáceres was assassinated. Subsequently, political rivals vied for office and served in the presidency for short terms, but long enough to loot the treasury. Given this instability, Wilson insisted on new financial and military reforms and that U.S. Marines supervise the 1916 presidential elections. The task fell to General Harry Knapp. He reorganized the government to carry out his reform directives, which included establishing a U.S.-style court system and creating a national guard to act as a local police force. Over time the North Americans modernized the nation's decrepit transportation and communications systems, constructed schools, and carried out fiscal reform. But the countryside remained rich with bandits who continually made life uncomfortable for the North Americans.

Wilson's effort to impose constitutional order took another form in Costa Rica in 1917, when he refused to extend recognition to Federico Tinoco, who had seized the presidency. Despite appeals from Minor Keith of the United Fruit Company and other U.S. businessmen, authorities in the Panama Canal Zone, and special emissary John Foster Dulles, Wilson refused to budge. He maintained that Tinoco had come to the presidency illegally and was not worthy of recognition. Neither U.S. diplomatic pressure nor the concomitant financial adversity forced Tinoco out, but an unauthorized act by U.S. Naval Commander L. B. Porterfield did. In June 1914, Porterfield took the USS *Castine* to Limón and threatened to land marines. Tinoco feared the worst and resigned. Julio Acosta won the subsequent presidential elections and quickly received U.S. recognition.

Wilson's moralizing was not limited to the smaller states of the Caribbean region. Relations were good with Mexico while Porfirio Díaz ruled for three decades. As a Latin American liberal, Díaz turned Mexico into a safe haven for investment. North American entrepenuers - J. P. Morgan, William Randolph Hearst, James J. Hill, and the Guggenheims - took full advantage of it. By 1913, there were over 500,000 Americans in Mexico, and their investments totaled $1 billion. Despite the outward appearance of order and prosperity, some fifteen million Mexicans lived in poverty and were reduced to a state of peonage. Between the poor and the upper class was a growing middle sector that wanted participation in the political process. This group found a leader in Francisco Madero, who led a democratic movement to replace the elderly Díaz in the 1911 presidential sweepstakes. But within two years, Madero was deposed by General Victoriano Huerta, representing the propertied classes. Huerta's action touched off a rebellion by the *caudillos* (chiefs) who represented the rural poor. The Taft administration did respond to the crisis, but the idealistic Wilson determined that nonrecognition would teach the Mexicans to elect a good man. In November 1913, when Huerta refused Wilson's demand that he resign, the United States lifted its arms embargo so that supplies could reach Huerta's two chief opponents, Venustiano Carranza and Francisco "Pancho" Villa. Mexico again plunged into an internal war that wrought much havoc and damage to North American life and property in Mexico.

The hostile atmosphere intensified and on April 9, 1914, a group of U.S. sailors at Tampico were arrested for allegedly violating martial law. Although quickly released and an apology issued, the naval commander there, Admiral Henry T. Mayo, demanded more, and Wilson used the incident to coax congressional approval of U.S. armed intervention. As war seemed inevitable, U.S. investors in Mexico joined with Huerta's political opponents and Latin Americans to protest Wilson's intentions. In face of such opposition, Wilson accepted the ABC powers' (Argentina, Brazil, and Chile) offer to mediate the crisis. Although the Niagara Falls conference met with failure, the Latin American effort prevented another U.S.-Mexican war. Finally, in 1915, Wilson grudgingly extended recognition to the Carranza government, although he still faced the insurrectionist Pancho Villa. When Villa sacked the town of Columbus, New Mexico, on March 9, 1916, killing seventeen North Americans, Wilson severed relations and ordered General John J. Pershing to pursue the bandit into Mexico. He never caught up with Villa, but the penetration again brought Mexico and the United States to the brink of war. Events in Europe overtook Wilson, and in February 1917, he ordered Pershing's withdrawal, but confrontation with the Mexican government continued.

The end of the Mexican Revolution brought a new threat to U.S. interests. Carranza's 1917 constitution contained provisions for rural and urban labor and was most anti-Catholic and antiforeign. Most alarming was Article 27, which vested the government with all subsoil properties, including minerals and oil. Carranza declared that this provision was retroactive, a direct threat to U.S. private investment in Mexico. Patient negotiations led to a tacit Mexican government pledge that Article 27 would not be applied retroactively. Satisfied, the United States extended recognition.

The high-water mark of U.S. intervention came with the 1923 Central American conference in Washington, D.C. The conference was the product of continued political intrigue that threatened the region

with war in August 1922. Still concerned that Central American calamities might spill over into Panama, the United States convened the conference in December 1922. It ended in February 1923 with a series of agreements that more rigidly defined a revolutionary government not worthy of recognition, reiterated promises of not helping revolutionaries, established a new Central American Court, and forced arms limitations. The ink had barely dried on the treaties before the United States again found itself interfering in the internal affairs of Honduras, Nicaragua, El Salvador, and Guatemala. At the same time, currents surfaced that led to a new era in inter-American relations.

In Latin America there was a growing crescendo of opposition to U.S. policies. The Argentines, Brazilians, and Chileans, each viewing themselves as the leader of Latin America, criticized U.S. unilateral actions in the Caribbean. The Central American nations refused to extend the life of the Central American Court after it ruled against the United States over the Bryan-Chamorro Treaty and Washington then ignored the ruling. All of Latin America rushed to join the League of Nations in hopes that it would curtail U.S. domination of the hemisphere. When the United States did not join the world body, the Latin Americans lost interest. Instead, during the 1920s, they used the inter-American conferences at Santiago and Havana to demand U.S. withdrawal from the Caribbean.

Following World War I, the North American public also became tired of conflict and wary of obligations to other governments. It favored withdrawal from world affairs, including staying out of the League of Nations. The war also momentarily ended the European threat to the Caribbean region and weakened its commercial links to Latin America. The decreased European presence contributed to Secretary of State Charles Evans Hughes's belief that inter-American conferences should be gala affairs used to demonstrate harmonious hemispheric relations. The new environment prompted Secretary of Commerce Herbert Hoover to promote withdrawal of U.S. Marines from the several Caribbean countries in order to foster the goodwill that might enhance the North American trading position throughout all of Latin America. The mood change found its way into the 1924 and 1928 platforms of the Democratic party, which condemned intervention, a position repeated by Franklin D. Roosevelt in 1928. Within the State Department there was a growing frustration with U.S. interventions. Successive heads of the Latin American Affairs Division, Francis G. White and Edwin C. Wilson, believed that it was no longer necessary to meddle in the internal affairs of the

Latin American states. Others questioned the wisdom of the nonrecognition policy. President-elect Herbert Hoover's goodwill visit to Central and South America in late 1928 was followed by the J. Rueben Clark *Memorandum on the Monroe Doctrine*, which renounced U.S. intervention in Latin American domestic affairs under the terms of the Roosevelt Corollary to the Monroe Doctrine.

In the late 1920s, the public became increasingly frustrated with the continued loss of life in the marines' futile attempt to catch Augusto César Sandino in Nicaragua. The growing forces of change culminated with Roosevelt's 1933 presidential inaugural address, in which he proclaimed the "Good Neighbor" policy. At the 1933 Montevideo and 1936 Buenos Aires Inter-American Conferences, the United States repeated its pledge not to intervene, directly or indirectly, in the domestic affairs of Latin American states. From 1933 to 1954, the State Department only asked that a government control the nation's territory and administrative machinery, have popular support, and be able to meet its international obligations to receive U.S. recognition.

The Good Neighbor policy produced immediate results. The marines were withdrawn from Haiti, the Dominican Republic, and Nicaragua; a new canal treaty was concluded with Panama; the Platt amendment in Cuba was abrogated; and recognition was extended to Jorge Ubico in Guatemala, Maximiliano Hernández Martínez in El Salvador, Tiburcio Carías in Honduras, Anastasio Somoza in Nicaragua, Rafael Trujillo in the Dominican Republic, and Francois Duvalier in Haiti, all of whom illegally extended their presidential terms.

Just as the United States lost interest in its moral crusade in Latin America, changes in the global environment prompted Washington to pursue new policies. For fifteen years after Franklin D. Roosevelt announced the Good Neighbor policy, three successive world crises - the Great Depression, World War II, and the onset of the cold war - vaulted the United States into the leadership role in international affairs, and Latin America was incorporated into the larger framework of these global strategies.

The world staggered under economic collapse in 1933. Since 1929, world trade had declined 25 percent in volume and 66 percent in value. During the same period, U.S. trade declined 48 percent in volume and 68 percent in value. Trade with Latin America declined even more drastically: exports dropped 78 percent in value, and imports, 68 percent. The response to the economic calamity was not imaginative. In 1930, the U.S. Congress approved the Hawley-Smoot Tariff Act, which actually increased the cost of foreign imports. Many of the Latin American countries

pursued nationalistic policies, including the establishment of a complicated web of monetary devaluations, currency restrictions, higher tariffs, import licensing, exchange controls, quotas, embargoes, and bilateral arrangements with European trading partners. None of these measures stimulated commerce and, in fact, only frustrated it.

Convinced that economic nationalism worsened the depression, Secretary of State Cordell Hull sought to liberalize trade policies in an effort to improve the world's economy and in turn ease world tensions. At home, Hull found a gallery of supporters, including Assistant Secretary of State for Latin American Affairs Adolf A. Berle, Secretary of Commerce Henry A. Wallace, the International Chamber of Commerce, and the American Automobile Association. At the 1933 Montevideo Conference, Hull secured a resolution calling for liberalized trade policies, including the negotiation of reciprocal trade agreements. Congress resisted until June 1934, when it passed the Reciprocal Trade Agreements Act, which provided for the use of the unconditional most-favored-nation clause and the principle of active tariff bargaining. The act also empowered the president to raise or lower tariffs by 50 percent and enabled him to move goods on and off the duty-free list.

Latin America fit neatly into the plan because it did not have a competitive industrial sector, nor did its major exports— flaxseed, cane sugar, cocoa, castor beans, bananas, crude rubber, manganese, bauxite, and platinum—compete with U.S. commodities. In comparison, the United States was in a stronger bargaining position because it could serve as Latin America's chief supplier of manufactured goods, and, given the fact that reciprocal trade agreements favored the principal supplier, tariff negotiations would focus only on those products that constituted the chief source of supply. Because the United States practiced the most-favored-nation principle, it meant that if tariffs were lowered on Brazilian coffee or Guatemalan bananas, the same tariff reductions applied to all other suppliers. In sum, the act placed the State Department in a nonconcessionary negotiating position. Although several agreements were signed with Latin American countries, they failed to break existing trade barriers. Each side contributed to the program's failure. In Washington, the State Department lacked Hull's enthusiasm, while the Latin Americans continued to favor bilateral agreements with the Germans, British, and Japanese. World War II changed that. The world market closed to the Western Hemisphere.

Despite the storm clouds that steadily increased over Europe and Asia during the 1930s, the Latin Americans did not share the U.S. concern with German, Italian, and, to a lesser degree, Japanese influence in Latin America. The United States first raised the question of hemispheric defense at the Buenos Aires Conference in 1936, when it sought a hemispheric embargo on trade with belligerents. But led by Argentine Foreign Minister Carlos Saavedra Llamas, the Latin Americans accepted only an innocuous agreement to consult when an emergency arose that affected the common defense of the hemisphere.

At the Lima Conference two years later, after Austria and Czechoslovakia had succumbed to Nazi Germany, Spain had come under control of Francisco Franco, and China was engaged in a life-or-death struggle with Japan, the United States still was unable to convince the Latin Americans of the need for mutual defense. While some remained unconvinced of the danger, others charged that Washington was using Germany's aggression in Europe as a backdoor entrance to their internal affairs. Thus, the Latin Americans approved only the establishment of consultative machinery to respond to the threat of any extrahemispheric threat. The Latin Americans still remained hesitant after Hitler's invasion of Poland in September 1939 and the subsequent outbreak of total war. Not until the fall of France in 1940 did the Latin Americans agree to the U.S.-enforced three-hundred-mile-wide security belt around the hemisphere. They also accepted a U.S. proposal to occupy European colonies in the Western Hemisphere in order to save them from the Axis powers, and they approved a series of measures to combat fifth-column activities in their countries.

Given Latin America's lack of interest and preparedness, the United States acted alone. Its military planners drew their line of defense at a line north of the equator to secure the Caribbean and Panama Canal. With Europe engulfed in war, the United States determined to establish military missions in each Latin American country to improve the hemisphere's defense capabilities. The 1940 Uruguayan pact became the model. It provided for U.S. funds to construct facilities that remained under the host country's control, but open to the use of all hemispheric nations engaged in the common defense. To carry out military assistance and the construction of defense sites, Latin America was included in the Lend-Lease Act approved by Congress in March 1941. Some $400 million was allocated to Latin America over a three-year period, but only $171.7 million was delivered through May 1945, one month after the European war theater closed. The military assistance emphasized the strengthening of the southern defenses, particularly of the Caribbean and Brazil, and the development and protection of vital military and supply routes by air and water.

Not all Latin American governments quickly joined the Allied cause. Immediately after the Pearl Harbor attack, the five Central American countries, Cuba, and the Dominican Republic declared war on the Axis powers. By March 1942, all but Chile and Argentina had at least severed relations with the Axis countries. Chile demurred, owing to its long, defenseless, coastline. In Argentina, pro-Fascist military officers dominated politics, and they refused to bow to American pressure. Throughout the war, the Latin American nations, save Argentina and Chile, cooperated in stamping out Axis (particularly Nazi) influence by exploiting essential raw materials and by producing war goods for the Allied cause. Brazil, Colombia, Mexico, and Venezuela benefited the most, and the Caribbean and Central American states the least. In fact, Mexico's postwar industrial boom was jump-started by the infusion of U.S. capital during the war. Finally, in 1943, the Chileans succumbed to U.S. pressure and broke relations with the Axis powers. Argentina held out until the inter-American conference at Mexico City in 1945, when a deal was struck to permit its entrance into the United Nations. But Washington's distaste for Argentina's pro-Fascist military leaders prompted Ambassador Spruille Braden to labor unsuccessfully against the election of Juan Perón in 1945. The affair served to embitter U.S.-Argentine relations for some time.

Unfortunately for the Latin Americans, Washington made no plans for postwar economic adjustment. Wartime contracts and subsidies were abruptly canceled. Despite pleas from Latin American political leaders, Washington neglected to address the economic and social dislocations, in contradistinction to what it did with the European Recovery Program (popularly known as the Marshall Plan). Instead, the United States focused on incorporating Latin America into its cold war containment policies, which anticipated Soviet-inspired global expansion. By the Act of Chapultepec, signed in Mexico City in 1945, the American republics agreed to consult before responding to aggressive acts upon any hemispheric nation. Two years later, at Rio de Janeiro, the United States and Latin America agreed, in accordance with individual constitutional requirements, to act jointly in case of an external attack upon one nation. At Bogotá in 1948, the Inter-American Defense Board was established and charged with developing hemispheric defense plans. Finally, in 1951, following six years of debate, the U.S. Congress approved the Mutual Security Act, which initially appropriated $38 million for direct military assistance to Latin America for its participation in hemispheric defense. Through these measures, the United States sought to secure the Western Hemisphere from an external attack, something Washington policymakers considered most remote.

During the same period, 1945-1951, administration spokesmen —Secretaries of State George C. Marshall and Dean Acheson and Assistant Secretary of State for Latin American Affairs Edward G. Miller - continued to espouse traditional themes regarding inter-American relations: pleas for political stability and faith in democracy and promises of nonintervention in Latin America's internal affairs. While preaching such lofty ideals, the United States ignored many Latin Americans' demands for an end to dictatorship and an improvement in the quality of life for the less fortunate. Washington focused its attention on the Communist threat in Europe and Asia.

✴SUPPRESSING COMMUNISM: U.S.-LATIN AMERICAN RELATIONS SINCE 1954

In the immediate postwar years, U.S. policymakers were quick to compare demands for political and social change in Latin America with the activities of Communist movements in Europe and Asia. For example, during the 1948 Bogotá conference, when Colombia was wracked by violence, Secretary of State George C. Marshall placed responsibility with the Communists and cautioned that all of Latin America could be victimized. In reality, the violence stemmed from local political passions. That same year, Washington officials did not fully comprehend the nationalistic inclinations of the Costa Rican Civil War, in which José Figueres declared that he had saved the country from communism.

The most striking example of confusing the Communist-nationalist issue came in Guatemala in 1954. Historically, Guatemala's political history had been dominated by strong rulers with the support of the landed elite. At the beginning of the twentieth century, the United Fruit Company (UFCO) was formed and emerged as the dominant economic force in the country. Over time, UFCO and its leaders developed an informal alliance with the elite that prevented the lower socioeconomic groups from advancing economically and socially and denied them political and civil rights. The liberal accomplishments by 1920 and the management opportunities created by UFCO contributed to the development of a broad-based middle sector, which, influenced by U.S. democratic propaganda during World War II, forced the ouster of the last liberal dictator, Jorge Ubico, in 1944. At first, the democratic election of Juan José Arévalo appeared as a triumph for the middle sector. Arévalo's "spiritual socialism," however, promised economic and social justice for the lower classes at the expense of

the elite and the middle sector, prompting the latter to distance themselves from Arévalo. Given this vacuum, Arévalo brought local Communists into government positions. In 1950, when the presidential sash passed to Jacobo Arbenz, Guatemala's leftward political drift accelerated and the alleged influence of Communists in government increased. Arbenz's determination to implement a land reform program that called for the redistribution of idle lands held by the Guatemalan elite and UFCO proved to be his downfall.

Arbenz's actions came at a time when the United States was whipped into an anti-Communist hysteria by the Soviet victories in Europe, the fall of China to Mao Tse-tung, the stalemate in Korea, the anti-Communist moral crusade of President Dwight D. Eisenhower and Secretary of State John Foster Dulles, and the trauma of Senator Joseph McCarthy's Communist witch-hunt. In 1953, Milton Eisenhower and the Commission on Foreign Economic Policy recommended policy changes that gave hope for new directions in Latin American relations. Instead, the president accepted the advice of his closest advisers, businessmen who looked at the world as something that could be managed and who were advocates of private enterprise in a world increasingly turning toward revolution and socialism. Assistant Secretaries of State for Latin American Affairs John M. Cabot, Henry F. Holland, and Roy R. Rubottom echoed similar thoughts. Thus, the United States advised Latin American countries to create an environment conducive to private investment, and, if that was accomplished, the United States would provide funds for the necessary infrastructure.

Compatible with this approach, Secretary Dulles's strident anti-Communist campaign applied to Latin America. According to Dulles, communism, or anything that resembled it, was a threat to U.S. interests. Communists, however identified, were linked to the Soviet Union and viewed as agents of the international Communist conspiracy against the United States. In Guatemala, the Arbenz reform program paralleled what the Communists had done in Eastern Europe and on mainland China. Thus, at the tenth Inter-American Conference meeting in Caracas, Venezuela, in March 1954, Dulles warned that the hemisphere was imperiled by international communism. In response, the Guatemalan representative, Guillermo Toriello, charged that U.S. economic imperialism was responsible for the hemisphere's social and economic injustices. After a spirited debate, the conference adopted a U.S.-sponsored resolution asserting that any hemispheric nation subjected to Communist political control was considered suffering from foreign intervention and a threat to the peace of the Americas. As such, decisive collective action was called for, presumably under the terms of the 1947 Rio Treaty. What the delegates did not know was that the United States had already begun to plan the overthrow of Arbenz.

Without evidence of a clear link to Moscow, the Eisenhower administration began to plot the overthrow of Arbenz in the early summer of 1953. The Central Intelligence Agency (CIA) trained a ragtag army of about 300 men under Colonel Castillo Armas in Honduras and Nicaragua, while at the same time conducting a propaganda campaign inside Guatemala to convince Arbenz that the rebel force was much larger. A shipment of Czechoslovakian small arms to the Arbenz regime on June 18, 1954, became the trigger to action. That same day, Castillo Armas entered Guatemala from Honduras with 150 men, and the U.S. embassy in Guatemala City was turned into an operations center. From the embassy, Ambassador John Puerifoy directed the air assault, and the CIA jammed the Guatemalan airwaves with its own reports of a purported massive invasion by an army of liberation. At the same time, the State Department successfully worked to keep the United Nations and the Organization of American States from intervening in the affair. Arbenz succumbed on June 27 and fled the country. An interim government served until the September presidential election of Castillo Armas. In effect, the United States prevented the advance of the alleged international Communist movement from the Western Hemisphere.

The Latin American nations heaped an avalanche of criticism on the United States for its singlehanded intervention in the domestic affairs of an American republic. But these same governments also maintained that deep-rooted economic and social problems, not communism, threatened their political fabric. Yet, neither U.S. foreign policy nor Latin American domestic policies were aimed at correcting those disparities. Before the decade was out, these issues again surfaced in Cuba.

Throughout the 1950s, the Eisenhower administration indiscriminately granted military assistance to governments that demonstrated a favorable attitude toward the United States and expressed opposition to communism. Such actions contributed to the charge that the United States supported right-wing dictatorships that gave the illusion of stability in Latin America. That illusion was shattered in 1958 during Vice President Richard Nixon's eight-nation goodwill tour of Latin America. Early on, he encountered student demonstrators protesting alleged U.S. economic imperialism and support of repressive governments. But in Caracas, Venezuela, violence threatened his life. In response, Eisenhower put marines and paratroopers on alert as Nixon sought refuge in the U.S. embassy until the Venezuelan military gained control of the civilian disorders. Without proof, Eisenhower, Dulles, and his brother Allen (head of the CIA) publicly charged that local Communists at Moscow's direction instigated the riots. Privately, they admitted that they had no evidence of a Moscow connection. For the Latin American governments, Eisenhower's preparedness for military intervention gave recall to gunboat diplomacy.

Of greater significance was the rise of Fidel Castro to power in Cuba. Since Cuban independence in 1898, the connection between Cuba and the United States had tightened. North American investment on the island multiplied so much that U.S. private enterprise dominated the sugar industry, transportation, tourism, and the illegal operations in gambling, prostitution, and the like. The privileged position of the Cuban elite also depended on the North American presence. Ever since the "Sergeants Revolt" in 1933, Fulgencio Batista had increased his hold on the country's political apparatus. He controlled presidential elections, dismissed the national congress at will, and brutally suppressed political opposition. In so doing, Batista constructed a powder keg in which both the lower and middle sectors had reason to displace him. They found their catalyst to change in Fidel Castro, a young lawyer who in the early 1950s protested against Batista's political tyranny. Exiled for such activities in 1953, Castro went to Mexico, where he built a rebel force that returned to the island in 1956 to conduct a guerrilla war against Batista. With safe haven provided by the rural poor in the mountains and with financial support from the middle sector for the purchase of arms and other supplies, Castro successfully chipped away at Batista's power until January 1, 1959, when the dictator fled the country and Castro marched into the capital. For the moment, most Cubans and North Americans were happy with the change.

Over the next year, however, Castro moved to consolidate his hold on the nation. He slowly eliminated his political opposition, confiscated property (including North American-owned firms), and implemented social programs that benefited only the poor. Given these conditions, Cuban elites, fearing the loss of all their wealth, and the middle sector became disillusioned at the loss of democracy and fled the island The Eisenhower administration fretted over the drift leftward and Castro's failure to compensate the North American companies. When Castro demanded a drastic reduction in the size of the U.S. embassy staff in Havana, Eisenhower imposed a trade embargo against Cuba in hopes that Castro would conform to U.S. wishes. But Castro did not bend and,

Fidel Castro.

in fact, spoke of spreading his revolution elsewhere in the Americas. Near the end of the Eisenhower administration, the president gave his approval for yet another CIA plot. Cuban exiles were assembled in Guatemala and Nicaragua to prepare for an invasion of their homeland.

The invasion of Cuba was left for President-elect John F. Kennedy. When the invasion began at the Bay of Pigs in April 1961, there were hopes that the people within Cuba would rise against Castro and, in combination with the invading brigade, force Castro's ouster. But when the plan went awry, Kennedy called off badly needed air cover, leaving the Cuban exiles at Castro's mercy. The Bay of Pigs invasion marked a key turning point in Castro's career. Isolated in the Western Hemisphere, Castro found the essential economic support in Moscow that shortly made Cuba a Soviet client state. In 1962, Khrushchev decided to test the long-standing U.S. defense perimeter in the Caribbean region. He not only introduced Soviet troops to the island but also directed the construction of surface-to-air missile (SAM) sites. At first, the Kennedy administration dismissed the construction reports that came from the exiled Cuban community in the United States

because it was the same group that promised an internal uprising at the Bay of Pigs. But when U.S. intelligence planes confirmed the reports, Kennedy quickly acted. He imposed a quarantine on the introduction of offensive weapons into Cuba and clearly indicated that it would be enforced. For thirteen days in October 1962, the world appeared poised on the brink of nuclear war between the superpowers before Khrushchev backed off. A subsequent agreement provided the removal of the Soviet missiles from Cuba in return for a promise that the United States would not support an invasion of the island.

In the aftermath of Kennedy's death, the United States determined that economic coercion would ruin Cuba and destroy Castro. The U.S. economic blockade of Cuba became hemispheric policy, and in July 1964 at an OAS foreign ministers' meeting in Washington, the delegates voted to sever diplomatic and commercial relations with Cuba, except in food and medicine, and to impose restrictions on travel to Cuba. The Latin American governments went along with U.S. policy because many of them feared a similar revolution themselves.

Nixon's nearly disastrous trip and Castro's success ignited a policy change for the United States, and in Latin America the elite momentarily became more responsive to the need for economic and social change. Late in the Eisenhower administration, Secretary of Treasury C. Douglas Dillon convinced the president to propose the establishment of a hemispheric social progress fund, which Congress subsequently approved. In September 1960, Dillon announced at an OAS meeting a $500 million Social Progress Trust Fund to provide "soft" loans for housing, land settlement and use, water supply, sanitation, and similar social purposes. John F. Kennedy went a step further during the 1960 presidential campaign when he asserted that a joint effort was needed to develop the hemispheric resources, strengthen the democratic forces, and improve the vocational and educational opportunities of every person in the Americas. Kennedy intended to foster a social revolution within a democratic framework by appealing to the lower and middle social groups.

At the White House, before the Latin American diplomatic corps on March 13, 1961 - during the same week that 139 years before President James Monroe had urged U.S. recognition of Latin American independence - Kennedy announced the Alliance for Progress, an ambitious $100 billion, ten-year program to bring political reform and social and economic progress to the Southern Hemisphere. As expressed in the Charter of Punte del Este, the alliance called for 2.5 percent annual economic growth rate, a more equitable distribution of national wealth, trade diversification, emphasis on industrialization, greater agricultural productivity, an end to illiteracy, agrarian reform, increased life expectancy, public housing for the poor, stable price levels, tax reform, and economic development. All these were to be carried out within the processes of political democracy. The alliance failed to achieve its lofty goals, in part because the Latin American elites that controlled the government apparatus resisted social change, tax reform, and democratization, and in part, because the United States lost its idealism as the quagmire in Vietnam and domestic violence engulfed its energies. By 1971, there were few signs of improvement in the quality of life for the masses, and most of the Latin American governments had come under military control.

Despite Kennedy's idealism, he did not lose sight of the Communist military threat. From 1945 to 1961, U.S. military assistance programs to Latin America focused on the prevention of an external attack, security of the Panama Canal and Caribbean sea-lanes, and Mexican and Venezuelan oil. Kennedy altered the emphasis to a concentration on internal aggression. The 1961 Military Assistance Program demon-

Archbishop Oscar Romero of El Salvador. (Courtesy of the *Texas Catholic Herald*.)

strated the new emphasis by replacing heavy equipment with mobile light equipment and training troops in counterinsurgency. In its broadest sense, counterinsurgency included a wide range of economic, political, social, psychological, and military activities utilizing several U.S. government agencies. For example, the Agency for International Development (AID) was charged with responsibility for economic programs, and its Office of Public Safety with the training of police forces in interrogation and riot control. The United States Information Agency (USIA) worked with governments to improve the U.S. image both at home and abroad. The CIA engaged in intelligence, covert, and paramilitary activities. U.S. military missions provided training, advice, and supplies to the local armed forces. Emphasis was placed on "civic action" programs that were intended to stimulate counterinsurgency, nation building, and economic development by improving the image of the local military, which would now undertake the construction of bridges, hospitals, and schools, serve as medics for rural civilians, and clear jungle terrain for establishment of small farms. By the time of Kennedy's death, however, it became apparent that the counterinsurgency program had lost its idealistic direction. The military began to assert its independence as it often moved against the non-Communist Left. This was most vivid in Guatemala, where the army turned on rural Indian villages and by the 1970s brought the warfare to the capital at Guatemala City.

As other events demanded more U.S. attention, Presidents Lyndon B. Johnson, Richard M. Nixon, and Gerald R. Ford gave little attention to Latin American affairs, except for isolated incidents of alleged Communist expansion. In March 1964, Johnson signaled his policy change with the appointment of Thomas C. Mann as assistant secretary of state for Latin American affairs. Mann explained that the United States would give greater attention to its own security interests, its investments, and its desire to thwart communism in the hemisphere rather than attempt to promote democracy. Nixon entered the White House in 1969 without a clearly defined Latin American policy. Despite warnings that U.S. military assistance programs had contributed to the increased political role of the military in Latin American politics, Nixon, motivated by profit, not constitutionalism, obtained congressional approval to increase arms sales to the region. In 1974, Ford ignored the recommendation of a twenty-three member commission that the United States deemphasize hemispheric security as an issue of primary consideration and place greater attention on political and economic relations. Two events, one during Johnson's administration and the other under Nixon, clearly reflected the policy's determinant factor.

Following the assassination of Dominican Republic strongman Rafael Trujillo in 1961, the country was administered by Juan Bosch. In the spirit of the newfound freedom, Bosch permitted the Communists to organize in hope of preventing them from mounting a guerrilla war. Washington opposed the co-opting; and so too did the Dominican generals who ousted Bosch in 1963. The generals installed a triumvirate headed by Donald Reid Cabral. His subsequent austerity measures satisfied Washington's foreign economic policies, but not the Dominican business and professional leaders and the country's socially conscious elements. Soon strikes and demonstrations disrupted the nation. In this environment, a group of younger officers called for the restoration of constitutional order and looked to Bosch as their leader. When they ousted Reid Cabral in April 1965 and announced Bosch's imminent return, Washington officials and the old-line generals feared that Bosch would permit a Communist takeover of the country. In this tense atmosphere, the competing factions exchanged gunfire, prompting President Johnson to dispatch marines, ostensibly to protect U.S. lives and property, but in Johnson's mind to prevent another Cuba. Johnson justified his actions on the grounds, subsequently learned to be exaggerated, that the Communists had already infiltrated the revolution. The unilateral action brought a storm of protest from the Latin American nations. Even the subsequent placement of an OAS peacekeeping force in the country did not stem the protest. Eventually, an election was arranged, and Joaquín Balaguer was chosen to guide the U.S.-controlled democratic experiment.

The Dominican experience owed much to the end of the Trujillo regime, but the Chilean experience was quite different. With a long history of political democracy, the system had evolved into coalition politics after World War II, effectively negating the government's opportunity to implement necessary social reform for the urban and rural poor. This void provided the opportunity for a popular coalition front, FRAP, led by a self-proclaimed Marxist, Salvador Allende, to make inroads. As the country stagnated in the late 1950s and early 1960s, Allende's popularity increased. He nearly captured the 1964 presidential contest. Six years later he did, becoming the first freely elected Marxist head of state in Latin America. In Richard Nixon's view, Allende's victory not only threatened U.S. interests in Chile but also served as a symbolic challenge to U.S. political stature elsewhere on the continent.

Allende intended to socialize the economy. He began by nationalizing, without compensation, the largest symbol of U.S. presence in the country, the copper industries. Subsequently, the government intervened in other segments of the foreign-dominated economy. In an appeal to labor, Allende froze prices and decreed hefty wage increases. He implemented an agrarian reform program. Subsequently, he attempted to change the national legislature to one that represented the masses rather than the elite. Such programs prompted wholesale opposition from the foreign-owned companies, the Chilean landowners, the middle sector, and eventually the workers themselves, who could not keep up with inflationary prices for scarce goods. Allende did not help his own image when he invited Fidel Castro to visit Cuba and when he reached a barter trade agreement with mainland China. Nixon's policies exacerbated the situation. He severed U.S trade relations, forbade private bank loans, and used U.S. influence to prevent financial arrangements with the Inter-American and World Banks. Soon the country was beset by political protest, labor discord, and a general strike that led to Allende's ouster by the military in September 1973. In the violence of the coup, Allende lost his life. While the evidence to date does not support the argument that the Nixon administration played a direct role in Allende's overthrow, the administration's policies contributed to the worsening economic conditions that led to the overthrow.

Augusto Pinochet's repressive government in Chile paralleled the experiences of several other Latin American countries in the 1970s and 1980s. Brutal authoritarian regimes were found in Argentina, Brazil, Peru, and El Salvador. In its anxiety to rid their nations of Communists, the military arrested, tortured, exiled, and killed thousands of individuals on the slightest suspicion. Political and civil rights were denied. The U.S. Congress quickly responded to these violations. Provisions in the 1973 Foreign Assistance Act, 1975 Food Assistance Act, and 1976 Security Assistance authorized the withholding of aid wherever human rights violations existed. No action was taken until Jimmy Carter moved into the White House in January 1977. He brought with him a commitment to the improvement of human rights not found among his immediate predecessors. Through his assistant secretary of state for Latin American affairs, Terence A. Toddman, Carter made it clear that future U.S assistance would be contingent on improvement in human rights conditions. Subsequently, the administration singled out Argentina, Brazil, Chile, El Salvador, and Guatemala for aid cutoffs. Unfortunately, the aid cutoff did not prevent those governments from securing military assistance elsewhere.

Carter also came to the presidency promising a

new era in U.S.-Latin American relations. His intense efforts on behalf of the new canal treaties with Panama in 1977 dramatized that effort. The canal symbolized the highest form of U.S. imperialism in the hemisphere. The Canal Zone, which divided the nation, resembled U.S. suburbia and contrasted greatly with the poverty and injustice that characterized life for most Panamanians. The 1977 treaties provided for turning the canal operation over to Panama in the year 2000. While the Latin Americans applauded Carter's work, the treaties deeply divided the North Americans. Before the Senate's ratification of the accords, a prolonged debate gripped the nation. Carter's supporters argued that the canal could no longer be defended and that it was of decreased economic and military importance. His opponents viewed the treaties as a sign of weakness, the surrender of a U.S.-owned canal and concomitant rights. The critics incorrectly asserted that the United States owned the Canal Zone. The 1903 treaty never granted ownership.

If Carter offered a new hope to the Latin Americans at the start of his administration, he faced a crisis of the old order in Central America before it ended. In Nicaragua and El Salvador leftist guerrilla movements - the Sandinista National Liberation Front and the Farabundo Martí National Liberation Front (FMLN) - had gained much strength in the 1970s. In Nicaragua they challenged Anastasio Somoza, whose family power dated to the 1930s, and in El Salvador the infamous "14 families," who dominated the nation's economic, political, and social structures. At first, Carter expressed a degree of sympathy toward these movements, as they appeared to address the needs of the downtrodden. He resisted Somoza's appeal for support, and only near the end, in May and June 1979, did Carter attempt to broker a settlement. He was too late. Once in power, the Sandinistas moved leftward on the political scale. In actions parallel to Castro in Cuba and Allende in Chile, the Sandinistas nationalized properties, dictated economic policies for the private sector, opened trade with Eastern Europe, curtailed civil rights, and stymied political opposition. His idealism shattered, Carter directed the funding of political opposition groups in Nicaragua before leaving his own presidency.

In October 1979, El Salvador appeared on the verge of civil war when a group of young officers engineered a coup that ousted President Carlos Humberto Romero. The new junta promised an improvement in human rights and an agrarian reform package. But the violence continued as illustrated by the bloodbath that followed the assassination of Archbishop Oscar Romero. Nor was there any agrarian

Guerrillas of El Frente Farabundo Martí por la Liberación Nacional (FMLN) in El Salvador.

reform. Late in 1980, Carter lifted the U.S. ban on military assistance so that the Salvadoran government could suppress the violence and implement the agrarian reform package.

Central America appeared on the verge of self-destruction when Ronald Reagan arrived in Washington in January 1980. Reagan was convinced that the malaise of the Carter administration had contributed to a loss of U.S. global prestige and had permitted an advance of international communism. For Latin America, the Reagan administration put its affairs into the context of the East-West struggle, denying that such long-standing issues as the disparity of wealth, deprivation of social mobility, and restriction of political rights were responsible for the contemporary protest and violence. Instead, Reagan argued that the Soviet Union, through its Cuban proxies, capitalized on these issues to vault into political power local Marxists, who would destroy the economies and offer no hope for political reform. From these Communist outposts, Moscow threatened U.S. interests. Human rights became a policy of the past as military, not economic and social, solutions received first consideration.

Within this context, Reagan determined to maintain Central America's old order, except in Nicaragua, where he intended to restore it. To carry out this policy, Honduras was turned into an American military outpost, over $300 million in military aid was supplied to the government in El Salvador for its battle against the FMLN, and the Nicaraguan contras were supported in a counterrevolution designed to oust the Sandinistas from power. The policy soon became unpopular, both in the United States and in Central and South America. The U.S. public and Congress debated the righteousness of an armed solution to an indigenous problem and whether the Soviets had any real interest in these conflicts other than supporting the opposition to the United States. In Central America, the Guatemalan government refused to be drawn in for fear of becoming a victim of U.S. interference in its internal affairs. Costa Rica, long aloof to isthmian violence, also resisted Reagan's advances in order to maintain its neutrality. Colombia, Mexico, Panama, and Venezuela joined together in the so-called Contadora process in an effort to find a diplomatic solution to the crisis. All these factors led to a U.S. congressional cutoff of assistance to the contras in 1987. Without U.S. support, the movement waffled, and Costa Rican president Oscar Arias seized the moment to fashion a Central American peace plan. The process was accelerated after February 1990, when the ballot box accomplished what U.S. policy did not— removal of the Sandinistas from power in Nicaragua.

As much as the Central American crisis revived cries of gunboat diplomacy, two other incidents reinforced the perception. Grenada, an island nation of about 110,000 people at the western end of the Antilles, had gained its independence from Great Britain in 1974. Its initial prime minister, Eric Gairy, was overthrown in 1979 by the leftist-leaning New Jewell movement headed by Maurice Bishop. When Bishop identified with the world Socialist movement, the Reagan administration promptly cut off all aid. Bishop visited Washington in 1982 but failed to alter Reagan's course. In the meantime, Bishop had secured Soviet and Cuban assistance for the construction of a runway capable of handling jumbo jets, which Bishop argued were essential for developing the island's tourist industry. U.S. policymakers thought otherwise. They viewed the airstrip as stopover point for Cuban planes going to and from Africa and for Soviet aircraft to threaten the Caribbean sea routes and the Panama Canal. At the same time, Grenada's political rivalries led to the assassination of Bishop and the emergence of a more leftist faction of the New Jewell movement. Washington panicked. Under the guise of rescuing U.S. medical students

from the deteriorating situation on the island, Reagan ordered the invasion of the island on October 25, 1983. Like Lyndon Johnson before him, Reagan determined not to have another Cuba in the Caribbean. And like Woodrow Wilson seventy years earlier, Reagan intended to teach the Grenadians to elect good men and in the process prevent the completion of the ten-thousand-foot runway. The discovery of Soviet and North Korean advisers along with the Cubans and a large arms cache after the invasion was used to justify the U.S. action. Although Reagan subsequently explained that he was invited to act by the Association of Eastern Caribbean nations, in fact the planning for the attack came the day after Bishop's death, and the request for U.S. assistance was drafted in Washington. This explanation was received well only in the United States. Most Latin Americans paralleled the incident to Eisenhower's in Guatemala, particularly when the Reagan administration successfully labored to prevent the United Nations and the Organization of American States from taking any action.

Ever since Great Britain seized the Falklands/Malvinas Islands off the Atlantic coast of Argentina in 1832, the government at Buenos Aires has unsuccessfully sought hemispheric solidarity and the application of the Monroe Doctrine to remove the British from the islands. By 1982 internal factors prompted the Argentine military government to take aggressive action. A decade of repressive government produced political protest amidst a deteriorating economic situation. To divert the public's attention from these issues, Leopoldo Galtieri decided to seize the islands. He believed that the British, more concerned with European affairs, had lost interest in the Falklands/Malvinas, and he also thought that the United States would be neutral because the Argentine army was training the U.S.-backed contras. Despite admonitions to the contrary by Secretary of State Alexander Haig, Galtieri went ahead with the invasion in May 1982. When the British reacted militarily, the United States provided intelligence assistance and refueling of the Royal Navy en route to the South Atlantic. When the crisis was over, the British retained the islands, Galtieri was forced from office, and the United States suffered another setback in its relations with Latin America.

As the cold war came to an end, Reagan's policies made Latin Americans wonder if the United States had returned to the tactics of an earlier era. The Bush administration gave further credence to that impression by its invasion of Panama in December 1989, its apparent willingness to use U.S. force to curb the drug problem at its source of supply in Colombia, Peru, and Bolivia, and its proposed hemispheric free

Demonstrators on the U.S. capitol steps opposing U.S. military aid to El Salvador in 1980. (Courtesy of the *Texas Catholic Herald*.)

trade zone that smacked of "dollar diplomacy." The Bush administration has not aggressively addressed other key issues that disrupt society: a staggering collective Latin America debt of nearly $500 billion and the economic and social disparities that tear at the fabric of Latin American society. Yet, the absence of the United States has provided the Latin American governments the opportunity to work more harmoniously toward a solution to their own problems. As democratically elected governments returned to Latin America in the 1980s, there appeared a greater willingness to address issues on a regional basis. Clearly, as the world moves toward the twenty-first century, inter-American relations are embarking upon a new era.

References

Connel-Smith, Gordon. *The United States and Latin-America: An Historical Analysis of Inter-American Relations.* New York: Wiley, 1974.

Gil, Federico. *Latin American-United States Relations.* New York: Harcourt Brace Jovanovich, 1975.

Kryzanek, Michael. *U.S.-Latin American Relations.* New York: Praeger, 1985.

Leonard, Thomas M. *Central America and the United States: the Search for Stability.* Claremont, California: Regina Books, 1985.

Leonard, Thomas M. *The United States and Central America, 1944-1949: Perceptions of Political Dynamics.* Tuscaloosa: University of Alabama Press, 1984.

Lowenthal, Abraham. *Partners In Conflict: The United States and Latin America.* Baltimore: John Hopkins University Press, 1987.

Mecham, J. Lloyd. *A Survey of United States-Latin American Relations.* Boston: Houghton, 1965.

Stuart, Graham H., and James L. Tigner. *Latin America and the United States,* 6th ed. Englewood Cliffs, N.J.: Prentice Hall, 1975.

Thomas Leonard

7

Population Growth and Distribution

✴ Census Bureau Statistics and the Hispanic Population
✴ Demographics ✴ Hispanic Diversity

In the last twenty-five years Hispanics have received a great deal of attention and have become part of the national consciousness, for several reasons. One is the rapid increase in the size of the Hispanic population. As can be seen from the statistics presented in this chapter, Hispanics are increasing at a much higher rate than the total population and are expected to become the nation's largest minority group sometime early in the next century.

A second reason for the increased attention is immigration to the United States, especially undocumented migration from Mexico. The size of the immigrant population and its effects on society have been intensely debated. The political turmoil in Central America, especially in El Salvador, has added to the debate as Central Americans have migrated to the United States to escape the crises in their countries.

The bilingual-bicultural movement has also focused attention on Hispanic demands that society's institutions, especially those devoted to education, develop programs in Spanish as well as in English to meet their needs and reflect their culture. These programs are controversial among many non-Hispanics.

A fourth reason for the expanded awareness of Hispanics is the economic and political power that Hispanics have gained as their numbers have grown. The sheer size of the Hispanic population makes it an important economic group in areas where Hispanics are concentrated. Hispanics are also an important voting bloc and now elect members of their own to political positions in states such as Florida, California, Texas, New Mexico, and New York. In other states Hispanics play an important role in electing non-Hispanics to office.

These issues, among others, are pushing many Hispanic concerns to the forefront, and for many observers of American society portend a national minority group whose economic, political, and social influence can only continue to increase.

✴ CENSUS BUREAU STATISTICS AND THE HISPANIC POPULATION

Most of the statistics presented in this chapter are taken from U.S. Census Bureau publications. Census Bureau information about Hispanics is controversial because of undercounting, the criteria used to identify Hispanics, and the presence of undocumented immigrants.

Generally speaking, persons from the working class tend to be undercounted to a greater degree than others. Since most Hispanics tend to be working-class, they are likely to be affected disproportionately by an undercount. The Census Bureau estimates that approximately 5.8 percent of the total Hispanic population, or 1.2 million people, were not counted in the 1990 census.

The criteria used by the Census Bureau to identify the Hispanic population has changed over time. Such categories as foreign birth or parentage, Spanish mother tongue, Spanish language, Spanish surname, and Spanish heritage are some of the ways in which Hispanics have been identified since 1850. These different identifiers make it difficult to make comparisons over time because they do not precisely define the same population. Also, the various definitions have not always been used on a national basis. The Spanish surname criteria, for example, was restricted to the five southwestern states of Texas, New Mexico,

199

Arizona, Colorado, and California, where Mexican Americans constitute the main Hispanic group. Currently the Census Bureau uses a self-identification method. Persons are asked if they are of Spanish or Hispanic origin. If they answer yes, they are then asked to identify themselves as Mexican, Mexican American, Chicano, Puerto Rican, Cuban, or other Spanish/Hispanic origin.

The presence of undocumented immigrants is an issue not only because of the debate over their economic and social impact because no one really knows how many reside in the United States. Estimates of their number have ranged from half a million to 12 million. The Census Bureau estimates that there were approximately 3.3 million undocumented immigrants in the United States in 1989. Undocumented migrants from Mexico constitute the largest portion of such immigrants, but there are other undocumented immigrants from other countries as well, but again no one knows precisely how many.

In addition to uncertainty over the size of the undocumented population, there is also uncertainty about its demographics. For instance, undocumented immigrants tend to be young males, but the proportion of young males, relative to females and older people is not known.

These problems with undercounting, identifying criteria, and undocumented immigrants indicate that census information about Hispanics should be interpreted cautiously. Nevertheless, despite the limitations, the Census Bureau is the main source of such information, and much can be learned about the Hispanic population from analyzing the data. Also, the Census Bureau continues to refine its counting and reporting techniques in order to ensure a more accurate count of not only the Hispanic population but other groups as well.

Demographics

Hispanics and Non-Hispanics: Growth Rate

The Hispanic population is growing at a faster rate than the non-Hispanic. Between 1980 and 1990, it increased by 53 percent, in comparison with only 6.7 percent for non-Hispanics.

In 1991, Hispanics numbered approximately 22 million people and composed approximately 9 percent of the total U.S. population of 249 million. If the number of undocumented Hispanic immigrants could be accurately counted, the growth rate and size of the Hispanic population would be greater.

Senior citizens at the Domino Park in Little Havana, Miami.

Undocumented workers entering the United States at El Paso, Texas, 1990. (Courtesy of the *Texas Catholic Herald*.)

The ten states with the largest increase in the number of Hispanics are California, Texas, New York, Florida, Illinois, New Jersey, Arizona, New Mexico, Colorado, and Massachusetts, in that order. The increase in the size of California's Hispanic population is particularly noteworthy. It increased dramatically, from approximately 4.5 million in 1980 to 7.6 million in 1990, or by 69 percent. This rate of increase exceeded the national Hispanic increase of 53 percent. The size of California's Hispanic population is in fact larger than the total population of all but nine states.

Factors in Population Growth

A population increases its size through net migration and natural increase. Net migration is the number of immigrants minus the number of emigrants. Natural increase is defined as the number of births minus the number of deaths. One-half of the growth rate among Hispanics is attributed to net migration and one-half to natural increase. In comparison, 21 percent of the increase in the number of non-Hispanics is attributed to net migration and 79 percent to natural increase. Again, the contribution

A group of Hispanics have just been issued their temporary residence cards, 1991. (Photo by Les Fetchko. Courtesy of the *Texas Catholic Herald*).

of net migration to the growth of the Hispanic population is probably greater because of the number of undocumented immigrants.

Population Predictions

At the current rates of growth, Hispanics will double in size by the year 2020 and will number

The drive to legalize undocumented workers in Houston, Texas. (Photo by Curtis Dowell. Courtesy of the *Texas Catholic Herald*.)

approximately 43 million people. Most of the growth rate will occur among those thirty-five years of age and older. In contrast, it will take the non-Hispanic population 160 years to double. Non-Hispanics may peak in size by the year 2020 and then begin to decline in relative as well as absolute numbers.

States with Large Hispanic Populations

The majority of Hispanics are concentrated in the five southwestern states of California, Colorado, New Mexico, Arizona, and Texas. Approximately 63 percent of the total U.S. Hispanic population reside in these five states. Four states outside the Southwest account for 26 percent of the Hispanic population: New York (12.3 percent), Florida (8 percent), Illinois (4 percent), and New Jersey. Puerto Ricans are the largest group in New York and New Jersey, and Cubans are the largest in Florida. Puerto Ricans and Mexican Americans are the largest groups in Illinois.

Hispanics are more geographically concentrated than the total population. Approximately 53 percent of the population lived in California and Texas in 1990. In comparison, a majority of the total population of the United States lived in nine states.

Age

Hispanics are younger than the non-Hispanic population. The median age of Hispanics is 26.2 years, compared with 33.8 years for non-Hispanics. Another indicator of the youthfulness of the Hispanic population is the relative number of people under five and fifteen years of age. Hispanics under age 5 make up 11 percent of the population, and people under age 15 make up 30 percent. Among non-Hispanics the respective figures are 22 percent and 7 percent.

Birth Rates

Hispanics are younger than non-Hispanics because they have a higher birthrate. The average number of children among Hispanics is 3.6, in comparison with 2.4 for non-Hispanics. The high birthrate of Hispanic women is emphasized when different age groups are considered. Hispanic women between ages 15 and 24 have 43 percent more children than non-Hispanic women of the same age group. Hispanic women between ages 25 and 34 have 30 percent more children than non-Hispanic women of the same age

A poster for National Migration Week, issued by the U.S. Catholic Conference.

group, and Hispanic women 35 to 44 have 29 percent more children than non-Hispanic women.

Educational Attainment

Educational attainment differences between Hispanics and non- Hispanics are glaring. Approximately 12.5 percent of Hispanics over age 25 have completed fewer than five years of education, compared with 1.6 percent for non-Hispanics. In regard to high school, 51.3 percent of Hispanic adults have a high school education, in comparison with 80.5 percent of non-Hispanics. Only 9.7 percent of Hispanics have a college education, in contrast to 27.3 percent of non-Hispanics.

Labor Force Participation

The civilian labor force is defined as persons sixteen years of age and over who are employed or are actively seeking employment. According to this criteria, 78 percent of Hispanic males and 51 percent of Hispanic females were in the labor force in March 1991. The respective figures for non-Hispanic males and females were 74 percent and 57 percent.

Occupation

The occupational status of Hispanics is not as high as that of non-Hispanics. Over twice as many non-Hispanic males (27.6 percent) hold managerial and professional jobs as do Hispanic males (11.4 percent). At the lower end of the occupational hierarchy, there are more Hispanics (29.1 percent) than non-Hispanics (19.1 percent) working as operators, fabricators, and laborers.

A similar picture emerges when the occupational distribution of Hispanic and non-Hispanic females is compared. Approximately 15.8 percent of Hispanic females in the labor force hold managerial and professional occupations,in contrast to 28 percent of non-Hispanic females. At the lower end, Hispanic females make up 14 percent of the operators, fabricators, and laborers, in comparison with 7.6 percent of non-Hispanic females.

Unemployment

Unemployment rates are also greater for Hispanics. In March 1991, the unemployment rate for Hispanic males was 10.6 percent, and 9.2 percent, for Hispanic females. The unemployment rate for non-Hispanic males and females was 7.8 percent and 5.9 percent, respectively.

Income

Given the relatively low educational-attainment level and occupational status of Hispanics, it is not surprising that they earn less income than non-Hispanics. The median family income of Hispanics is $23,400, in comparison with $36,300 for non-Hispanics, or 64 percent of the non-Hispanic median family income.

The median income of Hispanic males is $14,100, and $22,000 for non-Hispanic males. Hispanic males are earning 64 percent of what non-Hispanic males earn.

Hispanics females earn 81 percent of what non-Hispanic females earn. The median income figures are $10,100 for Hispanic females and $12,400 for non-Hispanic females.

Poverty

More Hispanic than non-Hispanic families live in poverty. According to 1990 U.S. Census income figures, 25 percent of all Hispanic families were classified as living in poverty, compared with 9.5 percent of non-Hispanic families. Further, 17 percent of the Hispanic families living in poverty were headed by persons sixty-five years of age or older, 48.3 percent were headed by females, and 35.7 percent of the heads of household were high school dropouts. The rates for

Mexican Independence Day Parade, Houston, Texas, 1982. (Photo by Curtis Dowell. Courtesy of the *Texas Catholic Herald*.)

non-Hispanic families were 9.5 percent, 31.7 percent, and 21.2 percent, respectively.

Hispanic Diversity

The Hispanic population is not a homogeneous group. It shares a common culture, but beyond this, the groups that make up the Hispanic population differ significantly in many important ways. The three major groups are Mexican Americans, Puerto Ricans, and Cubans. Other Hispanic groups are the Central and South Americans and people of various other Hispanic origins. There are major historical, cultural, and demographic differences between these groups.

History

The history of Mexicans, Puerto Ricans, and Cubans is radically different. The Spaniards conquered the Indians of Mexico, and by mating with them, produced the mestizo or Mexican people. Mexicans, therefore, have a strong Indian as well as Spanish heritage.

The islands of Cuba and Puerto Rico were also conquered by the Spaniards. Both islands were originally populated with the Arawak and Carib Indians, whom the Spaniards forced into slavery to work in the mines and fields in Puerto Rico and the sugarcane fields in Cuba. The Spaniards began importing slaves from Africa to Cuba and Puerto Rico, and eventually the African slaves outnumbered and began to marry into the Indian population. Thus, Cubans and Puerto Ricans not only have an Indian and Spanish heritage but a strong African ancestry as well.

Immigration

Immigration patterns to the United States are also different for Mexican Americans, Cubans, and Puerto Ricans. The number of people who migrated to the United States from Mexico was small prior to 1900. After 1900, Mexican immigration began to increase. The factors that stimulated emigration from Mexico were the Mexican Revolution, poor economic conditions, and a rapid increase in the size of the population. The primary factor which pulls Mexican immigrants to the United States today is the demand for cheap labor. Constant migration from Mexico means that within the Mexican American community there is always a large number of Mexican immigrants.

Prior to 1959, the number of Cubans who migrated to the United States was very small. In 1959, Fidel Castro overthrew the Fulgencio Batista dictatorship, declared Cuba a socialist state, and began implementing measures that outlawed private property and individuals' accumulation of large amounts of wealth. Many Cubans fled Cuba and immigrated to Florida. This was the first wave of Cubans to migrate, and the majority were educated professionals and skilled technicians. A second wave of Cubans migrated to the United States in 1980. Unlike the first wave, most of these immigrants were from the poorer classes and were not as welcome or as well treated.

As a result of these two immigration movements, the number of Cubans in the United States increased rapidly. In 1959, there were only 30,000 Cubans in the United States, and in 1991 there were 1.1 million. Cubans have become a major economic, political, and cultural force in Florida, especially in Miami, which has the largest concentration of Cubans in the United States.

The pattern of migration from Puerto Rico to the United States is different from that of either Mexico or Cuba. Puerto Rico became a possession of the United States in 1899, and Puerto Ricans were granted United States citizenship in 1917. Thus, Puerto Ricans who migrate to the United States are not considered immigrants in the same sense as Mexicans and Cubans. Prior to 1940, Puerto Ricans did not immigrate to the United States in large numbers. After World War II, the economy of Puerto Rico began to deteriorate, and migration to the United States increased and has been constant ever since. Today there are approximately 2.4 million Puerto Ricans 3.5 million living in the United States and 3.5 million living on the island of Puerto Rico.

Geographical Concentration

Mexican Americans, Puerto Ricans, and Cubans tend to reside in different parts of the United States. As previously mentioned, the majority of Mexican-origin people live in the five southwestern states of Texas, New Mexico, Colorado, Arizona, and California. Puerto Ricans tend to live in New York, New Jersey, and Illinois, while the majority of Cubans reside in Florida.

Age

Cubans are the oldest Hispanic population, and Mexican Americans are the youngest. The median age for Cubans is 39.3 years, in comparison with 24.3 years for Mexican. Puerto Ricans are also a young population, but not as young as Mexican Americans; their median age is 26.7 years.

Birthrates

Mexican Americans have the highest birthrate of the three groups, followed by Puerto Ricans and then Cubans. Mexican-American women between the ages of 35 and 44, for example, have given birth, on the average, to 3.6 children. The average for Puerto Rican women in the same age group is 3.2 children, and for Cuban women, 2.0 children. The Cuban average is even lower than the 2.6 average of the total U.S. population.

Education, Occupation, and Income

Cuban Americans are primarily a middle-class population with relatively high levels of education, occupational status, and income. Mexican Americans are primarily a working-class population holding blue-collar occupations and have low levels of education and income. Generally, Puerto Ricans rank in between Cubans and Mexican Americans, but are closer to Mexican Americans than Cubans in terms of their educational attainment, occupational status, and income.

The high educational level of Cubans is seen in the number of Cuban high school and college graduates: 61 percent have a high school education and approximately 19 percent have a college education. Among Puerto Ricans, 58 percent have a high school education and 10 percent have completed college. Among Mexican Americans, 44 percent have completed high school and only 6 percent are college graduates.

The high level of education among Cubans reflects the middle- class status of the Cubans who migrated to the United States in the early 1960s. Later generations of Cubans, however, are continuing to achieve high levels of education as well. Among Cubans ages 25 to 34, for example, approximately 78 percent are high school graduates and 20.4 percent have a college education.

Mexican-American males are in the labor force in a larger proportion than either Cuban or Puerto Rican males; 80 percent of all Mexican-American males over age 16 are participating in the nations's work force, in comparison with 73 percent of the Cuban and 66 percent of the Puerto Rican males. What Mexican American, Puerto Rican, and Cuban males have in common is being concentrated in the skilled and semiskilled occupations. Approximately 50 percent of all Mexican-American males and 43 percent of all Cuban and Puerto Rican males hold skilled and semiskilled occupations. Where the

A mass citizenship swearing in ceremony at Hoffheinz Pavilion of the University of Houston in 1987. (Photo by Curtis Dowell. Courtesy of the *Texas Catholic Herald*.)

groups differ is in managerial and professional and technical sales and administrative support occupations. Cubans hold more of these types of occupations than either Puerto Ricans or Mexican Americans.

There are more Cuban females in the labor force than either Puerto Rican or Mexican-American females. Approximately 55 percent of all Cuban females over age 16 are in the civilian labor force, compared with 42 percent of Puerto Rican females and 51 percent of Mexican American females.

The female occupational distribution resembles that of the males in that Cuban females have a higher occupational status than Puerto Rican and Mexican-American females. One significant difference is the higher proportion of Mexican-American females in service occupations. Approximately 27 percent of the Mexican-American females hold service occupations, compared with 16 percent of Puerto Rican and Cubans females.

Cubans have the highest average family income and Puerto Ricans have the lowest. The figures for the three groups are $38,144, $27,879, and $25,066 for Cuban, Mexican-American and Puerto Rican families, respectively.

Poverty

There are more Puerto Rican families living in poverty than either Mexican American or Cuban families. Approximately 38 percent of all Puerto Rican families live in poverty, 65 percent of these, families are headed by a female, and 55 percent of the females are high school dropouts.

Mexican Americans have the second-highest proportion of families living in poverty, approximately 28 percent. Of these 46 percent are headed by a female, with 34 percent of the females being high school dropouts.

Only 14 percent of all Cuban families live in poverty. Unlike the Puerto Rican and Mexican Americans, relatively few of the poor Cuban families are headed by females. Rather, most are headed my males who are high school dropouts.

Central and South Americans and Other Hispanics

In addition to Mexican Americans, Puerto Ricans, and Cubans, the Hispanic population consists of Central and South Americans and people who are classified by the U.S. Census Bureau as "other Hispanic origins." This latter category includes those whose origins are in Spain and those identifying themselves generally as Hispanic, Spanish, Spanish American, Hispano, Latino, and so on. Central and South Americans make up 13.8 percent of the total Hispanic population, and those of "other Hispanic origins" make up 7.6 percent.

Generally, Central and South Americans and "other" Hispanics tend to have characteristics that resemble the Cubans rather than the Mexican-American or Puerto Rican populations. The median age of Central and South Americans and "other" Hispanics is 27.9 and 31.0 years, respectively. Both groups tend to be highly educated. Approximately 15.1 percent of Central and South Americans and 16.2 percent of "other" Hispanics have four or more years of college.

Both groups also have a relatively high occupational status, with 12.7 percent of males and 14.5 percent of females of the Central and South American groups holding managerial and professional occupations; the respective figures for "other" Hispanics is 20.5 percent for males and 19.8 percent for females. At the lower end of the occupational hierarchy, Central and South Americans and "other" Hispanics tend to mirror the situation of Cubans, Mexican Americans, and Puerto Ricans in that there is a relatively large number of males concentrated in the operators, fabricators, and laborers category and a large number of females concentrated in the service occupations.

The average family income of Central and South Americans is $31,415 and for "other" Hispanics the average is $35,474. These averages are higher than the averages for Mexican Americans and Puerto Ricans but lower than the average for Cubans.

Approximately 27.2 percent of Central and South American families are classified as living below the poverty level. Approximately 33.3 percent of the families who live in poverty are headed by a high school dropout, and 39.3 percent are headed by females. Among "other" Hispanics, 19.4 percent of the families live in poverty, 49.1 percent are headed by females, and 38.7 percent are headed by a high school dropout. These percentages are closer to the rates for Mexican Americans and Puerto Ricans than to those for Cubans.

References

American Statistical Association. *Estimating Coverage of the 1990 United States Census: Demographic Analysis.* Atlanta, Georgia: U.S. Government Printing Office, 1991.

Bean, Frank D., Barry Edmonston and Jeffrey S. Passel. *Undocumented Migration to the United States: IRCA and the Experience of the 1980s.* Santa Monica, California: Rand Corporation, and Washington, D.C.: The Urban Institute, 1990.

Bouvier, Leon F., and Cary B. Davis. *The Future Racial Composition of the United States.* Washington, D.C.: Demographic Information Services Center (DISC) of the Population Reference Bureau, 1982.

Flagin, Joe R. *Racial and Ethnic Relations.* Englewood Cliffs, New Jersey: Prentice Hall, 1989.

Hogan, Howard. *The 1990 Post-Enumeration Survey: Operations and Results.* Washington, D.C.: Bureau of the Census, 1991.

Passel, Jeffrey S. "Undocumented Immigration." *Annals, AAPSS.* 487 (September 1986).

Portes, Alejandro, and Robert L. Bach. *Latin Journey: Cuban and Mexican Immigrants in the United States.* Los Angeles, California: University of California Press, Berkeley, 1985.

U.S. Bureau of the Census, Current Population Reports. Series p-20, No. 434. *The Hispanic Population in the United states: March 1986 and 1987.* Washington, D.C.: U.S. Government Printing Office, 1988.

U.S. Bureau of the Census, Current Population Reports. Series p. 20, No. 455. *The Hispanic Population in the United States: March 1991.* Washington, D.C.: U.S. Government Printing Office, 1991.

U.S. Bureau of the Census, Gregory Spencer, Current Population Reports. Series p. 25, No. 995. *Projections of the Hispanic Population: 1983 to 2080.* Washington, D.C.: U.S. Government Printing Office, 1986.

U.S. Department of Commerce. *1990 Census of Population and Housing. Puerto Rico.* Washington, D.C.: U.S. Government Printing Office, 1991.

U.S. Department of Commerce, Economics and Statistics Administration, Bureau of the Census. No. 1. *1990 Census Profile. Race and Hispanic Origin.* Washington, D.C.: U.S. Government Printing Office, 1991.

Warren, Robert, and Jeffrey S. Passel. "A Count of the Uncountable: Estimates of Undocumented Aliens Counted in the 1980 United States Census." *Demography.* Vol. 24, No. 3., 1987.

Tatcho Mindiola

8

Language

꙰ Varieties of Spanish Spoken ꙰ English Usage among Hispanics
꙰ Spanish in Business, the Media and in Other Social Environments
꙰ Bilingualism and Code-Switching

꙰VARIETIES OF SPANISH SPOKEN

To a large extent, the varieties of Spanish spoken in the United States reflect the countries of origin of the Spanish-speaking communities and the conditions under which their language has evolved in the U.S. setting. It is frequent for groups sharing common national and social origins to live in the same neighborhoods, which reinforces the use of regional language features. If immigration continues in significant numbers, and new arrivals gravitate toward already established Hispanic communities, regional tendencies are further reinforced. Hispanic groups living in rural areas of the United States are nearly homogeneous with respect to country of origin, which, due to historical patterns of migration, is usually Mexico. In large urban areas many Spanish-speaking groups may coexist, sometimes even in the same neighborhoods. If one Hispanic group is numerically and economically predominant, other groups usually make some accommodation to the leading variety of Spanish, which sets the standard in local advertising, communications media, and education. Such is the case for Mexican-American Spanish in the Southwest and in some midwestern cities, for Cuban Spanish in South Florida, and for Puerto Rican Spanish in some northeastern cities. In Chicago, for example, several varieties of Spanish compete, and there is more variation in usage, even among speakers of a single ethnic community.

Spanish-speaking communities in the United States are, in approximate descending order of size, of the following origins: Mexican, Puerto Rican, Cuban, and Central American. In the latter category, Nicaraguans and Salvadoreans are the most numerous. The Dominican population of New York City is rapidly growing; Dominican Spanish is quite similar

to that of Puerto Rico, although members of each group are aware of differences. Large numbers of Colombians are found in Miami, New York City, and elsewhere, but they come from many dialect zones of Colombia and do not exercise a strong centralizing influence on any variety of U.S. Spanish. Finally, there are several small but close-knit Spanish-speaking groups whose use of Spanish does not fall under the four large categories previously mentioned. These include Sephardic (Judeo-) Spanish-speakers in New York, Miami, and other urban areas, the *Isleños* of southeastern Louisiana, descendants of Canary Island settlers who arrived at the end of the eighteenth century, and the preCastro Cuban-Spanish communities of Key West and Tampa, which have been overshadowed by more recent Cuban immigration.

Spanish of Caribbean Origin

Cubans, Puerto Ricans, and Dominicans can instantly identify their own form of Spanish, but outsiders note more similarities than differences among the varieties of Spanish that originate in the Caribbean. Pronunciation is the single most important unifying factor, since Caribbeans are known for "swallowing" the final consonants, which are clearly heard, for example, in Mexican Spanish and parts of Central America. This slurring over final sounds also contributes to the impression that Caribbean Spanish is spoken faster than other varieties. For example, final *s* may sound somewhat like English *h*, or may disappear altogether. *Mis vecinos americanos* 'my American neighbors' may come out as *mih vecinoh americano*. In careful speech, *s* may be pronounced more frequently, since schools often insist on giving the "correct" pronunciation to every written letter,

209

The Teatro Puerto Rico in October, 1960, where Spanish-language vaudeville survived into the 1960's, along with Spanish-language films. (Justo A. Martí Collection. Courtesy of the Center for Puerto Rican Studies Library, Hunter College, CUNY.)

but in colloquial speech the nearly total lack of final *s* is often baffling to students of Spanish who have learned only a "spelling-pronunciation," and even Spanish-speakers from Mexico and Central America often find Caribbean Spanish hard to decipher.

Many Puerto Ricans pronounce trilled *rr* rather like English *h*, causing *Ramón* and *jamón* "ham" to practically fall together. This pronunciation of *rr* is often identified with rural regions; among Puerto Ricans in the United States, this type of *rr* is more frequent among families that have migrated from interior regions of the island, although it crops up from time to time in all Puerto Rican communities. More recently in Puerto Rico, this pronunciation has undergone a partial reevaluation, and some consider it a unique symbol of Puerto Rican cultural identity. Educated urban speakers may pronounce *rr* like *h* in circumstances which only a decade or two ago would have been unthinkable.

Also found in the Caribbean, particularly among Puerto Ricans, is the replacement of *r* by *l* at the end of words or before consonants; *trabajar* 'to work' becomes *trabajal*, *carta* 'letter' becomes *calta*, and

verdad 'true' may sound like *velá*. Even the most educated speakers slip into this pattern at times, but conscious attempts are usually made to avoid it. Since this pronunciation does not occur in Mexican or Central American Spanish, even a few instances of *l* for *r* among Puerto Ricans are enough to create the stereotype that the entire Puerto Rican community speaks this way. Among Cubans, the change of *r* to *l* is rare among the first generation of highly educated immigrants, most of whom came from Havana. Among more recent arrivals, representing rural regions and the urban working class, this change is found, alongside what sounds like a doubling of the following consonant: *algo* 'something' becomes *aggo*, *puerta* 'door' becomes *puetta*, and so forth.

A few key words also set Caribbean Spanish-speakers apart from their mainland counterparts. *Guagua* 'city bus,' *goma* 'automobile tire,' and *chiringa* 'kite,' are ready identifiers of Caribbean origin. Words like *ají* 'hot or sweet pepper,' *maní* 'peanut,' and *caimán* 'alligator' have spread to other Spanish-speaking countries, but are seldom used in Mexico or Central America.

Several words are unique to Puerto Rico, and sometimes also the Dominican Republic. As in other countries, many involve food and cultural practices. Beans, the staple food of the Caribbean, are known as *habichuelas* in Puerto Rico. These habichuelas are pink, as opposed to the black (Cuban) or red (Mexican) *frijoles*. Puerto Ricans also eat *gandules*, small greenish-brown beans, the same way they eat habichuelas with rice. Puerto Ricans refer to oranges as *chinas*; orange juice is, predictably, *jugo de china*. Bananas of the eating variety are *guineos*, while cooked bananas are more frequently *plátanos*. Fried banana slices are *tostones*. The word *pastel*, which in other Spanish-speaking countries refers to sweet cakes or cookies, is in Puerto Rico a type of meat pie prepared with mashed tubors. The colloquial term for money is *chavos*, coming from the old Spanish *ochavos* 'pieces of eight.' As in other Latin American countries where the U.S. dollar is in common circulation, *peso* refers to the U.S. dollar, while *peseta* is a U.S. quarter. *Escrachao* means 'ruined, destroyed,' and a common interjection upon discovering something in this condition is ¡ay bendito! Puerto Ricans joke among themselves that this expression is sometimes an alternative to taking action, calling this attitude *aybenditismo*. In Puerto Rico, a *jíbaro* is a 'hillbilly' from the mountainous interior of the island; the recent cultural revival is bringing more respect and even veneration to this term, which in the past was used only derisively to describe rustics who failed to cope with urban customs. In Puerto Rico, *aguinaldos* are Christmas carols, and *mahones* are blue jeans. The latter word comes from the name of a town on the Spanish island of Menorca, where the blue denim cloth was originally produced. A wastebasket or garbage can is a *zafacón* in Puerto Rico; some have suggested English "safety can" as the source, but this is doubtful.

Cuban Spanish also contains many local words. Unlike fellow Antilleans, Cubans often prefer the diminutive *-ico* instead of the more general Spanish *-ito*: *momentico* 'just a minute,' *chiquitico* 'very little,' and so on. Cubans use *chico* as a common form of address, at times even when speaking to more than one person. Neither excessive familiarity nor a male listener is necessarily assumed; the usage is similar to colloquial American English *man*, or *hombre* as used in Spain. Corresponding to the Puerto Rican *jíbaro* is the Cuban *guajiro*, the country dweller immortalized in the popular song "Guantanamera." Cubans refer to small sacks or bags, such as used in grocery stores, as *cartuchos*. More recent arrivals from Cuba might have heard of the *por si acaso*, a bag carried (in Cuba) in case an unexpected supply of a rationed product is found. In western Cuba, including Havana, *papaya* is a taboo word, and this fruit is known as *fruta bomba*. Producers of tropical juices that are marketed among Cuban-Americans carry two versions of papaya juice, *jugo de papaya* for the general Latin American clientele, and *jugo de fruta bomba* for the Cuban population. Among other uniquely Cuban culinary terms are *arroz congrí*, prepared with red beans and rice in eastern Cuba, and *tocino del sol*, a type of custard. The *sandwich cubano* is a well-known food item in Cuban-American communities, as is the *café cubano*, a tiny cup of highly sweetened espresso coffee. In Cuban Spanish, twins are colloquially referred to as *jimaguas*, a word of African origin. A *chucho* is a light switch, much to the surprise of Spanish-speakers from other regions, where the term has much different meanings. Cubans use *fajarse* for 'to fight,' *fastidiarse* for 'to break, become ruined, run into trouble,' and *me luce* for 'it seems to me.' A highly charged issue among Cuban Americans is the word used to refer to those who arrived via the Mariel boatlift of 1980, among whom the lower socioeconomic classes and rural regions were strongly represented. At the early stages, the term *marielero* was used, in reflection of Cuban place-naming patterns, but this has been replaced by *marielito*, a term that most Cubans regard as at least mildly pejorative.

Central American Spanish

People frequently refer to "Central America" as though it were a single entity. Indeed, the countries that form modern Central America (with the exception of Belize) did enjoy a fleeting moment of unity: following independence from Spain in the early 1820s, the Central American republics formed the ill-fated Central American Union, an attempt to federate five tiny nations into a significant regional power. After several unsuccessful trial marriages, the union was definitively dissolved in 1854, and the Central American republics have gone their own way ever since. Even during the colonial period there were striking differences in the Spanish spoken in different regions of Central America, in fashions that do not always correspond to what might be supposed by looking at a map. For instance, Costa Rica, the southernmost Central American nation, shares more similarities with Guatemala, at the far north, than with neighboring Nicaragua. Honduran and Salvadoran Spanish blend together smoothly, but the contrast with Guatemalan Spanish is striking, and Nicaraguan Spanish is also rather different. Costa Rican Spanish bears no resemblance to neighboring Panamanian Spanish to the south, which is not surprising in view of the fact that Panama was formerly a province of Colombia, administered from Bogotá and largely populated from Colombia's coastal provinces, whose speech even today is very similar to that of Panama. Guatemalan Spanish, on the other hand, is similar to the Spanish of Mexico's Yucatán region, largely due to the common Mayan heritage.

All Central American nations have contributed to the U.S. Hispanic populations, in differing proportions and for different reasons. The Costa Rican contribution has been the least noticeable; this may perhaps reflect Costa Rica's relative prosperity and political stability within Central America. The Honduran contingent in the United States is also small, scattered across Miami, Houston, New York, and Los Angeles, but the largest group is found in New Orleans. This community results from the early years of the Central American banana industry, when companies based in New Orleans administered plantations on Honduras's northern coast.

Although there have always been Guatemalans from the middle and professional classes in the United States, the heaviest immigration has come in the form of political refugees from a nation torn by civil war. Many of these refugees are Mayan-speaking native Americans who speak little or no Spanish. Guatemalan communities are concentrated in Los Angeles, Miami, Houston, and New York. Small rural groups are found, for example, in southern Florida.

The Nicaraguan population in the United States is large, due mainly to the political uncertainty in Nicaragua. Prior to the Sandinista revolution of 1979, there were significant groups of Nicaraguans living in Miami and Los Angeles, but the mass exodus to the United States began in the 1980s, bringing tens of thousands of Nicaraguans, most of whom settled in Los Angeles, San Francisco, and particularly in Miami. In the latter city, Nicaraguans live in several well-defined neighborhoods, in which they have transplanted social, cultural, and economic structures from their homeland. Nicaraguan restaurants, stores, travel agencies, beauty shops, and medical facilities serve to reinforce the "little Nicaragua" image; several newspapers are published within the Nicaraguan community, and local radio stations air special programs produced by and for local Nicaraguans. Nicaraguan holidays are celebrated as fervently in Miami as in Nicaragua, and nearly any product or food found in Nicaragua can be found in the transplanted colonies in the United States. As with the Cubans, the first Nicaraguans to leave following the Sandinista revolution were the professionals, or those who had held high posts in the previous government. Subsequent arrivals include citizens from all walks of life, including English-speaking residents of the Caribbean shore, as well as Miskito Indians. Small communities of seafaring coastal Nicaraguans are found in Florida and along

the coast of Texas, and even within Miami the *costeños* 'coastal people' live and work in parts of the city different from those where the *ladinos* or Spanish-speakers from the highlands live. Although the post-Sandinista Nicaraguan government has put out a call for the return of all those who left during the previous regime, the Nicaraguan community in the United States shows no signs of shrinking, and may actually be growing larger.

The largest Central American group in the United States is the Salvadoran, concentrated in Los Angeles, Houston, Chicago and, Miami. Although the prolonged civil war in El Salvador has caused many professional and middle-class residents to move to the United States, there has not been a mass exodus such as occurred in Cuba and Nicaragua following the overthrow of earlier governments. Most of the several hundred thousand Salvadorans living in the United States come from the poorest groups, from rural areas of El Salvador and from squatter communities in San Salvador and other cities. They frequently have little or no formal education, and their speech patterns combine regional features with the results of social and cultural isolation. The contrast with Nicaraguans is striking; for the latter, it is the speech of the middle and professional class that sets the standard, while among Salvadorans, when a voice is raised to speak for the entire community, it is often from the opposite end of the social spectrum. Within the United States, the precarious situation of Salvadorans has kept many of their children from entering the school system, with the result that education in English or Spanish is comparatively limited. For these reasons, Salvadoran Spanish as found in the United States contains a high proportion of words and grammatical patterns representative of less-educated groups.

The pronunciation of Nicaraguan Spanish is in many ways similar to Cuban and Puerto Rican Spanish, particularly in the weak pronunciation of final *s*. Unlike Caribbean Spanish-speakers, Nicaraguans never interchange or drop *l* and *r*. On the other hand, Nicaraguans pronounce Spanish *j* very weakly, and for example *trabajo* 'work' may come out like *trabao*. Even more characteristic of Central American Spanish is the weak pronunciation of *y*; *gallina* 'chicken' sounds like *gaína*, and *silla* 'chair' like *sía*. Overcompensation is also heard, especially among Nicaraguans, so that *María* and *frío* 'cold' sound like *Mariya* and *friyo*. None of this occurs in the Spanish-speaking Caribbean, and this difference is a major contributor to the unique accent of the *nicas* 'Nicaraguans' and *guanacos* 'Salvadorans.'

To the casual listener, Salvadoran Spanish is closer to Mexican Spanish than to any of the Caribbean varieties, an impression that is confirmed by history. Salvadoran and Mexican Spanish share a large quantity of vocabulary items derived from native American languages, principally Nahuatl and to a much lesser extent Mayan. Like Nicaraguans, Salvadorans weaken *y* and *j*. Among many rural speakers, a heavy nasalization is noted, with entire words and even phrases being pronounced "through the nose." This nasality, easy to detect and imitate but difficult to describe in technical terms, is not heard among other U.S. Hispanic groups. Another idiosyncratic feature of many Salvadorans is the occasional and sporadic pronunciation of *s* like English *th* in *thick* or the *z* of Castilian Spanish *zapato* 'shoe.' Salvadorans weaken final *s*, but not to the extent found among Nicaraguans and speakers from the Caribbean. On the other hand, many Salvadorans pronounce *s* like *h* at the *beginning* of words, something not heard in other varieties of Spanish. This causes *la semana* 'the week' to sound like *la hemana*, and *cómo se llama* 'what is your name' like *cómo he llama*. Sometimes this change affects *s* in the middle of a word; *presidente* 'president' frequently comes out as *prehidente*, *necesario* 'necessary' is heard as *nehesario*, and *nosotros* 'we' as *nojotros*. Many rural Mexican and Nicaraguan speakers also say *nojotros*, but this is hardly ever found in the Caribbean. All these factors combine to make rural Salvadorans difficult for other Spanish-speakers to understand. Mexicans, for example, claim that Salvadorans speak *entre dientes* 'mumbling'; Salvadorans in turn say that Mexicans "sing" instead of talk! Cubans in Miami often make similar remarks.

All Central Americans share a word that is puzzling for other Spanish-speakers in the United States, although it is well known, for example, in Argentina. It is *vos*, used instead of *tú* as the familiar 'you.' This pronoun is accompanied by different verb conjugations, for example, *comés* instead of *comes* 'you eat,' *tenés* for *tienes* 'you have,' *decí* for *di* 'say,' *sos* for *eres* 'you are.' Nicaraguans, like all other Central Americans, prefer *vos* when speaking to one another, but many Nicaraguans in the United States comfortably switch to *tú* when speaking with non-Central Americans. Salvadorans may also use *tú*, sometimes even among one another, when a less-familiar relationship is perceived, but this is limited to more sophisticated urban speakers. Salvadorans from rural areas use *vos* nearly exclusively, and also use the formal *usted* to a greater extent than other Hispanic groups in the United States. Rural Salvadorans frequently use *usted* with small children to train them the respectful forms of address, and also use *usted* in situations where other groups would use a familiar pronoun. Central Americans in the United

States who wish to conceal their origin or simply avoid misunderstandings when talking to other Spanish-speakers avoid using *vos*, although some speakers cling to this word precisely because of its strong regional identification.

Nicaraguan Spanish has many unique words, some of which are becoming well known in Miami. These include such food items as *gallo pinto* 'red beans and rice,' *vigorón* 'type of salad,' and *pinol* 'a drink made from toasted corn.' Nicaraguans colloquially refer to themselves as *pinoleros*, reflecting their fondness for this drink, and this term vies with *nica* as a general reference to Nicaraguans. Like Salvadorans, Nicaraguans often refer to a turkey as *chompipe*, use the term *chele* to refer to blond-haired or fair-skinned individuals, and call dogs *chuchos* (which to Cubans means electric light switches). Nicaraguans employ the common interjection *idiay*, 'wow' or 'gosh.' To a Nicaraguan, *arrecho* means 'angry' and *dundo* means 'stupid'; neither term is used in this fashion by non-Central Americans.

Although sharing many similarities with both Mexico and Nicaragua, Salvadoran Spanish also has words not used by other U.S. Hispanic groups (although they may be used elsewhere in Central America). Some such words are *andar* 'carry, take along' (for example, *no ando mi cédula* 'I don't have my identification card with me'), *suelto* 'loose change,' *chompa* 'sweater,' *bolo* 'drunk,' *pisto* 'money,' *cipote* 'small child,' *pupusa* 'food made of tortillas filled with cheese or meat,' *andén* 'sidewalk,' *chero* 'friend, buddy,' *chinear* 'to baby-sit,' *colocho* 'curly, unkempt hair.' Many Salvadorans use expressions like *un mi amigo* 'a friend of mine, my friend,' where other Spanish-speakers would leave out *un*. They often use *hasta* 'until' to refer to the *beginning* of an event, rather than to the end: *Abrimos hasta las ocho* thus means 'we open *at* 8:00' and not 'we are open *until* 8:00.' This may cause confusion when Salvadorans talk to other Spanish-speakers, particularly in making and keeping appointments.

Mexican Spanish

Mexican varieties of Spanish share more similarities with Central American speech, particularly Salvadoran, than with any Caribbean dialects. The same native American language families had a strong influence on Mexican Spanish, and the patterns of colonial administration resulted in similar profiles in central Mexico and the highland capitals of Central America. "Mexican" Spanish existed in what is now U.S. territory several centuries before the nations of Mexico and the United States came into being. More Mexican Spanish was incorporated through U.S. territorial expansion (the Texas revolution and the

Mexican-American War), and still more Mexican varieties are the result of twentieth-century immigration. Each stage of Mexican Spanish presence in the United States has its own peculiarities, although the similarities outweigh the differences.

The Spanish expedition of Juan de Oñate eventually settled in what is now New Mexico in the 1600s, and "Spaniards" have lived in this region ever since. When Mexico won its independence from Spain, the lives of the "Spaniards" in New Mexico and southern Colorado scarcely changed, and when this region became a U.S. territory following the Mexican-American War, the effects were again minimal. When New Mexico and Colorado attained statehood, following the migration of English-speaking settlers, the original Spanish began to recede, but even today it is possible to find speakers of what is regarded as the oldest variety of Spanish continuously spoken in North America. Families who identify with the earliest Spanish settlements refer to themselves as "Spaniards," and reject labels such as "Mexican," "Latin," and "Chicano." In its purest form, the speech of these "Spaniards" provides a window to the past, a taste of the speech of Spanish settlers during the formative period of Latin American dialects. More so than most Mexican dialects of today, the old Spanish of New Mexico and Colorado weakens word-final s, as in the Caribbean. Spanish j and y are also weakened. The intonation is less typically "Mexican" than other "Mexican-American" varieties; in particular, the characteristic *norteño* accent is virtually absent. The old-Spanish-speakers of New Mexico and southern Colorado use words and expressions that have long since disappeared in other varieties of Spanish (*cócono* 'turkey' is a typical example), at the same time using fewer native American borrowings than does modern Mexican Spanish.

Another group of U.S. Spanish-speakers, all but unknown and rapidly disappearing, represents a somewhat later stage of Mexican Spanish. Long before the colonial wars of independence from Spain, the Texas revolution, or the Mexican-American war, *mestizo* soldiers from Mexico were sent to fortify the border between Texas and the French territory of Louisiana. In the early 1700s Spain established outposts at Los Aes (presently San Augustine,

Downtown El Paso, Texas, and all along the border, Spanish is just as much the language of business as is English, and bilingualism is even more valued in business than either language alone. (Courtesy of the *Texas Catholic Herald*.)

Texas), at Nacogdoches, Texas, and at Los Adaes, near modern-day Robeline, Louisiana; by the second half of the eighteenth century, the settlements were well established and the residents knew no other home. Spain had intended to settle eastern Texas to create a buffer zone against intrusion from French Louisiana, particularly the outpost at Natchitoches, but when the Louisiana territory was ceded to Spain, these defenses were no longer needed, and the Spanish government decided to withdraw all settlers. In 1773, the order arrived in eastern Texas to abandon the settlements, for immediate resettlement in San Antonio, and despite bitter protests most residents were forced to abandon homes and crops and make an onerous journey of more than three months to the principal Spanish settlement in Texas. Upon arrival, the newcomers were treated poorly, given inferior land, and left to languish, and immediately they began planning for a return to the only place they knew as home. Many settlers managed to move back to eastern Texas, founding the town of Nacogdoches in 1779 at the site of an old mission. Louisiana once again came under French sovereignty in 1800, and the United States purchased the Louisiana Territory in 1808, but the Spanish settlers remained.

When Mexico won independence from Spain in 1821, only three significant Spanish-speaking settlements remained in what is now Texas: San Antonio, Bahía del Espíritu Santo (Goliad), and Nacogdoches. By the time that Texas joined the United States in 1845, massive immigration of English-speaking residents into Nacogdoches was well established, and before long the population balance had tipped completely in favor of the Anglo-Americans. In Louisiana, the arrival of Anglo-Americans had begun following the Louisiana Purchase, and the Hispanic character of the old Los Adaes settlement soon became a thing of the past. Despite these adverse circumstances, tiny pockets of Spanish-speakers, descendants of the original expeditions, survived well into the second half of the twentieth century, in small communities deep in the pine woods of northern Louisiana and east Texas. The residents use rustic implements such as the *molcajete* 'mortar,' *comal* 'griddle for cooking tortillas,' and *metate* 'grinding stone'; they make *nixtamal* 'hominy,' tie up objects with a *mecate* 'rope,' cut *zacate* 'grass' and raise *guajolotes* 'turkeys.' The names of Mexican animals have been applied to similar small animals found in Texas and Louisiana: *tacuache* 'possum,' *tejón* 'raccoon,' *coquena* 'Guinea hen.' Other old or rustic words still remembered by old residents are *mercar/ marcar* 'to buy,' *calzón/calzones* 'pants,' *túnico* 'ladies' dress,' *calesa* 'horsedrawn buggy,' *la provisión* 'supplies, provisions,' *noria* 'water well,' *truja/troja*

'barn,' *palo* 'tree,' *encino* 'oak tree,' *peje* 'fish,' *fierro* 'iron, tool,' *lumbre* 'fire,' *prieto* 'black.' Currently only a handful of the oldest residents still speak Spanish, but a generation ago the total was much higher, and two generations ago there were still monolingual Spanish-speakers living in rural northwestern Louisiana, unknown even to their most immediate neighbors. A tiny settlement near Zwolle, Louisiana, bears the name Ebarb, a name still shared by some community residents; this is simply the Anglicized version of Antonio Gil Ybarbo, the leader of the rebellious settlers who returned to their homes more than two centuries ago.

Additional groups of Mexican speakers were incorporated into the United States as a result of the Mexican-American War, and their speech represents northern Mexican Spanish. Emigration across the Rio Grande, which was an artificial border at best, never slowed down following the Mexican-American War, so that until the turn of the twentieth century the Spanish spoken in the southwestern United States was identical with that of Mexico. The U.S.-Mexican border began to tighten up during the first decades of the twentieth century, creating the beginnings of a real separation between Mexicans and Mexican Americans. This gap was further widened with the advent of *bracero* recruitment programs in the 1930s, which recruited labor forces not from the nearby northern Mexican states, but from poorer central and southern areas such as Guanajuato, Michoacán, and Guerrero. These laborers, many of whom ended up staying in the United States, spoke Spanish differently from natives of the border regions. Although the braceros passed through the southwestern United States on their way to sources of employment, a large number of these Mexicans from the south ended up working in the midwestern states. The original braceros were principally agricultural workers, giving rise to the waves of migrant farm workers that even today travel across the country, following the harvest patterns of seasonal crops such as orchard fruits, melons, and truck vegetables. Many of these Mexicans settled in northern cities such as Chicago, Detroit, Milwaukee, and Cleveland, so that "northern" Spanish in the United States was actually from southern Mexico, and vice versa.

At the same time as immigrants from central Mexico were arriving in the Midwest, an increasing number of Mexicans from the border region were arriving in southwestern cities, a change from the predominantly rural settlement of the past. As emigration from Mexico came under tighter control, an urban language began to evolve. During this same period, negative feelings grew in Mexico toward compatriots living in the United States. A new vocabulary derisively referred to these expatriates or foreign-born Mexicans. One such word was *pocho*, a strongly derogatory term referring to Mexicans who, it was thought, had lost their identity in a hostile foreign environment. The old Spanish word *gabacho*, originally applied by Spaniards to the French, was revived by Mexicans to refer to Americans. The term *bolillo* was also used with the same meaning, presumably because of the white color of the bread referred to. This use of *bolillo* is not recent; it is found among the Spanish-speakers in northwestern Louisiana, representing Mexican Spanish of more than two hundred years ago. Mexicans and Mexican Americans began to use the word *chicano*, an old colonial word dating back to the time when *México* was pronounced as *Méshico* and *mexicano* as *meshicano*. In Mexico, this word continues to carry negative connotations, while in the United States it has undergone a more complex evolution. Its use by political and social activists, along with such terms as *La Raza* and *Aztlán*, has polarized feelings toward the word *chicano*, which many Mexican Americans do not accept. Even for those who accept *chicano*, the term is used freely only by members of the group in question, but is not so readily tolerated when used by outsiders, least of all by those who are perceived as unsympathetic to Mexican-American culture.

Within Mexico, there are many regional dialects, just as occurs with English in the United States. In the United States, Mexican-American Spanish is best divided along rural-urban lines, together with degree of fluency in English. Pronunciation is relatively uniform, representing a broad cross section of northern and central Mexican dialects. Some Mexican Americans pronounce Spanish *b* as *v*, not always in accordance with Spanish spelling. In Spanish, the letters *b* and *v* represent the same sound, and some have viewed the use of *v* among Mexican-Americans as a carryover from English. This is unlikely, however, since the same pronunciation is also found within Mexico, while not used by bilingual Cubans and Puerto Ricans. Also found in some Mexican-American communities is the pronunciation of Spanish *ch* as *sh*.

The vocabulary of Mexican Spanish differs from textbook versions of the language, principally due to the huge number of indigenous elements absorbed over a period of more than four centuries. Most such items are of Nahuatl origin, and a few have passed into general Spanish: *tomate* 'tomato,' *aguacate* 'avocado,' *chocolate*, *chile* 'green pepper.' The majority of indigenous borrowings are confined to Mexico and neighboring Central America; their number runs into the hundreds, but most refer to flora and fauna found in rural areas of Mexico, or to implements and objects used in rustic life. In the United States, these words are easily replaced by English equivalents, or dropped altogether. Some indigenous words are found in all varieties of Mexican and Mexican-American Spanish: *zacate* 'grass, lawn,' *elote* 'corn,' *papalote* 'toy kite,' *guajolote* (*jolote*) 'turkey,' *tecolote* 'owl,' *zopilote* 'vulture,' *camote* 'sweet potato,' *cuate* 'friend, buddy' (literally, 'twin'), *hule* 'rubber,' and many more. Other characteristic Mexicanisms found in the United States include: *camión* 'bus,' *combi* 'van, station wagon,' *güero* 'blond, fair complexioned,' *chamaco* and *huerco* 'child, baby,' *feria* 'loose change,' *chamba* 'job,' *nieve* 'ice cream,' *aventón* 'pick up, ride,' *banqueta* 'sidewalk,' *raspa/raspada* 'snow-cone,' and many others. Mexican Spanish commonly uses *ándale* 'let's go, OK' (and many other items ending in *le*, such as the expression of surprise *híjole*, *órale* 'come on, get going,' *dale* 'do it,' and so on). For many observers, *ándale* is as synonymous with Mexican Spanish as *chévere* is with Caribbean varieties. Vulgar/slang terms also strongly identified with Mexican Spanish, whose omission would seriously distort any account of MexicanAmerican Spanish, include *pinche* 'cursed, damned,' *lana* 'money,' *mordida* 'bribe,' *padre* 'excellent, great,' and that most Mexican of all the *malas palabras*: *chingar* and its derivatives, originally referring to sexual intercourse and now reduced to insults. Mexican Spanish uses *no más* in the sense of 'only, just' as in *no más quería platicar contigo* 'I just wanted to talk with you.' *Mero* is used where *mismo* occurs in other Spanish dialects, meaning 'very, same, one and only': *aquí mero* 'right here,' *él es el mero jefe* 'he's the boss,' *el mero mero* 'the big boss, the big cheese.' *Ya mero* means 'almost.' *Se me hace* means 'it seems to me,' and *¿qué tanto?/¿qué tan?* is preferred to *¿cuánto?* 'how much'; for example *¿qué tanto ganas?* 'how much do you earn?' *¿qué tan viejo es tu carro?* 'how old is your car?' Also typical of Mexican Spanish is *puro* in the sense of 'only, exclusively, predominantly': *son puras mentiras* 'nothing but lies,' *ahí va pura raza* 'only Mexican Americans go there.' All of these expressions are frequent in Mexican-American speech.

✳ENGLISH USAGE AMONG HISPANICS

The majority of Hispanics born or raised in the United States speak English, as a home language or a strong second language. Arrivals from Spanish-speaking countries also learn English, to a greater or lesser extent depending on such factors as age upon arrival, previous study of English, urgency of using English in the workplace or in the home environment, children in school who bring English into the home, and economic conditions that provide opportunities for acquiring English. As happens with speakers of other languages, Spanish-speakers who learn English during adolescence or later frequently retain an "accent," regardless of the level of fluency eventually attained. Even in bilingual communities where most residents learned English in childhood, a slight "Hispanic" flavor is often found in English. This ranges from a different intonation, to pronunciation shifts such as *v* to *b* (*bery* for *very*), *y* to *j* (*jes* for *yes*), *th* to *t* (*tank* for *thank*), *z* to *s* (making *does* sound like *duss*), and *sh* to *ch* (*chip* to *ship*), reflecting the phonetics of Spanish.

Grammatical interference from Spanish is only found among those who have never fully learned English. Some features of "Hispanic" English are also found in the speech of other Americans, such as pronunciation of *-ing* endings as *-in*, or the use of double negatives as in *I'm not doin' nothin'*. Not all Hispanics use this ethnic variety of English; many speak the prevailing regional form of English and cannot be distinguished from non-Hispanics. There are many reasons for the continued existence of Hispanic English among speakers who have spoken English since early childhood. In large bilingual communities, this may be the sort of English heard most often, so that speakers reinforce one another's use of English. Even in school, use of non-Hispanic English may be only passive, and there may be no attempt by teachers to change pronunciation patterns. Much as has happened in other ethnic neighborhoods in the United States, the Hispanic accent can persist for many generations, only fading away as the ethnic group itself becomes more integrated into the wider community, marriages take place outside the group, children interact at school with members of other groups, and so forth.

Traditionally, Hispanic English has been seen in a negative light, as a way of speaking that needs to be corrected. More recently, linguists have studied Hispanic English as it is actually used, without preconceived notions, and have discovered that it also has a role in maintaining community solidarity. The shift from Spanish to English is affecting all Hispanic groups in the United States, and maintaining an ethnically marked form of English is sometimes a semiconscious way of resisting total assimilation to the American "melting pot." Research has demonstrated that some speakers deliberately switch varieties of English depending on whether they are inside the ethnic neighborhood or in an Anglo-American setting. Community activists and grass roots political campaigners often find it more effective to use ethnic varieties of English, which arouse a more favorable response from their audience. Among educators and community leaders, there is ongoing debate as to the desirability of Hispanic English. Some feel that it is an impediment to economic and social advancement, while others insist that it is the attitudes of society that must be changed first. This controversy shows no signs of being resolved in the near future.

Whether or not they speak a Hispanic variety of English, Hispanics in the United States inevitably use more English as they enter wider economic and social structures, and when they work and live in the midst of non-Hispanics. Eventually, the daily use of Spanish becomes of secondary importance in defining and maintaining Hispanic identity, and many individuals who identify strongly with Hispanic culture prefer to use English in most of their activities. Older, Spanish-dominant community members may feel that this represents alienation and loss of cultural identity, while those who take a negative attitude toward maintenance of Spanish see increased use of English as an encouraging sign of social integration. Neither viewpoint is necessarily correct, and the history of the United States provides many examples that show that the shift away from an ancestral language does not automatically entail abandonment of ethnic identity. A significant proportion of literature written by U.S. Hispanics is in English, and peer role models adopted by young Hispanic Americans freely speak English without compromising their ethnicity. In the United States, the concept of being Hispanic does not necessarily require frequent use of, or even fluency in Spanish. At the same time, given the increasingly large numbers of non-Hispanics learning Spanish, in New York City, south Florida, and the Southwest, speaking Spanish is no longer the exclusive property of Hispanics, either.

✱SPANISH IN BUSINESS, THE MEDIA AND IN OTHER SOCIAL ENVIRONMENTS

Spanish as used in radio, television, and the written media parallels regional varieties found throughout the United States, particularly in areas where a single Spanish-speaking group prevails. As in other Spanish-speaking nations, radio and television announcers adopt a "neutral" speech, including careful articulation, precise grammar, and few regional or colloquial words. Many Spanish-speaking news announcers and talk-show hosts have received broadcast training or professional experience in other countries. It is not uncommon to find announcers in Miami with experience in Cuba, announcers in New York who have worked in Puerto Rico, or broadcast personnel in the Southwest who have worked in Mexico. This collective experience gives U.S. Spanish-

A typical Hispanic grocery store in New York City. (Justo A. Martí Collection. Courtesy of the Center for Puerto Rican Studies Library, Hunter College, CUNY.)

language broadcasting a professional sound and an international flavor. Not all Spanish-speakers in the United States prefer this approach; some feel that the unique situation of the Spanish language in the United States and the people who use it should receive greater emphasis. In response to this need, Spanish-language broadcasting in the United States comes into its own with community action programs, popular music programs, political and social commentary, and programs with an artistic focus. In such programs, regional and casual varieties of Spanish are used more prominently. Broadcast personnel may accentuate regional features of their speech to strengthen the emotional bond with their audience. Many community-oriented programs include participation by individuals not involved in broadcasting and media production, who bring to the airwaves the speech of all segments of the community. Talk shows and call-in programs are particularly representative of communitywide speech patterns, and by listening to these programs the "special" nature of U.S. Hispanic broadcasting can be appreciated.

The use of English and of anglicisms varies widely in Spanish-language broadcasting. When programs aimed at U.S. Spanish-speakers were first aired, they were entirely in Spanish, and public pressure to maintain "pure" Spanish resulted in avoidance of anglicisms. As U.S. Hispanic broadcasting developed its own profile, closer approximations to community language usage became more frequent. This can be clearly seen in advertising, where products, services, and brand names with no easy Spanish equivalent require borrowing from English. Sportscasting is also instrumental in enhancing the use of Anglicisms, but the most important single factor that has put U.S. varieties of Spanish on the airwaves is audience participation. Active community involvement has even brought language-switching to the airwaves, and popular programs on many Hispanic radio stations freely use this format.

The language styles used in U.S. Hispanic broadcasting are frequently a factor of the commercial orientation. Large, powerful stations in big cities are often conservative in matters of language. Such stations may discourage all but the most neutral forms of Spanish, may have a high proportion of advertising and prerecorded material produced in other cities, or overseas, and may downplay controversial social issues in favor of a more consumer-oriented menu of news, musical variety, and sports. Small stations, publicly sponsored stations, and stations run by colleges and universities may have more flexible programming, including announcers (sometimes unpaid volunteers) with little professional training in broadcasting. Such stations tend to have a higher percentage of locally produced material, some of which is aired without rehearsal. Although the most powerful Spanish-language stations are as slickly modern as their English-language counterparts, U.S. Hispanic broadcasting as a whole retains a "family" sound that has largely been lost in mainstream commercial broadcasting in English.

Spanish-language newspaper and magazine publishing in the United States affords a wider range of options of language usage, given the relatively small capital investment needed to publish a local newspaper or newsletter and the lack of government licensing requirements, which have often impeded the establishing of Hispanic broadcasting stations. A Spanish-language press has existed in the United States for more than a century. Many of the early newspapers, concentrated along the Mexican border, have long since disappeared. Innumerable parish papers and bulletins have appeared; labor unions, political action groups, and social organizations have also

Two scenes from the *Villa Alegre* television series, which used scripts with extensive code-switching.

produced Spanish or bilingual publications. The language of all these publications has followed the same evolution as English-language newspapers. The earliest publications used a stiffly formal language based on European Spanish, and some current papers still do. The articles in the early publications were directed to an elite, socially active sector of the community, the assumption being that less affluent community members could not read well enough to benefit from such publications. News reporting was confined to local affairs and personalities, and with the exception of such major events as wars, depressions, or natural disasters, nothing beyond the pale of the ethnic community was included. Such papers continue to exist, in areas where the Hispanic community is small and localized, or where recent immigrants from a single region attempt to recreate a bit of their homeland. For example, the Nicaraguan community in Miami publishes several small newspapers. There have also been, from time to time, Salvadoran newspapers in Houston and Los Angeles, Honduran newspapers in New Orleans, and newspapers aimed at Mexicans and Puerto Ricans in the Midwest. The language used by these small newspapers varies

A customer buying *La prensa*, the Spanish-language daily newspaper which survives today as *El diario-La prensa* in New York City. (Justo A. Martí Collection. Courtesy of the Center for Puerto Rican Studies Library, Hunter College, CUNY.)

widely. Some use highly formal, journalistic prose, while others use a closer approximation to community language.

In the United States today, there are numerous large Spanish-language newspapers with regional or national circulation. The language used in these papers is professional and international, reflecting the standards of Spanish-language journalism worldwide and not giving preference to any regional variety of Spanish. Common to all Hispanic newspapers in the United States is use of anglicisms, particularly in advertising. Most Spanish-speakers born and raised in the United States use English words for many items advertised in newspapers, and may fail to recognize "legitimate" Spanish equivalents. Advertisers and publishers must balance the attitudes of educators and community leaders and the reality of effective communication; the results vary widely. Some advertisers invent new Spanish expressions, in hopes that they will be accepted as translations of English terms, while others go to the opposite extreme, including more English words than would ever be done by a bilingual speaker. In general, the lan-

guage of advertising, classified announcements and editorial commentary as found in Spanish-language newspapers provide a good window on actual usage.

Many Hispanics in the United States use English in business and professional activities, particularly if they are surrounded by English-speaking co-workers and clients, but in cities with large Spanish-speaking populations, professional services are also offered in Spanish. Bilingualism is a highly desirable commodity for companies doing business with an increasingly affluent Hispanic community, and non-Hispanics in cities like Miami find that learning and using Spanish is advantageous. Commerce with Latin America is also a major source of revenue for many American cities, and financial and industrial transactions conducted in Spanish represent hundreds of millions of dollars for American businesses. Finally, at the neighborhood level, Spanish is used in thousands of small businesses, such as grocery stores, gas stations, travel agencies, banks, restaurants, and any place that provides products and services to a Hispanic clientele. It is difficult to calculate the volume of trade that these businesses involve, but taken as a whole, the Spanish-speaking market represents a large and important share of the American economy.

✳ BILINGUALISM AND CODE-SWITCHING

Except for recent arrivals, or in a few isolated rural areas, the majority of Hispanics in the United States speak English. A gradual but definite shift from Spanish to English occurs in most Hispanic communities, the same course followed by every other immigrant language brought to the United States, and the speed with which this language shift takes place is increasing. Europeans arriving in the nineteenth and early twentieth centuries often settled in rural areas of the United States and were able to maintain their own languages and traditions for a considerable time, while experiencing little pressure to learn English. Immigrants who moved to urban areas learned English, as did their children, but settlement in ethnic neighborhoods made retention of the ancestral language easy. With the breakup of the tight mosaic of ethnic neighborhoods, the increase of mixed-ethnic marriages, and the greater penetrating power of public education, radio, and television, the shift to English is increasingly rapid among new immigrants, and the period of stable bilingualism is steadily decreasing. Often one generation is sufficient for the ancestral language to disappear from a family and even from a neighborhood.

Hispanics currently have a higher retention rate of the ancestral language than any group in the United States. Ironically, at a time when the United States is emphasizing international economic and political cooperation and promoting proficiency in foreign languages to gain a competitive edge, the high rate of retention of Spanish is viewed by some Americans as threatening. Throughout the country, nearly all "English only" campaigns and amendments have targeted Spanish-speakers, and in many cities there is strong public sentiment against bilingual education, the use of Spanish in official government documents and institutions, and the high priority accorded to bilingual fluency in job descriptions.

There is no single answer to the question of why Spanish-speakers have successfully maintained their language in the United States, but there are several obvious contributing factors. Circumstance of arrival in the United States is a major influence on language retention. The original Mexican Americans did not move to the United States, but were enveloped by a new government and language following U.S. territorial expansions. The same occurred with Puerto Ricans, whose government and citizenship changed due to circumstances beyond their control. The first migrations from Puerto Rico to the

mainland United States did not fit the pattern of European immigration, which had a much higher voluntary component, although most European arrivals in the nineteenth and twentieth centuries were impelled by economic necessity. Beginning in 1901, Puerto Ricans were recruited as sugar plantation laborers in Louisiana and, in much greater numbers, in Hawaii. Descendants of the original Puerto Rican cane-cutters are found in Hawaii even today, and Puerto Ricans contributed words and cultural items to Hawaiian life. The Puerto Ricans became known as *Pokoliko, Poto Riko,* or *Borinki,* and the Puerto Rican *arroz y gandules* 'small green beans cooked with rice' became transmuted to *gandude rice.*

From the end of the Spanish-American War (1898) to the present, the Puerto Rican population in the United States has steadily grown. While the community in New York had its origins in the revolutionaries who were organizing the rebellion from Spain, by the beginning of the twentieth century there were numbers of Puerto Ricans (and Cubans) in the cigar manufacturing industry in New York. Puerto Ricans involved in service and manufacturing industries grew, with greater migration spurred by the authorization of U.S. citizenship in 1917, under the Jones Act. U.S. trade and business relationships during the twentieth century continued Spain's practices of encouraging mono-culture in one failing agricultural product after another: coffee, tabacco, sugar. Each failed industry produced greater waves of labor migration. But the largest mass migration, which was stimulated by labor recruiters and free airfare, took place during World War II labor shortages in the United States. From the 1940s to the middle 1950s, one-third of Puerto Rico's population migrated to the continental United States. These landless and homeless Puerto Ricans ended up in the cold, industrialized cities of the Northeast, where they frequently suffered even worse conditions than those left behind in Puerto Rico. The plight of these displaced Puerto Ricans, who cannot be considered voluntary immigrants in the true sense of the word, is poignantly covered in many literary works, including the collection of stories *Spiks,* by Pedro Juan Soto, and the play *La carreta,* by René Marqués. Forced by economic hardship and racial prejudice to live in ghettos and tenements, and deprived of the opportunity to be educated in their home language, many Puerto Ricans dropped out of school, and by returning to their home neighborhoods, consolidated the retention of Spanish.

The landless Mexicans recruited in the bracero program of the 1950s also fail to fit the definition of voluntary immigrants, and their retention of Spanish is a natural outgrowth of the circumstances of their

A voter registration drive in New York City. Hispanics cherish the right to vote in the Spanish language. (Justo A. Martí Collection. Courtesy of the Center for Puerto Rican Studies Library, Hunter College, CUNY.)

life in the United States. Recent immigrants from border regions of Mexico maintain close contacts with their original homeland, through visits and additional migration, and a sense of continuity with Mexico can be maintained indefinitely under such conditions.

The large number of Spanish-speakers who immigrated to the United States because of political or social problems in their homelands constitutes another source of Spanish-language retention, since such groups initially harbor the intention to return to their country of origin, and see their presence in the United States as transitory. At first, some may even consciously resist learning English or teaching it to their children, since learning English symbolically represents accepting a prolonged stay outside their homeland. Cubans arriving in the 1960s and 1970s were predominantly from the professional classes, and insisted that their children learn and retain Spanish. These same Cubans intended to return to their homeland shortly, and the awareness that this would not be possible in the near future came only slowly and painfully. The relatively positive reception given to these Cubans in the United

States, in contrast to the harsh treatment often afforded to Puerto Rican, Mexican, and Central American arrivals, might have added to the feeling of self-assurance in maintaining Spanish as the language of the community as well as of the home. To this day, more than thirty years after the first immigration of Cubans spurred by the Cuban Revolution, young Cuban Americans, particularly in South Florida, continue to learn and use Spanish at a higher rate, and with less shift in the direction of English, than many other U.S. Hispanic groups.

The Nicaraguan community in the United States shows patterns similar to those of Cuban Americans. The Sandinista Revolution of 1979 brought several hundred thousand Nicaraguans to the United States, most from professional and middle classes, although in recent years the number of rural and working-class residents has increased. Most Nicaraguans, planning to return to their homeland, have maintained a high level of Spanish. Although their children learn English in school, Spanish is maintained without difficulty. This situation is different among Salvadorans who come from the ranks of the rural poor. In cities with a large Salvadoran population, Salvadorans live and work in Spanish-speaking neighborhoods and drift toward jobs that do not require learning English. However, those young Salvadorans who do go to school may shift to English faster than other Hispanic groups, at times with the active encouragement of their parents.

Even though Spanish remains a strong home language in U.S. Hispanic communities, English is always present. It is the first language for some, the second language for others, and for most U.S.-born Hispanics, bilingualism begins in earliest childhood. Spanish and English in such close contact inevitably influence one another, but despite this natural process, any evidence of language mixing is often criticized and ridiculed. It is the hybrid varieties of Spanish that receive the most criticism; terms like "Tex-Mex," "Spanglish," and "pocho" are used to describe a wide range of language, ranging from only limited abilities in Spanish by English-dominant speakers, to fully fluent Spanish that has simply absorbed some English words. Although often based on prejudice and intolerance, these terms do arise from several types of English influence that can be noticed in U.S. Spanish.

Spanish has borrowed many words from English. At first, English words were modified to fit Spanish patterns, sometimes capitalizing on already existent patterns. *Lunch* became *lonche*, a term that is now found well into South America. In all instances, *lonche* refers to the light lunch eaten in the United States, for example, by schoolchildren or by employees at work, and not to the large *almuerzo* or *comida* consumed at midday in Hispanic countries. *Lonche* therefore represents a borrowing for a new cultural concept. Derived from *lonche* are *lonchera* 'lunch box,' *lonchar* 'to eat lunch,' and *lonchería* 'lunchroom, cafeteria,' all words based on productive patterns of Spanish word formation. Sometimes an existent Spanish word was replaced for no apparent reason. For example, in many countries *estacionar* 'park an automobile' has been replaced by *parcar*, *aparcar*, or *parquear*, all derived from 'park.' This extends to *parquímetro* 'parking meter,' and *parqueo* or even *parking* 'parking lot.' Other anglicisms widely known in Latin America are *líder* 'leader' (together with *liderar* 'to lead' and *liderazgo* 'leadership'), *guachimán* 'watchman,' *flirtear* 'to flirt,' *esnob* 'snob' (together with *esnobismo* 'snobbishness'), *esquí*

Catholic churches in Hispanic populated areas quite often offer masses in both English and Spanish, as does Our Lady of Guadalupe Church in Queen Creek, Arizona. (Courtesy of the *Texas Catholic Herald*.)

'ski,' *esmóquin* 'tuxedo' (from 'smoking jacket'), *bluyins* 'blue jeans.' *livin* 'living room,' *estándar* 'standard,' *sanuiche* (with variants *sánuich*, *sánuiche*, *sanduche*, and so on) 'sandwich,' and so on. Sports terminology is full of anglicisms, some of them unmodified. This is particularly true in baseball, where Spanish terms (all of which were originally translated from English) are largely replaced by English words in live commentary, although the Spanish forms may be used in written form: *pícher* (*lanzador*), *cácher* (*receptor*), *lef fílder* (*jardinero de izquierda*), *jonrón* 'home run' (*cuadrangular*), and so forth. Some baseball terms were made over into plausible-sounding Spanish words right from the beginning: *base* 'base,' *bate* 'bat,' *bateador* 'batter.'

In the United States, borrowing from English is naturally more frequent and penetrates further into Spanish. Early borrowings like *troca* 'truck' have spread into Mexico, but most remain confined to the United States. Verbs are usually formed by adding *-ear* or *-iar*: *güeldiar* 'to weld,' *taipiar* 'to type,' *espelear* 'to spell.' *Frizar* 'to freeze,' *tochar* 'to touch,' *fixar* 'to fix,' and so forth, add only *-ar*. Sometimes Spanish *hacer* 'to make, to do' is followed by an English word: *hacer fix* 'to fix,' but this is not done often. Anglicisms in U.S. Spanish do not detract from the communicative potential of the language, and are in no way different from indigenous words in Latin American Spanish, which are often not understood outside a limited region. Most U.S. Hispanics who use the words just mentioned alternate with words from the general Spanish vocabulary.

Another common aspect of language appropriation is word-by-word translation. Colorful expressions like "kick the bucket," "spill the beans," and "toe the line" started out with concrete meanings, but ended up signifying something that cannot be predicted by looking at the individual words. On the other hand, an expression like "think it over" is also idiomatic, since "over" is not operating with its normal meaning. Colorful idiomatic expressions are seldom translatable, although cultural contact may cause some to enter another language. For example, *patear el balde* 'kick the bucket' is sometimes used outside the United States. In Texas, "redneck" is often semiseriously rendered as *pescuezo colorado* or *nuca colorada*. Speakers who use such expressions are aware of their idiomatic nature and usually do so jokingly, and only with other bilingual speakers who will appreciate the humor. In expressions that are part of everyday language, speakers may not be aware that a word-by-word translation is not possible. In bilingual communities, word-by-word translations are used more frequently, but grammatical rules of Spanish are hardly ever broken. What does

change is the meaning of individual words. Thus, when a bilingual speaker says that a politician *está corriendo para sheriff* 'is running for sheriff,' nothing about the Spanish expression is out of place, except that *correr* ordinarily refers to the physical act of running, and not to a political campaign. Spanish-English bilinguals in the United States frequently use expressions based on *para atrás* (usually pronounced *patrás*) as a translation of English "back": *te llamo patrás* 'I'll call you back,' *fuimos patrás* 'we went back,' *no me hables patrás* 'don't talk back to me.' *Para atrás*, is a legitimate Spanish combination, but only in the sense of backward motion: *el hombre se echó para atrás* 'the man jumped backward.' The "new" use of *patrás* has occurred under the influence of English. The grammar is Spanish, the words are Spanish, but the meaning can only be interpreted in a bilingual environment.

Among fluent bilinguals, rapid switches between languages commonly occur in a single conversation. Linguists refer to this behavior as "code-switching," where "code" refers to the language or communicative system that is changed. This may happen at a logical break in the conversation, for example when answering the telephone or welcoming a newly arrived participant. Language switching also takes place in direct quotes, or to underscore a personal identification with the group represented by the language in question. This is a strategy used by bilingual speakers worldwide, and even individuals with only a slight knowledge of a second language engage in this strategy (for example, in the foreign language classroom). Bilinguals may slip in short tag expressions in the opposite language: *tú sabes* 'you know,' *ándale* 'OK, right,' *de acuerdo* 'all right,' *ay bendito* 'my goodness,' *qué chévere* 'that's great,' and in English, "wow, right on," "that's incredible," and so forth. These switches are not always conscious, but they are invariably short and colloquial, a way of reaffirming one's identity and of reassuring the listener of solidarity and intimacy. In the U.S. setting, inclusion of Spanish phrases in the midst of a conversation in English is the more common case, even among English-dominant bilinguals. In these circumstances, English is perceived as the neutral language, spoken by everybody and carrying no connotations of ethnicity, while Spanish is the "special" half of a bilingual conversation.

The type of language shifting that arouses the most controversy is the switch in the middle of a sentence. The titles of recent research articles illustrate the process: "Sometimes I'll Start a Sentence in English *y termino en español* [and I finish up in Spanish]." "*Ta bien* [it's OK], you can answer me *en cualquier idioma* [in either language]." Such combinations are baffling to the outsider, incomprehensible to the monolingual speaker of either language, and bewildering to foreign language learners. This fluent switching in midsentence has been taken by many as the deterioration of English and Spanish, evidence of the undesirability of bilingualism. Some have even used bilingual language switching as an argument to convince Spanish-speakers to abandon their native language, on the assertion that it is already corrupted beyond reclamation. Midsentence language shifting is the sort of shift most often associated with pejorative terms like "Spanglish" and *pocho*.

Although bilingual code-switching has often been criticized when practiced by Hispanics in the United States, language switching is not regarded so negatively in all other bilingual communities throughout the world. It is an effect of the lopsided social status accorded to English, as opposed to Spanish, in the United States. In bilingual societies where a more nearly even balance exists between languages, switching, even in midsentence, is seldom criticized. The residents of Gibraltar, nearly all of whom are Spanish-English bilinguals (although English is the only official language), switch languages in the same fashion found in the United States, arriving at many of the same bilingual combinations. During the height of the Napoleonic Empire, aristocratic Russians freely switched in and out of French, which was regarded as highly prestigious behavior, since in Russia, only the elite knew French. Code-switching is the order of the day in countries such as India and the Philippines, and in areas of Belgium, Switzerland, the Soviet Union, and Canada. During the Norman occupation of England, Anglo-Saxons who were forced to learn the French of their conquerors actually spoke a code-switched mixture. French and English intellectuals of the time condemned this mixed language as vulgar and depraved, but after withstanding the test of time, it went on to become a world language—modern English—with its hundreds of French words. Spanish absorbed hundreds of Arabic words during the nearly eight centuries of Moorish occupation of Spain, from 711 to 1492, during which time bilingualism was the rule in southern Spain, and language shifting undoubtedly occurred. Attitudes toward language mixing and shifting reflect social power rather than actual communicative value. Languages of powerful nations are respected and imitated, and when a nation or society loses power, its language loses prestige and is learned by fewer people.

After the fact, a bilingual speaker may not be exactly sure where in a sentence the shift occurred, and may even be unaware (until reminded) of having switched languages at all. This is not evidence of confusion or the inability to keep the two languages apart, since bilinguals take care to not shift languages with nonbilinguals or those who object to this style of speaking. This crucial fact, combined with the maintenance of grammatical rules during language shifting, is evidence that bilingual speakers are manipulating two separate language systems. Serious research into bilingual code-switching reveals that, far from being a random jumble of two languages, this way of speaking is governed by the same types of rules as determine the acceptability of sentences in Spanish or English. Bilingual language shifting is not a "mix and match" strategy of randomly alternating Spanish and English words. Segments in Spanish and segments in English contain no internal grammatical errors; each portion is minisentence" produced in a single language. The transition from one language to the other creates no grammatical violation; the same parts of speech are used in the same basic order, and in general the only thing that changes is the language from which they are taken. The transition is smooth, and each half of the sentence sounds acceptable with respect to the language in which it was produced. When the beginning of a sentence in one language would not be compatible with a continuation in the other language, the shift does not occur. For example, one might say in English, "This is the record that I was telling you about" ending with "about." In Spanish this word order is not possible: *Este es el disco de que te hablaba.* If languages were to be switched in such a sentence, likely possibilities would be *Este es el disco que I was telling you about,* or *This is the record de que te hablaba,* since the same grammatical patterns are followed after the language shift as would have been had the sentence remained in the first language. However, *This is the record that te hablaba,* would hardly ever occur, because there would be no way of adding the meaning of English "about" in an acceptable way in Spanish. Similarly, we might hear *my red carro,* but not *mi carro red,* since in English the adjective does not usually follow the noun that it modifies.

The reasons for language switching in the middle of a sentence are complex and not yet fully understood. One common cause is unavailability of a word in the initial language due to a momentary memory lapse, a word with no equivalent in the first language, or a proper name. The switch will often 'pull' the rest of the sentence along; it may not occur exactly at the point where a word from the second language is introduced, but may anticipate the triggering element. A typical example is *Mucha gente no sabe where Magnolia Street is* 'Many people don't know where Magnolia Street is,' where the speaker, thinking of a street name in English, switched languages at the first clause boundary before the English name. Although some language switching is triggered by words or expressions that are untranslatable or momentarily forgotten, many more cases simply reflect the expanded combinations available to bilingual speakers during a relaxed conversation. Such switching reinforces ethnic solidarity, allows for greater subtlety of expression, and gives bilingual speakers the pleasure of having an additional "language" of their own, not shared by monolingual speakers of either language.

Bilingual language switching is not simply a way of speaking, it is a way of writing, and the use of Spanish-English alternations is increasingly common in literature written by bilingual authors. This strategy is most frequently used in poetry but has also found its way into novels and stories depicting the life and language of Spanish-speakers in the United States. One of the best-known novelists to extensively use language switching is Rolando Hinojosa (for example in *Mi querido Rafa*). Many prominent poets and playwrights also use this technique, reflecting the real language of U.S. Hispanic communities.

It is frequently asked whether or not there is a uniquely "U.S." variety of Spanish. It seems, after considering the full panorama of Spanish language usage in the United States, that the answer in general is no. Spanish in the United States continues to be divided mainly according to the country of ancestral origin: Mexican, Puerto Rican, Cuban, and so forth. Even in cities where more than one large Hispanic group is found, a single language variety usually prevails. In a few cities, such as Chicago, more than one variety of Spanish is represented in the communications media, but this has little effect on Spanish used in individual neighborhoods. Similarly, and despite dictionaries that claim to describe such dialects, it is almost impossible to justify the existence of "American" varieties of Spanish: "Mexican-American," "Puerto Rican-American," "Cuban-American," and so forth. What is found in the United States is greater use of English, and shifting of some Spanish words to match equivalent English terms. This does not make for separate dialects of Spanish, especially since the use of English elements is not consistent from speaker to speaker. In fact, the claim of a special U.S. Spanish is often a by-product of negative attitudes toward Spanish-speakers in the United States, as held by Spanish-speakers from other nations as well as by many Americans.

The nonexistence of a unique U.S. Spanish dialect is not a negative result. Spanish use in the United States is expanding rather than shrinking, and this expansion involves styles and ranges of language in addition to the number of speakers. U.S. Spanish is, more than ever, closely tied both to the international Spanish-speaking community and to American society and culture. What *is* uniquely American U.S. Spanish is the complex pattern of bilingual language usage, which finds its highest form of expression in bilingual literature. By being able to communicate bilingually, U.S. Spanish-speakers command an extraordinarily rich language repertoire, which is at once part of Latin American and U.S. society and also uniquely Hispanic-American.

References

Amastae, John and Lucía ElíasOlivares, eds. *Spanish in the United States: Sociolinguistic Aspects.* Cambridge: Cambridge University Press, 1982.

Berger, John, ed. *Spanish in the United States: Sociolinguistic Issues.* Washington, D.C.: Georgetown University Press, 1990.

Elías-Bowen, J. Donald and Jacob Ornstein, eds. *Studies in Southwest Spanish.* Rowley, Mass.: Newbury House, 1976.

ElíasOlivares, Lucía, ed. *Spanish in the U.S. Setting: Beyond the Southwest.* Rosslyn, Va.: National Clearinghouse for Bilingual Education, 1983.

———, Elizabeth Leone, René Cisneros, John Gutiérrez, eds. *Spanish Language Use and Public Life in the USA.* The Hague: Mouton, 1985.

Fishman, Joshua, Roxanna Ma, Eleanor Herasimchuk, eds. *Bilingualism in the Barrio.* The Hague: Mouton, 1972.

Hernández Chávez, Eduardo, Andrew Cohen, Anthony Beltramo, eds. *El lenguaje de los chicanos.* Arlington, Va.: Center for Applied Linguistics, 1975.

Lipski, John. "Spanish World-wide: Toward a More Perfect Union." *Revista Chicano-Riqueña* 12, no. 1 (1984): 4356.

———. "Central American Spanish in the United States: El Salvador." *Aztlán* 17 (1986): 91-124.

———. *Linguistic Aspects of Spanish-English Language Switching.* Tempe: Arizona State University, Center for Latin American Studies, 1985.

———. "Salvadorans in the United States: patterns of Sociolinguistic Integration." *National Journal of Sociology* 3 (1989): 97-119.

Metcalf, Allan. *Chicano English.* Arlington, Va.: Center for Applied Linguistics, 1979.

Ornstein-Galicia, Jacob, ed. *Form and function in Chicano English.* Rowley, Mass.: Newbury House, 1980.

Peñalosa, Fernando. *Chicano Sociolinguistics.* Rowley, Mass.: Newbury House, 1980.

———. *Central Americans in Los Angeles: Background, Language, Education.* Los Alamitos, Calif.: National Center for Bilingual Research, 1984.

Poplack, Shana. "Sometimes I'll Start a Sentence in English y termino en español." *Linguistics* 18 (1980): 581-618.

Sánchez, Rosaura. *Chicano Discourse.* Rowley, Mass.: Newbury House, 1983.

Timm, Leonra. "Spanish-English Code-Switching: el porque y how-not-to." *Romance Philology* 28 (1975): 473-82.

Zentella, Ana Celia. "Ta bien, You Could Answer Me en cualquier idioma: Puerto Rican Code-Switching in the Bilingual Classroom." *Latino Language and Communicative Behavior*, edited by Roberto Durán, 95-107. Norwood, N.J,: Ablex, 1981.

John M. Lipski

Illustrations

A Historical Overview: *p. 5:* Map of early European penetration of the United States (courtesy of the U.S. Department of the Interior and the National Park Service); *p. 13:* San José de Tumacacori Mission, Arizona (courtesy of the U.S. Department of the Interior and the National Park Service); *p. 14:* A *vaquero* in early California (courtesy of the Bancroft Library, University of California); *p. 15:* Rules issued by King of Spain regarding presidios on the frontier; *p. 18:* Soldier at the Monterey presidio in 1786 (courtesy of the Bancroft Library, University of California); *p. 19:* Wife of a presidio soldier in Monterey, 1786 (courtesy of the Bancroft Library, University of California); *p. 19:* A *patrón* in early California (courtesy of the Bancroft Library, University of California); *p. 20:* Presidio and pueblo of Santa Barbara in 1829 (from a lithograph by G. & W. Endicott. Courtesy of the Bancroft Library, University of California); *p. 21:* Ferdinand VII, King of Spain, 1814-1833 (from Manuel Rivera Cambas, Los gobernantes, 1872); *p. 23:* Pío Pico (1801-1894), last governor of California under Mexican rule (courtesy of the California Historical Society); *p. 24:* Confederate officers from Laredo, Texas: Refugio Benavides, Atanacio Vidaurri, Cristóbal Benavides and John Z. Leyendecker (courtesy of the Laredo Public Library); *p. 25:* Viceroy Francisco Fernández de la Cueva Enríquez, Duke of Albuquerque; *p. 25:* General Manuel Mier y Terán, Laredo, 1928; *p. 27:* Map of European claims in the United States to 1763 (courtesy of the U.S. Department of the Interior and the National Park Service);

p. 30: Albizu Campos at a press conference on December 16, 1947; *p. 30:* Luis Muñoz-Rivera; *p. 44:* Luis Muñoz Marín, architect of the present commonwealth status of Puerto Rico; *p. 47:* Fidel Castro; *p. 49:* The first flight of American citizens repatriated from Cuba on December 19, 1966 (courtesy of the *Texas Catholic Herald*); *p. 50:* Cubans arriving in Miami during the Mariel boat-lift (courtesy of the *Texas Catholic Herald*); *p. 51:* A legally immigrating Cuban woman is reunited with her granddaughter in Miami in 1980 (courtesy of the *Texas Catholic Herald*).

Spanish Explorers and Colonizers: *p. 60:* Queen Isabella la Católica; *p. 60:* Frontispiece from original 1493 edition of Cristóbal Colón's letter to the Catholic Kings describing his discoveries; *p. 66:* The title page of Cabeza de Vaca's *La relación* (*The Account of His Trip*), 1542; *p. 69:* A portrayal of Hernando de Soto by an unknown eighteenth-century artist (courtesy of the U.S. Department of the Interior and the National Park Service); *p. 71:* Pedro Menéndez de Avilés; *p. 71:* Drawing of free black militia (1795).

Historic Landmarks: *p. 138:* Royal Presidio Chapel, Monterey (courtesy of the U.S. Department of the Interior and the National Park Service); *p. 139:* San Francisco de Asís Mission (Mission Dolores) (Oriana Day Painting. Courtesy of the De Young Museum, San Francisco); *p. 140:* San Luis Rey de Francia Mission, Oceanside (photo by Henry F. Whitey, 1936. W.P.A.); *p. 140:* Santa Barbara Mission (photo by

Henry F. Whitey, 1936. W.P.A.); *p. 141:* General Vallejo House (photo by Roger Sturtevant, 1934); *p. 141:* Castillo de San Marcos, St. Augustine; *p. 142:* The Cabildo in New Orleans (courtesy of the U.S. Department of the Interior and the National Park Service); *p. 144:* The Convent of Porta Coeli in San Germán; *p. 144:* The Alamo, San Antonio (courtesy of the Department of the Interior and the National Park Service); *p. 145:* San Francisco de la Espada Mission, San Antonio; *p. 145:* La Bahía Mission (courtesy of the U.S. Department of the Interior and the National Park Service); *p. 146:* Monument honoring the fallen at the Alamo, San Antonio (courtesy of the U.S. Department of the Interior and the National Park Service); *p. 147:* A reconstruction of the San Francisco Mission in East Texas (courtesy of the *Texas Catholic Herald*); *p. 148:* San Miguel Mission, Santa Fe, New Mexico (courtesy of the U.S. Department of the Interior and the National Park Service); *p. 148:* San José y San Miguel Aguayo Mission (photo by Arthur W. Stewart, 1936. W.P.A.).

The Family: *p. 152:* The Lugo Family, circa 1888 (courtesy of Los Angeles County Museum of Natural History); *p. 153:* A child's birthday party in New York City (Justo A. Martí Collection, Center for Puerto Rican Studies Library, Hunter College, CUNY); *p. 154:* United Bronx Parents, Inc. (Records of the United Bronx Parents, Inc. Courtesy of the Center for Puerto Rican Studies Library, Hunter College, CUNY); *p. 154:* A Puerto Rican mine worker and his family, Bingham Canyon, Utah (Historical Archive, Departamento de Asuntos de la Comunidad Puertorriqueña. Courtesy of the Center for Puerto Rican Studies Library, Hunter College, CUNY); *p. 155:* Mexican Mother of the Year, 1969: Mrs. Dolores Venegas, Houston, Texas (courtesy of the *Texas Catholic Herald*); *p. 157:* A Hispanic family attends mass, Houston, Texas (photo by Curtis Dowell. Courtesy of the *Texas Catholic Herald*); *p. 158:* A *posada* rehearsal, Houston, Texas, 1988 (photo by Curtis Dowell. Courtesy of the *Texas Catholic Herald*).

Relations with Spain and Spanish America: *p. 177:* Rally in East Lower Harlem (El Barrio) in Manhattan in support of the independence of Puerto Rico (The Jesús Colón Papers. Courtesy of the Center for Puerto Rican Studies, Hunter College, CUNY; Benigno Giboyeaux for the Estate of Jesús Colón and the Communist Party of the United States of America); *p. 193:* Fidel Castro; *p. 194:* Archbishop Oscar Romero of El Salvador (courtesy of the *Texas Catholic Herald*); *p. 196:* Guerrillas of El Frente Farabundo Martí por la Liberación Nacional (FMLN) in El Salvador; *p. 198:* Demonstrators opposing U.S. military aid to El Salvador in 1980 (courtesy of the *Texas Catholic Herald*).

Population Growth and Distribution: *p. 200:* Senior citizens at the Domino Park in Little Havana, Miami (courtesy of the *Texas Catholic Herald*); *p. 201:* Undocumented workers entering the United States at El Paso, Texas, 1990 (courtesy of the *Texas Catholic Herald*); *p. 201:* A group of Hispanics have just been issued their temporary residence cards, 1991 (photo by Les Fetchko. Courtesy of the *Texas Catholic Herald*); *p. 202:* The drive to legalize undocumented workers in Houston, Texas (photo by Curtis Dowell. Courtesy of the *Texas Catholic Herald*); *p. 203:* A poster for National Migration Week; *p. 204:* Mexican Independence Day Parade, Houston, Texas, 1982 (photo by Curtis Dowell. Courtesy of the *Texas Catholic Herald*); *p. 206:* A mass citizenship swearing in ceremony at Hoffheinz Pavilion of the University of Houston in 1987 (photo by Curtis Dowell. Courtesy of the *Texas Catholic Herald*).

Language: *p. 210:* The Teatro Puerto Rico in October, 1960 (Justo A. Martí Collection. Courtesy of the Center for Puerto Rican Studies Library, Hunter College, CUNY); *p. 214:* Downtown El Paso, Texas (courtesy of the *Texas Catholic Herald*); *p. 218:* A typical Hispanic grocery store in New York City (Justo A. Martí Collection. Courtesy of the Center for Puerto Rican Studies Library, Hunter College, CUNY); *p. 219:* Two scenes from the *Villa Alegre* television series; *p. 220:* A customer buying *La prensa* (Justo A. Martí Collection. Courtesy of the Center for Puerto Rican Studies Library, Hunter College, CUNY); *p. 222:* A voter registration drive in New York City (Justo A. Martí Collection. Courtesy of the Center for Puerto Rican Studies Library, Hunter College, CUNY); *p. 223:* Our Lady of Guadalupe Church in Queen Creek, Arizona (courtesy of the *Texas Catholic Herald*).

Law and Politics: *p. 240:* Four charts on law school enrollment (*Consultant's Digest*, May 1991); *p. 242:* Wilfredo Caraballo; *p. 243:* Antonia Hernández; *p. 244:* Mario G. Obledo; *p. 246:* Table 9.1, Hispanic Judges in State Courts (courtesy of the Hispanic National Bar Association Nationwide Summary of Hispanics in the State Judiciary, 1992); *p. 247:* Judge Reynaldo G. Garza; *p. 249:* Judge Raymond L. Acosta; *p. 249:* Justice John A. Argüelles; *p. 250:* Justice Joseph F. Baca; *p. 251:* Judge José A. Cabranes; *p. 253:* Judge George La Plata; *p. 254:* Judge Federico A. Moreno; *p. 255:* Chief Judge Manuel L. Real; *p. 256:* Justice Dorothy Comstock Riley; *p. 257:* Judge Joseph H. Rodríguez; *p. 257:* Chief Justice Luis D.

Rovirá; *p. 260:* Ben Blaz. Delegate to the U.S. Congress from Guam; *p. 261:* E. (Kika) de la Garza, U.S. Congressman (D-Texas); *p. 261:* Ron de Lugo. Delegate to the U.S. Congress from the U.S. Virgin Islands; *p. 262:* Matthew G. Martínez, U.S. Congressman (D-California); *p. 263:* Solomon *P. Ortiz, U.S. Congressman (D-Texas); p. 263:* Bill Richardson, U.S. Congressman (D-New Mexico); *p. 264:* Ileana Ros-Lehtinen, U.S. Congresswoman (R-Florida); *p. 264:* Edward R. Roybal, U.S. Congressman (D-California); *p. 265:* José E. Serrano, U.S. Congressman (D-New York); *p. 266:* Esteban E. Torres, U.S. Congressman (D-California); *p. 267:* Hispanic Members of the House of Representatives (courtesy of the Congressional Hispanic Caucus); *p. 268:* Herman Badillo, Former U.S. Congressman (D-New York); *p. 273:* Cari M. Domínguez, Director, Office of Federal Contract Compliance Programs; *p. 273:* Manuel Luján, Jr., Secretary of the Interior; *p. 274:* Robert Martínez, Director, Office of National Drug Control Policy, and Former Governor of Florida; *p. 275:* Antonia C. Novello, M.D., M.P.H., Surgeon General, United States Public Health Service; *p. 275:* Catalina Vásquez Villalpando, Treasurer of the United States; *p. 278:* Stephanie González, Secretary of State, New Mexico; *p. 279:* Ygnacio D. Garza, Mayor, Brownsville, Texas; *p. 280:* Gloria Molina, Los Angeles County Supervisor; *p. 281:* Federico Peña, Mayor, Denver (photo by Larry Lazlo); *p. 281:* Louis E. Saavedra, Mayor, Albuquerque; *p. 282:* Xavier L. Suárez, Mayor, Miami.

Education: p. 287: Children at recess, the Guadalupe Aztlán alternative school, Houston, 1981 (photo by Curtis Dowell. Courtesy of the *Texas Catholic Herald*); *p. 299:* Mexican fourth-graders at Drachman School (circa 1913) (courtesy of the Arizona Historical Society); *p. 300:* A poster encouraging Hispanics to register to vote; *p. 302:* Children at the Guadalupe Aztlán alternative school, Houston, 1981 (photo by Curtis Dowell. Courtesy of the *Texas Catholic Herald*); *p. 303:* A sixth-grade classroom in the Huelga School, an alternative school set up in St. Patrick's Chapel, Houston (photo by Curtis Dowell. Courtesy of the *Texas Catholic Herald*); *p. 304:* A poster encouraging affirmative action and equal opportunity in education in California; *p. 305:* Dr. Manuel Pacheco, President of the University of Arizona.

Business: p. 309: Table 11.1, Hispanic and Nonminority Businesses; *p. 309:* Poster for the 1985 United States Hispanic Chamber of Commerce convention; *p. 310:* Figure 11.1, Origin of U.S. Hispanic Business Owners; *p. 310:* Table 11.2, Number of Businesses, Sales Volume, Number of Employees, and Payroll by Hispanic Origin of Owners (source: United States Bureau of the Census, 1991); *p. 311:* Table 11.3, Hispanic Businesses by Major Industry Category (source: United States Bureau of the Census, 1991); *p. 311:* Table 11.4, Number and Sales Volume of Hispanic Businesses in the Ten Largest Metropolitan Statistical Areas versus Those in the Entire State (source: United States Bureau of the Census, 1991); *p. 312:* Table 11.5, Number of Employees in Hispanic Businesses (source: United States Bureau of the Census, 1992); *p. 312:* Table 11.6, Sales Volume of Hispanic Businesses (source: United States Bureau of the Census, 1987); *p. 313:* Table 11.7, The Thirty Largest Hispanic Businesses (courtesy of "The 500," 1991); *p. 314:* Table 11.8, Hispanic and Nonminority Business Owners by Age (source: United States Bureau of the Census, 1987); *p. 314:* Table 11.9, Hispanic and Nonminority Business Owners by Years of Education (source: United States Bureau of the Census, 1987); *p. 314:* Table 11.10, Hispanic and Nonminority Business Owners Across Four Characteristics (source: United States Bureau of the Census, 1987); *p. 315:* Table 11.11, Start-up Capital Required for Hispanic and Nonminority Business Owners; *p. 315:* Figure 11.2, Sources of Start-up Capital for Hispanic and Nonminority Business Owners; *p. 316:* Table 11.12, Profit and Loss for Hispanic and Nonminority Businesses (source: United States Bureau of the Census, 1987); *p. 316:* Table 11.13, Minority Employees in Hispanic and Nonminority Businesses (source: United States Bureau of the Census, 1987); *p. 318:* Gilbert Cuéllar, Jr; *p. 319:* Roberto C. Goizueta; *p. 319:* Frederick J. González; *p. 320:* Edgar J. Milán; *p. 322:* Lionel Sosa; *p. 323:* Clifford L. Whitehill.

Labor and Employment: p. 325: César Chávez exhorting people to start a new grape boycott in 1986 (courtesy of the *Texas Catholic Herald*); *p. 326:* Mexican women working at a commercial tortilla factory in the 1930s (courtesy of the Library of Congress); *p. 327:* A cotton picker in 1933 (photo by Dorothea Lange. Courtesy of the Library of Congress); *p. 328:* Mexican mine workers in the early 1900s (courtesy of the Arizona Historical Society); *p. 329:* Puerto Rican garment workers in New York City; *p. 329:* A Mexican worker being finger-printed for deportation (courtesy of the Library of Congress); *p. 330:* Southern Pacific railroad workers during World War II in Tucson, Arizona (courtesy of the Arizona Historical Society); *p. 332:* Unemployed workers at a relief office during the Depression (courtesy of the Library of Congress); *p. 332:* A fruit picker in California (courtesy of the *Texas Catholic Herald*); *p. 333:* A parade ending National Farm Workers Week, Union Square, New York, 1975 (courtesy of the *Texas Catholic Herald*); *p. 334:* A United Farm Workers picket line in Coachella,

California, 1973 (courtesy of the *Texas Catholic Herald*); *p. 336*: A scene from the Bracero Program (courtesy of the Library of Congress); *p. 337*: A field worker in the Bracero Program (courtesy of the Library of Congress); *p. 339*: A migrant work camp (courtesy of the Library of Congress); *p. 340*: The interior of a migrant labor shack (courtesy of the *Texas Catholic Herald*).

Women: p. 354: Poster advertising a Hispanic women's conference in Texas in 1987; *p. 354*: A beauty queen for the Fiestas Patrias celebration, Houston (photo by Curtis Dowell. Courtesy of the *Texas Catholic Herald*); *p. 357*: A workshop at the 1980 California Governor's Chicana Issues Conference; *p. 361*: Teresa Bernárdez, M.D; *p. 363*: Emyré Barrios Robinson; *p. 365*: Carmen Delgado Votaw, Director, Washington Office, Girls Scouts, USA.

Religion: p. 368: A Catholic charismatic prayer meeting (courtesy of the *Texas Catholic Herald*); *p. 369*: The Franciscan method of teaching the Indians by pictures (from an engraving based on Fray Diego Valdés, o.F.M., in his Rhetorica Christiana, Rome, 1579); *p. 369*: Bartolemé de las Casas (1474-1566); *p. 370*: San Juan Capistrano Mission, San Antonio, Texas (photo by Silvia Novo Pena. Courtesy of the *Texas Catholic Herald*); *p. 372*: The Image of Our Lady of Guadalupe (photo by Curtis Dowell. Courtesy of the *Texas Catholic Herald*); *p. 380*: Feast of the Crowning of Mary, Sacred Heart Cathedral, Houston, 1987 (photo by Curtis Dowell. Courtesy of the *Texas Catholic Herald*); *p. 382*: Annual mass on the feast day of Our Lady of Guadalupe, Houston, Texas (courtesy of the *Texas Catholic Herald*); *p. 383*: The celebration of the feast day of Our Lady of Caridad del Cobre, the patron of Cubans, Houston, 1986 (photo by Curtis Dowell. Courtesy of the *Texas Catholic Herald*); *p. 384*: A Christmas posada, Houston, 1988 (photo by Curtis Dowell. Courtesy of the *Texas Catholic Herald*); *p. 385*: Diversity in Hispanic evangelism (photo by Curtis Dowell. Courtesy of the *Texas Catholic Herald*).

Organizations: p. 388: A march from the Lower East Side of New York City over the Brooklyn Bridge to protest the poor conditions of public schools in the Puerto Rican community (Historic Archive of the Department of Puerto Rican Community Affairs in the United States. Courtesy of the Center for Puerto Rican Studies Library and Archives, Hunter College, CUNY); *p. 388*: A celebration of the Three Kings (Jesús Colón Papers. Courtesy of the Center for Puerto Rican Studies Library and Archives, Hunter College, CUNY); *p. 389*: A parade organized by the

Tucson's Alianza Hispano-Americana (courtesy of the Arizona Historical Society); *p. 390*: President Ronald Reagan presents the Medal of Freedom to Dr. Héctor García; *p. 394*: Brooklyn Chapter of the Liga Puertorriqueña e Hispana (Puerto Rican and Hispanic League), circa 1927 (Jesús Colón Papers. Courtesy of the Center for Puerto Rican Studies Library and Archives, Hunter College, CUNY); *p. 396*: Poster for the Spanish-Speaking Coalition Conference of October, 1971.

Scholarship: p. 400: Albert Michael Camarillo; *p. 400*: Arthur León Campa; *p. 401*: Carlos E. Cortés; *p. 402*: Rodolfo J. Cortina; *p. 403*: Margarita Fernández Olmos; *p. 404*: Erlinda González-Berry; *p. 405*: Olga Jiménez-Wagenheim; *p. 406*: Luis Leal; *p. 407*: Raúl Moncarraz; *p. 408*: Sonia Nieto; *p. 408*: Julián Olivares; *p. 410*: Ricardo Romo; *p. 411*: Ramón Eduardo Ruiz.

Literature: p. 414: Miguel Antonio Otero (Miguel A. Otero Collection, Special Collections, General Library, University of New Mexico, Neg. No. 000-021-0004); *p. 415*: Eusebio Chacón (Miguel A. Otero Collection, Special Collections, General Library, University of New Mexico, Neg. No. 000-021-0168); *p. 415*: Title page of El hijo de la tempestad by Eusebio Chacón (Special Collections, General Library, University of New Mexico); *p. 416*: Cuban literary and patriotic figure, José Martí; *p. 418*: The cover of Daniel Venegas's satirical newspaper, *El Malcriado*; *p. 418*: Fray Angélico Chávez (Special Collections, General Library, University of New Mexico); *p. 419*: Cover of the first issue of *Gráfico* newspaper; *p. 421*: Lola Rodríguez de Tió (archives, Arte Público Press); *p. 423*: Abelardo Delgado, Ron Arias and Rolando Hinojosa at the Second National Latino Book Fair and Writers Festival, Houston, Texas, 1980 (archives, Arte Público Press); *p. 424*: The original manuscript of the Tomás Rivera poem, "When love to be?" (archives, Arte Público Press); *p. 425*: Evangelina Vigil-Piñón, reciting at the Third National Hispanic Book Fair, Houston, 1987 (photo: Julián Olivares. Archives, Arte Público Press); *p. 425*: The cover of Rudolfo Anaya's best-selling novel, *Bless Me, Ultima* (archives, Arte Público Press); *p. 426*: A vendor at the First National Latino Book Fair, Chicago, 1979 (archives, Arte Público Press); *p. 427*: Ana Castillo, 1979 (archives, Arte Público Press); *p. 427*: Helena María Viramontes, 1986 (photo by Georgia McInnis, Archives, Arte Público Press); *p. 428*: Luis Dávila at the First National Latino Book Fair, 1979 (archives, Arte Público Press); *p. 429*: The cover of Rudolfo Anaya's *Cuentos: Tales from the Hispanic Southwest* (archives, Arte Público Press); *p. 429*: Pat Mora, 1986 (archives, Arte Público Press); *p. 430:* The cover of Denise Chávez's *The Last of the Menu Girls* (archives, Arte Público Press); *p. 430:* The cover of *This Bridge Called My Back* (archives, Arte Público Press); *p. 431:* Gary Soto and Evangelina Vigil-Piñón, Third National Hispanic Book Fair and Writers Festival, Houston, Texas, 1987 (archives, Arte Público Press); *p. 432:* Ricardo Sánchez, Alejandro Morales, critic Salvador Rodríguez del Pino and Victor Villaseñor at a book fair in Mexico City, 1979; *p. 433:* Julia de Burgos; *p. 434:* José Luis González (archives, Arte Público Press); *p. 434:* Luis Rafael Sánchez (archives, Arte Público Press); *p. 435:* Pedro Juan Soto (archives, Arte Público Press); *p. 436:* Jesús Colón ca. 1950s (archives, Centro de Estudios Puertorriqueños, Hunter College); *p. 436:* Bernardo Vega in 1948 (archives, Centro de Estudios Puertorriqueños, Hunter College); *p. 437:* Sandra María Esteves, 1979 (archives, Arte Público Press); *p. 438:* Second National Latino Book Fair and Writers Festival, Houston Public Library Plaza, 1980 (archives, Arte Público Press); *p. 439:* Nicholasa Mohr, Nicolás Kanellos and Ed Vega at the Bookstop, Houston, Texas, 1985 (archives, Arte Público Press); *p. 440:* Virgil Suárez, 1991 (archives, Arte Público Press); *p. 441:* José Sánchez-Boudy; *p. 442:* Miguel Algarín reciting his poetry at the First National Latino Book Fair, Chicago, 1979 (archives, Arte Público Press); *p. 443:* Alurista, 1980 (archives, Arte Público Press); *p. 445:* Denise Chávez, 1989 (photo by Georgia McInnis. Archives, Arte Público Press); *p. 446:* Lorna Dee Cervantes, 1990 (photo by Georgia McInnis. Archives, Arte Público Press); *p. 446:* Judith Ortiz Cofer, 1989 (archives, Arte Público Press); *p. 447:* Victor Hernández Cruz, 1980 (archives, Arte Público Press); *p. 448:* Abelardo Delgado, 1979 (archives, Arte Público Press); *p. 449:* Roberto Fernández, 1989 (archives, Arte Público Press); *p. 450:* Lionel G. García, 1989 (archives, Arte Público Press); *p. 451:* Rolando Hinojosa, 1987 (archives, Arte Público Press); *p. 452:* Tato Laviera, 1990 (photo by Georgia McInnis. Archives, Arte Público Press); *p. 453:* Nicholasa Mohr, 1990 (archives, Arte Público Press); *p. 454:* Alejandro Morales, 1991 (archives, Arte Público Press); *p. 456:* Album cover of a live poetry recital by Pedro Pietri; *p. 457:* Ricardo Sánchez, 1987 (archives, Arte Público Press); *p. 457:* Gary Soto, 1991 (photo by M.L. Marinelli. Publicity Department, Chronicle Books); *p. 459:* Sabine Ulibarrí, 1989 (archives, Arte Público Press); *p. 460:* Ed Vega, 1991 (archives, Arte Público Press); *p. 461:* Victor Villaseñor, 1991 (photo by Tony Bullard. Archives, Arte Público Press).

Art: *p. 465:* Figure 18.1. Bell wall, San Juan Capistrano Mission, 1760-87. San Antonio, Texas (photograph by Jacinto Quirarte); *p. 466:* Figure 18.2. Facade, San José y San Miguel de Aguayo Mission, 1768-82. San Antonio, Texas (photograph by Kathy Vargas); *p. 467:* Figure 18.3. *Saint Joachim* portal sculpture (left side of the doorway), 1768-82, San José y San Miguel de Aguayo Mission. San Antonio, Texas (photograph by Kathy Vargas); *p. 467:* Figure 18.4. *Saint Anne* portal sculpture, 1768-82. San José y San Miguel de Aguayo Mission. San Antonio, Texas (photograph by Kathy Vargas); *p. 468:* Figure 18.5. Facade, 1783-97, San Xavier del Bac Mission. Tuscon, Arizona (photograph by Jacinto Quirarte); *p. 468:* Figure 18.6. *Saint Lucy.* Portal sculpture, 1783-97, San Xavier del Bac Mission. Tucson, Arizona (photograph by Jacinto Quirarte); *p. 469:* Figure 18.7. Main Portal, 1755, Nuestra Señora de la Purísma Concepción de Acúna Mission. San Antonio, Texas (photograph by Kathy Vargas); *p. 469:* Figure 18.8. Polychromy, 1768-82, San José y San Miguel de Aguayo Mission. San Antonio, Texas (photograph by Kathy Vargas); *p. 472:* Figure 18.9. José Benito Ortega. *Saint Isidore the Farmer,* 1880s-1907. Denver Art Museum; *p. 473:* Figure 18.10. José Dolores López. *Expulsion from the Garden of Eden; p. 476:* Figure 18.11. Theodora Sánchez. *Nicho* (Yard Shrine), dedicated to Saint Dymphna. 1957. Tucson, Arizona (photograph by Jacinto Quirarte); *p. 477:* Figure 18.12. Octavio Medellín. *Xtol* print (photograph courtesy of the artist); *p. 478:* Figure 18.13. Edward Chávez. *Indians of the Plains.* 1943. Egg Tempera on Plywood (photograph courtesy of the artist); *p. 482:* Figure 18.14. Rafael Ortiz. *Piano Destruction Concert, Duncan Terrace.* September 1966, London (photograph courtesy of the artist); *p. 486:* Figure 18.15. Judy Baca. Detail of *The Great Wall of Los Angeles.* 1980 (photograph by Jacinto Quirarte); *p. 487:* Figure 18.16. Carmen Lomas Garza. *Lotería—Table Llena,* 1974 (photograph courtesy of the artist); *p. 488:* Figure 18.17. Víctor Ochoa. Gerónimo, 1981, San Diego, CA (photograph by Jacinto Quirarte); *p. 489:* Figure 18.18. Víctor Ochoa. *Chicano Park,* 1981, San Diego, CA (photograph by Jacinto Quirarte); *p. 490:* Figure 18.19. Cesar Martinez. *La Pareja,* 1979 (photograph courtesy of the artist); *p. 491:* Figure 18.20. Jesse Treviño. *Panadería,* late 1970s (photograph courtesy of the artist); *p. 492:* Figure 18.21. José González. *Barrio Murals.* 1976. Cover design for *Revista Chicano-Riqueña* (photograph courtesy of the artist); *p. 493:* Figure 18.22. Marcos Raya. *Stop World War III* (photograph courtesy of the artist). Mural. Chicago, IL; *p. 497:* Figure 18.23. Willie Herrón and Gronk. *Black and White Mural,* 1973 and 1978. Estrada Courts, Los Angeles, CA (photograph by Jacinto Quirarte); *p. 497:* Figure 18.24. Willie Herrón and Gronk. *Black and White Mural,* 1973 and 1978.

Estrada Courts, Los Angeles, CA (diagram by Jacinto Quirarte); *p. 499:* Figure 18.25. Raymond Patlán and others. *History of the Mexican American Worker, 1974-75.* Blue Island, IL (photograph by Jose Gonzalez); *p. 499:* Figure 18.26. Raymond Patlán and others. *History of the Mexican American Worker, 1974-75.* Blue Island, IL (diagram by Jacinto Quirarte); *p. 500:* Figure 18.27. Raúl Valdez and others. *La Raza Cósmica,* 1977. Austin, TX (photograph by Jacinto Quirarte); *p. 500:* Figure 18.28. Raúl Valdez and others. *La Raza Cósmica,* 1977. Austin, TX (diagram by Jacinto Quirarte); *p. 501:* Figure 18.29. Raúl Valdez and others. *La Raza Cósmica,* 1977. Austin, TX (diagram by Jacinto Quirarte); *p. 501:* Figure 18.30. Raúl Valdez and others. *La Raza Cósmica,* 1977. Austin, TX (diagram by Jacinto Quirarte); *p. 501:* Figure 18.31. Raúl Valdez and others. *La Raza Cósmica,* 1977. Austin, TX (diagram by Jacinto Quirarte); *p. 502:* Figure 18.32. Rogelio Cárdenas. *En la lucha ponte trucha,* 1978. Hayward, CA (photograph by Jacinto Quirarte); *p. 502:* Figure 18.33. Rogelio Cárdenas. *En la lucha ponte trucha,* 1978. Hayward, CA (diagram by Jacinto Quirarte); *p. 503:* Figure 18.34. Gilberto Garduño and others. *Multicultural Mural,* 1980. Santa Fe, NM (photograph by Jacinto Quirarte); *p. 503:* Figure 18.35. Gilberto Garduño and others. *Multicultural Mural,* 1980. Santa Fe, NM (diagram by Jacinto Quirarte).

Theater: *p. 507:* Don Antonio F. Coronel, ex-mayor of Los Angeles, and early theater owner and impresario (courtesy of Los Angeles County Museum of Natural History); *p. 507:* Los Angeles's California Theater; *p. 509:* The Mason Theater, Los Angeles; *p. 510:* Actress Rosalinda Meléndez; *p. 512:* The García girls chorus line from the Carpa García Tent show; *p. 513:* Don Fito, the Carpa García *peladito* from the Carpa García tent show; *p. 517:* The cover of a program for the performance of an operetta at the Centro Español in 1919; *p. 518:* Centro Asturiano, with director Manuel Aparicio at the center front of the audience in 1937 (courtesy of the Dorothea Lynch Collection, Special Collections, George Mason University Library); *p. 519:* A scene from *El niño judío* at the Centro Asturiano (courtesy of the Dorothea Lynch Collection, Special Collections, George Mason University Library); *p. 520:* Manuel Aparicio directing a rehearsal of Sinclair Lewis's *It Can't Happen Here* in Spanish at the Centro Asturiano (courtesy of the Dorothea Lynch Collection, Special Collections, George Mason University); *p. 521:* Manuel Aparicio in Jacinto Benavente's *La Malquerida* (courtesy of the Dorothea Lynch Collection, Special Collections, George Mason University Library); *p. 522:* A scene from El Teatro Urbano's *Anti-Bicentennial Special* in 1976; *p. 524:* A scene from El Teatro de la Esperanza's production of Rodrigo Duarte Clark's *Brujerías; p. 524:* New York's Teatro Hispano in 1939; *p. 525:* Poster from La Farándula Panamericana theater group's 1954 production of *Los árboles mueren de pie,* starring Marita Reid; *p. 526:* Postcard photo of the Bronx's Pregones theater company in 1985; *p. 527:* The elaborate costuming of a Miami production of José Zorrilla's *Don Juan Tenorio; p. 529: Romeo and Juliet* in Spanish in Miami; *p. 537:* A scene from the Los Angeles production of Dolores Prida's *Beautiful Señoritas* (archives, Arte Público Press); *p. 539:* Playwright-director Luis Valdez; *p. 540:* Actress-director Carmen Zapata portrays Isabel la Católica in *Moments to Be Remembered.*

Film: *p. 548:* María Montez, an early Hispanic film star; *p. 551:* Henry Darrow as Zorro; *p. 560:* Carmen Miranda; *p. 561:* The late Freddie Prinze; *p. 561:* Erik Estrada, star of "CHiPs"; *p. 563:* The Sharks face off with the Jets in *West Side Story; p. 564:* A scene from *Boulevard Nights; p. 565:* Anthony Quinn in *The Children of Sánchez; p. 567:* Andy García in *The Godfather, Part III; p. 569:* The poster for *El norte; p. 570:* Raúl Juliá as Salvadoran Archbishop Oscar Romero in *Romero; p. 571:* Jimmy Smits; *p. 574:* Director Jesús Salvador Treviño in 1978; *p. 583:* The late Academy-Award-winning cinematographer, Nestor Almendros; *p. 585:* Producer-Director Moctezuma Esparza; *p. 588:* Ricardo Montalbán in the T.V. series, "Fantasy Island"; *p. 589:* Silvia Morales, director-cinematographer; *p. 590:* Rita Moreno receives her second Emmy in 1978; *p. 591:* Edward James Olmos.

Music: *p. 596:* Mexican musicians in the 1890s in California (courtesy of the Huntington Library, San Marino, California); *p. 596:* Xavier Cugat and his orchestra in the 1940s; *p. 597:* Augusto Coen and his Golden Orchestra, ca. 1930s-1940s; *p. 599:* Lidia Mendoza with Marcelo, comic Tin Tan and Juanita Mendoza in Chicago in the 1950s; *p. 600:* A working-class *orquesta,* circa 1930 (courtesy of Thomas Kreneck); *p. 606:* An *orquesta típica* in Houston (courtesy of Thomas Kreneck); *p. 609:* Beto Villa y su Orquesta, circa 1946 (courtesy of Chris Strachwitz); *p. 610:* Alonzo y su Orquesta, circa 1950 (courtesy of Thomas Kreneck); *p. 611:* Octavo García y sus GGs, circa 1952 (courtesy of Octavio García); *p. 612:* An outdoor *salsa* concert in Houston, Texas (courtesy of the Arte Público Press archives); *p. 613:* Celia Cruz at the Hollywood Palladium; *p. 614:* The Joe Cuba Sextet; *p. 615:* A Machito album cover; *p. 616:* A Tito Puente album cover; *p. 616:* Eddie Palmieri.

Media: *p. 628:* Wanda de Jesús as "Santa Andrade" in NBC's "Santa Barbara"; *p. 629:* A. Martínez as "Cruz Castillo" in NBC's "Santa Barbara"; *p. 630:* Henry Darrow as "Cruz Castillo's" father in NBC's "Santa Barbara"; *p. 633:* Ignacio E. Lozano, Jr., Editor-in-Chief of La Opinión; *p. 634:* Mónica Lozano-Centanino, Associate Publisher of *La Opinión; p. 634:* José I. Lozano, Publisher of *La Opinión; p. 635:* Marti Buscaglia, Director of Marketing, *La Opinión; p. 635:* Peter W. Davidson, President, *El Diario-La Prensa;p. 636:* Carlos D. Ramírez, Publisher, *El Diario-La Prensa;p. 637:* Phillip V. Sánchez, Publisher, *Noticias del Mundo* and *New York City Tribune; p. 640:* Cover of *Temas* magazine; *p. 640:* Cover of *Réplica* magazine; *p. 641:* Cover of *Más* magazine; *p. 641:* Cover of *La Familia de Hoy* magazine; *p. 642:* Cover of *Hispanic* magazine; *p. 643:* Cover of *Hispanic Business* magazine; *p. 643:* Charlie Erikson, founding editor of Hispanic Link News Service; *p. 644:* Cover of *Saludos Hispanos* magazine; *p. 645:* Pedro J. González; *p. 646:* Pedro J. González's singing group, "Los Madrugadores"; *p. 646:* Banner headlines in *La Opinión* newspaper announcing the guilty verdict in the Pedro J. González case; *p. 648:* Table 22.1, Radio Stations Owned and Controlled by Hispanics (sources: National Association of Broadcasters, Department of Minority and Special Services, Minority Telecommunications Development Program of the National Telecommunications and Information Administration, U.S. Department of Commerce); *p. 649:* McHenry Tichnor, founder of the Tichnor Media Systems; *p. 650:* Amancio V. Suárez of the Viva America Media Group; *p. 656:* Gustavo Godoy, Hispanic American Broadcasting Corporation, founder; *p. 657:* Henry R. Silverman, Telemundo founder; *p. 658:* Saul P. Steinberg, Telemundo founder; *p. 660:* Table 22.2, Stations Owned and Operated by the Univisión Spanish-Language Television Group (Late 1991); *p. 658:* Table 22.3, UHF Affiliates of the Univisión Spanish-Language Television Group (Late 1991); *p. 661:* Joaquín F. Blaya, president of Univisión; *p. 661:* Rosita Perú, senior vice president and director of programming, Univisión; *p. 662:* Univisión news studio; *p. 663:* Jorge Ramos and María Elena Salinas of "Noticiero Univisión"; *p. 664:* Table 22.4, Univisión Programming (Mid-1991); *p. 665:* Cristina Saralegui, host of Univisión's "El Show de Cristina";*p. 665:* Don Francisco, host of Univisión's "Sábado Gigante" (Giant Saturday); *p. 666:* Luca Bentivoglio, host of Univisión's "Desde Hollywood," with Julio Iglesias; *p. 666:* Table 22.5, Stations Owned and Operated by the Telemundo Spanish-Language Television Group (Late 1991); *p. 667:* Table 22.6, Stations Affiliated with the Telemundo Spanish-Language Television Group (Late 1991); *p. 668:* Table 22.7, Telemundo Program-

ming (Mid-1991); *p. 669:* Enrique Gratas, host of Telemundo's"Ocurrió Así"; *p. 669:* Andrés García and Rudy Rodríguez, of "El Magnate"; *p. 670:* Table 22.8, Affiliates of the Galavisión Spanish-Language Television Group (Late 1991); *p. 671:* Table 22.9, Galavisión Programming; *p. 672:* Laura Fabián, of Telemundo's "El Magnate";*p. 672:* María Laria, host of Telemundo's "Cara a Cara"; *p. 673:* Milagros Mendoza, Host of "Esta Noche con Usted"

Science: *p. 678:* Dr. Angeles Alvariño de Leira; *p. 679:* Alberto V. Baez;*p. 680:* Graciela Candelas;*p. 681:* Manuel Cardona; *p. 682:* David Cardús; *p. 683:* Guillermo B. Cintrón; *p. 684:* Antonio E. Colás;*p. 684:* Francisco Dallmeier; *p. 685:* George Castro; *p. 685:* José Alberto Fernández-Pol; *p. 686:* Jorge Fischbarg; *p. 687:* Celso Ramón García; *p. 688:* José D. García;*p. 690:* Teresa Mercado;*p. 691:* Isabel Pérez-Farfante;*p. 693:* Pedro A. Sánchez; *p. 694:* James J. Valdés.

Sports: *p. 697:* Ramón Ahumada, known as "El Charro Plateado." (photo, circa 1890. Courtesy of the Arizona Historical Society);*p. 699:* A baseball team of Mexicans and Anglos, Los Angeles, 1870s (courtesy of the Huntington Library, San Marino, California); *p. 703:* Rod Carew; *p. 704:* Roberto Clemente; *p. 704:* Dave Concepción; *p. 705:* Roberto Durán;*p. 706:* Sixto Escobar;*p. 707:* Tom Flores;*p. 707:* Pancho González, U.S. Men's Singles Lawn Tennis Championship, 1948 (courtesy of the National Archives); *p. 708:* Keith Hernández; *p. 709:* Nancy López; *p. 710:* Amleto Monacelli; *p. 711:* Anthony Muñoz; *p. 712:* Jim Plunkett; *p. 713:* Juan "Chi Chi" Rodríguez; *p. 713:* Alberto Bauduy Salazar;*p. 715:* José "Chegüi" Torres (José A. Martí Collection. Courtesy of the Center for Puerto Rican Studies Library, Hunter College, CUNY); *p. 715:* Lee Treviño.

Prominent Hispanics: *p. 717:* Michael Jules Aguirre; *p. 718:* Tomás A. Arciniega; *p. 718:* Philip Arreola; *p. 719:* Tony Bonilla; *p. 720:* Harry Caicedo; *p. 720:* Vikki Carr; *p. 721:* Lynda Carter; *p. 722:* César Chávez; *p. 723:* José R. Coronado; *p. 724:* Jaime Escalante;*p. 725:* Joseph A. Fernández; *p. 726:* Archbishop Patrick F. Flores; *p. 726:* Ernesto Galarza; *p. 727:* Elsa Gómez; *p. 728:* Carolina Herrera; *p. 729:* Dolores Fernández Huerta;*p. 730:* Tania León; *p. 731:* Modesto A. Maidique; *p. 732:* Eduardo Mata; *p. 733:* Julián Nava; *p. 734:* Miguel A. Nevárez; *p. 735:* Katherine D. Ortega; *p. 735:* Manuel Pacheco (photo by Julieta González); *p. 735:* Guadalupe C. Quintanilla;*p. 736:* Mario E. Ramírez (photo by Gittings); *p. 736:* Paul Rodríguez; *p. 737:* Luis Santeiro;*p. 738:* Cristina Saralegui; *p. 738:* Alberto Serrano; *p. 739:* Roberto Suárez.

Glossary

A

acto – a one-act Chicano theater piece developed out of collective improvisation.

adelantado – the commander of an expedition who would receive, in advance, the title to any lands that he would discover.

agringado – literally "Gringo-ized" or Americanized.

audiencia – a tribunal that ruled over territories.

Aztlán – originally the mythological land of origin of the Mechica nations, to which the Toltecs and the Aztecs belong. Chicanos identify this land of origin as the geographic region of the American Southwest, figuratively their homeland.

B

babalao – a spiritual healer, witch, or advisor, especially in *santería*.

barrio – neighborhood.

batos locos – See *pachuco(s)*.

behareque – thatched huts used by Indians of the Caribbean.

bodega – a small general store.

bohíos – thatched-roofed huts used by the Caribbean Indians.

botánica – a shop that specializes in herbs and folk potions and medicines.

bracero – from *brazo*, arm, literally someone who works with their arms or performs manual labor; originally applied to temporary Mexican agricultural and railroad workers, it is also occasionally used to refer to any unskilled Mexican worker.

bulto – a wooden sculpture in the image of a Catholic saint.

C

cacique – the American Indian village chieftain.

caló – a Mexican-American dialect, often associated with *pachucos*.

canción – song.

capilla – chapel.

carpa – from the Quechua word meaning an "awning of branches;" in Spanish it has come to mean a tent. Circuses and tent theaters have come to be known as *carpas* by extension.

carreta – cart.

caudillo – chief, leader, originally of the rural poor, but today quite often used to refer to any grass-roots political leader.

charrerías – contests of the Mexican cowboys.

charro – a Mexican cowboy of the Jalisco region, maintaining the dress and customs often associated with *mariachis*.

Chicano – derivative of *Mechicano*, the same Nahuatl word that gave origin to the name of Mexico. The term originally meant Mexican immigrant worker in the early twentieth century, but became the name adopted by Mexican Americans, especially during the days of the civil rights and student movements.

chinampa – a man-made island or floating garden, developed by Meso-American Indians as an agricultural technique.

cimarrones – runaway slaves.

colonia – literally a "colony," it refers to the enclave of Hispanic population within a city, much as the term *barrio* is used today.

compadrazgo – godparenthood, usually through the baptism of a child. *Compadrazgo* is the extension of kinship to non-relatives and the strengthening of responsibilities among kin.

compadres – co-parents; godparents.

confianza – trust, the basis of the relationships between individuals in many spheres of social activity, but especially among kin.

conjunto – said of a Texas, northern-Mexico musical style as well as of the ensemble that plays it, usually made up of a guitar, a base guitar, a drum, and a button accordion.

corrido – a Mexican ballad.

criollo – a Creole, that is, someone of Spanish (European) origin born in the New World.

crónica – a local-color newspaper column often satirizing contemporary customs.

cronista – the writer of a *crónica*.

curandero – a folk healer who combines the practices of the Mexican Indians and Spanish folk-healing.

E

encomendero – the owner of the *encomienda*.

encomienda – the system by which a Spaniard held in high esteem by the King and Queen was given ownership of land in the New World and authorized to "protect" the Indians who had occupied the land in exchange for their free labor. This failed attempt at establishing feudal baronies was marked by the exploitation of the Indians.

ex-voto – a gift presented to a saint as a show of gratitude for a favor conceded.

F

familia, la – the greater family, which includes the immediate nuclear household and relatives that are traced on the female and male sides.

finca – farm, ranch.

G

gallego – in Cuban farce, the stock Galician Spaniard, known for his hard head and frugality.

H

hacendados – the owner of a *hacienda*.

hacienda – a large ranch derivative of the *latifundia* system.

hermandad – brotherhood.

I

indigenismo – an emphasis on American Indian and Pre-Colombian origins and identity.

ingenios – plantations, especially of sugar.

Isleños – descendants of the Canary Island settlers in southern Louisiana.

J

jíbaro – originally an American Indian word for "highlander," it is what Puerto Ricans call the rural mountain folk, but has also come to be symbolic of the national identity of Puerto Ricans.

K

kiva – a secret underground ceremonial chamber, especially as used in Pueblo culture for ceremonies and meetings.

L

latifundia – a large estate or ranch originating in ancient Roman civilization.

lectores – professional (hired) readers who would read books, magazines, and newspapers to cigar-rollers as they performed their laborious tasks.

M

macana – a wooden war club.

manda – a sacrificial offering to a saint in order to receive some favor.

maquiladora – a factory on the Mexican side of the border that performs part of the manual assembly of products at the comparatively lower wages offered by the Mexican economy. These products would then be shipped back to the United States for finishing and marketing by the partner company.

Marielito – a Cuban refugee who arrived in the United States as a result of the Mariel boatlift in the 1980s.

mestizo – an individual of mixed Spanish (or European) and American Indian heritage.

milagro – a charm made of tin, gold, or silver, and shaped in the form of an arm, a leg, a baby, or a house, representing the favor (usually of healing) that is desired from a saint.

morada – the meeting house of the *Penitente* lay brotherhood.

mulata – the stock female Mulatto character in Cuban farce.

música norteña – *conjunto* music from the northern region of Mexico (also includes Texas).

mutualista – mutual aid society, an organization that engaged in social activities and provided basic needs for immigrant workers and their families, including insurance and death benefits for members.

N

nacimiento – a nativity.

Nañiguismo – membership in the secret society of Abakúa, which combines elements of the Efik culture of the southern coast of Nigeria and Freemasonry.

negrito – in Cuban farce, the stock character in black face.

nitainos – principal advisors among the Arawak Indians, quite often in charge of the labor force.

nopal – the prickly pear cactus.

norteño – of northern Mexican origin.

Nuyorican – literally "New York-Rican," a term developed colloquially by Puerto Ricans born or raised in New York to distinguish themselves from those identifying solely with the island.

O

orishas – the African deities of *santería*.

orquesta – a Mexican-American musical ensemble that develops its style around the violin.

P

pachuco – the member of a Mexican-American urban youth subculture, which characteristically developed its own style of dress (zoot suit), its own dialect (*caló*), and its own bilingual-bicultural ideology during the 1940s and 1950s.

padrinos – godparents.

parentesco – kinship sentiment.

parientes – blood relatives.

pastorela – the shepherds play; a folk drama reenacted during the Christmas season.

patria – fatherland.

patria chica – the home region within the fatherland.

pelado – literally the "skinned one" or shirtless one, he was the stock underdog, sharp-witted picaresque character of Mexican vaudeville and tent shows.

Penitente – literally "penitent;" it is the name of a religious brotherhood in New Mexico.

piraguas – a narrow, high-prowed canoe used by the Caribbean Indians.

posada – a community Christmas pageant where carolers go door to door asking for shelter in reenactment of Joseph and Mary's search for lodging.

presidio – a fort, especially characteristic of frontier settlements.

promesa – literally a "promise," it is a sacrificial offering to a saint in order to receive some favor.

R

renegado/a – a renegade, someone who denies his or her Mexican identity.

repartimiento – a form of the *encomienda* which vested the rights over the Indians in the civil authorities.

reredo – altar screen.

retablos – paintings on panels behind the altar in a Catholic church.

revista – a vaudeville musical revue.

S

salsa – literally "sauce," it refers to Afro-Caribbean music.

santería – a synchretic religious sect growing out of the original African religion and the Catholicism of slaves.

santerismo – the same as santería.

santero – in the Southwest, a sculptor of wooden saints; in the Caribbean, a devotee of an *orisha* in *santería*.

santos – the sculpted figures representing saints of the Catholic church; used in worship and prayer.

T

Taino (also Nitaino) – a group of sedentary tribes native to the Caribbean.

V

vaquero – cowboy.

vegas – plantations, especially of coffee.

Y

yerberías – shops specializing in medicinal plants, herbs and potions.

yerberos – folk healers and spiritualists who use herbs in their practices.

yuca – manioc root.

Z

zarzuela – a type of Spanish operetta.

zemíes – gods of the Arawak Indians, also the small Taino religious figure made of clay that represented these gods.

General Bibliography

A

Acosta-Belén, Edna, ed. *The Puerto Rican Woman.* New York: Praeger, 1986.

Acuña, Rodolfo. *Occupied America: A History of Chicanos.* New York: Harper & Row, 1981.

Alvarez, Robert R. *Familia: Migration and Adaptation in Alta and Baja California 1850-1975.* Berkeley: University of California Press, 1987.

B

Barrera, Mario. *Race and Class in the Southwest: A Theory of Racial Inequality.* Notre Dame, Ind.: University of Notre Dame Press, 1979.

Bean, Frank D., and Marta Tienda. *The Hispanic Population of the United States.* New York: Russell Sage Foundation, 1988.

Beardsley, John, and Jane Livingston. *Hispanic Art in the United States: Thirty Painters and Sculptors.* New York: Abbeville Press, 1987.

Boswel, T.D., and J.R. Curtis. *The Cuban American Experience.* Totawa, N.J.: Rowan and Allenheld, 1984.

C

Camarillo, Albert. *Chicanos in a Changing Society.* Cambridge, Mass.: Harvard University Press, 1979.

Cotera, Marta P. *Latina Sourcebook: Bibliography of Mexican American, Cuban, Puerto Rican and Other Hispanic Women Materials in the USA.* Austin, Texas: Information Systems Development, 1982.

E

Elías Olivares, Lucia, ed. *Spanish in the U.S. Setting: Beyond the Southwest.* Rosalyn, Va.: National Clearinghouse for Bilingual Education, 1983.

F

Fitzpatrick, Joseph P. *Puerto Rican Americans: The Meaning of Migration to the Mainland.* Englewood Cliffs, N.J.: Prentice Hall, 1987.

Furtaw, Julia C., ed. *Hispanic American Information Directory 1992-1993.* Detroit, Mich.: Gale Research, 1992.

G

García, Mario T. *Mexican Americans.* New Haven, Conn.: Yale University Press, 1989.

H

Hendricks, G.L. *The Dominican Diaspora: From the Dominican Republic to New York City.* New York: Teacher's College Press of Columbia University, 1974.

History Task Force of the Centro de Estudios Puertorriqueños. *Labor Migration under Capitalism: The Puerto Rican Experience.* New York: Monthly Review Press, 1979.

K

Kanellos, Nicolás. *A History of Hispanic Theater in the United States: Origins to 1940.* Austin: University of Texas Press, 1990.

————, ed. *Biographical Dictionary of Hispanic Literature.* Westport, Conn.: Greenwood Press, 1985.

Knight, Franklin W. *The Caribbean.* New York: Oxford University Press, 1990.

L

Llanes, J. *Cuban Americans, Masters of Survival.* Cambridge, Mass.: Harvard University Press, 1982.

Lomeli, Francisco and Julio A. Martínez. *Chicano Literature: A Reference Guide.* Westport, Conn.: Greenwood Press, 1985.

M

McKenna, Teresa Flora and Ida Ortiz, eds. *The Broken Web: The Education Experience of Hispanic American Women.* Berkeley, Calif.: Floricanto Press and the Tomás Rivera Center, 1988.

Meier, Kenneth J. and Joseph Stewart. *The Politics of Hispanic Education.* New York: Russell Sage Foundation, 1987.

Meier, Matt S. and Feliciano Rivera. *Dictionary of Mexican American History.* Westport, Conn.: Greenwood Press, 1981.

Moore, Joan, and Harry Pachón. *Hispanics in the United States.* Englewood Cliffs, N.J.: Prentice Hall, 1985.

Morales, Julio. *Puerto Rican Poverty and Migration: We Just Had to Try Elsewhere.* New York: Praeger, 1986.

P

Pedraza-Bailey, S. *Political and Economic Migrants in America.* Austin: University of Texas Press, 1985.

Portes, Alejandro, and Robert L. Bach. *Latin Journey: Cuban and Mexican Immigrants in the United States.* Berkeley: University of California Press, 1985.

R

Rodríguez, Clara. *Born in the U.S.A.* Boston, Mass.: Unwin Hyman, 1989.

Ryan, Bryan. *Hispanic Writers.* Detroit, Mich.: Gale Research, 1991.

S

Sánchez-Korrol, Virginia. *From Colonia to Community.* Westport, Conn.: Greenwood Press, 1983.

Sandoval, Moisés. *On the Move: A History of the Hispanic Church in the United States.* Maryknoll, N.Y.: Orbis Books, 1990.

Schorr, Edward Allen. *Hispanic Resource Directory.* Juneau, Alaska: Denali Press, 1988.

Shirley, Carl F., ed. *Chicano Writers: First Series.* Detroit, Mich.: Gale Research, 1989.

Suchliki, Jaime. *Cuba: From Columbus to Castro.* Washington, D.C.: Pergammon Press, 1986.

U

United States Commission on Civil Rights. *Puerto Ricans in the Continental United States: An Uncertain Future.* Washington, D.C.: U.S. Commission on Civil Rights, 1976.

Unterburger, Amy L., ed. *Who's Who among Hispanic Americans, 1992-1993.* Detroit, Mich.: Gale Research, 1992.

V

Veciana-Suárez, Ana. *Hispanic Media: Impact and Influence.* Washington, D.C.: The Media Institute, 1990.

Vivó, Paquita, ed. *The Puerto Ricans: An Annotated Bibliography.* New York: R.R. Bowker, 1973.

W

Wagenheim, Kal. *A Survey of Puerto Ricans in the U.S. Mainland in the 1970s.* New York: Praeger, 1975.

Weber, David. *The Mexican Frontier, 1821-1846: The American Southwest under Mexico.* Albuquerque, University of New Mexico Press, 1982.

Index

Colmenares, Margarita Hortensia: 361
Colón, Jesús: 421, 434, 436, 447, 526
Colón, Miriam: 525, 526, 530, 580, 581
Colón-Morales, Rafael: 491
Colón, Willie: 615
colonia: 34, 37, 38, 39, 41, 42, 43, 47, 171
colonization: 14-18, 21, 413
Colorado Institute for Hispanic Education and Economic Development: 284
Colorado, Rafael J.: 579
Columbia Broadcasting System Hispanic Radio Network: 652
Columbus, Christopher: 4, 5, 6, 7, 58, 59-61, 62, 149, 229, 367, 432
Columbus, Diego: 61, 65
Columbus Landing Site: 149
Comanches 15, 16, 21
comisiones honoríficas: 38
Comisión Femenil Mexicana Nacional: 389, 390
Comité Hispano de Virginia: 285
Commission on Foreign Economic Policy: 191
commonwealth (*see also* Constitution of the Commonwealth of Puerto Rico): 45
communism: 48, 175, 191-198, 231, 232, 233, 237, 421
Community Action Program (CAP): 340, 341
compadrazgo: 155, 156-159, 162, 163, 164, 167, 171, 172
Compañía Dramática Española de Pedro C. de Pellón: 507
Compañía Española de Angel Mollá: 506
Compañía Española de la Familia Estrella: 506
Compañía, La: 523
Compañía Periodística del Sol de Ciudad Juárez: 639
Comprehensive Employment and Training Administration (CETA): 341-342
Concepción, Dave: 704
Concepción Mission: 144
Confederación de Trabajadores Generales (CGT): 332
Confederacy: 24
confianza: 155, 157-158, 162, 163, 164, 171
Congregationalists: 294
Congreso de Artistas Chicanos en Aztlán: 487, 493, 494-495, 496
Congreso Mexicanista: 38
Congressional Hispanic Caucus: 259, 387, 390
congressmen: 259-271, 335
Congress of Industrial Organizations (CIO): 331, 332
Congress of Mexican-American Unity: 562
conjunto: 29, 575, 596, 603
Conjunto Bernal, El: 604-605
Connecticut Association for United Spanish Action: 285

conquistador: 383
Consortium of National Hispanic Organizations: 391
Constitution of the Commonwealth of Puerto Rico: 120-134
Contadora: 197
Convent of Porta Coeli: 144
conventos: 465
Cordero, Angel: 705
Cordero, Julio: 684
Cordero y Bustamante, Antonio: 147
Córdova, Arturo de: 556, 580, 585
Córdova House: 135
Córdova, Pedro de: 585
Corea, Chick: 617
Corona, Bert: 723
Coronado, Francisco. *See* Vásquez de Coronado, Francisco
Coronado, José R.: 723-724
Coronado National Memorial: 135
Coronel, Antonio F.: 506, 507
Corpi, Lucha: 427
Corporation for Public Broadcasting: 631
Corpus Christi de la Ysleta: 144
Corpus Christi de la Ysleta Mission: 145
Corral, Edward A.: 724
corrido: 414-415, 597-603, 522
Cortés, Carlos E.: 401-402
Cortés, Hernán: 6, 7, 9-10, 14, 56, 57, 64, 65, 66-67, 75, 368
Cortez, Gregorio: 601
Cortez, Raúl: 653-654
Cortina, Juan Nepomuceno: 601
Cortina, Rodolfo J.: 402, 441, 528
Cossío, Evangelina: 416
Costello, Diana: 575
Cotera, Manuel: 511
cotton: 32, 34, 327, 331, 335, 338
Council of Puerto Rican Organizations: 388
Council of the Indies: 62, 66
court cases: 237-238
cowboys: 697, 701-702
Cremata, Ernesto: 528
Crespi, Juan: 136
criollo: 14, 30, 41
Cristal, Linda: 562, 584, 627
Cristo el Salvador: 381
Cristo Negro de Esquipulas: 381
Crockett, Davey 22
crónica: 417
Crusades: 3
Cruz Azaceta, Luis: 491-492
Cruz, Celia: 612, 613, 615
Cruz, Nicky: 435
Cruz-Romo, Gilda: 724

media (*see also* magazines; newspapers; periodicals; radio; television): 217-220, 621-673; electronic, 645-673; print, 632-645
medicine: folk medicine 17, 676; among the Indians 17
Medina, Harold R.: 253
Meléndez, Manuel Gaspar: 690
Meléndez, Rosalinda: 510
melting pot: 217
Memorandum on the Monroe Doctrine: 189
Méndez Avilés, Pedro: 372-373
Méndez, José: 690, 700, 701, 709
Méndez-Longoria, Miguel Angel: 243
Méndez, Miguel: 422
Mendoza, Antonio de: 11, 68, 72, 73, 75
Mendoza, Lydia: 512, 598, 599
Mendoza, Tomás: 513
Mendoza, Vicente: 493, 498-499
Menéndez de Avilés, Pedro: 70-72
Menéndez, Ramón: 578, 579, 625
Mercado, Teresa: 690-691
Merry, William L.: 184
Mesa-Baines, Amalia: 485, 486
Mesa-Lago, Carmelo: 407
Mesilla Plaza: 143
mestizo: 6, 11, 12, 14, 18, 25, 28, 61-62, 214, 288, 371, 383, 432, 433, 505, 547, 697, 701
Mestre, Ricardo: 566
Methodists: 294-295, 379
Mexican American Culture Center: 378
Mexican American Democrats of Texas: 284
Mexican American Generation: 608, 611
Mexican American identity: 39-40
Mexican American Legal Defense and Education Fund (MALDEF): 241, 243, 243, 247, 257, 258, 283, 392, 573
Mexican-American Political Association: 283, 388
Mexican American War: 22-25, 31, 168, 214, 216, 326, 413, 464, 600
Mexican-American Women's National Association: 284
Mexican Farm Labor Supply Program: 335
Mexican identity: 12
Mexican Labor Agreement: 327, 335
Mexican League: 699
Mexican Revolution of 1910: 28, 34-36, 37, 170, 188, 230, 472, 507, 509, 550, 558, 676
"Mexican Spitfire": 552
"México de afuera": 416, 417, 419
"México Lindo": 37, 38, 39, 41, 42
Michigan Commission on Spanish-Speaking Affairs: 285
Mier y Terán, Manuel: 21
migrant farm labor: 171, 301, 338-339
Migrant Legal Action Program: 241, 283

migration: Hispanics in general 156, 157, 159, 328-329, 334-339; Dominicans 163; Mexican 326; Puerto Rican 41-46, 161, 299, 328, 420
milagro: 475-476
Milagro Bean Field War, The: 567, 568
Milán, Ed: 320
Miles, Nelson: 42
Military Assistance Program: 1948
Miller, Edward G.: 191
Mina, Xavier de: 178
mining: 2, 12-13, 14, 16-17, 24, 32, 33, 34, 38, 137, 154, 170, 230, 235, 326, 328, 331, 332
Minority Business Development Agency: 317
minority status: 199, 258, 543-547, 698, 702
Minority Telecommunications Development Program: 648
Minnesota Spanish-Speaking Affairs Council: 285
Miñoso, Orestes "Minnie": 701, 710
Miranda, Carmen: 560, 624
Miranda, Francisco de: 178
Miruelo, Diego: 64
Misisipí, El: 633
Miskito Indians: 212
missile crisis: 48
missionaries: 13, 16, 17, 18, 413, 505
Missionary Catechists of Divine Providence: 379
missions: 13, 15, 17, 18, 76-78, 136-148, 288-291, 369-377, 465-469, 506
Mobile Act: 176
Moctezuma II: 9-10, 74, 385
Modernistic Editorial Company: 420-421
Mohr, Nicholasa: 438-439, 453-454
Molina, Gloria: 280
Molina, Luis: 582
Mollá, Angel: 507
Monacelli, Amleto Andrés: 710
Moncarraz, Raúl: 407
Monroe Doctrine: 84-90, 177, 178, 180, 182, 186, 187, 193, 197
Monroe, James: 177, 193
Montalbán, Ricardo: 554, 565, 569, 573, 578, 588, 624, 627
Montalván, E.: 414
Monterey Old Town Historic District: 137
Monteros, Rosenda: 566
Montes de Oca López, Diana: 689
Montes Huidobro, Matías: 440, 533
Montevideo Conference: 189
Montez, María: 548, 589, 624
Montoya, José: 577
Montoya, Joseph Manuel: 260, 265, 270
Montoya, Malaquías: 486
Montoya, Nestor: 270
Moors: 3, 4, 5-6, 60, 61
Mora, Francisco Luis: 478-479

Our Lady of Guadalupe: 38, 45, 371-372, 381, 382, 383, 385, 470, 475, 476
Our Lady of La Caridad del Cobre: 381
Our Lady of Providencia: 381
Our Lady of San Juan de los Lagos: 381, 382, 385, 475
Our Lady of Sorrows: 381
Our Lady of Talpa: 471
Outdoor shrines: 474-476
Ovando, Nicolás de: 61
Oviedo, Gonzalo Fernández de: 61

P

Pacheco, Johnny: 615
Pacheco, Manuel Trinidad: 305, 733-734, 735
Pacheco, Romualdo: 271
Pachón, Harry: 409
Pact of El Zajón: 29
Padilla, Amado Manuel: 409
Padilla, Benjamín "Kaskabel": 417
Padilla, Heberto: 440, 441
Padilla, Nancy: 321
padrino: 156
Paine, Thomas: 178
Pakira Fils: 580
Palace of the Governors: 143
Palacio, Adolfo: 135
Palés Matos, Luis: 433, 437, 580
Palés, Vicente: 420
Palma, Chief: 76
Palmieri, Charlie: 615
Palmieri, Eddie: 615, 616
Palo Alto Battlefield: 145
Palomino, Ernesto: 480, 481
Pan American Union: 182
Panama Canal: 86-88, 114-119, 175, 181, 184-187, 189, 194, 196, 197
Panchito: 553
Papago Indians: 17
Papp, Joseph: 523, 525
Paredes, Américo: 396, 409, 418, 600
parentesco: 157-158, 161, 163, 164, 171
pariente: 156-157
Parra, Richard: 578
Partido Liberal Mexicano: 387
Pasquel Family: 699
pastorela: 389, 505
patio process: 12
Patlán, Raymond: 493, 498-499
patria, la: 415
patria potestad: 12
patriarchy: 172
patrón: 18
Peace Corps: 275
pecan shellers: 331

pelado: 509, 510, 512, 523, 536
Pellicer, Pina: 554
Pellón, Pedro C. de: 507
Pelton, John: 297
Penichet, Carlos: 577
Penichet, Jeff: 577
penitente: 377, 383, 471
Pennsylvania Governor's Advisory Commission on Latino Affairs: 286
Pentecostalism: 380
Peña, Elizabeth: 571, 626
Peña, Federico: 280-281
Peña House (Vacaville, California): 137
Peña, Juan: 137
peonage: 187
Peralta House (San José, California): 137
Peralta, Pedro de: 74, 374
Perea, Francisco: 271, 296
Perea, Pedro: 272
Perea, Pedro de: 16, 296
Perenchio, A. Jerrold: 658
Pérez de Almazán, Fernando: 75
Pérez de Villagrá, Gaspar: 413
Pérez del Río, José (Pepe): 653
Pérez et al. versus Federal Bureau of Investigation: 341
Pérez-Farfante, Isabel Cristina: 691
Pérez-Firmat, Gustavo: 408-409
Pérez-Giménez, Juan M.: 254
Pérez, Ignacio: 136
Pérez-Méndez, Víctor: 6918
Pérez, Minerva: 733
Pérez, Severo: 523, 574
Perfecto de Cos, Martín: 21
Periodicals (*see also* newspapers and media): 639-645
Perón, Juan: 190
Pershing, John J.: 188
Perú, Rosita: 661
Petaluma Adobe State Historic Park: 137
Phillip, Prince of Austria: 11
Phillip II: 70, 147
Philip IV: 374
Phoenicians: 2
Phos Press: 419
Pico, Andrés: 139
Pico Hotel (Los Angeles, California): 137
Pico House(s) (Mission Hills and Whittier, California): 137
Pico, Pío: 23, 137
Pieras, Jr., Jamie: 254
Pierce, Franklin: 183
Pietri, Pedro: 435, 455-456, 526
Pike, Zebulon: 20
Pima Indians: 16, 17

Index